COMPUTER BOOK SERIES FROM IDG

ATM For Dummies®

D1170420

Important ATM Terms and Definitions

- **Adaptation:** Defined methods for packaging user information into ATM cells. The most common adaptation scheme is AAL5.

- **ATM (Asynchronous Transfer Mode):** A high speed networking technology that utilizes packets of a fixed size (cells). ATM uses logical connections to provide quality of service guarantees which enable disparate traffic such as data, voice, and video to be carried over the same local or wide area network.

- **ATM Forum:** The most important standards organization for ATM has over 700 members. Fourteen technical working groups generate a variety of key specifications for building and enhancing ATM networks and services.

- **B-ISDN (Broadband-Integrated Services Digital Network):** A high speed (above 1.544 Mbps) network standard that grew from traditional Narrowband ISDN. The ITU standards for ATM are its B-ISDN recommendations.

- **Cell:** The fixed length packet used to carry data across an ATM network, a cell consists of 53 bytes, 5 of which carry header information.

- **LANE (LAN Emulation):** Specification allowing devices attached to existing LANs (such as Ethernet and Token Ring) to communicate with devices connected to ATM networks. The specification is also essential for building ATM-based LAN backbones.

- **MPOA (Multiprotocol over ATM):** Specification connecting virtual ATM LANs together using cut-through routing.

- **PVC (Permanent Virtual Circuit):** A logical connection manually defined by network administrators. The ATM network maintains the connection at all times, regardless of actual traffic flows. Compare with SVC.

- **QoS (Quality of Service):** A unique feature of ATM compared to most other networking technologies, QoS parameters ensure minimum levels of network performance for carried traffic.

- **Router:** A computer that forwards packets through a network using information contained in the packet headers. A router typically maintains *routing tables* which enable it to select the best outgoing link for forwarding the packet to the next router.

- **Service Category:** A known grouping of generally defined network performance attributes (that is, QoS parameters).

- **SVC (Switched Virtual Circuit):** A logical connection established via signaling. Users request SVCs through messages sent to the network, identifying the destination address and desired performance attributes (similar to dialing a phone number). The network tears down SVCs after the users complete their calls.

- **Switch:** A computer that maintains circuits by matching an input port to an output port for each connection. The switch contains *switching tables* to track this information.

- **UNI (User-to-Network Interface):** A protocol which defines how ATM end users connect to private and public ATM networks. The UNI defines the available capabilities for ATM transport.

- **VTOA (Voice and Telephony over ATM):** Specification defining a standard method for carrying traditional voice circuits over an ATM network.

- **Winsock 2:** An API (Application Programming Interface) allowing software applications to request the quality of service and bandwidth of their networking connections.

...For Dummies: #1 Computer Book Series for Beginners

ATM For Dummies®

Cheat Sheet

A Transportation Analogy for ATM

Transportation Element	Its ATM Counterpart
Materials to construct the roadway	Physical medium
Driving rules	Transmission protocols
Transportation vehicles	Cells
Packing instructions	Adaptation
Painted guidelines pointed to the destination	Virtual connections
Specialized lanes for getting to the destination on-time, safe and sound	Virtual paths and virtual channels
The needs that the specialized lanes must meet	Quality of service
Getting on the highway	Multiplexing
Changing from one highway to another	Switching

ATM Service Categories

Category Name	Its Description
CBR (Constant Bit Rate)	Supports a constant or guaranteed rate to transport information. Used for services such as traditional video or voice, which require rigid bandwidth and low latency.
VBR (Variable Bit Rate)	Supports predictable data streams within bounds of average and peak traffic constraints. Used for delay and loss-sensitive data transmissions and packetized voice/video. This category may be broken into two: VBR Real-Time and VBR Non-Real-Time.
ABR (Available Bit Rate)	Supports bursty applications such as LAN interconnect and Internet access. ABR uses internal and external network feedback mechanisms to manage traffic.
UBR (Unspecified Bit Rate)	Offers no traffic-related service guarantees.

Quality of Service (QoS) Parameters

Parameter	What It Means
Cell Loss Ratio	The percentage of cells lost during a transmission.
Cell Transfer Delay	The end-to-end delay introduced by transmission across the network.
Cell Delay Variation	The change in the interarrival times between cells at the peak cell rate.

Where Can I Use ATM?

- Local Area Network (LAN): A high speed network connecting personal computers, printers, and other data equipment within an office.

- Campus Network: A high speed network connecting multiple LANs within a building or close cluster of buildings.

- Wide Area Network (WAN): A high speed network connecting communications equipment nationally and internationally.

...For Dummies: #1 Computer Book Series for Beginners

®

COMPUTER BOOK SERIES FROM IDG

References for the Rest of Us! ®

Are you intimidated and confused by computers? Do you find that traditional manuals are overloaded with technical details you'll never use? Do your friends and family always call you to fix simple problems on their PCs? Then the *...For Dummies*® computer book series from IDG Books Worldwide is for you.

...For Dummies books are written for those frustrated computer users who know they aren't really dumb but find that PC hardware, software, and indeed the unique vocabulary of computing make them feel helpless. *...For Dummies* books use a lighthearted approach, a down-to-earth style, and even cartoons and humorous icons to diffuse computer novices' fears and build their confidence. Lighthearted but not lightweight, these books are a perfect survival guide for anyone forced to use a computer.

> *"I like my copy so much I told friends; now they bought copies."*
>
> **Irene C., Orwell, Ohio**

> *"Quick, concise, nontechnical, and humorous."*
>
> **Jay A., Elburn, Illinois**

> *"Thanks, I needed this book. Now I can sleep at night."*
>
> **Robin F., British Columbia, Canada**

Already, hundreds of thousands of satisfied readers agree. They have made *...For Dummies* books the #1 introductory level computer book series and have written asking for more. So, if you're looking for the most fun and easy way to learn about computers, look to *...For Dummies* books to give you a helping hand.

7/96r

ATM FOR DUMMIES®

by Cathy Gadecki and Christine Heckart

Foreword by Allen Robel

IDG Books Worldwide, Inc.
An International Data Group Company

Foster City, CA ♦ Chicago, IL ♦ Indianapolis, IN ♦ Southlake, TX

ATM For Dummies®

Published by
IDG Books Worldwide, Inc.
An International Data Group Company
919 E. Hillsdale Blvd.
Suite 400
Foster City, CA 94404
http://www.idgbooks.com (IDG Books Worldwide Web site)
http://www.dummies.com (Dummies Press Web site)

Library of Congress Catalog Card No.: 96-79277

ISBN: 0-7645-0065-1

Printed in the United States of America

10 9 8 7 6 5 4 3 2 1

1E/TQ/QR/ZX/IN

Distributed in the United States by IDG Books Worldwide, Inc.

Distributed by Macmillan Canada for Canada; by Transworld Publishers Limited in the United Kingdom and Europe; by WoodsLane Pty. Ltd. for Australia; by WoodsLane Enterprises Ltd. for New Zealand; by Longman Singapore Publishers Ltd. for Singapore, Malaysia, Thailand, and Indonesia; by Simron Pty. Ltd. for South Africa; by Toppan Company Ltd. for Japan; by Distribuidora Cuspide for Argentina; by Livraria Cultura for Brazil; by Ediciencia S.A. for Ecuador; by Addison-Wesley Publishing Company for Korea; by Ediciones ZETA S.C.R. Ltda. for Peru; by WS Computer Publishing Company, Inc., for the Philippines; by Unalis Corporation for Taiwan; by Contemporanea de Ediciones for Venezuela. Authorized Sales Agent: Anthony Rudkin Associates for the Middle East and North Africa.

For general information on IDG Books Worldwide's books in the U.S., please call our Consumer Customer Service department at 800-762-2974. For reseller information, including discounts and premium sales, please call our Reseller Customer Service department at 800-434-3422.

For information on where to purchase IDG Books Worldwide's books outside the U.S., please contact our International Sales department at 415-655-3023 or fax 415-655-3299.

For information on foreign language translations, please contact our Foreign & Subsidiary Rights department at 415-655-3021 or fax 415-655-3281.

For sales inquiries and special prices for bulk quantities, please contact our Sales department at 415-655-3200 or write to the address above.

For information on using IDG Books Worldwide's books in the classroom or for ordering examination copies, please contact our Educational Sales department at 800-434-2086 or fax 817-251-8174.

For press review copies, author interviews, or other publicity information, please contact our Public Relations department at 415-655-3000 or fax 415-655-3299.

For authorization to photocopy items for corporate, personal, or educational use, please contact Copyright Clearance Center, 222 Rosewood Drive, Danvers, MA 01923, or fax 508-750-4470.

is a trademark under exclusive license to IDG Books Worldwide, Inc., from International Data Group, Inc.

About the Authors

Cathy Gadecki lives in Richmond, Virginia with her husband and three kids — two boys and a girl — with another boy on the way. She is a senior consultant with TeleChoice, Inc., a telecommunications consulting and market research company. Prior to joining TeleChoice, Cathy was Group Manager - ATM Services with Sprint's Long Distance Division. Cathy has over ten years of industry experience in both local and long distance services that includes strategy development, product development, management, and marketing of data communication services.

Cathy's background with ATM began in 1990, with efforts to gain approval of an ATM research testbed sponsored by Sprint, DOD, various universities, and other organizations. The testbed was later dubbed MAGIC. In 1993, she was the product manager responsible for launching Sprint's ATM services, the first long distance ATM services in the U.S. For the next three years, Cathy lead Sprint's ATM product group working with early users and enhancing the initial service to keep pace with the rapidly evolving technology.

Cathy earned her Master degree in Electrical Engineering from the Georgia Institute of Technology where she specialized in data communications course work. She earned her Bachelor of Science degree in Engineering Sciences at Pennsylvania State University.

Christine Heckart lives with her husband, her two year old son, and a dog named Jake, in a house they built on five acres in the booming metropolis of Claremore, Oklahoma. She leads the broadband consulting practice at TeleChoice, Inc. as Vice President of the company. She has assisted many clients in developing strategic business and marketing plans, defining price structures and rates, assessing strategic market positioning, developing product features that provide differentiation and competitive market advantage, and developing advertising and marketing communications strategies.

Chris's work on ATM began in 1990, when she served as the marketing product manager at WilTel and worked on the frame relay services rollout. At that time, WilTel undertook the assembly of a special task force aimed at defining the requirements for an ATM network switch and customized object-oriented management system. Chris worked interactively with the group over a four year span to launch ATM-based services for high-speed remote channel extension and LAN interconnectivity. She became group manager for broadband services and was involved in all areas of product positioning and definition, customer needs analysis, and product launch.

Chris graduated Phi Beta Kappa and Magna Cum Laude with her Bachelor of Arts degree in Economics from the University of Colorado at Boulder.

ABOUT IDG BOOKS WORLDWIDE

Welcome to the world of IDG Books Worldwide.

IDG Books Worldwide, Inc., is a subsidiary of International Data Group, the world's largest publisher of computer-related information and the leading global provider of information services on information technology. IDG was founded more than 25 years ago and now employs more than 8,500 people worldwide. IDG publishes more than 275 computer publications in over 75 countries (see listing below). More than 60 million people read one or more IDG publications each month.

Launched in 1990, IDG Books Worldwide is today the #1 publisher of best-selling computer books in the United States. We are proud to have received eight awards from the Computer Press Association in recognition of editorial excellence and three from *Computer Currents'* First Annual Readers' Choice Awards. Our best-selling *...For Dummies®* series has more than 30 million copies in print with translations in 30 languages. IDG Books Worldwide, through a joint venture with IDG's Hi-Tech Beijing, became the first U.S. publisher to publish a computer book in the People's Republic of China. In record time, IDG Books Worldwide has become the first choice for millions of readers around the world who want to learn how to better manage their businesses.

Our mission is simple: Every one of our books is designed to bring extra value and skill-building instructions to the reader. Our books are written by experts who understand and care about our readers. The knowledge base of our editorial staff comes from years of experience in publishing, education, and journalism — experience we use to produce books for the '90s. In short, we care about books, so we attract the best people. We devote special attention to details such as audience, interior design, use of icons, and illustrations. And because we use an efficient process of authoring, editing, and desktop publishing our books electronically, we can spend more time ensuring superior content and spend less time on the technicalities of making books.

You can count on our commitment to deliver high-quality books at competitive prices on topics you want to read about. At IDG Books Worldwide, we continue in the IDG tradition of delivering quality for more than 25 years. You'll find no better book on a subject than one from IDG Books Worldwide.

John Kilcullen
CEO
IDG Books Worldwide, Inc.

Eighth Annual
Computer Press
Awards ≥1992

Ninth Annual
Computer Press
Awards ≥1993

Tenth Annual
Computer Press
Awards ≥1994

Eleventh Annual
Computer Press
Awards ≥1995

Dedication

This book is dedicated to working telecom parents that somehow preserve time and energy for their families after a challenging day of climbing the technology mountains to wrestle with the gods of complexity, and to the telecom spouses (especially Steve and Doug) who provide us safe haven when the winds of chaos blow and who understand that we must climb the mountains because they are there.

Author's Acknowledgments

Providing easy-to-understand, practical information on a topic as complex, diverse, and fast-changing as ATM was a very challenging task. We wish to thank the many individuals who made our job a little easier by sharing their knowledge, suggestions, and support.

Thanks to our contributing authors for their thoughtful features sharing their unique insights and perspectives. And thank you for being ready resources when we needed additional information.

Chris Baldwin,
ATM Business Manager,
Cascade Communications, Inc.

David Beering, Senior Staff
Telecommunications Analyst,
Amoco Corporation

David Benham, ATM Product
Manager, Cisco Systems

Tim Dwight, Senior Engineer-
ATM Engineering,
MCI Telecommunications, Inc.

John Fjeld, Vice President of
Marketing, NetEdge

Beth Gage, Broadband
Consultant, TeleChoice, Inc.

Robert Gourley, Technical
Program Manager,
LDDS WorldCom

Mike Grubbs, ATM Group
Manager, Product Marketing,
Sprint

Tim Hale, ATM Program
Manager, Cabletron

Liza Henderson, Broadband
Consultant, TeleChoice, Inc.

Richard Klapman, Product
Director, Networking Services
Division, AT&T

Claire Lewis, Senior Manager
Broadband Cell Services,
MCI Telecommunications, Inc.

Martin McNealis, IP Product
Manager, Cisco Systems

Tony Rybczynski, Director
of Strategic Marketing,
Nortel Multimedia Networks

Joe Skorupa, Senior Director
of Product Marketing,
FORE Systems

Kieran Taylor, Broadband
Consultant, TeleChoice, Inc.,

Martin Taylor, VP Network
Architecture, Madge Networks

Thanks to the end users and service providers who shared their ATM implementation stories with us so that we could pass along real-world experiences and tips to our readers.

Bill Brasuell, Network Technologist, Tandem Computers, Inc.

Daniel Gasparro, Chief Technologist, Booz-Allen & Hamilton

Dr. Frederick George, MD, University of Southern California, Professor Emeritus of Radiology and of Radiation Oncology

Steve Glick, Manager of Networking and Distributed Communications, Dallas Community College

Phil Lawlor, President and CEO, AGIS

Alex Tashayoud, Senior Communications Analyst, Royal Bank of Canada

Martha Wendel, Network Architecture Planning, Cincinnati Bell Telephone

Thanks to the many individuals from the vendors who spent substantial time answering our questions as we tried to make heads or tails of the many aspects of the ATM market and technology, especially Cecil Christie, Morgan Littlewood, and George Swallow from Cisco Systems; Andrew Miazga from Ipsilon; Ravi Narayanan from Nortel Multimedia Networks; and Rich Borden, M. Vijay Raman, Andrew Reid, Jack Reinhart, Robert Schiff, Scott Searcy, Rebecca Thompson, Jacques Welter, and Jeffrey White from FORE Systems.

Cathy would like to thank the many individuals (too numerous to mention) from the ATM team at Sprint who taught her much about the development, implementation, and launch of an ATM network (as they all cut their teeth together on a brand new technology).

We would especially like to thank the individuals who spent long hours alongside us managing the project, writing text, and closely editing our work: Leah Cameron, who was our tireless, patient project editor at IDG Books; Pat Hurley who wrote our Cheat Sheet, Introduction, Chapter 20, Appendix A, and sections of Appendix B and who offered many helpful hints, suggestions, and edits as the first pair of eyes to review our text; Victor Frost who offered many helpful, informed suggestions as our Technical Editor; Leslie Lake who wrote the end-user case studies and coordinated the contributions of the feature writers; Fannie Davidson who wrote the sidebars on the Internet and intranets; Allen Robel who wrote an entertaining Foreword to introduce our book; Christy Beck and Nancy DelFavero, our copy editors at IDG Books; and the many others at IDG Books Worldwide, Inc. who made it all come together.

And finally, we owe an unpayable debt of gratitude to our husbands, Steve and Doug, who pulled many extra hours of babysitting duty so that we could finish the book this century!

Publisher's Acknowledgments

We're proud of this book; please send us your comments about it by using the Reader Response Card at the back of the book or by e-mailing us at feedback/dummies@idgbooks.com. Some of the people who helped bring this book to market include the following:

Acquisitions, Development, and Editorial

Senior Project Editor: Leah P. Cameron

Acquisitions Editor: Gareth Hancock

Product Development Director: Mary Bednarek

Copy Editors: Christine Meloy Beck, Tina Sims

Technical Editor: Victor S. Frost

General Reviewer: Tracy Barr

Editorial Manager: Mary C. Corder

Editorial Assistants: Chris H. Collins, Michael D. Sullivan

Production

Project Coordinator: Regina Snyder

Layout and Graphics: Dominique DeFelice, Maridee V. Ennis, Ruth E. G. Loiacano, Drew R. Moore, Brent Savage

Proofreaders: Nancy L. Reinhardt, Rachel Garvey, Karen York, Carrie Voorhis

Indexer: Richard Shrout

Special Help

Heather H. Dismore, Associate Permissions Editor
Nancy DelFavero, Project Editor,
Constance Carlisle, Copy Editor

General and Administrative

IDG Books Worldwide, Inc.: John Kilcullen, CEO; Steven Berkowitz, President and Publisher

IDG Books Technology Publishing: Brenda McLaughlin, Senior Vice President and Group Publisher

Dummies Technology Press and Dummies Editorial: Diane Graves Steele, Vice President and Associate Publisher; Judith A. Taylor, Brand Manager; Kristin A. Cocks, Editorial Director

Dummies Trade Press: Kathleen A. Welton, Vice President and Publisher; Stacy S. Collins, Brand Manager

IDG Books Production for Dummies Press: Beth Jenkins, Production Director; Cindy L. Phipps, Supervisor of Project Coordination, Production Proofreading and Indexing; Kathie S. Schutte, Supervisor of Page Layout; Shelley Lea, Supervisor of Graphics and Design; Debbie J. Gates, Production Systems Specialist; Tony Augsburger, Supervisor of Reprints and Bluelines; Leslie Popplewell, Media Archive Coordinator

Dummies Packaging and Book Design: Patti Sandez, Packaging Specialist; Kavish+Kavish, Cover Design

◆

The publisher would like to give special thanks to Patrick J. McGovern, without whom this book would not have been possible.

◆

Contents at a Glance

Cartoons at a Glance

By Rich Tennant • Fax: 508-546-7747 • E-mail: the5wave@tiac.net

page 131

page 295

page 207

page 339

page 11

Table of Contents

Foreword

I remember first reading about ATM on March 30, 1987, as a graduate student at Indiana University. For idle amusement, I used to go to the university's main library and pick books off the shelves at random, then open them to any page at all and start reading. On that particular night, the library's TK-TL section (where Mr. Dewey and his Decimals kept engineering texts) looked enticing and I happened upon the "Conference Record of the International Conference on Communications," dated June 1977, which contained Forgie and Nemeth's paper on "An efficient packetized voice/data network using statistical flow control." In 1977, the acronym *ATM* hadn't been concocted yet, but this paper, and others like it, introduced me to such concepts as *virtual circuit* and *uniform-sized packets*. I was fascinated and remain so to this day.

Now, the reason I can pinpoint this night with such certitude is because — while I was inside reading about this strange new technology (and wondering why the library was all but vacant) — the Indiana Hoosiers were busy winning the NCAA championship in New Orleans. The rest of the population of Bloomington, ablaze in rapturous giddiness, had taken temporary leave of its collective sanity. Inside the library's windowless walls, I was oblivious to all of this. Indeed, I didn't even realize our university had a basketball team to speak of. At 11:30, a voice on the speaker system interrupted the quiet solitude: "The library will be closing in 15 minutes." Reluctantly, I packed my book bag, slung it over my shoulder, and walked out the front door into...utter pandemonium! I watched with a mixture of confusion, awe, and trepidation as bumper-to-bumper cars, their horns blaring and crammed to the gills with way too many overly exuberant students, stood deadlocked in the worst traffic jam I'd ever seen. I guess my book bag gave me away because cries of "Whatta geek!" and "You nerd!" accompanied me all the way home.

You won't find much argument with the assertion that in 1987, ATM's intrigue was limited to hard-core geeks and nerds. At that time, ATM existed merely as ink on a small but increasing number of very dry research papers on queuing theory, switch fabric design, and other heady matters — topics that held zero relevance to the daily concerns of network managers and planners. After several years, however, ATM slowly coalesced, and articles began to surface in the popular trade press. (My guess is that the 10baseT versus Token Ring wars were subsiding and telecommunications geeks had to have something controversial to write about.)

By 1992, the hype surrounding ATM was beginning to escalate and, still very much interested in the technology, I formulated (petitioned?) a Usenet Call For Votes to create a newsgroup called *comp.dcom.cell-relay.* I intended to provide a discussion forum for All Things ATM. The vote passed, and in May of that year, the first messages started flowing. As is often the case on Usenet, the hype melted like butter against the fiery words of many of the newsgroup's contributors.

While the newsgroup has been a blessing in the years since, I have often wished for a book about ATM that would distill the relevant pieces of this multifaceted and complex technology into a manageable form and present it in a way that clarifies its application in real-world networks. In other words, a book that provides, in a layperson's terms, answers to questions like: How do I use this stuff? What does it buy me? What do I need to get started? *ATM For Dummies* is that book! My thanks go out to the authors and to the folks at TeleChoice for a job well done.

Allen Robel
Senior Network Analyst
Indiana University

Introduction

....

Welcome to *ATM For Dummies*. Asynchronous Transfer Mode (ATM) is one of the newest and most technically complex set of standards, products, services, and protocols in the communications industry. Nearly everyone, including the authors and contributors of this book, can be baffled by ATM in at least one respect or another — because ATM is not just one thing, but instead, is many things.

Many? Yes, ATM is a communications protocol suite for the desktop, the local area network (LAN), the campus backbone network, and the wide area network (WAN). (By the way, we explain the preceding networking terms and concepts — along with many others — throughout this book.) Although the ATM protocol is basically the same in all these environments, the issues, obstacles, and alternatives regarding ATM can differ greatly. Therefore, someone who is an expert in ATM for wide area networking may not feel nearly as confident when discussing ATM in the local area or campus backbone environments.

Whatever your level of expertise (or NOT) with ATM, you should only bother reading this book if:

- You are in a marketing, operations, or engineering department, or are a financial analyst, manager, director, president, stock investment enthusiast, or wannabe, in the computer, communications, cable, or utility industries and need to get in touch with one of the many cosmic forces converging to shape the astrological charts for networking in the '90s and beyond.

- You are the CIO of an organization and your networking people keep talking about ATM and asking for a lot of money to go out and implement this technology, and you want to better understand what you're paying for.

- You are an MIS director, network manager, or other laborer in a data communications or MIS department and are tired of getting all of your information about ATM from sales people, trade publications, and advertisements. We give you the real inside scoop — not some over-hyped marketing pabulum.

- You are interested in networking and have heard about the supposedly magical networking properties of a modern-day talisman called ATM, but don't have a local witch doctor to consult about getting some for yourself.

- You are new to the telecommunications industry and need an overview of this acronym you constantly hear bantered about.

✔ You, your boss, and/or your company are looking for ways to gain a competitive market advantage, and buying out your largest competitors is out of the question for this fiscal year.

✔ You are a byte-junky, computer nerd, Internet geek, enginerd, or other techno-minority just interested in finding alternatives to social activities and interaction with other humanoids. (Don't feel bad, some of our best friends are just like you.)

✔ You are a student looking for an exciting, stressful, fun-filled, stressful, fast-moving, (did we mention stressful?) career in the ever-changing, always-interesting communications industry.

✔ You are involved in the telecommunications industry on the voice side of the house and want to understand what all the ATM hype is about.

✔ One of your self-proclaimed *cutting-edge* friends told you that ATM stands for Another Tragic Mistake — and you've learned to always believe the opposite of what he or she says. (We have a few friends like this, too.)

✔ You are married to any one of the above, or you are married to the authors of this book (Hi, Steve and Doug!), and you want to know what we do for a living! (Not! :+)

If you own or operate a 9.6 Kbps network between fewer than 20 sites, or are using modems to send information between network locations, you can read this book, but you may want to look into buying frame relay (not ATM) to improve your network's price/performance. (See, we really are looking out for your interests.)

If you own and operate an Ethernet or token ring LAN and it works fine, never gets congested, and supports the applications you need supported for the foreseeable future, you, too, can read this book. But you probably don't need ATM and you may be better off sticking with what you have today, even if you're looking into some packet-based desktop video applications just for fun.

If you are in the banking industry and picked up this book to find out more about Automatic Teller Machines, put this book down. YOU ARE IN THE WRONG SECTION OF THE BOOKSTORE.

About This Book

Like all ...*For Dummies* books, this book takes a refreshing approach to a difficult technical subject. We don't intend to fill page after page with minutia and detail, and we don't expect you to read the book from cover to cover. But we do plan on telling you what you need to know to understand ATM and to make an intelligent decision about how, when, why, and even whether ATM is for you and your network.

Look in the Table of Contents and find a topic that interests you. Turn to the index in the back of the book and find your area of interest there. Or just open the book to any page and start reading.

The important point is that you don't need to read the chapters in order. But to help you in your *ATM For Dummies* adventure, you find sections in the book with topics like these:

- ✔ What ATM stands for and what *that* means
- ✔ Who determines the all important standards that make ATM work
- ✔ *Some* technical details of the ATM standard, but in user-friendly language
- ✔ Where ATM is or can be used in various areas of the network — and to what benefit
- ✔ How competing technologies stack up against ATM
- ✔ Who's using ATM today — and how it's working for them
- ✔ Where to go (beyond this book) to learn more about ATM

Conventions Used in This Book

Remember that *ATM For Dummies* is a reference book! That means that you can refer back to the book any time you want. Don't try to memorize the information, but feel free to mark your favorite spots in the book (you know, dog-ear the page, get out your trusty highlighter, and so on) so that you can easily find them again.

This book is a bit unique in the *...For Dummies* book arena. That is, the book isn't exactly swimming with conventions that we use to show you what keys to press on your keyboard, what to type into a text box on-screen, and so on. However, we'd like to point out one convention to watch for: We like to give you references to online resources on the World Wide Web (WWW) that may give you more information about ATM. When we include the online resource addresses, or URLs (Uniform Resource Locators), they appear in monospaced font like this: `http://www.atmforum.com`

Or if the URL is on a separate line, it may look like this:

```
http://www.atmforum.com
```

What You're Not to Read

We want to demystify ATM for you, and strip away the hype that surrounds this most eagerly anticipated and talked-about communications technology. While we aren't going to discuss the technological issues that large groups of PhDs spend years arguing about, we must discuss some aspects of ATM in technical terms — with an emphasis on technical issues that most effect the decision to become an ATM user or ATM avoider. We also include a few tips and considerations for implementing ATM networks.

Because ATM is such a complex topic, at times the book's discussions may seem a bit *over*-technical — but we warn you when that happens (before your eyes glaze over). We clearly mark the affected paragraphs with an icon that identifies the passages as *Technical Stuff*. And we tell you what's really important to understand and what you can gloss over if you wish.

Foolish Assumptions

We don't assume that you have an encyclopedic knowledge of telecommunications and networking, but we do assume that you understand the basics — things like the basic makeup and usage of networks. And we do assume that you're knowledgeable about the needs of your organization's network and that you want to know whether ATM can meet those needs.

We don't just want you to take our word about ATM either, so interspersed throughout the book you find editorials, testimonials, and opinions from lots of different people — including other TeleChoice consultants, ATM vendors, ATM service providers, and real-life ATM end users — to give you a good idea where ATM stands and where its headed.

A word of warning — we've both been up to our ears for a bit too long in the telecommunications world, the place that spawned the Dilbert cartoons (which often mirror our working lives a bit too closely), so if our humor seems a bit skewed to the techie, please oblige us and laugh anyway. And we both have small children (Cathy has three, Alex, Eric, and little Kara) and Chris has one (Ty). We, like many of you, have seen too many hours of children's TV, so if a reference to the purple dino or any other similar character slips in, don't say we didn't warn you.

How This Book Is Organized

The rest of this introduction outlines the layout and contents of the book. We hope that this organization makes finding exactly what you're looking for on the subject of ATM even easier. The book is divided into four main parts, with two supporting appendixes at the end.

Part I: Finding Out Why, What, Where, Who, And When

The only way to get into a complex technology like ATM is to start at the ground floor. In Part I, we'll break down ATM for you — and explain what the pieces and parts are all about, and why you should know about them. We'll give you a good overview of ATM, including what it's used for, and who's pulling the strings that make ATM happen. Part I is the place to get started if you know absolutely nothing about ATM.

This part is less technical than the remaining parts of the book and provides a good overview without requiring prior knowledge of a lot of networking terms. We even give you a chapter to read if you just want to be able to converse in ATMese — that's the secret language known only to those fully initiated in the deep, dark secrets of ATM. (We'll even share with you the special right of initiation into ATM's secret club.)

Part II: Finding Out How ATM Works

Part II of the book digs into the components and standards of ATM in more technical detail. Do you like fun networking stuff like protocols, interoperability, service quality, network usage, and so on? Well then, this is the part for you.

Do you hate stuff like that, but still need to get a handle on it? Our goal is to present this information in a way that keeps you from pulling out all your hair and keeps you away from that huge container of ice cream, hot fudge, or your indulgence of choice. (Of course, after you successfully get through the chapters in Part II, you have reason to dig into these delicacies in celebration!) So dig in, discover ATM, and (we hope) have a bit of fun.

You can also use this part as a technical resource to look up technical terms as you need them. If you don't need to understand a lot about technology in your job, you can skip this section. Just use it as a handy reference on those rare occasions that you have to understand how something works.

Part III: Investing In ATM: Decisions, Decisions!

In Part III, we discuss many risks and benefits that adopting ATM carries with it. Our goal is to give you the tools you need to make a sound decision about using ATM yourself. We cover considerations for both your local and wide area networks and include a few practical thoughts on justifying and implementing your network.

This part adds a bonus: real-world case studies of companies and organizations that are using ATM right now — today! We let you know what trials and tribulations these organizations went through and what payoffs they're getting from their investment.

Part IV: The Part of Tens

Although we're big fans of a well-written chapter that digs into detail and provides a thorough explanation of an important subject, we recognize that sometimes a short, quick reference is what you need. This part of the book is designed to be just that — a place to dig up some quick facts or to find the answers in a nice, easy, distilled format. This is also the part where you can find a list of additional resources and references for ATM.

Part V: Appendixes

Just because the appendixes come last doesn't mean you should ignore them. In Part V of the book, we provide you with detailed information about the ATM Forum (the international body that provides a lot of the standards and marketing support for ATM) — including information on how you can (and whether you should) join the Forum.

We also provide a glossary of ATM terms, so that you have a place to find out the difference between a FUNI and a UNI.

Icons Used in This Book

Just in case you've never read a ...*For Dummies* book before (we're sure most of you have, but maybe there's someone out there who hasn't!), we'd like to highlight the icons that we use throughout the book. Each icon has a specific meaning, but in general, they serve to point out something important or unique — something that you probably want to take note of.

Each of the *Inside ATM* features that we include in the book is accompanied by an icon that carries the name of that feature's author.

The Key Concept icon flags an aspect of ATM or networking that is essential to understanding the technology.

Our friend the Multiplicity octopus marks the instances where the multiple-personality of ATM technology or networking is most apparent.

The Remember icon marks information that you need to keep in mind as you continue your discovery of ATM.

With the Technical Stuff icon, we point out extra-neat stuff that makes this technology actually work. But you don't have to read it to understand the basics.

The warning icon flags areas of ATM that are potentially troublesome.

In addition to icons, we include several diagrams in *ATM For Dummies* to help us explain the complexities of ATM. The wonderful graphics and design team at IDG Books has prepared the following standard components that bring consistency and meaning to these diagrams. Feel free to refer back here to refresh your memory of what these diagram elements mean.

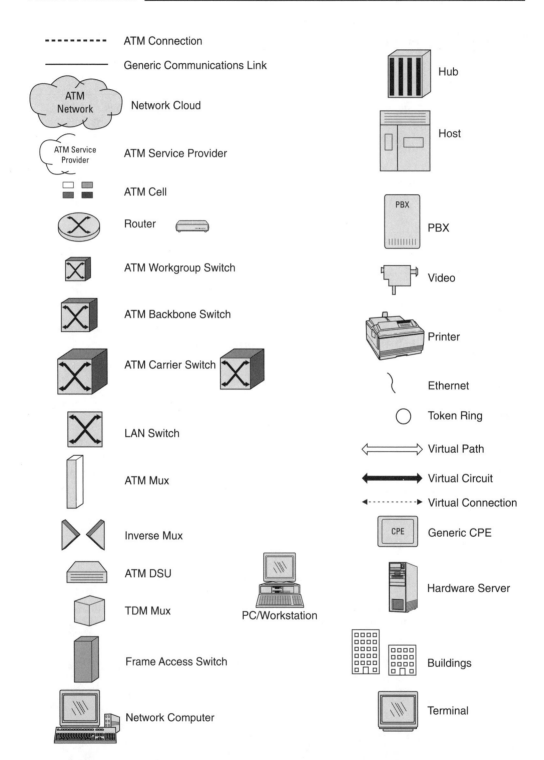

Where to Go from Here

Open the book anywhere and forge ahead into the realm of ATM!

But on your journey, we ask that you keep us (your authors) in mind. We want to finish this introduction with a request for your opinions, experiences, nightmares, triumphs with ATM — whatever. Let us know what you think of *ATM For Dummies*, and what we can do to make it even more useful to you. We'll do our best to incorporate your comments and experiences into the next version of the book.

We wrote this book based on our experiences in developing and launching ATM (and non-ATM!) products and services, and from working with earlier ATM users. Both of us began working with ATM as product managers for major service providers, but we have also developed and launched many services that compete head-to-head with ATM in the wide area network. We hope that our experience gives us a balanced and realistic perspective that we pass along in this book.

We now spend our days consulting with service providers and equipment vendors around the world, helping to craft ATM and other data communications strategies, products, and services that we hope will be successful and meet a real market need. We've drawn on the resources of industry insiders, ATM standards, and the advice and guidance of friends. We openly welcome any additional ATM information or insight that you may have.

Our company is based in New Jersey, but many of the data folks are in our other U.S. offices. If you want to contact us, please feel free to do so at the following address:

TeleChoice, Inc.
8555 N. 117th E. Ave, Suite 100A
Owasso, OK 74055

Or send us an email at any of these addresses

atmdummies@telechoice.com
checkart@telechoice.com
cgadecki@telechoice.com

We look forward to hearing from you.

Part I

Finding Out Why,
What, Where, Who,
And When

In this part . . .

ATM is a complex, multifaceted technology for networking. Part I takes you on a whirlwind tour where you can meet the many faces of ATM. You get the eight-part definition of ATM, a description of ATM in different networking environments, a discussion of who needs ATM (and why), and even a glimpse into the jargon-infested networking jungle. Go ahead — delve into this part and discover the scope of ATM.

Chapter 1

Why All the Fuss about ATM? An Executive's Summary

*I*f you've been living in a closet or on a mountaintop, you may not have heard that society is headed for a bright, new world where interactive information technology brings everything you need or want to know to your desktop, your doorstep, and even your bedside. We all hope that the changes brought about by this information explosion have a strong positive influence — making our lives richer, healthier, and happier.

The World Wide Web (WWW), a worldwide network of computers, offers a shining potential for exchanging and distributing information, ideas, goods, and services that has already attracted millions of consumers and thousands of businesses like love-sick moths. (We sure hope that's not a bug light at the end of the tunnel!) Although the World Wide Web (WWW) has a long way to go, it offers a glimpse into a future full of fantastic possibilities. Every day, people become more comfortable with and more addicted to electronic interaction.

As users of information technology, individuals and businesses are figuring out how to send and receive information efficiently. And handling information is what ATM is all about, which leads us to what this book is all about . . . ATM.

ATM stands for *Asynchronous Transfer Mode* — a communications networking technology that carries information (voice, video, data, or whatever) in 53-byte chunks known as *cells*. The fixed-length cell allows a network to carry any type of information within the cell and also provide stringent service qualities that can differ by application. In this book, we spend lots of time telling you about the details of the technology, about how you can tell whether you need ATM, about who can help you implement ATM, about the benefits and costs of implementing ATM, and so on.

More Information, NOW!

Although the business community tends to blaze new communication trails first, the advanced products and services of the information industry eventually find their way into people's homes. And when they do, they transform daily lives — just look at the way business and personal communications revolve around the telephone, computer, and TV. Your parents and grandparents couldn't have imagined how dependent their descendants' lives would be on these technologies. Neither can you imagine how your life may change over the next decade as technological miracles are translated into practical products and services.

These changes will affect you regardless of your industry, your title, your expectations, or your understanding. And ATM can play a fundamental role in bringing about many changes in the way new communications services evolve. ATM's high bandwidth is essential for building large carrier backbones, the networks over which voice and data services are delivered. ATM also promises to be the first communications protocol that extends seamlessly from the computer through the LAN (local area network) and the WAN (wide area network). But first ATM must show that it can improve upon the price/performance capabilities of competing options such as IP and frame relay.

Running a Business Electronically

The electronic exchange of information with customers and suppliers, and also between employees, is now a basic business requirement whether you work for yourself in your garage or work for a multinational conglomerate. You no longer just need a phone and fax, but also an Internet address, and probably a Web page as well (and maybe a fax-on-demand network, and videoconferencing, and collaborative whiteboards, and — well, you get the idea).

ATM can have a significant impact on information exchange in areas that are important to modern businesses, like the following:

✔ **ATM can support business process re-engineering:** Corporations are continually exploring how new telecommunications capabilities can lower costs, improve productivity, sell goods and services, and bring new ideas to market. In this rapidly changing global community, long-term survival means discovering the answers to these questions before your competitors do.

✔ **ATM improves the flow of information:** The competitive importance of accurate, timely information significantly elevates its strategic value in the business. The ability to better organize, distribute, control, and leverage the growing stockpile of information creates a new maze of challenges. These challenges reach far beyond the walls of the information systems department into the core of the business strategy.

✔ **ATM offers fast communications for decentralized organizations:** New corporate business structures (the new virtual corporation) support the fluid, dynamic, and often chaotic business environment of today. Through the magic of networking, remote employees can access the same resources and tools that the employees in the ivory tower of corporate headquarters use.

✔ **ATM provides communication linkage for effective collaboration:** Many people, from down the hall to around the globe, can electronically come together on a project-by-project basis to solve a problem or develop a new product. This shrinking of distance through communication links lets an organization take advantage of resource pools across the nation and around the world. (For example, we're working on this book from different offices, from our homes, and while on the road — with only our telecommunications resources holding us together.)

✔ **Networking with ATM can speed up market response and product development:** Setting up (and using) great communications infrastructures enables businesses to respond quickly to new market conditions, collaborate on new projects, implement organizational changes, add new partners or even owners, and reach new customers. Business partnerships can exist for the life of a project and then quickly melt away . . . only to be established again (with new faces and new ideas) to conquer the next opportunity.

Is ATM Really All That?

The words *Asynchronous Transfer Mode* don't intuitively communicate much outside of the tech labs that spawned them. And defining ATM's bits and bytes alone does not provide a complete picture of what ATM represents. Some true believers think that ATM may literally revolutionize our daily existence a few decades hence. Others wonder whether ATM can ever get very far beyond the lab and question its practicality and cost-effectiveness.

What is this technology that's causing such an eruption of industry news coverage and controversy, not to mention billions of dollars of research investment? Does it represent the future of telecommunications, or a technologist's fantasy dream world?

ATM is simply a new way to transmit information from one point to another. In some ways, ATM is much more efficient than more traditional networking mechanisms; in other ways, less. All the following concepts accurately describe ATM, highlighting its scope and its potential for being misunderstood.

- ✔ **ATM is a set of rules** for handling the transmission of electronic information between two (or more) points. (ATM is the etiquette for how you greet an associate, conduct a meeting, and say "Good-bye.")

- ✔ **ATM is a communications process** that segments information into fixed-length cells of 53 bytes for rapid distribution. (ATM is the cafeteria worker that quickly doles out even portions to every hungry kid in line — and makes sure that the line keeps moving!)

- ✔ **ATM is a communications protocol** for sharing transmission resources through asynchronous multiplexing and interconnecting those resources with switching. (ATM is the dock manager that organizes the flow of goods off the boats, through the warehouses, onto the trucks, and out to the retailers.)

- ✔ **ATM is a replacement technology for local area networks** that provides very high-speed dedicated connections (bandwidth) to individual users/ workstations. (ATM is the express lane to downtown.)

- ✔ **ATM is a replacement technology for campus networks** that increases the size of the LAN backbone to handle more traffic and more users. (ATM is the interstate that replaces the highway.)

- ✔ **ATM is a high bandwidth service of public carriers** providing virtual networking between many locations. ATM meets the broad information needs of the enterprise by supporting many different traffic types. (ATM is the Cadillac of carriers, offering advanced features and lots of room to those wishing to travel in style.)

- ✔ **ATM is a transfer mode** in which the information is organized into cells. It is asynchronous in the sense that the recurrence of the cells containing information from an individual user is not necessarily periodic. (ATM is the segmented conveyor belt that carries different components to the assembly line workers in a random order.)

- ✔ **ATM is a telecommunications concept** defined by ANSI and ITU standards (refer to ATM Forum UNI 3.1) for carriage of a complete range of user traffic — including voice, data, and video signals — on any *user-network interface* (UNI). (ATM is the freight train delivering a variety of goods in standardized shipping containers.)

We can create a lot of different definitions for ATM, but the idea behind ATM is simple. ATM creates a faster, more efficient way to electronically move information in mass quantities, while treating different types of information in an appropriate manner.

Transferring Information — and How to Do It

When you talk about sending and receiving information over communications networks, you can refer to the information as *traffic*. And you must recognize that different kinds of traffic need different handling. Also, as more people use the network, the amount of traffic increases, which in turn can cause slower transmission of the traffic. ATM addresses both the required differences in traffic handling and the issue of speed.

Getting your information across

When voice traffic is sent over a network, it needs to be treated differently than data traffic. But different types of data traffic need different network treatment; video traffic acts like voice traffic in some respects, and like data in others. And because the needs of the communications traffic types are so different, a separate network is typically built to support each unique set of application needs.

ATM networks help to simplify information traffic control by providing common traffic vehicles (the ATM fixed-length cell) and rules of the road (the ATM protocol). The result is that the different types of traffic can all share the same roadway — some get the fast lane, some get the right-of-way, and most get where they're headed without incident.

Seeing the need for speed in your network

The use of networks is increasing, and with this increase comes additional demands on a network capacity for traffic-handling. As applications require more bandwidth and more people use the network for more things, traditional network solutions (such as Ethernet and token ring LANs and T1/E1 connections) may not be fast enough. Even fast Ethernet and FDDI (fiber distributed data interface) stop at 100 Mbps, which may not be enough in some networks. (Can you ever have too much network speed?)

ATM offers an increased capacity to handle more network traffic at greater speeds (in excess of 622 Mbps), as well as the capacity to handle a variety of different traffic types.

Looking at other technologies

Networks come in many sizes and with many designated uses. Throughout the book, we talk about the requirements of these different networks: LANs (local area networks), WANs (wide area networks), MANs (metropolitan area networks), and so on. Although ATM is designed so that it can be used in any of these network types, implementing ATM in each type has its own challenges.

Other technologies, such as Ethernet and token ring for LANs and private lines and frame relay for WANs, compete with ATM to satisfy the user's networking needs. The different networking technologies come with different specifications for hardware, different price points, and various capabilities and benefits. The point is that you have many options for setting up a network and many choices that you must make. ATM is one of several available technologies.

Okay, So Where Does ATM Fit In?

Communications industry *problems* such as the information glut, instantaneous collaboration, and process re-engineering have been oversimplified and overhyped. But elements of truth and huge pockets of potential lie behind the headlines. Few people question that the future holds more information needs, more interactive applications, and more and different ways to communicate, learn, buy, sell, and entertain. Billion-dollar fortunes and losses are riding on *when* and *how* these *more* and *different* communications systems develop.

ATM is an important part of the mix of technologies that may enable profound changes in the application of information technologies over the next decade and beyond. ATM offers ways to move information faster and potentially more cost-effectively than ever before. In fact, ATM's expectation to meet so many of the future world's requirements may now be its greatest liability. While ATM developers struggle to add fancy features and functions to meet every networking problem known to man and woman, network managers have been aggressively implementing other relatively new technologies that work just fine today. These technologies are also under intense development, quickly catching up to the promised capabilities of ATM.

Over the next decade, the marketplace is the battleground where ATM fights with other networking technologies for its role in the new information infrastructure. ATM is sure to become a common element of large enterprise and carrier backbones over time. Other segments of the network may also benefit from ATM and depend on the supported application, existing equipment, costs of ownership, and implementation time frames. When and where you use ATM in your network depends upon your future requirements and ATM's success in delivering not only the best solution at the best price, but also at a price that you are willing to pay.

Inside ATM with Cathy Gadecki
Senior Broadband Consultant
TeleChoice, Inc., (Corporate Headquarters) Verona, NJ
`cgadecki@telechoice.com`

The Price of Bandwidth

When you look at all the reasons given by ATM vendors, experts, and fans for the ultimate success of ATM in the marketplace, you can trace each back to a single root: the price of bandwidth.

The price of bandwidth today is just too high for all the things we want to do, like link into online industry conferences from anywhere through real-time video, tap into multimedia Web sites full of valuable information without having time to run around the block while our screen paints the images, use intelligent agents to search corporate databases for just the right slide for the presentation we have to do in an hour, or even work at our homes in the mountains (or on an island) with faster access than we get with our modems and ISDN lines.

What we could do if the price of bandwidth were free!

ATM's high speed; its ability to simultaneously meet the quality of service demands of voice, data, and video; its use in both the LAN and the WAN; its virtual connectivity; and its interoperability with existing protocols all contribute towards the goal of lower-priced bandwidth. Indeed, much of ATM's complexity comes from this goal and getting as much information as possible out of every bandwidth bit.

Some people question whether ATM's high overhead penalty and technical complexity are worth the incremental bandwidth gains it may achieve. They also wonder how much ATM's elaborate schemes are really helping. In fact, ATM is now just beginning to deliver on its promises of providing statistical bandwidth gain that lowers bandwidth costs.

Other people argue that the price of bandwidth is already falling rapidly without ATM. They point to technologies such as SONET

(synchronous optical network) and WDM (wave division multiplexing). SONET optical systems can increase the speed of a single fiber pair from a previous maximum of 1.7 Gbps to 9.6 Gbps, and a gigabit per second (Gbps) is 1000 megabits per second (Mbps) — that's a lot of bandwidth! Using WDM to support multiple optical systems on a single fiber pair can multiply the available capacity by another 16 times to give nearly 100 times more bandwidth than was available just two years ago. And research labs are pushing both the SONET and WDM numbers even higher.

Looking at these facts, one has to ask whether the ATM effort is really worth it. Will its improvements in the utilization of bandwidth be worth its costs?

It is my opinion that the answer to this question must be "Yes," at least in certain segments of the network. I give this answer for two reasons in the wide area network. First, the installation of SONET and WDM technology does not come without cost, so don't expect your phone bill to drop 99 percent in the next few years. Second, even if bandwidth bills did drop 50 percent or more in the next five years (not an unlikely scenario with new technology and competition), our insatiable appetite for bandwidth would quickly erase the gains, and we'd all be looking for even further improvement — that is, we'd be looking for ATM. I can think of many ways to use even 100 times the bandwidth that my 28 Kbps modem currently supplies.

But the discussion in the preceding paragraph is really only relevant for the wide area. What about the campus network?

I believe that the bandwidth costs of even the campus can justify the installation of ATM. Making the most of existing wiring can be

(continued)

very important in a campus or building. Ripping up walls, floors, and ceilings to add new wiring can be very expensive and disruptive to the work environment. Sometimes, doing this ripping-up is not even possible in older or leased buildings. Laying new wiring between buildings can be even more challenging if doing so requires that you cross easements. Many times, getting the necessary right-of-way from the municipality isn't possible, especially in congested city blocks.

If bandwidth were free, unlimited capacity could solve almost any networking problem. But because it's not free (nor will it be anytime in the near or even long-term future), cost-effective solutions which better utilize bandwidth are (and will be) useful. ATM is such a solution, providing bandwidth efficiencies without sacrificing performance of different traffic types.

So if you agree that lowering the cost of bandwidth is a truly worthy goal for ATM, I move on to the second argument raised against ATM: Other available technologies can achieve the goal for better price/performance. These other available technologies include Ethernet, frame relay, and IP, with their emerging enhancements.

On this second point, ATM and its supporters have a more difficult task ahead, at least at the edges of the network. In the WAN and campus backbone, ATM's scale, service integration capabilities, and costs set it above the competitors. IP is just beginning to try and meet the service integration challenges which ATM has been working to resolve for the past five years, and IP's inherent connectionless operations impose immediate technical constraints and costs to solutions. Frame relay's long packet lengths ultimately require more bandwidth than ATM to avoid congestion so that real-time traffic can move quickly through the network. Ethernet shares this same difficulty.

On the edge of the network, whether it be from the local switch to the desktop or from the wide area switch to the customer location, these alternative technologies will probably be able to deliver the required capabilities. ATM will only be successful in these segments of the network if it can beat the cost and ease-of-use of the alternatives, or if the needed bandwidth speed just becomes too great for these options.

So ATM's challenge is to deliver on its promise of a lower price of bandwidth at a cost and ease that make it worth all the effort, while beating the price/performance of the alternatives. If ATM cannot meet this challenge in the targeted segments of the network, it will never gain widespread use. But if it ultimately comes through, we may all someday join those lucky few who already work at home on an island!

Chapter 2

Just Give Me the Scoop (How to Sound Like an ATM Expert)

● ●

In This Chapter

▶ Talking ATM like a pro

▶ Looking at definitions galore

▶ Making the ATM connection

▶ Going to ATM service class

▶ Quality of Service is (ATM's) job one

▶ Using ATM in all the different types of networks

▶ Hey Rocky, watch me pull a standard out of my hat

● ●

The telecommunications industry, like most other industries, has its own language. The language is not quite English, although someone who speaks English could pick up and understand at least every other word. When you talk about ATM, however, it's like speaking a foreign language. The uninitiated don't understand one word in ten. In fact, you can put together entire sentences that are meaningless outside the ATM circle. For example:

> The QoS parameter to control jitter is CDV, and for a VBR-RT VCC or VPC is typically 1 msec in a long distance network.

Think of using ATM jargon as sort of like being in junior high when you used *in* words in front of your parents and they didn't have a clue as to what you were talking about. You were cool; they were nerds. Of course, we're adults now and no one in the telecom industry would make up a bunch of words and acronyms just to needlessly confuse other people and have a little chuckle. (Or would they? When you get through with this chapter you may just wonder.)

The sources (culprits?) that coined many of these terms are the ATM Forum and the International Telecommunications Union (ITU). The ATM Forum is an international non-profit organization formed with the stated objective of "accelerating the use of ATM products and services through a rapid convergence of interoperability specifications" (their words). You can find out more about the Forum (as it is commonly known by the ATM inner circle) in Appendix A. The ITU is an international organization providing specifications in all aspects of telecommunications.

Several key concepts make up ATM, and each concept is surrounded by a plethora of acronyms and buzzwords. In this chapter, we hit the key concepts of ATM and describe the associated acronyms and buzzwords for you. After you have the ATM secret decoder ring, know the special handshake, and run naked through a cemetery at midnight with whipped cream on your nose and egg in your hair, you know the real meaning of each of these words and can carry on complex-sounding discussions with yourself while your peers look on enviously.

In this chapter and throughout the book, we do our best to explain away the mysteries of ATM. But if you still have questions after you read this book, you may find that you can't avoid this ATM initiation ritual. (We suggest waiting for a warm, moonless night.)

Cell That Network

If you knew that this book was not about bank machines when you picked it up, then you may already know that ATM has a basic structure called a *cell*. (For all you Tim-The-Tool-Man fans we are sorry to report that this has nothing to do with batteries. ATM is not the latest technology for wireless power to your circular saw.)

The *cell* is the most fundamental element of the ATM network and the nucleus around which all the benefits of ATM revolve. (You can't expect us to talk about cells without using some sort of biology reference, now can you?) The ATM cell is very important. In fact, sometimes ATM is referred to as *cell relay* because it uses these special cells. If you have ever read a book or sat through a training class about ATM, you probably spent a lot of time hearing about the length of the ATM cell and the information contained at the beginning of the cell. After you know this information, everything is supposed to become clear because, after all, now you know the definition of the ATM cell. Anytime you hear something about ATM, you hear about these silly cells.

CELLS! CELLS! CELLS! What's the big, fat, hairy deal about cells?

The *cell* is how ATM packages information to be sent over the network. All cells happen to be the same size (that's why this structure is called a *cell* and not a *packet* or a *frame* as in other networking technologies). The size of the cell is always 53 bytes, which is a relatively small package for transmitting data. (In the *Inside ATM* feature located at the end of this chapter, you find out about the reason behind the 53-byte cell size.)

The cell is what makes ATM unique compared to other networking protocols. The switching of cells enables two important benefits of ATM:

- ✔ The ability to intermingle voice, data, and video without compromising the unique needs of each application.
- ✔ The ability to switch the information very quickly in hardware.

You may hear an ATM cell compared to a boxcar on a train. The analogy is overused, but effective. Basically, the analogy says that the cell is like the container (hopper car) on a coal train. Each container is the same size for ease of loading and transmission. Imagine that the train is at a coal mine and the train goes by the loading dock at a consistent speed so that each hopper car (container) can be filled with coal. Some containers may get more coal than others, but the train keeps chugging away at the same speed. This method is a fast and highly efficient way to fill the train and get the coal transported to its destination.

Packaging information into a cell is typically referred to as *cellification*. (This word may bring to mind *cellophane* for some and *putrification* for others, but it actually has nothing to do with either. Really!)

Cellification enables voice, data, and video support

This ATM method of packaging information, or cellification, allows ATM networks to handle a combination of voice, data, and video information and still provide an optimized transmission environment for each information type.

When voice traffic is sent over a network, it needs to be treated differently than data traffic. And different types of data traffic need different network treatment. Video traffic acts like voice traffic in some respects and like data traffic in others. Because the needs are so different, a separate network is typically built to support each unique set of application needs.

By putting the information from these different applications into cells, the cells can share the same network but still be treated in a manner that provides adequate performance to the end user. Depending on the requirements of the application, some cells can be treated in a high-priority manner and transmitted with a high level of consistency and predictability (which is desirable for voice traffic). Other cells may receive a lower priority, be held back momentarily in preference of higher-priority cells, and have less consistency and predictability in their transmission. Many data applications operate just fine under the lower-priority conditions.

You can find out more about the magical properties of voice, data, and video in Chapters 3 and 9.

Cellification enables fast switching in hardware

The cellification of information has a second advantage, which solves a problem that more network managers are facing today: the need for more speed. As applications require more *bandwidth* and more people use the network for more applications, traditional network solutions such as Ethernet and token ring LANs, and T1/E1 connections are not fast enough. Even fast Ethernet and FDDI (fiber distributed data interface) stop at 100 Mbps, which may not be enough in some networks. (Can you ever have too much network speed?)

ATM gets its speed from the cells' fixed length. Unlike most other networking technologies with variable length packets or frames (including Ethernet, FDDI, token ring, frame relay and TCP/IP), the ATM switching hardware always knows where each cell ends and begins. The hardware doesn't have to waste time and processing power to find these critical delineators. The switch also always finds the cell addressing information in the same place — in the cell header making up the first few bytes of the cell.

To determine the right output port for each incoming cell, the switch has to read only some very basic information in the cell *header*. The cell header identifies the logical connection (see the following section "It's All in Your Connections") that takes the cell to its destination. The switching hardware does not have to make a routing decision for each and every cell; this is done only once — at connection setup. Because the handling of each cell is so simple, it can be automated and built right into the network switch as an automatic function. This automation enables tremendous switching speeds — the cells move in and out of switches like greased lightning.

The equipment used by other networking protocols requires much more processing-intensive functions, like finding start and stop bits or determining the right output port through complex routing functions. You can find out more about this routing process and the complexity that it adds to internetworking protocols in Chapter 3.

Now you know everything

Surely after you understand that ATM uses cells that are 53 bytes, everything about ATM becomes perfectly clear? No? Well, if ATM is still a little fuzzy, you could try sitting like a pretzel in a small white room with incense burning and Tibetan music playing, while you silently meditate on the cosmic powers of the 53-byte cell. I'm sure we could find many amazing coincidences of the number 53 throughout human history, which would help to explain the powerful significance of this number and why ATM is destined to intertwine fates with mankind — numerology is a hobby of ours.

Or, you can just continue reading and we can do our best to enlighten you in the old-fashioned way.

It's All in Your Connections

You have many ways to send information from one point to another. You can use the postal service (known as *snailnet* in networking circles). You can walk (otherwise known as *sneakernet*). You can send information over a LAN (such as Ethernet). You can wake up at 4 a.m. and channel a light-being that claims to be from the lost city of Atlantis (that gives new meaning to the word *ethernet*). But, if you are using an ATM network, you send information over virtual connections. A *virtual connection* defines a logical networking path between two endpoints on the network, and the ATM cells going from one point to the other travel over this connection. Virtual connections are *logical* because they are defined in software or in the memory of the networking devices.

An ATM network can have two types of virtual connections, depending on the addressing used to switch the traffic:

- ✔ **Virtual Channel Connection (VCC):** A VCC uses all the addressing bits of the cell header to move traffic from one link to another. The VCC is formed by joining a series of *virtual channels* which are the logical circuits uniquely defined for each link of the network.

- ✔ **Virtual Path Connection (VPC):** A VPC uses the higher order addressing bits of the cell header to move traffic from one link to another. A VPC carries many VCCs within it. A VPC can be set up permanently between two points, and then switched VCCs can be easily and quickly assigned within the VPC as need arises. The VPC is formed by joining a series of *virtual paths* which are the logical groups of circuits uniquely defined for each link of the network.

To connect, or not to connect

In general, networks can be classified as either connection-oriented or connectionless, depending upon the physical path (or paths) that carries data from point to point. Probably the most well-known example of a connection-oriented network is the Public Switched Telephone Network (PSTN), while the most famous connectionless network is the Internet.

✔ **Connection-oriented:** Connection-oriented networks rely on end-to-end connections to send information. ATM networks are connection-oriented and use VCC and VPC connections. Cells traveling over a connection (VCC or VPC) always take the same set of physical links in the same order in which they are sent by the source to the network. The cells don't have to be resequenced at the receiving end. If a failure occurs along the physical path of a virtual connection, the network temporarily changes the connection's route to an alternate physical path. This is called *automatic rerouting* and typically occurs within a second or two of the physical outage.

✔ **Connectionless:** Connectionless networks rely on each individual packet to find its own way through the network to its destination. Often, individual packets in the same transmission may take a slightly different set of physical links to reach the destination. Because of this, each packet may not arrive in the same order sent. The packets have sequence numbers so that the receiving end can put everything back together in the right order. Putting the packets back together can be a real problem if you are sending delay-sensitive traffic, like voice, because the recipient may have to wait to get the packets reorganized and in order, causing latency in the playback of the voice.

The use of these connections is why ATM is considered a connection-oriented technology. In contrast to this orientation, some competing technologies, like TCP/IP, send their data over connectionless paths — in other words, the data may flow from point A to point B over any number of different paths instead of traveling over a fixed route.

The virtual connections in ATM are *bidirectional* and *full duplex*. Information can travel in both directions (bidirectional) of the connection at the same time (full duplex) without bumping into each other. However, the bandwidth properties of the connection may be defined uniquely for each direction.

The virtual connections in an ATM network can be predefined and left in place all the time, as in the case of a *permanent virtual circuit* (PVC). Or, they can be set up at the instant that information needs to be sent between communication endpoints and then taken down after the transmission is finished, as in the case of a *switched virtual circuit* (SVC).

- ✔ **Permanent Virtual Circuit (PVC):** A PVC is a VCC or VPC that is pre-defined and left up all the time. If information is not being transmitted over it then it does not take up space on the network (that is, it doesn't use any bandwidth). However, a PVC is ready and waiting to receive cells. Service providers and network managers typically limit the total amount of assigned PVC bandwidth on a given physical link to ensure sufficient capacity for all. *Oversubscription* occurs when the sum of the assigned bandwidth is greater than the physical line rate.

- ✔ **Switched Virtual Circuit (SVC):** An SVC is a VCC that is established on demand through a signaling procedure between the premises equipment and the network. Using SVCs does not mean that the network environment is connectionless; it is still connection-oriented, but the connections are set up and torn down on demand.

The Unique Needs of Voice, Data, and Video

Much of the complexity of ATM exists because the protocol is designed to support many different applications within an enterprise network and to treat each application according to its needs. We discuss in section "Cell That Network" that the unique properties of the fixed-length ATM cell allow all three major applications (voice, data, and video) to be combined over the same network. But just using cells isn't enough. ATM has rules that define how cells carrying different types of information need to be treated by the network. These rules add to the complexity (and the flexibility) of ATM networking.

Imagine trying to build a single house that is functional and appealing to a flamingo, a woolly mammoth, and an octopus. Woolly's bedroom needs mountain murals, little blow-up Neanderthals in the corner for company, a glacier or two for sleeping, and so forth. Pinkie flamingo would want a humid climate, a soft marsh for sleeping, with company provided by cockroaches that are big enough to swallow a small dog. The octopus wants — well it's hard to tell what an octopus wants, but it's surely different than the others. You couldn't really have common areas because Woolly would bully his way to the temperature control and freeze out Pinkie flamingo or step on the octopus and squash it by accident.

Voice, data, and video traffic on a network are similar to the flamingo, the mammoth, and the octopus living together.

The transmission needs of each application are very different, and mixing and matching these applications in the same network can't be done by just allowing a free-for-all. Some forms of data, like remote client-server traffic or an e-mail with a harmless little 50 slide Microsoft PowerPoint presentation attached, may freeze out the voice calls. Meanwhile, both types can step on the special needs of real time video.

The approach to networking without ATM involves giving each application it's own set of rooms, almost like building a house for each. Very little sharing occurs, which increases costs for the network. The technology typically used (for giving each type of information its own house) is known as Time Division Multiplexing (TDM), or Synchronous Transfer Mode, and is how private leased lines are delivered. You hear more about this technology in Chapter 3.

With ATM, more sharing of network resources can occur because the network is more flexible. The network adapts to the needs of each application. If we consider building a house that Woolly, Pinkie, and Salty (that's the Octopus, by the way) can all share, then each room needs to change as each of our friends uses it. When Woolly walks into the kitchen it automatically increases in size and drops the temperature. Woolly takes up the available space, and the space conforms to his needs. If Pinkie needs the kitchen, it becomes steamy and marshy. And if they both need the kitchen at the same time, a divider wall emerges, giving a percentage of the room to Woolly and a percentage to Pinkie.

The allocation and sharing of resources is handled on a connection-by-connection basis in an ATM network, through the definition of a *traffic contract* and an assigned *quality of service* (QoS). The traffic contract of each connection is defined by selecting the service category and associated bandwidth rate(s). The selected service category and bandwidth rates determines the supported QoS.

ATM is a Classy Act

ATM supports different classes of service, known as *service categories,* to support different applications with different levels of performance. The assigned service category of each connection determines how the network prioritizes and allocates resources (primarily link bandwidth and switch buffer space) during a transmission. Each virtual connection (VCC or VPC) in an ATM network has a service category. The performance of the connection is measured by the established *QoS parameters.* You can find out more about ATM's service categories and QoS parameters in Chapter 9.

Service categories

The ATM standard defines different service categories to support different application needs. You may also hear the term *service class* used; it means the same thing. The defined service categories are as follows:

✔ **Constant Bit Rate (CBR):** CBR is the service category designed to support applications that need a highly predictable transmission rate. Private lines can be carried over an ATM network in a mode called *circuit emulation* and use the CBR service category. CBR service maintains the timing relationship between each end during the transmission.

✔ **Variable Bit Rate (VBR):** In the simplest terms, VBR simply means that the rate of transmission can vary. But just stopping at that definition doesn't give the whole picture because the rate of transmission can also vary in other service categories — plus two different types of the VBR service category exist. With VBR service, a standard rate of transmission (the SCR) is assigned to the VBR connection, but the connection rate can momentarily exceed this standard rate by bursting up to a peak rate known as PCR. (Yeah, we know we're throwing in a bunch of new acronyms. We try to give you definitions for them all, and we promise not to spin you into the twilight zone with an endless reference circle of definitions.)

- **Real Time:** With VBR-RT the application is assumed to operate in a real-time environment in which people (or computers) on each end of the connection are waiting for something to happen. Each end of the connection maintains a timing relationship. Desktop videoconferencing is an example of an application that may use a VBR-RT connection. Voice implementations using compression and silence suppression to allow statistical bandwidth gain are another example. Although CBR was originally targeted to support voice applications, now most expect voice to use the VBR-RT service category.

- **Non-Real Time:** With VBR-NRT the application is assumed to be tolerant of network delays and not require a timing relationship on each end of the connection. An example of a non-real time application is information stored for later retrieval, such as store-and-forward video. Also, data applications requiring very high performance (that is, low cell loss) but not needing a timing relationship on each end can feasibly use a VBR-NRT connection. A terminal-to-host data application in which spoofing is employed is a potential candidate for the VBR-NRT service category. *Spoofing* is a technique for locally responding to communication status queries from an end device versus waiting for the response from the far end.

✔ **Available Bit Rate (ABR):** ABR is the service category designed for data applications that need a high level of performance (that is, low cell loss) but can tolerate variation in transmission speed and network delay. With ABR, the minimum amount of network resource is made available to the connection when needed. However, if idle network capacity exists, then the connection can send even more information (bursting). The connection assumes that this excess capacity is available until it notices a slow-down in received traffic or receives congestion notification messages from the network.

✔ **Unspecified Bit Rate (UBR):** The UBR service category is like flying standby on an airplane. If space is available, you get to travel on the plane. If no space is available, you don't. If congestion occurs in an ATM network, the UBR cells are the first to be dumped into the infamous bit bucket in the sky (that is, these cells are the first ones lost.)

If you ever get the opportunity to present a training class on ATM, a fun way to start is by rattling off these service category acronyms very quickly at the beginning of the session. (Fun for you anyway, the audience tends to get a bit nervous at this point.)

SO . . . you thought frame relay was complicated, huh? With frame relay networking, you have only one service class, and you assign a committed information rate. With ATM, you have *five* choices — CBR, VBR-RT, VBR-NRT, ABR, and UBR. And with each choice, you may have to assign a PCR, SCR, and/or MCR (yes, more acronyms to learn in a moment) in addition to quality of service (QoS) parameters such as CLR, CDVT, and MBT. By the way, in case you were wondering, *frame relay* is a popular wide area service for connecting LANs and more recently other communications equipment at dial-up to T3 speeds. It is similar to ATM in many ways, and we refer to frame relay frequently in this book — look for the most detailed description in Chapter 12.

ATM's many qualities

The ATM networking structure isn't as simple as just assigning the service category for the network traffic. For each connection, you also must assign the rate of maximum and/or minimum (or alternatively, average) transmission bandwidth. If you compare an ATM network with a highway system, the transmission bandwidth rates correspond to speed limits on a highway.

Bandwidth attributes to assign include the following:

✔ **Peak Cell Rate (PCR):** Peak cell rate is the maximum transmission speed of a virtual connection. PCR is assigned for all service categories. The PCR is the rate of transmission on a CBR connection, and the maximum burst rate of VBR, ABR, and UBR connections. When connecting to a public ATM service, PCR is often the same as the port connection speed for non-CBR connections, but it does not have to be the same. The peak cell rate can be set at a speed lower than the port connection speed, but it cannot be set higher than the port speed.

✔ **Cell Delay Variation Tolerance (CDVT):** CDVT defines the maximum tolerance for variation in the time between the arrival of one cell and the next cell (immediately following it). If cells are transmitted from one point to another with a high level of consistency in the time between each cell transmitted, then the network connection has a low level of delay variation between cells. The CDVT is typically very low for CBR and VBR-RT connections, a bit higher for VBR-NRT connections, and very high for ABR and UBR connections.

- ✔ **Bursting:** When extra network resources are sitting idle, these resources can be temporarily used by VBR, ABR, and UBR connections. The connections burst above their assigned rate of transmission (as defined by the SCR or MCR).

- ✔ **Sustained Cell Rate (SCR):** Sustained cell rate is the average rate of transmission on a VBR connection. The duration of bursting above the SCR is limited to the first initial moments of each transmission. The majority of information travels across a VBR connection at the SCR or lower, unless the application transmits very short bursts of information intermittently. ATM services requiring the definition of an SCR typically call it a committed information rate (CIR) instead. The CIR terminology is a throw back to frame relay services and reduces by one the number of new terms a user must learn. (Aren't the carriers swell?)

- ✔ **Minimum Cell Rate (MCR):** Minimum Cell Rate is the minimum rate of transmission on an ABR connection. The ABR connection can burst above the MCR, up to the PCR if the network has spare bandwidth resources.

- ✔ **Maximum Burst Size (MBS):** MBS defines the amount of bursting allowed for an individual connection during a single transmission. This amount is measured by number of cells. The same variable can also be measured in time, in which case it is sometimes referred to as Maximum Burst Tolerance (MBT). The two acronyms (MBS and MBT) mean about the same thing and define the amount of allowed bursting.

We're not through yet. For each connection you should also know two more QoS parameters.

- ✔ **Cell Loss Ratio (CLR):** CLR is the acceptable percentage of cells that the network can discard due to network congestion. An example of a cell loss ratio is 10^{-4}. This particular ratio allows the network to loose 1 in every 10,000 cells (not a great cell loss ratio, by the way, as a single DS3 can send 96,000 cells every second).

- ✔ **Cell Transfer Delay (CTD):** Cell transfer delay refers to how long the network can take to transmit a cell from one endpoint to another. Sources of delay in a network are physical propagation time, buffer queuing time, and switching time. CBR and VBR-RT connections require low CTD.

These two parameters further define and quantify exactly how the network handles the transmission of information over the virtual connection so that the performance of the application is acceptable. If you are subscribing to a public carrier service, each service category generally has default values for these two QoS parameters. The network meets these criteria through its engineered design. Critical aspects of the design include the switch matrix and buffer design, load on the backbone links, virtual connection distances, and number of switches through which each connection must pass.

Statistical bandwidth gain

ATM allows higher utilization of network bandwidth by supporting statistical bandwidth gain. For most ATM service categories, the network does not reserve the full bandwidth of the connection. The network expects these connections to have bursty traffic, allowing the sharing of bandwidth among many different connections. The amount of sharing determines the statistical bandwidth gain of the network link. If many connections share the bandwidth, the network has a high statistical gain; if only a few connections can share the bandwidth, the statistical gain is lower. Higher statistical gain means lower bandwidth costs but also increases the risk of congestion if multiple connections send a large amount of traffic at once. The right balance of cost versus performance is a careful consideration in engineering a large ATM network.

The CBR service category is like time division multiplexing and causes no statistical bandwidth gain. The network always reserves the full bandwidth of the CBR connection just in case the connection has traffic to send. Reserving the bandwidth is necessary because CBR applications can tolerate only minimal delay and loss. This flexibility of the ATM network to allocate resources appropriate to each application's needs while allowing sharing where possible to lower networking costs is its most important benefit.

Measuring the specific values of these two QoS paramenters (CLR and CTD) for a given connection in a given time is very difficult. Measurements generally require intrusive testing. Cell loss requires knowledge of the transmitted set of cells and the ability to measure the loss at the ATM layer versus the applications layer. CTD measurements are usually done through *ping tests* and are therefore subject to processing delays at the remote end. These limitations makes isolation of the ATM layer performance very difficult.

UNI's, FUNI's, and LUNI's

In the preceding sections, we talk about what happens to information traffic within an ATM network. In this section, we talk about how to connect *to* the ATM network, or how to connect two or more ATM networks together. As you may guess by now, if the process were simple, it wouldn't be ATM.

Currently, six different connection types (for connecting to or between ATM networks) are defined. At the time that we're writing this book, only a few of these connection types are actually being implemented and used.

> ✔ **User-to-Network Interface (UNI):** The interface between a user's equipment and an ATM public network service or into an ATM switch on a private enterprise network.

✓ **Frame User Network Interface (FUNI):** Developed to accommodate low speed user connections into an ATM network (such as T1/E1 and below), the FUNI uses variable length packets (frames) instead of cells. Frames avoid the high overhead percentage required (by ATM) for the cell header (almost 10 percent) on the access portion of the connection.

✓ **Network-Network Interface (NNI):** NNI is a generic term that refers to a connection between two ATM switches or two ATM networks. NNI is not a specifically defined ATM standard, but the term still gets used a lot because it is a part of the frame relay standards and jargon. NNI may also stand for Network Node Interface.

✓ **Private Network-to-Network Interface (PNNI):** The interface between two ATM switches or group of switches. The PNNI defines how switched virtual connections are established and then automatically rerouted (if necessary) between network switches.

✓ **Broadband (ISDN) Inter-Carrier Interface (B-ICI):** An interface defined for connecting two public ATM networks (such as the interface between different service providers).

✓ **LAN User-to-Network Interface (LUNI):** The interface between a user and an emulated LAN network. (And you thought we just made this one up! Only engineers would actually call something a loony and expect their sales people to be widely successful at selling it — actually the engineers refer to it as *L UNI*, pronounced *ell-yoonie*.)

The Story of HAN, LAN, MAN, and WAN

Once upon a time, there were four brothers: HAN, LAN, MAN, and WAN. They went to an ATM Forum meeting just to see what kind of wild party could attract 600 attendees, 6 times per year (to all kinds of locations like Anchorage, Alaska). The brothers were surprised to find mainly engineers in attendance and discovered that the attendees spent a lot of time arguing about small, seemingly irrelevant details that seemed contrary to the invitation they had received from the ATM Forum. (The invitation said that they were invited to the meeting to define usable standards quickly.) But at the meeting, everyone liked very much to hear themselves talking, and the attendees were able to repeat earlier points with profound insight by just flipping around a couple of words in a sentence. (We shouldn't be so hard on the Forum meeting actually — it sounds just like every meeting we've ever attended.)

Yet, the brothers knew that they each must learn about ATM because they had all heard that it was an important technology. As they continued to attend ATM meetings, they found that many of the ATM definitions and acronyms changed over time. They decided that ATM still has a little maturing to do — that it was still in its adolescence, growing and changing quickly. They understood that all technologies go through this stage, and that they, as more mature acronyms, needed to be there to support ATM as it grows — like a big brother or sister.

- ✔ **Home Area Network (HAN):** High speed network connecting personal computing equipment, printers, and possibly other networked devices (such as the TV of the future) within the home.

- ✔ **Local Area Network (LAN):** High speed network connecting personal computing equipment, printers, servers, mainframes, and other devices within an office or a small group of buildings.

- ✔ **Metropolitan Area Network (MAN):** High speed network connecting personal computing equipment, printers, servers, mainframes, and other devices within a local region that does not extend over 50 kilometers.

- ✔ **Wide Area Network (WAN):** High speed network connecting personal computing equipment, printers, servers, mainframes, PBXs, video equipment, and other networked devices nationally and internationally.

ATM's format can run over any of these networks without change. The ATM technology marks the first time that a protocol has been specifically designed to operate in all four network domains. This key characteristic of ATM is to make everything simpler for network managers. However, ATM's proponents are finding that satisfying all four network environments is very challenging. A very long time may elapse before ATM seamlessly connects users from desktop-to-desktop in every network across the globe, as originally envisioned. (And indeed, this vision will probably never be realized.)

Nothing but net (management)

Managing an ATM network presents unique challenges, particularly if you are using ATM to manage connections from desktop-to-desktop. No other existing network management platform has ever taken on such an ambitious task. The current day solutions focus on one particular protocol or segment (such as the LAN or WAN) of the network.

The ATM Forum is defining specifications for network management in their Network Management technical working group (surprise . . . you can actually figure this group out by its name!). This group has defined a model for network management that includes five interfaces, all designated by the letter *M* and a number (straight forward naming conventions don't last long in ATM — but we can hope that this one does!)

- ✔ **M1:** Defines the interface between a private ATM switch and a corporate management system.

- ✔ **M2:** Defines the interface between a private ATM network and a corporate management system.

- ✔ **M3:** Defines the customer interface to a carrier's management system. Ultimately this interface will support real-time control by the customer over their network (with necessary checks and balances by the carrier of course).

✔ **M4:** Defines the interface between the public network and the carrier's management system.

✔ **M5:** Defines the interface between two (or more) different management systems of a carrier.

Knowing that the completion of all these specifications may take years (early versions of M3 and M4 are actually complete), the Forum included a specification for basic network management functionality in its UNI specification. This basic management functionality is known as *Integrated Layer Management Interface* (ILMI). ILMI allows ATM devices to exchange fault and performance management information over a UNI interface using a limited subset of *Simple Network Management Protocol* (SNMP) capabilities. SNMP is a widely implemented network management protocol.

The UNI devices share rudimentary management information over preassigned virtual channels through specifically defined *Operations, Administration, and Maintenance* (OAM) cells. Eventually OAM cells can allow ATM network devices to gather end-to-end statistics, thereby reducing the number of needed *Management Information Bases* (MIBs) throughout the network. MIBs are simply databases in equipment and network management systems which store collected statistics and network information. You can find out more about ATM's network management in Chapter 10.

The interoperability groupies

Because we're trying to give you the whole ATM scoop in this chapter (or least a taste from all the many different scoops) we really need to add a whole slew of terms for protocols that allow ATM users to interoperate with non-ATM users. These protocols are generally called *internetworking protocols* and include the following. You can find out more about each protocol in Chapter 11.

✔ **Frame Relay to ATM Service Internetworking:** Specification allowing a frame relay site to seamlessly connect to an ATM site. The network handles all conversions between the two wide area networking protocols.

✔ **LAN Emulation (LANE):** Specification allowing a non-ATM LAN user (such as a user on an Ethernet or token ring LAN) to connect to an ATM LAN user or server. The LANE specification introduces even more new terms, including LAN Emulation Client (LEC), LAN Emulation Server (LES), LAN Emulation Configuration Server (LECS) and Broadcast and Unknown Server (BUS).

✔ **RFC 1483:** Specification for encapsulating internetworking protocols such as IP (Internet Protocol) into ATM.

✔ **Multiprotocol over ATM (MPOA):** Specification for connecting ATM LANs and ATM emulated LANs from different subsets (that is, subnets) of an IP network using cut-through routing. MPOA adds more functionality for connecting ATM LANs as compared to the more fundamental LANE standards.

✔ **Voice and Telephony over ATM (VTOA):** Specifications defining standard methods to carry traditional voice traffic over ATM.

✔ **Winsock 2:** Even though Winsock 2 is not really an internetworking protocol, we throw its definition into this section. Winsock 2 is an Application Programming Interface (API) that allows software applications to request the quality of service and bandwidth of their networking connection. This important specification allows Windows-based computing systems to take advantage of the new networking capabilities introduced by ATM and other emerging protocols that support multiple service types.

The standing standards

Most existing implementations of ATM in late 1996 conform to the ATM Forum's UNI version 3.0 ratified in 1993. UNI 3.0 includes specifications for different physical layers, traffic management, and signaling. The Forum approved a subsequent UNI in 1994 known as 3.1. This new UNI changed the ATM signaling to match the definition adopted by ITU after 3.0 was defined.

As we are writing in late 1996, the Forum members have recently approved a potpourri of new standards building on UNI 3.1. Instead of grouping the growing behemoth of UNI standards, the Forum decided to release the 4.0 specifications according to function. Hence we have UNI Signaling 4.0, Traffic Management 4.0, and ILMI 4.0.

We include a list of organizations defining ATM standards in Chapter 21. These groups include the ATM Forum, the IETF (Internet Engineering Task Force), ANSI (American National Standards Institute), and ITU (International Telecommunication Union). If you are counting all of the relevant ATM standards, you better be able to move beyond your ten fingers and ten toes. In fact, centipedes may have an advantage here.

ATM lingo, along with standards, is like the song that never ends! (That's an inside joke to all parents of preschoolers who love Lambchop.)

Inside ATM with Robert Gourley
Technical Program Manager
LDDS WorldCom, Tulsa, Oklahoma

A Brief History of ATM and Its Standards

Standards? Now there's a dry subject. I can't believe that they want me to write an editorial on standards and make it interesting and humorous! First, I don't think that's even possible, but here goes anyway.

First the history

The ATM fundamentals were developed by Bell Laboratories and France Telecom's Research Center—the companies were working independently in the early to middle 1980s on packetizing voice communications. Both organizations wanted to transmit voice and data across one switching fabric. Those Bell Lab guys, first they invent the transistor back in the 1950s, the laser in the 1960s, and now ATM; what will they think of next! That's about it for the ATM history part. (Pretty short for a history lesson, huh?)

Now for the standards stuff

ATM was first standardized in 1988, by the Consultative Committee on International Telephone and Telegraph (CCITT), which is now known as the International Telecommunications Union (ITU). ATM was later standardized by the American National Standards Institute (ANSI).

In addition to the ITU and ANSI, which have developed standards for ATM, a group called the ATM Forum also develops standards for ATM. The ATM Forum was founded in October, 1991, with four members. (I wonder if those four guys are still around?) The Forum (the group's nickname) now has over 750 member companies representing all sectors of government and industry. The ATM Forum mission is to promote ATM within industry and the end-user community; the Forum primarily performs its mission by developing ATM specifications (which are, in fact, *standards* for everybody to follow). Actually, those

four ATM Forum founding members are still around . . . they're Cisco Systems, NET, Nortel Multimedia Networks, and Sprint.

Besides the ATM Forum, you find the Internet Engineering Task Force (IETF), which is the standards body for the international Internet. The IETF is primarily concerned with TCP/IP and LAN standards, but they've developed some standards (called *requests for comment*, RFCs) for ATM. (You wonder why they call them requests for comment when no one ever comments much on them, anyway.) The most important RFCs for ATM are RFC 1483, the RFC that details Multiprotocol Encapsulation Over ATM Adaption Layer Five, and RFC 1577, which defines Classical IP and ARP over ATM. The IETF also has a specific working group that is exploring and defining new RFCs to expand multiprotocol functionality over ATM.

The ANSI and ITU ATM standards specify a fixed length 53-byte frame called a *cell*. This cell length was determined as a result of a political compromise in the ITU: North America wanted a 64 byte cell (which was better suited to data applications) while Europe and Japan wanted a 32 byte cell (which reduced echo cancellation problems in voice packets). The result of the compromise was a 48-byte payload cell with a 5-byte header resulting in a 53 byte cell. (Neither side was happy with the compromise, but that's the way compromises work out sometimes.)

Specifying the ATM cell length and format turned out to be the easy part. The hard part has become defining classes of service. Unlike frame relay and X.25, which have only one class of service (except for some proprietary and other minor stuff), ATM is capable of carrying more than one type of traffic such as data, voice, and video. That flexibility makes ATM really interesting, but harder to deal with and understand.

(continued)

So, the standards guys came up with a scheme for providing for these classes of service. They first called the classes A, B, C, and D and defined them using the concern for timing, whether a constant or variable bit rate was required, and whether the service used connection-oriented or connectionless technology.

Nobody could really understand much of how this all was going to come together, so the A, B, C, and D stuff disappeared and you don't hear much about it any more. In case you ever stumble across someone still in the dark ages of ATM, here is a chart outlining the old definitions:

Class Elements	Class A	Class B	Class C	Class D
Timing concern	Required	Required	Not required	Not required
Bit rate	Constant	Variable	Variable	Variable
Connection mode	Connection oriented	Connection oriented	Connection oriented	Connectionless

(You see why nobody could figure out this stuff?)

Next, the standards guys tried to define these classes of service in terms of ATM Adaptation Layers (AALs) which is a method or protocol for mapping data into ATM cells. They came up with AAL 1, 2, 3, and 4. It wasn't long until they combined 3 and 4 as 3/4 because there was very little difference between them, and they added AAL 5, which is somewhat similar to AAL 3/4 except AAL 5 is simpler and easier to implement than AAL 3/4. No one started developing applications using AAL 1 or AAL 2, and for a while it looked like AAL 3/4 and AAL 5 was where all the action was going to be. But, because AAL 3/4 was a more complex protocol, soon AAL 5 was being used specifically to replace AAL 3/4.

AAL 5 is used in almost all ATM applications today. Recently, the ATM Forum chose AAL 1 as the adaption layer for circuit emulation services (CES). All the above may be true, but this still doesn't help us define the classes of service that we are looking for.

Finally, someone thought up the idea of using the ATM traffic provisioning parameters to specify class of service. But they don't even call them classes of service anymore — they're now called service categories and have the acronyms CBR, VBR, ABR, and UBR. The *BR* stands for bit rate and the *C* means constant or continuous; *V* means variable, *A* means available, and *U* means unspecified. The traffic parameters and QoS parameters that serve to provision services categories are as follows:

Peak Cell Rate (PCR)

Cell Delay Variation Tolerance (CDVT)

Sustainable Cell Rate (SCR)

Maximum Burst Size (MBS)

Minimum Cell Rate (MCR)

Peak-to-peak Cell Delay Variation (CDV)

Maximum Cell Transfer Delay (Max CTD)

Cell Loss Ratio (CLR)

Traffic and QoS parameters are pretty heavy stuff and more complicated than we really want to discuss right now, but let it suffice to say that you can make the ATM equipment provide one of the service categories by setting the traffic and QoS parameters in a particular way.

The bottom line is that the ATM standards have been — and constantly are — in a state of flux since the early 1990s (and the end is still not in sight).

The main reason that this ATM standards stuff is so important is that it provides a format for one vendor's equipment to talk to another vendor's equipment. Without that format, each vendor would have a proprietary ATM implementation and could not communicate with any other vendor's implementation. The switch guys couldn't talk to the customer premise equipment (CPE) guys and they couldn't talk to the host equipment (adapter) guys and ATM would never get off the ground. But because all the vendors build their equipment to the standards, then everybody's equipment talks to everybody's equipment, and we all will live happily ever after. THE END.

Chapter 3

What Makes Up ATM?

In This Chapter

▶ Looking at ATM as a transportation system

▶ Mapping out the different parts of a network

▶ Finding where the ATM pieces fit in a network

ATM is a complex technology, and defining what makes up ATM is no simple task. So to help out with the task, we use the analogy of building a highway system (and then taking a trip via the highway) to describe putting together an ATM network.

Through the building-a-highway analogy, we further describe the key concepts of ATM (like ATM's cell structure and quality of service) that we introduce in Chapter 2. And we add some new network-related definitions to the story (like traffic management, routing, and signaling), just to keep you entertained on our ATM road trip.

So buckle up, and we can be on our way!

Custom Building an ATM Network

Communications networks are analogous to another type of network . . . the diverse infrastructure of roads that carry us from one place to another. To explain ATM, we are going to build a new road and then take a trip. The endpoints of our road are Cathy's house in Midlothian, Virginia, Chris's house in Claremore, Oklahoma and the beautiful Kona Coast of Hawaii. Performance specifications for the highway system are as follows:

1. Construction costs on the highway meet our budget of $1,000.

2. Travel on the highway is very safe so that we can bring the kids.

3. Via the highway, our families can get to Hawaii in 30 minutes or less before the kids start getting cranky.

   (We told you that ATM may just be a fantasy dream world).

Physical medium . . . dirt, gravel, and concrete

To begin construction, we first need to select the roadway materials. Roads can be made of many different materials including dirt, gravel, and concrete. Different materials may be best suited for different locations. For example, dirt roads may be the best choice for mountain sites to ease construction and preserve the environment. Gravel may let you reach your mountain retreat faster but can be more expensive. Concrete is best for well-traveled city or interstate roads. If you want to go fast, then concrete offers the best alternative. Have you ever tried to drive 100 mph on a gravel road? If the road is a narrow gravel passage and many cars travel in each direction, the likelihood of collision is quite high because of these conditions.

Similarly, telecom networks can be built from different material, or medium. Copper may be the best choice for small, remote locations with occasional network traffic. Fiber may be the best choice for heavily loaded network links, and wireless may be the only choice for reaching roaming users.

You can build an ATM network from many different kinds of *physical medium*. ATM networks may use copper wire, coaxial cable, fiber, wireless, and even satellite links. The choice for your ATM network is yours and depends on your existing physical medium, speed requirements, tools and test equipment, right-of-way, and budget.

ATM does not provide for correction of errors during the transmission of information. The end equipment eventually corrects for the corrupted (or errored) information, but this correction takes some time. Therefore, choosing an ATM medium that minimizes potential damage to the information being transmitted is important, especially when distances are long and retransmissions have a greater impact on application performance and network congestion. To use our road analogy — the dirt or gravel road may prove too bumpy and cause too much structural damage to the vehicles. Therefore, concrete may be a better choice.

For our dream road, we are selecting a wondrous new material called *tugor*. Tugor is a durable, magnetic composite that holds the car close to the road for safety while supporting speeds up to 250 miles per minute. Tugor also floats for easy roadway construction over water. And it costs less than 10 cents per mile . . . ZOOM!

Transmission protocols . . . side streets, boulevards, and highways

Now that we have selected tugor as the physical medium for our highway, we must determine what kind of road to build. Tugor is suitable for building boulevards or highways. We want to get to Hawaii quickly, so we are choosing to build a limited access highway. However, we decided that we don't want a highway in our neighborhoods, so we can build a one-mile street of asphalt connecting each of our driveways to the Hawaiian dream highway.

Next, we need to determine the rules that will govern traffic on our highway. A *protocol* is a set of rules for governing a process. The set of driving rules for a highway in London may include the following:

- Do not exceed the speed limit of 100 kilometers per hour.
- Drive on the left side of the highway.
- Do not stop in the middle of the road.

In the U.S., the protocol differs. The speed is 65 mph, you drive on the right side of the road, and there is no stopping in the middle. If you use the wrong protocol, you are in for some trouble. (Fortunately, collisions of information on an ATM network have much shorter-term consequences than do collisions on a real highway!)

Network managers can choose to run various transmission protocols on the network medium. A *transmission protocol* is the set of rules guiding the exchange of information on the physical medium. Some common transmission protocols are DS0, T1, E1, T3, E3, TAXI, and SONET/SDH. Each of these protocols are suitable for various medium, and we talk more about them in Chapter 8.

Just as your car can travel over various medium and road types, ATM can easily move across different physical medium and transmission protocols. This flexibility is a key benefit of ATM. ATM is a single scheme throughout the communications system and is useful in the local, campus, and wide area network. ATM faithfuls say that it simplifies network management and operations and reduces sparing and training requirements — all of these savings can result in lower networking costs.

ATM critics point out that the overhead associated with ATM makes it inefficient for some transmission protocols, especially those that operate at low speeds, such as DS0 and T1. This overhead is equivalent to a "toll" that is paid per car on the roadway, regardless of the number of people in the car. The ATM overhead is sometimes referred to as ATM's *cell tax*. In reality, the justification of ATM over any specific media and transmission protocol must be made on a case-by-case basis when all the conditions of the situation can be taken into account.

Cells . . . your transportation vehicle

Now that we've built our physical roadway infrastructure, we want to share it with all of you. We are therefore extending our dream highway to each of your towns.

We want you all to come to Hawaii with us. The first step is to determine what kind of vehicles we want to travel on our road. We don't want to be snobbish, but we plan to travel very fast, and we remember the kind of clunkers we drove in college. Everyone can travel much more quickly, safely, and efficiently if everyone uses the same type of vehicle. Mixing cars, buses, motorcycles, and trucks on one highway can cause traffic jams and accidents and result in slowdowns for everyone. Therefore, we want to specify a vehicle that is fast, relatively cool (after all, a lot of nerdy engineer types may want to travel on our road, and we have to give them all the help we can), capable of traversing different terrains, and able to carry a lot of stuff.

We believe that a sports utility vehicle offers the best compromise of speed, flexibility, loading capacity, and cost. A Corvette is sportier, but the sports utility vehicle is generally considered cool among high school and college types. Although a full-sized four-wheel-drive truck may be preferred by "real men," the sports utility vehicle also offers the ability to go four-wheeling. Though not as handy for kids as the minivan, the sports utility choice still offers parents room to pack a lot of people and stuff for the trip.

We think that ATM is a lot like the sports utility vehicle that we've chosen for our highway. The developers of ATM also realized that a common transportation vehicle could speed delivery, improve efficiency, and lower costs in their communications systems. They thus devised a consistent electronic packaging known as an ATM cell. The ATM *cell* consists of *user information* along with a *header* that identifies where the cell is going.

The ATM cell, which is the fundamental concept of ATM, is special because of its fixed, 53-byte length and the resulting benefits of having the fixed length. (Chapter 2 also includes a discussion of the ATM cell.)

The speed and adaptability for information transfer that are provided by the fixed-length ATM cell result in a more basic benefit — lower cost — that is, at least lower than other methods for carrying vast amounts of different types of information very quickly from one point to another.

Just as the sports utility vehicle may not be the optimum choice for every transportation need, the ATM cell is not the perfect choice for every telecommunication need. Computers typically prefer longer, variable-length packets, while voice calls prefer steady, constant transportation streams. The fixed-length cell for ATM was selected as a compromise between these two fundamentally different communications requirements. ATM's developers expected that the benefits of mixing different traffic types would outweigh any disadvantage experienced by any particular information type.

Adaptation . . . packing for the trip

As we continue preparing for our trip, we are going to insist that all drivers ride in the left front seat, navigators go in the right front seat, babies ride in rear-facing child seats in the back, and all other passengers go in the remaining seats. However, if you were born on a Tuesday, then you have to sit in the back right seat unless you are the driver or you are traveling on Sunday or at night. If your eyes are brown, then you have to travel in the back left seat unless you were born on a Tuesday or you are traveling on a Friday. If you are a *Star Trek* or *Star Trek: The Next Generation* fan, then no rules apply, and you can sit anywhere you like.

Similar to our loading instructions, ATM *adaptation* provides a set of instructions for packing information into the ATM cell. Each different type of information, such as voice, video, and computer transmissions (also known as data) can have a different packing scheme, depending on its transportation requirements. Sometimes the ATM rules seem as complex as those on our Hawaiian highway, but in most cases the rules exist for a very good reason and ultimately serve to make the travel experience overall more efficient and safe for everyone.

The ATM cell is typically not large enough to carry most communication exchanges, so the information must be broken up to fit into the fixed-length cells. This slicing and dicing is known as *segmentation. Reassembly* puts all the pieces back together again at the receiving end. Again, a very detailed set of rules exists for each of these functions.

You can discover more about the amazing ATM cell and adaptation in Chapter 8.

Now that we have chosen our transportation vehicle and packing instructions, everyone jump into their cells, or, um . . . sports utility vehicles, and we can start our trip over the Hawaiian dream highway.

Virtual connections . . . painted guidelines

For your convenience while travelling, we include brightly colored, painted guidelines on the highway for you to follow. The guidelines identify a known route from each U.S. city to different destinations in Hawaii. You don't have to bring a road map or a navigator. Just tell us your destination address. We assign you the right colored guideline, and you follow the markings to your destination!

This navigation is what *virtual connections* do in an ATM network. This feature cuts down on complexity and makes the drive much faster because you don't have to stop and make decisions about which way to go. And getting lost is pretty difficult. The downside to the painted guidelines is that after a while, you may end up with a whole lot of different connections that have to be maintained. And if an accident happens on one path, or new construction occurs, or a pothole requires repairs (and shuts down the lanes partially or completely), then alternate routes are necessary, which makes things just a bit more complicated.

In ATM, the cells ride on the transmission protocol using known, end-to-end routes identified as virtual connections. *Virtual connections* link one communicating entity to another through a series of physical medium links. Each transmission link can support thousands of virtual connections, depending on how much and how often each entity has traffic to send.

Virtual paths and channels . . . specialized lanes

Because many different types of travelers use our Hawaiian highway, we have specific lanes to meet everyone's unique needs. HOV lanes are available for heavy users. (For you rural-dwellers, HOV stands for High Occupancy Vehicle — see, telecommunications doesn't have claim to all three-letter acronyms, just 99 percent of them.) If you are carrying kids in your vehicle and are likely to have to stop a lot, you have to drive in the far-right lane, except to pass. If you have a surfboard or bike strapped to the roof, you must travel in one of the two right lanes.

In ATM, the lanes are known as virtual paths or virtual channels. Actually, *virtual channels* are a sublane in the *virtual path*. Network managers or management software determine the defined virtual paths and channels for each link of the transmission path. Yes, we still have to keep the virtual connections. And yes, even the most experienced ATM guru can get tired and confused by all these different virtual names with subtle but important differences in meaning. But we hope that our roadway analogy is helping to keep it all straight for you.

On our Hawaiian highway, we have assigned the colored guidelines to the appropriate lanes for each segment of the highway. We only let you travel in the lanes meeting your needs. Similarly, each virtual ATM connection uses a series of virtual paths and/or channels on various transmission links to reach its destination. Each path and channel is assigned based on the performance requirements of the virtual connection.

Quality of service . . . meeting your needs

The unique need that each virtual path or channel meets is known as the *quality of service* (QoS). QoS allows ATM to meet the performance requirements of many different types of applications. A set of needs is known as a *service category*. Each service category is specialized to carry a different traffic type.

Cells carrying real-time traffic such as voice or video have highest priority. Real-time traffic is very sensitive to delays. Delays in voice delivery over 100 msec hinder the natural flow of conversation. The small cell size of ATM assures that a voice cell does not have long to wait before gaining access to the transmission path. No one application is able to hog the transmission resource, unlike other communications protocols which allow large packet sizes. *Constant bit rate* (CBR) is a service category that can carry real-time traffic.

Alternatively, computers can be very tolerant of more delay, especially for applications such as file transfers or e-mail. The problem that drives most computer applications crazy is information loss. In fact, most data exchanges have strict assurances that no information is lost and can request retransmission from the network if loss has occurred. These retransmissions can quickly add intolerable load to the network. ATM virtual connections carrying data are therefore engineered to limit cell loss to an acceptable level. *Available bit rate* (ABR) is a service category that can carry data traffic.

Multiplexing . . . the on-and off-ramps

We need to determine how we are going to share the limited lanes of our Hawaiian highway.

> "Uh, Houston . . . Houston, we have a problem!"

> "Look out! !%#*!" (We had to censor that last comment.)

Looks like we have a little more work to do.

Everyone receives a time and place to ride on the highway, depending upon your importance and personal preferences. HOV lanes allow you to enter the road almost immediately because you are very important. Surfers and bikers can only use the roadway at night when there is little traffic. The extreme left lane is open at any time, but you'll have to fight with the rest of the road warriors so as to not be bumped off to the side.

ATM also provides a means for sharing the physical medium. The transmission protocol is still necessary to define how the medium carries the cell, that is, at what speed it travels. The virtual connections are still necessary so that each cell knows where it is going. The virtual connections share the physical medium through a process known as *multiplexing*. Figure 3-1 illustrates a physical resource (such as a fiber pair) supporting multiple users through multiplexing. The cells associated with each virtual connection wait in line until it is their turn to ride the transmission link. This is like waiting in line at the on-ramp until the light turns green so that you can enter your lane on the Hawaiian highway.

You can find much more detail on virtual connections, quality of service, service categories, virtual paths and channels, and multiplexing in Chapter 9.

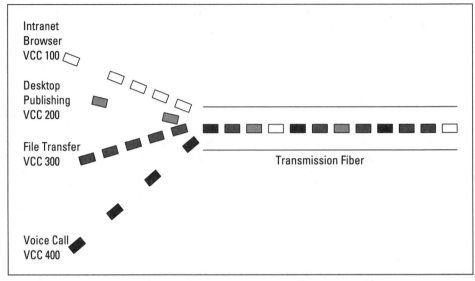

Intranet
Browser
VCC 100

Desktop
Publishing
VCC 200

File Transfer
VCC 300

Transmission Fiber

Voice Call
VCC 400

Figure 3-1:
Multiple
connections
over one
physical
connection...
pretty neat,
huh?

Switching . . . adding the traffic circles

We have one more thing to tell you about driving on our Hawaiian roadway system. We have traffic circles interconnecting our highways. These are automated circles so you don't have to worry about where to get off. Based on which lane you travel, the circle dumps you out on the right outgoing lane so that you can continue your trip. The automated traffic circles include deep pull-offs where travelers can wait for their turn on the next highway. With all this help, even your teenagers could probably make it to Hawaii on their own, but we don't suggest it.

In ATM, switches provide the services of our automated traffic circles. Switches join transmission resources together and ensure that a cell travels safely from one transmission link to the next. The switches have large buffers where cells can wait in queues for their turn on the outgoing link.

Figure 3-2 shows a sample network with transmission links interconnected by ATM switches. ATM's developers creatively dubbed the interface between the ATM user and the network as the *UNI* (user-network interface). The interfaces between switches also have clever names depending upon their function. These names include *NNI* (network-network interface), *PNNI* (private network-network interface), and *B-ICI* (B-ISDN inter-carrier interface). Aren't acronyms a pain? Unfortunately, they're a fact of life in the telecommunications world.

How did ATM get its name?

So you really want to know how ATM got its name. To provide your answer, we are going to have to explain the traditional multiplexing scheme known as Time Division Multiplexing (TDM) and also known as Synchronous Transfer Mode (STM). STM is the multiplexing method used by most existing digital communications systems.

STM/TDM divides an available transmission resource into fixed channels. Each connection uses one channel, as shown in the next figure. In our example, the resource supports three users: Alex, Eric, and Kara. The channel is always available to the assigned connection regardless of whether these three have traffic to send. Because communication is rarely continuous (Alex likes to talk, Eric is brief, and Kara likes to sleep), the transmission resource is often idle.

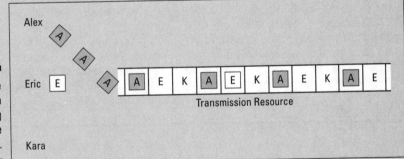

Time division multiplexing looks like this.

If Alex, Eric, and Kara were all driving on our Hawaiian highway, they would have to travel at one set speed during the entire trip. If someone decided to pull off the road, this system would not be a very efficient way to use the available highway space.

ATM improves upon STM's fixed allocation of the resource. Each connection can use the resource as it has traffic to send. We have redrawn the example using asynchronous transfer in the next figure. Now the transmission path has free resource to support fast-talking Tyler in addition to Alex, Eric, and Kara.

In terms of our highway, as each driver needs to pull over for a break on our road, he or she can do so. And everyone left on the road can then go a little faster if they'd like. ATM is more flexible than STM.

The asynchronous sharing of physical resources can allow greatly improved efficiencies. The average utilization of most STM links is between 15 and 30 percent. Network designers must oversize these links to handle the peak demand of the supported connections. However, if the peak demand time of many different connections has a wide variation, then they can all more efficiently share a resource using ATM.

(continued)

(continued)

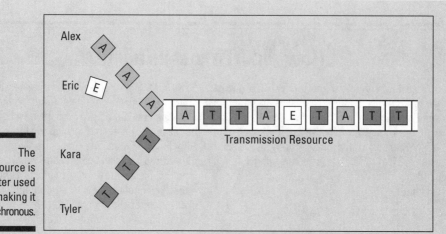

The resource is better used by making it asynchronous.

Transmission Resource

No one knows yet exactly how much improvement ATM can give to average utilization, and it may vary greatly from network to network. ATM's developers hope that average utilization may reach as high as 60 percent for a very large network with wide variation in peak demand times. Networks in which different traffic types such as voice, data, and video are all integrated onto the same facility should have higher utilization. Thus, the concerted effort by ATM's developers is to ensure that it could carry all traffic types, even if a cell may not be anyone's first transportation choice.

Unlike our Hawaiian roadway system where we painted the guidelines for all to see, in ATM the switches and their management systems are the only elements with knowledge of the virtual connections. Based on the cell's incoming virtual channel or path (as identified in the cell's header address), the switch determines the next outgoing channel and path and switches accordingly. The cell really has little intelligence stored in its header but makes its journey safely based on all the intelligence in the switches.

The switch makes its determination by looking up the directions in its switching tables. These tables may be static or dynamic. In static tables, network managers must enter all directions long before a cell needs them. Such static connections are known as *permanent virtual connections* (PVCs). Alternatively, the switch may determine the directions for a connection at the time needed. Such instantaneous connections are called *switched virtual connections* (SVCs).

Switches establish SVCs on a call-by-call basis. *Signaling* messages between the user and the originating switch provide information about the type of connection required. SVCs are very similar to the connections established each time you use your phone. With each call, you enter a dialed number representing the destination of your call. The network then determines what network links to use

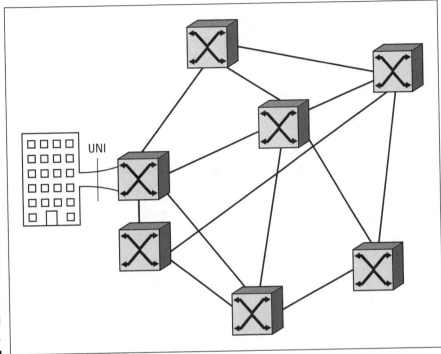

Figure 3-2:
ATM
switches
connecting
physical
medium.

and establishes your phone connection. The connection stays in place for the duration of your call and delivers all call traffic to the terminating end in the same order in which it was sent.

Routing . . . the gas station approach

Switching contrasts to an another important technology known as *routing*. In switching technology, all cells associated with a given communication exchange use the same virtual connection and traverse the same series of virtual paths or channels. This contrasts with how information moves across transmission links in routing.

To explain this concept, we are going to remove the automated traffic circles from our Hawaiian roadway system and add gas stations at all intersections. At every intersection you must get out and ask the local gas station attendant where to go next. Each attendant can't tell you the entire way to Hawaii, but he or she probably can point you in the general direction. You presumably get to Hawaii someday, but you may not have gone the most direct way in the shortest time. If a crash or traffic jam occurs on the road ahead, the attendant may suggest another road. If you are traveling with another family, you may each receive different directions and become separated, arriving at different times and by way of different routes. But again, you are both likely to arrive in Hawaii. If the gas station attendants have to help enough travelers, they may actually become very efficient at providing directions.

In *routing,* equipment known as *routers* provide directions to each information packet. Each junction of the network transmission links must have a router. The routers provide the best directions possible based on information stored inside their routing tables. This information can change quickly, so the different packets can receive different directions. The packets often arrive out of order, and the remote end of the communications exchange must know how to put the packets back together again. The time to take the trip is unpredictable because the packets are never sure which route they may take. Routing can also be more inefficient because each packet must be routed individually, whereas switches determine an itinerary just once for all the cells in each virtual connection. The benefits of routing technology are easy load balancing of traffic and simple bypassing around failures.

Some alternative technologies to ATM depend on routing instead of switching to move information across junction points of transmission links. The most famous alternative technology is TCP/IP (transmission control protocol/Internet protocol) — which you no doubt recognize from the Internet. The distinction between the switching versus routing approaches is important to understand as you consider where each technology fits into your network. We further explore the differences between switching and routing in Chapter 11.

ATM Sounds Simple Enough

So ATM is just building a road and defining some rules to use it — that sounds simple enough!

- ✔ We have picked out our materials to construct our roadway — the transmission media.

- ✔ We have built our roadways and assigned the driving rules — transmission protocols.

- ✔ We have chosen our vehicles — cells.

- ✔ We have loaded our vehicles according to our packing instructions — adaptation.

- ✔ We know to follow the painted guidelines to our destination — virtual connections.

- ✔ We have identified specialized lanes so we can get to Hawaii on time, safe and sound — virtual paths and virtual channels.

- ✔ We have identified sets of needs that our specialized lanes must meet — quality of service.

✔ We know how to get on the highway — multiplexing.

✔ And lastly, we know how to change from one highway to another — switching.

Yes, the basic concepts of ATM are logical and straightforward, even though ATM is the brainchild of techie PhDs working too late into the middle of the night in telecom labs around the world. ATM's developers drew heavily upon existing telecommunications protocols, keeping the best concepts while trying to find new solutions for the worst. But our short story in this chapter has not even begun to touch the implementation details necessary to deploy ATM as a viable, working solution.

Defining all the methods and rules for sharing the physical and virtual resources while offering the right quality of service for each traffic type has turned into a monstrous task known as *traffic management*. The scale and youth of ATM networks have further compounded this issue. Because all existing ATM networks are small compared to projected designs, many traffic behaviors for heavily loaded networks are only theoretical models dependent upon specified

ATM and the infamous layers

We have made it through our whole description without ever once mentioning layer or data link or any other OSI gobbledygook. But, we also realize that a few of you may be curious as to how ATM stacks up against the infamous OSI Layers.

This figure shows the OSI Layers and the corresponding ATM Layers. These are rough comparisons (as ATM does not fit perfectly into the OSI model). As an example, ATM's adaptation layer is shown having some layer 2 functions, yet adaptation occurs only at the edge as opposed to at every node of the network for user information. As another example, some would argue that the ATM layer contains layer 3 functionality, such as end-to-end connection control.

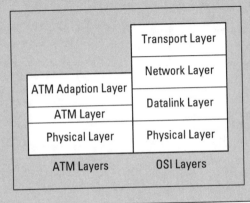

ATM Layers	OSI Layers
	Transport Layer
	Network Layer
ATM Adaption Layer	Datalink Layer
ATM Layer	
Physical Layer	Physical Layer

assumptions. Details for signaling and *call admission control* have hardly been a breeze either. And interoperability with existing technologies has been a necessary challenge — adding pages and pages of detail to the specifications and causing one to wonder whether users would be better off just sticking with what they have.

Consideration of the details (exponentially multiplied by ATM's youth, bandwidth scale, and interoperability prerequisites) makes ATM the most complex networking technology ever defined. But if your job or some strange burning desire requires that you understand these details, don't stress. We present all the important technical facts and implementation considerations in Parts II, III, and IV of this book. We step you through ATM's intricacies and idiosyncrasies so that you, too, can make rational, informed decisions regarding this complex technology.

Inside ATM with Richard N. Klapman
Product Director, Networking Services Division
AT&T, Holmdel, NJ

ATM LAN Emulation — The Power Web

Now that you know the basics of ATM, you can find out where you might use it in a real-life business application and how its *LAN emulation* (LANE) specification makes ATM easy and safe to add to your existing network.

Today, many companies are centralizing their computing power into what are known as *server farms.* Here's a bit of the history behind why companies are doing this.

In the 1970s, computing power was centralized on mainframes, such as those from IBM, and desktop terminals were used to access data from the mainframes.

By the 1980s, personal computers arrived on desktops. These PCs were connected by local area networks (LANs) to allow sharing of printers and files. Then, corporate departments, such as finance and personnel, deployed other small but powerful computers called *file servers* that were attached to the departmental LAN.

Today in the 1990s, we're seeing many companies reversing the trend and re-centralizing their computing power for two reasons:

✔ To reduce operations and administration costs

✔ To gather all strategic data into one place to improve their competitive edge. (*Data warehousing* and *data mining* are terms often associated with this strategy.)

As more and more computing power is centralized into *server farms,* networks also need to keep up the pace. Networks need to grow two-dimensionally:

✔ For increased power to carry huge volumes of data in and out of server farms.

✔ For increased connectivity to form a high-mesh web that links any computer with any other computer to support collaboration across various corporate locations and organizations.

You'll see how ATM LAN emulation creates this *power web* in just a moment, but first, here's how ATM technology delivers the power and web connectivity needed to support the creation of server farms:

✔ The most desirable characteristic of ATM technology is its power. ATM has the ability to transport information at high capacity (also known as high-speed bandwidth), but few companies can afford to lease an entire OC-3 line (which runs at 155 Megabits per second) to get that capacity. However, if you think of an airline analogy, an ATM cell is like a seat on a plane. You can rent ATM cells on a high-speed OC-3 line, which gives you at least 100 times the power of a private T1 line.

✔ The second most desirable characteristic of ATM is its high degree of connectivity. ATM lets any computer make a phone call to any other computer on the network. One computer signals the network with an address of another computer it wishes to reach, a process similar to dialing a phone number. The ATM network then sets up a *switched virtual circuit (SVC)* to make this connection. So, at any point in time, one computer can talk with any other computer on the same network. ATM provides the any-to-any connectivity needed to centralize computing power into server farms.

There's one problem, however. ATM speaks a different language than your existing LANs, such as Ethernet or token ring. That's when LANE steps in.

LAN emulation is an ATM technology software application. LANE examines the cells flowing in a network and helps ATM look like, or emulate, the traffic patterns in a LAN. This software also provides a type of directory assistance function: If you know the name of a computing device on an ATM switch, the software gives you the device's LAN address, and vice versa. This software also sets up a conference call of sorts that allows a computing device attached to an ATM switch to participate in broadcast discussions (which are typical on LANs). LANE makes extensive use of signaling and SVCs to perform these functions.

Basic LANE Benefits

✔ Computing power can be centralized in server farms to reduce operations and administration costs and gather corporate data into one place for a competitive advantage. Other related uses include disaster recovery, Internet hosting, data warehousing, image publishing, and software development environments.

✔ LANE is evolutionary, not revolutionary. You can add the power of ATM technology to support high-speed servers while preserving your investment in existing LANs and applications at the desktop PC level.

✔ You get web connectivity to support communities of interest across the network through ATM's any-to-any signaling connections. Desktop PCs can easily connect to computing power in centralized server farms (and with each other).

As a whole, LAN emulation is an application of ATM technology that gives you a simple evolution path to build a power web (a high-performance *intranet*) to meet your business needs.

LAN emulation seems pretty great, but who is going to provide it? We already see leading companies in key sectors of networking responding to customer needs for LANE products and services:

✔ **Customer Premises Equipment:** Just about every LAN, hub, switch, and router vendor supports LAN emulation today. You can use these vendors' products to build your own private LANE network, or you can connect these LANE-capable products to public LANE services from telecommunications carriers.

✔ **Telecommunications Carriers:** As LAN emulation is becoming widely adopted on premises, carriers are offering public LANE services. Like public voice services, carrier-based LAN emulation service may offer you better scalability, increased reliability, and lower costs than building your own private network.

✔ **Internet Services Providers:** These companies provide a variety of hosting functions that are, in reality, server farms. In addition, when you dial into an Internet services provider network, your connection often travels over a LAN to an ATM-connected host.

So, should you adopt LAN emulation now? As with any new technology, you need to weigh the risks and rewards of getting on the technology train.

(continued)

LAN Emulation Risks

✔ The main risk has been reduced significantly. LAN emulation standards have advanced to the point that most equipment and services actually work together (that is, they *interoperate*). Also, early LANE performance concerns are being solved by recent vendor advances. So we know LANE itself works.

✔ The second risk is one of timing. LAN emulation helps you build a power web at layer 2 using ATM technology while the Internet creates a similar, though less powerful, web at layer 3. The jury is still out on how ATM and the Internet protocol (IP) will interoperate. Some of the more promising technologies, such as *IP switching*, *resource reservation protocol* (RSVP), and *multi-protocol over ATM* (MPOA) with *non-hierarchical routing protocol* (NHRP), will enable IP to work in conjunction with ATM. So, while some technology zealots now advocate either an ATM-only or IP-only solution, we believe the networking industry will soon resolve this debate so you can adopt LANE now — and not wind up in a cul-de-sac with no way out.

LAN Emulation Rewards

✔ LAN emulation is simple and it works now.

✔ LANE provides you with an evolutionary way to migrate your servers to higher-speed ATM connections with fewer bottlenecks.

✔ LANE lets you optimize your server topology and provides interoperability to preserve your existing investment in desktop applications and LAN equipment.

✔ Through ATM, LANE supports new multimedia applications that require Quality of Service signaling (although the ATM Forum must first complete some additional standards work).

✔ LANE helps your telecommunications manager reduce the cost of reconfiguring the network when users move to new locations.

A good course of action is to get started with a LANE trial now. We know of more than 100 companies testing LAN emulation in a few locations for noncritical applications. A handful of other companies have been so satisfied with their tests in noncritical areas that they are moving LANE into their mission-critical networks as we write this.

Start building your own power web (or intranet if you prefer!) by calling several of your favorite telecommunications carriers and network equipment providers. Their advice is free. Then you can make your own decision whether LAN emulation works for you.

Chapter 4

Where Can I Use ATM Locally?

*H*ave you heard the story about the aliens who come to Earth to gather information about what is here and report back to the mother ship? (This is a different story from the one told in the *Independence Day* movie. These aliens are friendly.)

Anyway, the alien who lands in the middle of the Pacific Ocean reports back that the entire world is covered with salt water and that the only life forms are non-tool-using sea creatures of varying size.

The alien who lands in the middle of the Sahara Desert reports back that the whole Earth is covered by sand and that few life forms exist. The planet is very hot and very dry.

Another alien reports that the earth is incredibly overcrowded and impoverished, with only a basic utilization of technology. Yet another reports that the earth is covered by huge mountains of ice and that the primary residents are little tuxedo-wearing birds (as it turns out, tuxedos are the same around the universe).

Get the picture? The report changed based on the perspective of the observer, but all reports were correct in part. ATM is very much the same. Yes, ATM is intended to be a unifying technology that stretches from your desktop to the local area network (LAN), through the campus backbone network connecting your LANs to the wide area network (WAN). Yes, ATM is a single protocol that doesn't need to go through gateway devices and be modified or translated as it passes through different networking environments. However, you don't *have* to use ATM from the desktop through the WAN.

Instead, ATM can be used in just one environment or another, wherever you may need it. This flexibility enables you to slowly integrate ATM into different parts of your network, whenever integrating makes sense. ATM can be used within the local area network, as a campus backbone, or across the wide area network, and the important attributes and benefits of ATM in each area change accordingly. In this chapter we discuss using ATM on your premises, in either a local area network or a campus backbone network. If you want to find out more about ATM's implementation in a wide area network, you can skip to Chapter 5.

Acronyms Used in This Chapter

Acronym	What It Stands For
BUS	Broadcast and Unknown Server
CSMA/CD	Carrier-Sense Multiple Access/Collision Detection
FDDI	Fiber Distributed Data Interface
IETF	Internet Engineering Task Force
IP	Internet Protocol
LAN	Local Area Network
LANE	LAN Emulation
LECS	LAN Emulation Configuration Server
LES	LAN Emulation Server
MPOA	Multiprotocol Over ATM
NIC	Network Interface Card
QoS	Quality of Service
RFC	Request for Comment
SVC	Switched Virtual Circuit
TCP/IP	Transmission Control Protocol/Internet Protocol
VLAN	Virtual LAN
WAN	Wide Area Network

Three Takes on ATM

As you may have discovered in the preceding chapters, explaining ATM in layman's terms is nearly impossible. Many ATM insiders avoid cocktail parties for fear of hearing the dreaded question, "So, what is it that you do?"

"I'm the product manager for a new technology called ATM," you say as you try to casually slide toward the peanut bowl and avoid further discussion.

"Oh, what's ATM?" says the cocktail party person. (Darn! You'd hoped to avoid answering that one! However, this person is rather attractive, and while remaining introspective and sitting alone looking contemplative about the wall art for the rest of the evening would be much easier, you decide to make the effort required for verbal communication. Too bad you can't go hop on a computer and have this conversation over the Internet.)

How you answer this question depends on whether your job and your involvement with ATM is centered around a local, campus, or wide area network and on whether you are an end user of ATM or a provider of ATM goods and services. Of course, we can't cover every possible scenario — our time warp device only works a few times before we have to recharge the dilithium crystals.

Take 1: The Wide Area Network

Activate Time Warp: If you happen to be in charge of ATM from a marketing or technical perspective for a major service provider, you may answer that question like this:

> ATM stands for Asynchronous Transfer Mode, which means nothing to a layman. So now that you know it, just forget it.

Of course, if this answer is a bit too harsh, you may try the following explanation:

> A very basic description of ATM in a WAN is that ATM represents a new way for a service provider to handle many different traffic types such as audio, text, image, and video over a single network. The network itself — the fiber and copper lines — does not change. However, the way in which information is sent over these lines is different with ATM than with other technologies. ATM was developed to make sending information faster and cheaper for service providers.

> Traditionally, service providers (and end users building WANs) have built separate networks for the many different types of services they offer. This separation lets them tailor the network to the specific needs of the applications they aim to support, but it is not very efficient from an operations and costs perspective. ATM, in theory, lets the service providers build one network and support many different services (audio, text, image, and video) over it. Again in theory, this merge lowers their costs and eventually lowers the price of communications services, too.

Stop here. This explanation is a very basic description of ATM in the WAN (we promise more details for the masochistic in Chapter 5 and in Part III of this book), but it only applies to one of ATM's several personalities. ATM is like Sybil; it has many personalities, and each one is unique. Now that you understand personality number one of ATM, we can introduce personalities number two and three.

Take 2: The Campus Backbone

Activate Time Warp: Now you are a network manager for a company that is installing ATM in its campus backbone network, and you are back at the cocktail party. That same attractive someone says, "Oh, what's ATM?"

In this case, your answer may be:

> I help manage my company's communications network, which connects computers at our three main locations just outside town. This campus network supports many local area networks, called LANs, that are used to connect computers and computer users so that they can easily share information, send e-mail, and so forth.
>
> ATM is a new way to connect these LANs more cost-effectively and at much higher speeds than the system that was used before ATM.

Take 3: The Local Area Network

Activate Time Warp: Now you are a LAN manager in charge of implementing ATM to the desktop to support new applications. "So, what's ATM?"

In this case your answer may be:

> ATM is a new way of giving each computer user very fast access to other computers on the network. Before ATM, several computer users shared a rather slow connection called an Ethernet connection, and each user was limited to sending 10 million bits of information per second. Now, each computer has a dedicated network connection and can send over 150 million bits of information per second.
>
> Before ATM, the network was too slow and didn't let us implement some of the newest scientific visualization and development tools that our engineering department has been screaming about. So this new technology has been deployed to meet this and other future needs, and I'm the lucky one in charge of putting it all together. Now can we please change the subject? If not, I think I hear the wall art calling my name.

Figure 4-1 shows ATM used in the WAN, the campus backbone, and the LAN.

We take a closer look at ATM in each of these segments of the network in the remaining sections of this chapter and in Chapter 5, starting at the desktop and stretching out into the wide area. If you want even more details, flip to Chapters 12 and 13 for additional coverage of ATM in the WAN and LAN.

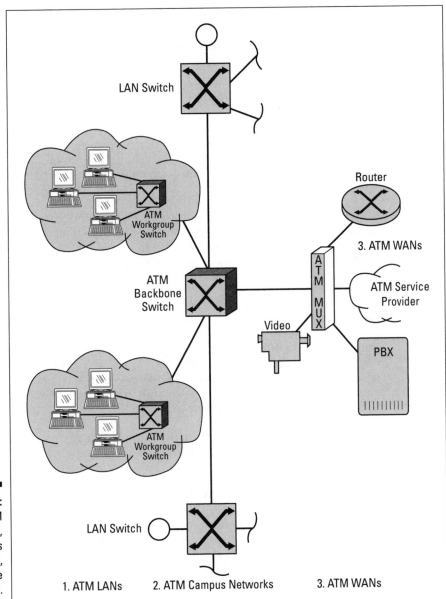

Figure 4-1:
Finding ATM in the LAN, the campus backbone, and the WAN.

How Traditional LANs Work and How to Get More out of Them

Unless your company is very young, your corporate data network has probably gone through an evolutionary process, beginning with the mainframe. Mainframe networks are strictly hierarchical, and the traffic patterns are slow and highly predictable. Within the past ten years, personal computers probably infiltrated your workplace as each department began developing documents and applications specific to its needs. Over time, work groups had to deploy LANs to provide a way for these personal computer users to share files and resources such as printers.

Most of the corporate world has now taken the next step into the era of client-server computing. Client-server computing enables your company or department to centrally store files on a server or in a collection of many servers. Companies can segregate servers to support specific needs, so now you may have file servers, application servers, and most recently, intranet servers.

You and the other hundreds or thousands of cube dwellers in your company are the clients, and you all require frequent access to these servers. Unless you like the excuse to go grab a cup of coffee with each push of the enter key, you want your LAN to be fast enough to drop the requested contents to your disk or screen in a few seconds, preferably faster. If your LAN can't keep up with the demand, the first place you notice the slowdown is in your server links. For bandwidth-intensive applications, such as ones that use a great deal of graphics and video, the slowdown can be much more noticeable.

For many of you, traditional LAN solutions provide adequate speed and capacity to support your client-server environments. Traditional LAN solutions, such as Ethernet and token ring, work like the old party lines in the telephone network. Several users, in this case desktop computers, printers, servers, and so forth, all share a "party line." LANs allow only one party to seize the line and transmit information at any given point in time. When a device on the LAN wants to transmit information, it must first find out whether the channel is available. An Ethernet LAN uses the Carrier-Sense Multiple Access with Collision Detection (CSMA/CD) standard to see whether the coast is clear. With token ring and some other LANs, a token moves around the LAN, and any device needing to transfer information seizes the token as it passes by.

These days, your firm is likely adding more users to the LAN, and everyone is sending more information more often. If you are in a large office, all this extra traffic may be causing congestion on your LAN, slowing your networked applications to a crawl. You (well, actually, your company) own the LAN wiring, so local optimization efforts can center on speeding up the LAN connectivity to the desktop. This focus on speed contrasts to the focus in the WAN, where you try to minimize connectivity costs by maximizing line utilization.

You may be able to solve the problem of a congested LAN fairly easily. Install more LANs and put fewer user devices on each. This process is referred to as *segmentation*. In fact, you can dedicate an entire LAN to just one user device, such as in the case of switched LANs for Ethernet or token ring. In switched Ethernet, each user, printer, or server is given full-time, dedicated access to a 10 Mbps connection. A centralized switch is at the hub of several dedicated Ethernet connections. This solution is one example of how a switched network architecture can increase the effective bandwidth available to an individual network device without changing the technology being used, upgrading the wiring, or modifying the application protocol stacks.

Still, a few applications require transmission speeds of more than 10 Mbps, such as high bandwidth applications with tons of graphics and video. For these applications, approaches like switched Ethernet are not enough, and alternatives such as fast Ethernet or fiber distributed data interface (FDDI) — each of which operate at 100 Mbps — or ATM become viable solutions.

How ATM LANs Work

The promise which ATM holds for the LAN is higher speed networking and support of real-time traffic along with the traditional data traffic on the LAN. ATM can provide a new LAN infrastructure offering advanced networking capabilites not available from other solutions. Although other solutions do provide an easier upgrade path to higher speeds, they can't provide ATM's quality of service guarantees to each application or exceed throughput over 100 Mbps — although Ethernet developers say they are well down the path toward cost-effective gigabit (1000 Mbps) Ethernet.

Figure 4.2 shows a typical configuration for an ATM LAN, in which several desktop computers each have direct interfaces to the local ATM switch. If you deploy ATM on an island of users, then life is probably fairly simple. The complexities arise when you must connect the new ATM users to legacy networks of Ethernet and token ring desktops. To achieve interoperability, the ATM switch must include specialized software to move information between the traditional and ATM environments.

An ATM LAN provides a duplex 25, 155, or 600 Mbps physical connection to the desktop. A *duplex* connection is two-way compared to a *half-duplex* connection which is one-way. Duplex is an important modifier because vendors give other LAN throughputs as a half-duplex measurement. Thus a quoted bandwidth rate for ATM is actually twice the same quoted rate for another LAN technology.

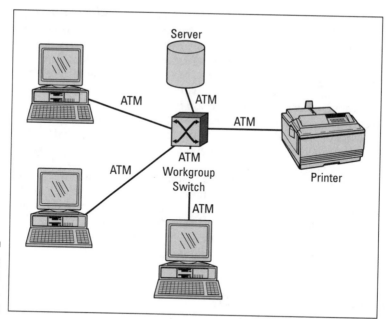

Figure 4-2:
An ATM
LAN.

If you do choose to make the move to ATM, you won't find existing application software capable of talking directly to the ATM network. New Applications Programming Interfaces (APIs) for Windows and UNIX include hooks for application developers to use ATM networks and request different qualities of service. However, it will take several years before a large number of advanced applications are programmed to use these hooks.

Until then, you can take advantage of ATM's speed and power (but not multiple service categories) by using the TCP/IP protocol stack in your desktop machines. The TCP/IP protocol stack is a well-known set of protocol layers which support communication over an IP network. ATM transports TCP/IP by using the Internet Engineering Task Force's (IETF's) RFC 1483 which provides the standard recommendations for encapsulating IP and other internetworking protocols into ATM cells for transport over an ATM network.

Introducing ATM into Your LAN

At the time we write this, users are deploying ATM LANs in only a very small percentage of companies, and these few firms are limiting ATM's use to a small number of advanced applications that are critical to their business and highly bandwidth intensive or requiring real-time communications. *Scientific visualization* (using computer-generated images to analyze problems) is one example of a specialized program that uses a great deal of bandwidth. Desktop conferencing for training is an example of a specialized application requiring real-time communications. ATM is not widely implemented because so many other solutions are available for the desktop which are better known and available at lower costs.

Introducing ATM in the LAN is very different than implementing traditional LAN protocols because it is connection-oriented as compared to the connectionless environments of other LANs. ATM does not, by nature, assume that it should broadcast all information to all other devices on the network. Carrying higher layer protocols designed for connnectionless networking environments on ATM introduces many challenges.

Faked ya out! Emulating traditional LANs over ATM

Most companies that deploy ATM implement it slowly into the local network sections where it is needed. If you decide to deploy ATM to support a few advanced applications requiring the bandwidth or service qualities of ATM, you probably need a way to interconnect the existing LAN users to the ATM users.

The LANE standards define how ATM can transparently support and interoperate with legacy LANs such as Ethernet, token ring, and FDDI. Because LANE joins ATM and existing networks at the LAN networking layer, it includes support for all higher layer protocols using the LANs. Thus protocols such as TCP/IP, Novel's IPX and SPX, IBM's LLC2, and DEC's DECnet can operate over the joined networks. With LANE, ATM LAN deployment does not require vast changes in the existing applications.

Ethernet, token ring, fast Ethernet, and FDDI all operate using connectionless environments, a hallmark of traditional LANs. Standard applications and most of today's installed protocol stacks assume a connectionless environment. They also rely on broadcasts for functions such as service advertising. With broadcasts, all devices on the LAN have access to the broadcasted information. Whether the LAN traffic has to be broadcasted or not, traditional LANs make the information available to all the devices on the LAN.

ATM LANE consists of two software-defined functions:

- ✔ A client function
- ✔ A services function

The client is a device on the ATM network and is an ATM end station or a proxy representing the end stations of a traditional LAN. Clients communicate with each other through switched virtual circuit (SVC) connections using known destination addresses.

If a client does not know the destination address or must broadcast information, it relies on the services function of LANE. Three defined elements known as the LAN Emulation Configuration Server (LECS), LAN Emulation Server (LES), and Broadcast and Unknown Server (BUS) provide these and other services. The broadcasting function can result in a high level of network traffic, depending upon the number of devices and broadcast messages generated, and this function limits the practical size of the emulated LAN network.

We provide further information about emulating LANs in Chapter 11. Fortunately, vendors are implementing the LANE specifications in software that hides much of its complexity from the user. You don't necessarily have to understand all the details to implement LANE, although understanding certainly does help in troubleshooting.

Now that's a switch!

A side benefit of both LAN switching and ATM LANE is the capability to assign individual users to *communities of interest* regardless of their physical location. The network treats each community of interest as its own LAN, even if the people are in different parts of the building, the city, the country, or the world. This setup is referred to as a *virtual LAN,* or VLAN, because the LAN segmentation is logical rather than physical.

One of the biggest benefits of VLANs is that a person's VLAN address and membership does not change when that person physically changes locations. In a world where up to a third of the professional work force experiences a physical office move each year, this benefit can result in substantially lower network operation and administrative costs. If you are a network manager in a company that likes to move around, this capability may also let you actually take your vacation this year.

It'll cost ya

When comparing and contrasting your alternatives for upgrading your LAN, you need to consider the costs of each solution. We can give you the economic comparison for late 1996, but ATM's prices continue to fall, so the comparison may be different as you read this book. A few phone calls to some vendors should provide you with the updated situation.

ATM is currently more expensive than many of the alternatives. For example, if you already have an Ethernet or token ring network interface card (NIC) in the back of your desktop machine, upgrading to a switched Ethernet or token ring LAN requires only a change in your wiring hub. This solution enables you to preserve the investment in the hundreds and possibly thousands of NICs used in your network. And thousands of NICs is not a meager investment.

Using (or not) your existing cards and wires

If you need new NICs for the devices on your LAN, you may want to consider a 25 Mbps ATM LAN — you can purchase it for about the same cost as switched token ring. A 25 Mbps ATM LAN enables you to use your existing Category 3 wiring and gives you ATM's service categories, in case your network (now or someday) needs to support multimedia applications.

Traditional LANs typically run on Category 3 unshielded twisted pair wires. High speed LANs, conversely, typically require Category 5 twisted pair or multimode fiber. If you are now installing a LAN, then the incremental cost to install Category 5 wiring or fiber is probably worth the investment, unless you are pretty sure that the users, individually and collectively, will not require more than 4, 10, or 16 Mbps within five years. A few high speed LAN alternatives are available, including 100VG-AnyLAN and 100BaseT-4 that can run over Cat 3 (that's short for Category 3), but they require an additional pair of wires.

An addition to the capital costs are the costs in time and training (and sometimes in mistakes) encountered while learning a whole new protocol and a new networking paradigm. ATM brings a new learning curve to climb to maintain the network, optimize application performance, and troubleshoot and resolve problems. You may view these challenges as an advantage. A small deployment of ATM in the LAN enables you to gain experience and familiarity with this technology before committing to a large investment in the campus backbone or WAN. You may also view the steep curve as a definite negative, if you live by the credo, "Go with what you know!" (Not a bad way to stay out of trouble.)

Finally, because ATM standards are still maturing, the risk exists that the equipment, protocol, management, and so forth will change, requiring you to upgrade your network and re-ascend part of the learning curve. This risk is the price of implementing a new technology that is still in its adolescence, still growing.

Using ATM in the Campus Network

Many of the issues and standards discussed earlier for ATM in the LAN also apply to ATM as a campus backbone solution. Your campus network technology is probably based on LAN technology, although it may mimic a WAN as a short-term option. The issue of scalability to support future higher bandwidth needs is even more critical in the campus than in the LAN, because the backbone is the aggregator of all high-speed LAN-to-LAN traffic within the campus, and its traffic can quickly multiply. So, for the most part, if you just read the previous section discussing ATM in the LAN, you have a good understanding of the issues of ATM as a campus solution.

A *campus backbone* connects many LANs throughout a building or group of buildings over a single high-speed network. As with the LAN, the physical wiring is owned, not leased on a monthly basis, so if you're the network manager for the campus backbone, you probably focus the network design parameters on optimizing speed and throughput, not on minimizing bandwidth cost or maximizing utilization.

Several fast packet options are available today for building the campus backbone, including fast Ethernet, 100VG-AnyLAN, and FDDI. FDDI has been widely deployed as the campus backbone solution of choice up to this point, and it overcomes the distance limitations faced by other high-speed LAN technologies such as fast Ethernet. These technologies are very similar to traditional LAN technologies in that they use a variable length packet, qualities of service are not specifically supported, and delays are non-deterministic (that is, they can vary from packet to packet).

ATM is a fourth alternative, and as discussed earlier, it is quite different from traditional LAN technologies, a fact that has both positive and negative implications. ATM does support qualities of service, multimedia applications, and deterministic traffic expecting fixed delay. It is also scaleable from 25 Mbps to as much as 2.4 Gbps and perhaps beyond. Nearly all the campus backbone technologies are expensive to implement, so cost is not a major hurdle for ATM (on a relative basis, anyway). It is a new technology requiring you to learn the new jargon and rules. And, you may have to deploy LAN emulation to support traditional LANs over the ATM backbone.

Figure 4-3 shows a campus backbone using an ATM switching solution. In most configurations, the central ATM switches have only native ATM interfaces. The local workgroup devices handle all needed conversions to ATM.

Shakin' up IP over ATM

Transporting IP and other higher layer protocols over the ATM campus backbone requires implementation of one or more of the specifications designed to support this interoperability. These include RFCs 1483 and 1577, LANE (LAN Emulation), and MPOA (Multiprotocol over ATM). Flip to Chapter 11 if you need more information than we provide here.

The first step in transporting the higher layer packets is to encapsulate them into the ATM cells. IETF defined its RFC1483 to perform this function for IP and other protocols. The other defined interoperability specifications generally all use this same encapsulation.

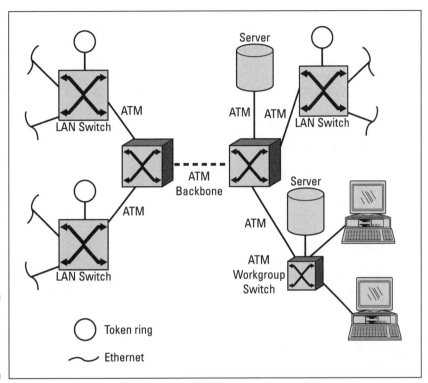

Figure 4-3:
An ATM
campus
backbone.

We've already discussed LANE in this chapter. It provides transparent connectivity of LANs within a single subnet (an IP network which can be reached through a single IP address) and, by default, any of the higher layer protocols, such as IP, that use the services of the LAN. LANE is a good way to carry traditional LAN traffic over an ATM campus network.

An alternative is RFC 1577. RFC 1577 provides a way to map IP addresses into ATM addresses and carry IP over ATM within a single subnet. If SVCs are being used, 1577 also provides a way to set up and tear down the virtual circuits as well as to automate address resolution (mapping between IP and ATM addresses).

The advantages of 1577 are that users may see better performance, and it's implementation may be easier for network managers familiar with configuring IP networks. The drawback to 1577 is that it can only carry IP traffic, has no inherent support for IP *multicast* (sending a packet to a group of users), and is difficult to manage. Most ATM campus implementations are using LANE as opposed to 1577 to overcome these drawbacks and offer the added benefit of providing virtual LANs.

And finally, Multiple Protocol Over ATM (MPOA) exists to carrying IP and other internetworking packets from multiple subnets over an ATM network. MPOA complements the functionality provided by LANE. Its purpose is to allow devices attached to an ATM network to communicate directly with each other, even if they are on two different subnets, as opposed to communicating through a router. This is known as cut-through routing.

Did you say repeat?

Many users are finding that because of its rapid growth, the campus network is the first portion of their network requiring the high speeds of an ATM solution. If your campus backbone is experiencing frequent network congestion, you'll want to consider changing it to ATM.

Instead of rehashing all the same issues, we want to emphasize that all the issues discussed earlier in this chapter regarding the deployment of ATM in the LAN apply to most campus environments, including the use of switching technology, as well as the costs and considerations of upgrading to ATM.

Inside ATM with Joe Skorupa
Senior Director of Product Marketing
FORE Systems, Warrendale, PA

Integration Not Migration

The word *migration,* that is, moving from one place to another, commonly describes the process by which organizations adopt ATM technology. The word *migration* in this context is misleading because it implies that organizations must abandon their current network technology to move to ATM. Not only is the migration approach unrealistic due to the investment companies have in their current network infrastructures; it is also disruptive both to the network and to the business operation overall.

In reality, a complete migration to ATM is neither a required nor recommended approach. In fact, the more realistic approach is to integrate ATM technology into the existing network infrastructure, protecting investments in existing equipment. You can integrate ATM into your network in a planned, phased approach that reduces risk, decreases costs, and increases productivity.

Given this, the next logical question is, "How should I integrate ATM in my network?" History tells us that users typically add new network technology to upgrade the network infrastructure or to support a key application. Infrastructure technology is the long-term underlying foundation of the network, while application technology solves a specific business problem; for example, improving the response time for a financial trading application. ATM is well-suited to support both the infrastructure and applications. Simply put, you should deploy ATM where it makes sense and you need it most.

ATM as an Application Technology

ATM's speed, capacity, and quality of service (QoS) make it the right choice to support core business applications. The unique features of ATM make existing applications perform better, and enable new applications. Today, users depend upon ATM in a variety of high-performance applications for engineering, scientific, and technical computing. And you'll also find growing use in many different vertical industries — from financial services to health care.

A key advantage of integrating ATM as an application technology is that it works well in isolated workgroups. Historically, users have implemented ATM installations from the bottom-up, driven by the needs of the workgroup in support of a specific application.

If you identify a particular workgroup or department as a networking bottleneck (see Figure 1), they are a prime candidate for the use of ATM. By moving these users from the existing network to an ATM workgroup (Figure 2), you realize two benefits immediately.

✔ The users on the ATM workgroup get an improvement in network performance.

✔ With the bottleneck removed from the existing network, the rest of the users notice better performance, too.

The following illustrations show how this works:

The ATM workgroup simply interoperates within the existing corporate backbone, as shown in Figure 2. From this small, initial project you may find it beneficial to further explore ATM's use in your network. The true challenge in a dynamic, internetworked enterprise is to rapidly develop and deploy new applications that improve enterprise-wide performance. Internet access, high-speed intranets, multimedia front-ends to existing databases, and videoconferencing are all applications that organizations need to support — if not now, soon.

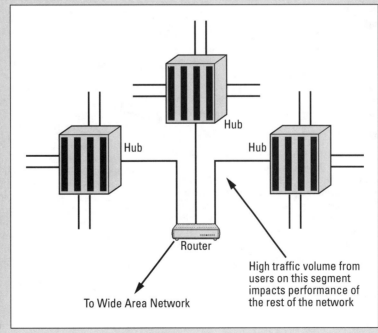

Figure 1:
The existing network with a performance bottleneck.

Hub

Hub

Hub

Router

To Wide Area Network

High traffic volume from users on this segment impacts performance of the rest of the network

(continued)

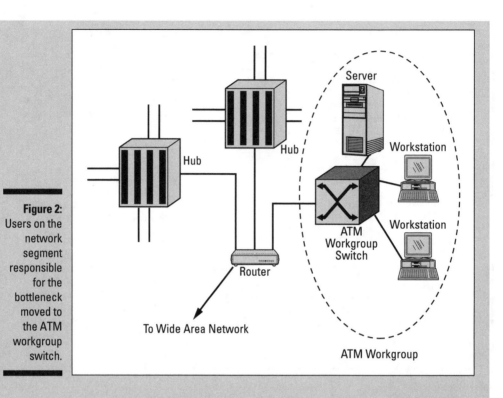

Figure 2:
Users on the network segment responsible for the bottleneck moved to the ATM workgroup switch.

Many organizations have found that once they've installed an island of ATM, they can expand it to other parts of the network — from the department level to the backbone. This is also the initial step toward integrating ATM as the infrastructure technology.

ATM as an Infrastructure Technology

ATM's scalability, reliability, and interoperability also make it the right choice for the enterprise infrastructure. Traditionally, when users deploy a new technology in a network, they integrate it at the core. As time passes, however, an existing infrastructure technology that was once suitable will probably lack support for newer, more sophisticated applications, like voice or video.

As the network grows, then the existing infrastructure technology moves to the edge of the network as newer core technologies become available. Routers are a good example. Today they are moving from the core of the network to the edge, and switching is becoming the standard infrastructure technology.

Returning to the example, Figure 3 shows that, as time passes, more of the network segments have moved to the ATM network. Depending on the level of traffic volume they generate, users and/or servers either directly attach to the ATM workgroup switch (high traffic volume) or indirectly attach (lower traffic volume) via a LAN switch equipped with an ATM uplink to the workgroup switch.

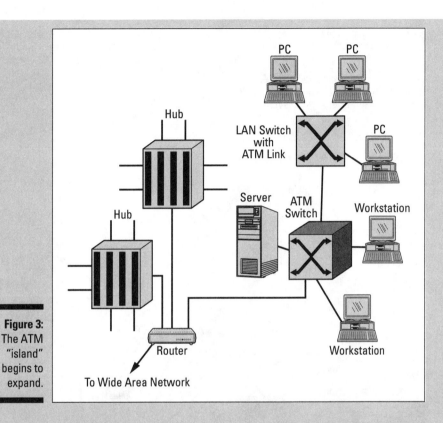

Figure 3: The ATM "island" begins to expand.

As you build and then interconnect multiple ATM workgroups your ATM backbone network begins to emerge (see Figure 4). Common servers and centrally-located routers can also directly attach to the growing ATM backbone. The network integrates ATM gradually, by operating in parallel with the existing backbone.

As an infrastructure technology, ATM functions across both the local and wide area network. By eliminating multiple overlay networks (that is, separate networks for voice, video, and data traffic), organizations can reduce their overall network costs by as much as 50 percent.

The Advantages of Integrating ATM

By integrating ATM as you need it, you are protecting your organization's existing network investments. You can introduce ATM gradually into the current network infrastructure as it makes sense.

This approach provides you with three benefits:

- You can improve the technology with little or no disruption to the existing network.

- You can provide an opportunity to train the staff in phases, just as you integrate the technology in phases.

(continued)

✔ You demonstrate a pilot ATM application to management and future users — all with little or no risk.

Whether integrated as an application technology or as an infrastructure technology, ATM provides a scalable networking technology that will meet the increasing demands of both today's and tomorrow's business requirements. Organizations can integrate ATM technology today with the confidence that it will "future-proof" their networks, taking them well into the next century.

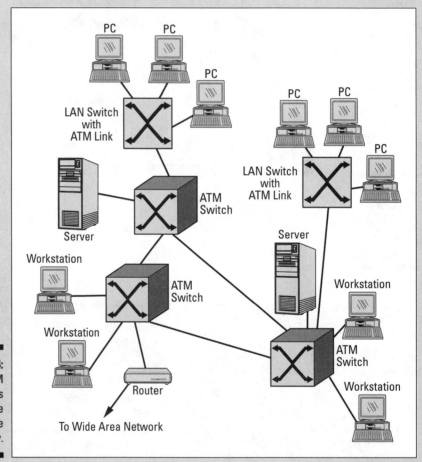

Figure 4:
ATM
becomes
the core
infrastructure
technology.

Chapter 5

Where Can I Use ATM in the Wide Area?

. . . .

In This Chapter

▶ Revisiting Darwin: The evolution of the WAN

▶ Understanding how ATM works in the WAN

▶ Comparing ATM in the WAN to ATM as an infrastructure

▶ Extending ATM into the residential network

▶ Integrating ATM into your WAN

▶ Deciding whether to put ATM in the WAN

▶ Connecting new ATM locations to existing private line, frame relay, and IP locations

. . . .

ATM was initially designed for wide area networks (WANs) as part of the Broadband-Integrated Services Digital Network (B-ISDN) standards to meet the need for infrastructure capable of providing high-speed services for carrier-class networks. Later, developers expanded ATM to benefit other network environments, including private enterprise, local area, and campus backbone networks. The result of this diverse range of uses is the most complicated protocol for networking ever developed by the telecommunications industry (but you've probably figured that out by now!).

Luckily, deploying ATM as a unifying backbone transport on the WAN may actually be less complicated than using it in other ways. If ATM is just providing raw transport on a network, you don't need the complex ATM solutions for routing and protocol support.

By the way, in this chapter we include metropolitan area networks (MANs) in our use of the term WAN. The only difference between MANs and WANs is one of geography — MANs are typically within a city; WANs operate between cities. But the issues for ATM are very similar for MANs and WANs.

Acronyms Used In This Chapter	
Acronym	**What It Stands For**
ADSL	Asymmetrical Digital Subscriber Line
B-ISDN	Broadband-Integrated Services Digital Network
CAP	Competitive Access Provider
CBR	Constant Bit Rate
CPE	Customer Premises Equipment
DSL	Digital Subscriber Line
FDDI	Fiber Distributed Digital Interface
FRF	Frame Relay Forum
IAM	Inverse ATM Mux
IETF	Internet Engineering Task Force
IMA	Inverse Multiplexing for ATM
IP	Internet Protocol
IXC	Interexchange Carrier
LAN	Local Area Network
LEC	Local Exchange Carrier
MAN	Metropolitan Area Network
MPOA	Multiprotocol over ATM
NT	Network Terminator
POTS	Plain Old Telephone Service
RBB	Residential Broadband
RBOC	Regional Bell Operating Companies
RSVP	Resource Reservation Protocol
SMDS	Switched Multimegabit Data Services
SNA	Systems Network Architecture
TCP/IP	Transmission Control Protocol/Internet Protocol
TDM	Time Division Multiplexing
TII	Technology Independent Interface
UNI	User-Network Interface
VBR	Variable Bit Rate
VPN	Virtual Private Network
WAN	Wide Area Network

How Traditional WANs Work

Describing the traditional WAN isn't as straightforward as you may think because each network must meet the unique needs of the organization which it serves. How different groups deploy wide area networking technologies depends on the number of locations, geographic distribution, traffic volume, existing network equipment and protocols, communication applications, and many other factors.

Private fortresses

For over twenty-five years, companies have been building and operating private networks to connect corporate and remote locations. Your company probably has a whole department that sprang up to support this function. The Telecom department typically is responsible for buying, building, and operating the part of the network that supports the voice applications, and the Information Systems (IS) department usually takes responsibility for the computer network and data applications.

These two networks are often physically separate and have different premises equipment, access lines, and long haul networks. In the traditional wide area network, private leased lines connect privately owned premises equipment on each end. During the 1980s, this equipment became very sophisticated, enabling companies to reduce the amount of money spent on expensive leased lines by increasing the average use of those lines. This customer equipment also provided advanced features, such as automatic rerouting and time of day routing, to increase network availability as the networks and their applications became critical to the business.

The most common technology used to build a private infrastructure is Time Division Multiplexing (TDM). TDM enables companies to integrate different applications, such as voice and data, onto the same T1 (also called DS1) circuit. Each application uses one or more of the 24 different low-speed circuits within the T1, known as DS0s.

In the 1980s, the point-to-point voice applications usually justified the cost of buying the high-speed T1 network between major business locations. Companies found the leased T1 lines provided substantial savings over using standard 1+ dial phone services. The data applications used leftover network bandwidth, essentially riding on the network for free.

The TDM approach has two big drawbacks:

 ✔ Each DS0 within the T1 supports only one application. If the application isn't using its allotted bandwidth at a given point in time, the bandwidth just goes to waste.

    ✔ Each individual corporation has the full burden of operating and optimizing the network.

For some organizations, the mission of the network applications is so critical that they feel that they cannot afford to give up control over the WAN, even if costs can be reduced by doing so. Other corporations, especially those under competitive pressures to reduce costs, find that the resources of the organization are more effective when concentrating on the core business problem — such as making shoes or selling ice cream (a personal favorite of ours) — not on operating a network. For many years, the phone companies did not offer many options for businesses fitting this profile, but today public network services, as well as managed network services, provide an attractive alternative to private fortresses.

Public services

In the late 1980s and early 1990s, public *virtual* voice and data services began to flourish. Designed specifically to meet the needs of large organizations, these public services are said to be virtual because they logically — as opposed to physically — dedicate networking resources to customers. The new services provided network managers with alternatives that increased speed, connectivity, and reliability, and in many cases, substantially lowered the cost of owning and operating the network.

Virtual private network (VPN) services for voice traffic were the first major step toward dismantling the TDM-based private networks of the 1980s. VPNs offer a way to substantially lower networking and administrative costs while still retaining the sophisticated functions of a private voice network. As more and more voice traffic migrated from private networks to VPNs, the private networks filled up with burgeoning data traffic. Operating these private networks continued to be expensive and required specialized organizations, but the mission-critical nature of the applications justified the dollars.

In the early 1990s, a new breed of public data service, called *frame relay,* emerged to meet the specific needs of bursty and intermittent data traffic — the kind of traffic generated by connected LANs. Frame relay provided a virtual data network to users by fairly sharing networking resources through logical connections. Companies began to question the capital and personnel expenditures associated with maintaining a private network. Some applications — especially mainframe connectivity — justified a private network, but justifying the allocation of private network bandwidth to the ever-increasing but sporadic capacity requirements of remote LAN (and later remote client-server) applications became more difficult.

Frame relay services became the best option to fill this need, offering low-cost CPE (Customer Premises Equipment) and network services. Frame relay provided the additional benefit of alleviating the corporation from the responsibility of designing and managing the WAN backbone, delivering automatic rerouting functions, troubleshooting problems, and so forth. Later, customer equipment emerged that enabled other applications, such as terminal to host traffic, traditional SNA (Systems Network Architecture) traffic, and even voice and desktop video, to share the frame relay network. Sounds like ATM, doesn't it? Well, in many ways it is, only at slower speeds and using a different protocol.

At the same time, the Internet began to grow in popularity, and the World Wide Web was born. It looked as if IP might take over the world, especially as the Web's multimedia applications made use of IP. The IETF (Internet Engineering Task Force) began work on a protocol — known as RSVP or Resource Reservation Protocol — that enables applications riding an IP network to ask for reserved bandwidth.

As the use of frame relay networks and the Internet has grown exponentially over the last five years, these networks have developed the very problems that ATM is designed to solve: They need a highly scaleable architecture, and in time, they will need to offer users with different requirements, different qualities of service. In other words, they need an ATM backbone.

If you purchase networking equipment and services, you can choose among two or more of these protocols. However, each protocol has its own zone of advantage in which its benefits outweigh those of the other two. Frame relay, IP, and ATM cooperate more than compete, and so standards exist for transparently supporting and interoperating the protocols in a single, integrated network. We talk much more about these options in Chapter 12.

Hidden world: The underlying infrastructure

So now you've had your history lesson on the evolution of wide area networks. Wasn't it exciting! Well, maybe not exciting, but hopefully interesting. Like all history, the WAN network story provides perspective on what may happen in the future. The past 20 years have left most corporations and the public carriers with a legacy of diverse networks and services meeting different needs. The private line network infrastructure is different from the IP network, the frame relay network, the X.25 network, the VPN network, and even the POTS network (that's *plain old telephone service* — you know, the dial tone that you take for granted in your home until it's gone for a day, and then you'd give most anything to get it back).

This legacy has its benefits and a few drawbacks. On the plus side, designers built each network to the exact specifications and requirements of the target applications. On the down side, private organizations and the carriers usually had to erect separate engineering teams, operations groups, maintenance teams with their associated equipment and test processes, and sometimes even billing systems for each and every service. This sort of behavior creates jobs for the economy, but it also substantially increases the costs to provide these services and, therefore, the prices that we pay.

As you read in the next section, ATM is intended to offer an alternative to this legacy, one that enables these separate networks, and many of the supporting departments, to consolidate.

How ATM WANs Work

The promise that ATM holds for the WAN is one of consolidation. Your company or carrier can combine previously segregated networks onto a single network infrastructure while providing each separate application a guaranteed quality of service.

If you need more bandwidth at a single location than two T1 lines can provide, you may want to consider ATM or ATM-based technologies and services in your evaluation.

If you already have a large frame network and data will be the only application using the network for the next several years, NxT1 or T3 frame relay services are possible alternatives to ATM. Or if your local carrier is an aggressive provider of switched multi-megabit data services (SMDS) and you need to connect over twenty regional locations, then SMDS may also be a potential solution. Native LAN services are another option. They typically offer Ethernet, token ring, or FDDI interfaces to the customer using an ATM backbone. The carrier then takes care of all the design and operations complexities of adopting these native LAN interfaces into ATM for transport across the network. We compare and contrast all these different solutions in Chapter 12.

Private ATM fortresses

If you already operate a wide area network based on T3 (or DS3) and/or multiple T1 private lines, then you probably use intelligent multiplexing equipment to transport multiple traffic types over your private lines. Moving to a private ATM network infrastructure can mean a relatively simple equipment upgrade or, more likely, may require investing in new equipment and redeploying the existing intelligent *muxes* (multiplexers, that is) elsewhere in the network.

Already a few dozen companies use ATM as the underlying foundation for the private WAN. A percentage of these companies are supporting not just data applications and possibly a little video, but on-net voice calls as well. In fact, some are using the VBR-RT class of service or proprietary approaches for these voice applications. These solutions are bringing the statistical multiplexing advantages of ATM to voice traffic, further improving network utilization and reducing costs — something we all like to do.

Figure 5-1 shows a private ATM network configuration. If you build an ATM private WAN, you have to purchase ATM equipment, typically a router or switch for data or an ATM multiplexer for data with voice. Private leased lines (usually T3s) provide the facilities to tie the equipment together.

Setting up a private ATM network sounds easy, and frankly, compared with using ATM in most other network environments, it is. However, ATM still represents a whole new protocol and a new approach to building, operating, managing, and optimizing the WAN. You have a definite learning curve to ascend, and the protocol is still maturing, even in the relatively stable area of raw transport.

Public ATM services

Selecting public services over owning and maintaining the private fortress is often less expensive and more reliable. The carriers have multiple engineering teams operating the network, and they can quickly address any troubles that occur. In the U.S. today, the interexchange carriers (IXCs) have the most experience, but a few of the competitive access providers (CAPs) and regional Bell operating companies (RBOCs) offer widely available ATM that you can trust. ATM is following the trend started by frame relay: Most corporations find the public solutions superior to private frame implementations.

Today's ATM service is typically defined in technical terms which closely mirror the standards themselves. The service providers offer little packaging or value-added services beyond building and maintaining the wide area networking infrastructure for you.

An ATM inverse mux by any other name . . .

We're finding that using ATM-related terms consistently is difficult (and we're really trying, too). That is, ATM (and networking technology in general) lives up to its multiple-personality reputation by using different names for the same entity. The continuing development of new technologies and standards in the networking industry makes acronyms fair game for redefinition.

For example, we may not have consistently used the same term for inverse multiplexing on ATM. You may see the same concept referred to as ATM Inverse Multiplexing (AIMUX), Inverse Multiplexing for ATM (IMA), or Inverse ATM Mux (IAM). Because we recently found IAM on the

ATM Forum home page, we're trying to get the book's terminology in line with this *latest* acronym. And we're hoping that the imminent straw ballot on this standard will bring about a standardization of terminology, too.

IAM isn't the only networking term that you may see referenced in multiple ways. The term ILMI moved from the description Interim Link Management Interface to Integrated Layer Management Interface. And what used to be the ATM *class of service* designations are now known as ATM *service categories*.

Go figure!

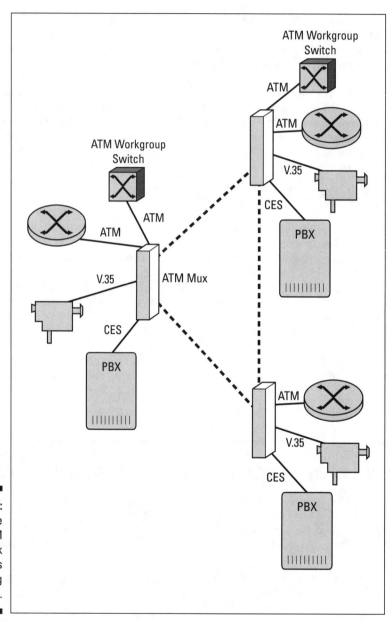

Figure 5-1:
A private
ATM
network
looks
something
like this.

The carriers are positioning these native ATM services primarily for data applications targeted to a very small percentage of customers. Companies that use these services today commonly need a very high-speed backbone or want to solve a very specific business problem. Using a native ATM service lessens, but does not eliminate, your need to invest in ATM equipment or train a team of network technicians that understand and can troubleshoot the network.

Over time, the service providers may hide the underlying complexities of the ATM service and take on a greater level of responsibility for optimizing the performance of individual applications and user network environments over their services. Until that time, however, installation of public ATM service requires a team effort between the service provider and the customer. To further complicate matters, the ATM processes are far from old hat for the carrier employees. Most networks are handled on a case-by-case basis, and even getting prices from the service provider can be difficult.

Figure 5-2 shows an example configuration for a public ATM network. You usually purchase an ATM router, multiplexer, or switch and connect to the network by using the ATM UNI protocol over a high-speed access line. The access is usually a T3 (or E3) connection, although it can be a single DS1 (or E1).

The network uses ATM cells all the way to the premises equipment, so the service is levying the *cell tax* over the access as well as the backbone. At lower speeds, the bandwidth efficiency gained compared to the ATM overhead is often questionable and is usually justified only when the location must communicate with other ATM locations. In this case, using the same protocol end-to-end can have advantages outweighing the disadvantages of the additional overhead. A few enterprises are also using T1/E1 solutions to support multiple traffic types, although most companies choose to achieve this support through advanced frame relay premises equipment and service.

In almost all cities and countries, the cost of a T3 or E3 access circuit is very high — high enough to take ATM out of the reach of the typical company even if the price of the ATM service itself is very affordable. The high cost of the access circuit is why the ATM standard was scaled down to T1/E1, although not without controversy. But another solution is on the horizon, to be finalized in 1997.

The Forum is developing a new ATM standard called Inverse ATM Mux (IAM). IAM lets users needing more than 1.5 or 2.0 Mbps but less than 32 or 45 Mbps of ATM port speed worth of access into an ATM network to buy multiple T1 or E1 circuits and use the aggregate bandwidth to access the ATM network service. Most configurations use two to eight T1 lines — with more than eight T1s, costs start to the match the price points of a T3. Using multiple T1s or E1s to access the ATM network is possible already, but it requires a proprietary solution with an additional layer of inverse multiplexing equipment on each end of the access circuits, as shown in Figure 5-3. The cost of these units typically makes the solution too expensive to be feasible.

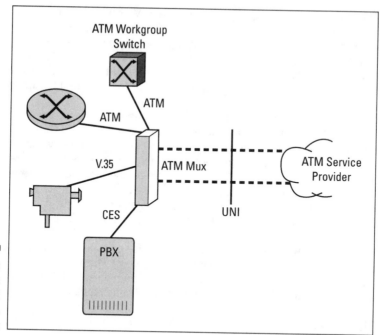

Figure 5-2:
A public
ATM
network.

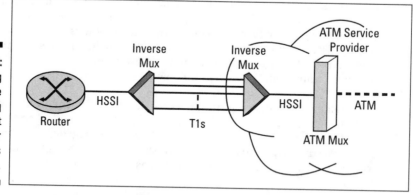

Figure 5-3:
Adding
inverse
multiplexing
equipment
to your
access
circuits.

With IAM, the inverse multiplexing function is embedded into the ATM equipment at one or both ends of the access connection, as shown in Figure 5-4. While this capability does incur an incremental equipment cost, the cost is expected to be less than that of stand-alone devices. This lower cost, combined with the lower cost of T1 compared to T3 access and the rather aggressive prices that many service providers are offering with ATM public services (that is, aggressive relative to T3 or E3 dedicated lines), may help to spur the use of IAM over the next few years.

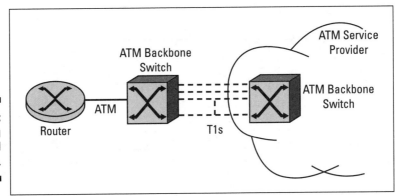

Figure 5-4:
Using
IAM ATM
connections.

Most public services have two separate components in addition to the access line. These components are the port connection and the virtual connections, shown in Figure 5-5. The port connection is the high-speed physical interface for a given site into the ATM network. The virtual connections, which may come in several different sizes and flavors, provide connectivity between locations. The capacity of the port connection is the bandwidth available for the accumulative virtual connection traffic into and out of the location at any given point in time. The port connection's capacity is also the maximum transmission speed for any of the virtual connections into or out of the location. You can find out more about the details of ATM public services in Chapter 12.

Hidden world: The underlying infrastructure

While ATM public services may not take off in a big way for a few years yet, ATM as an underlying infrastructure for frame relay, Internet, intranet, native LAN, and other services is well accepted.

Some of the largest carriers are exploring how they can use a single ATM infrastructure to support many different data services simultaneously, just like the theory says. They are just beginning to investigate the organizational, engineering, operations, and other support issues that go along with this type of move. Few service providers are exploring the merits of putting switched voice services over an ATM backbone, although a few have researched the achievable theoretical savings — with impressive results, especially if bandwidth costs are high. As competitive pressures to reduce costs in order to improve competitive positioning and profit margins mount, the use of ATM as an underlying infrastructure continues to increase.

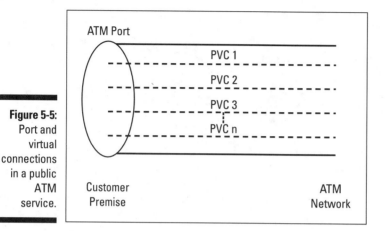

Figure 5-5:
Port and
virtual
connections
in a public
ATM
service.

One of the best ways to get the benefits of ATM is to look for public services that use ATM as the underlying infrastructure. Some service providers are even beginning to put small ATM service multiplexers in multiclient buildings, enabling individual companies to buy one or more ATM-based services, such as native LAN services, without making a big investment in ATM itself.

We share more information on the use of ATM in carrier backbones in Chapter 6.

Residential Broadband Networks

A subset of underlying infrastructures is ATM as a platform for delivering and supporting high-speed, multimedia, and/or interactive services to the home. Initial residential broadband trials focused on interactive TV and video services, but recently the focus has shifted to include high-speed Internet access and even home office (remote LAN) services.

Cable television companies are entering the telephony and Internet services market with cable modems that can use ATM as the network backbone. (Cable modems are like the modems you use for your phone, except that they can provide up to 10 Mbps instead of the present-day maximum 28.8 Kbps on your phone line.) TCI's @Home (a new cable modem-based online service) is a good example.

Additionally, U.S. RBOCs and other independent local exchange carriers (LECs) will probably use ATM backbones for new services competing with cable companies for entertainment, high-speed Internet, and work-at-home services. Many of the trials already underway include the use of a new technology called Asymmetrical Digital Subscriber Line (ADSL) and other DSL technology variations.

The reason that ATM is being considered as a backbone for these networks is traced directly to ATM's core competencies:

- ✔ Support for multiple carrier services simultaneously

- ✔ Delivery of different qualities of service

- ✔ Capability to scale for cost-effectively supporting very high speeds

The ATM Forum's Residential Broadband (RBB) technical working group is developing specifications to take ATM a bit farther — all the way into your home. This group is defining a complete end-to-end system to use ATM for both residential and in home distribution. The target delivery date for the initial specification is mid-1997. Not surprisingly, Microsoft is chairing this effort.

Figure 5-6 shows a simplified version of the reference model for the RBB specification. The networks consists of three parts:

- ✔ **The ATM Core Network** provides access to far-flung resources such as video servers and uses the existing specifications of the ATM forum.

- ✔ **The ATM Access Network** delivers the ATM services to the home. Distribution and Final Drop are the two subcomponents of this network. The underlying physical access technology varies depending upon the local factors of the network and may include ADSL, cable modems, and other solutions.

- ✔ **The Home ATM Network** delivers the ATM services to various devices in the home. The network terminator (NT) terminates the access network and separates this network from the home network. The variety of interfaces possible in the home necessitates the need for a technology independent interface (TII) within the attached devices to the home ATM network. The TII enables vendors to develop common equipment available for use in the home ATM network through the addition of a suitable adapter.

Most of ATM's use in these networks is still experimental, and other technologies may prove to be a more realistic choice in the short or long term. However, ATM is well-positioned to become the default backbone infrastructure for high-speed, next-generation residential services. The biggest hurdles in this market, in fact, are not the network technologies; the hurdles are the capability of the service providers to provision, install, maintain, bill, and market these services. The most difficult hurdle of all is offering these services at a price point that consumers are willing to pay. But we are diverging into what could be a whole different book. . . .

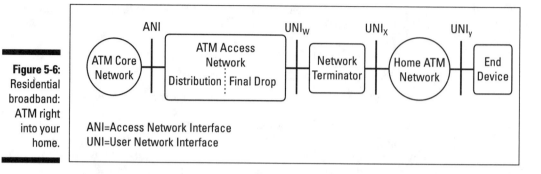

Figure 5-6:
Residential broadband: ATM right into your home.

ANI=Access Network Interface
UNI=User Network Interface

Introducing ATM into Your WAN

If you do decide to introduce ATM at the locations in your WAN requiring higher speeds, you're going to need some techniques to connect these sites to the rest of your network. Just as in the LAN, where LANE supports interoperability between the old and the new, the ATM WAN has some special interoperability standards.

The carriers have taken steps to provide a means to connect remote locations needing a low-speed service with primary locations needing a high-speed ATM service. The general term used for this type of process is *service interworking,* which refers to the capability to use different protocols at different points on a network and have them interoperate smoothly and seamlessly. The network service is responsible for converting between the different protocols, so that the equipment on each end thinks that it is communicating with similar equipment at the other end of the connection.

Three of the more common types of service interworking are circuit emulation, frame relay interworking, and IP. We introduce all below. You can find out more about each in Chapter 11.

Faked ya out! Emulating traditional leased lines over ATM

What if you have already made a huge investment in private line technology but need to introduce ATM into your network to support new applications? Is there any hope for a smooth migration path to ATM that does not require forklift upgrades of all the networking equipment simultaneously?

Circuit emulation is the idea that a traditional private line, such as a T1 (or E1) circuit, can ride transparently over an ATM network, and the circuit termination equipment on each end can remain exactly the same.

The purpose of circuit emulation is to provide a migration path for integrating the traditional applications of the private line network seamlessly into a new ATM backbone. The constant bit rate (CBR) service category supports this type of application.

Circuit emulation enables the existing private line applications to continue using the same infrastructure after you upgrade to an ATM backbone. The existence of the ATM backbone is transparent to the traditional applications. The benefits of this approach are many, enabling you to

✔ Require only a single access connection

✔ Manage a single network

✔ Protect your existing investment in equipment

✔ Slowly migrate each set of applications to native ATM as appropriate

However, we cannot add bandwidth savings to the list of benefits because the CBR connection does not support any statistical multiplexing gain.

Figure 5-7 diagrams the use of circuit emulation at a new ATM location. The other end of the private line can remain the same if you are using a carrier ATM service that includes circuit emulation services.

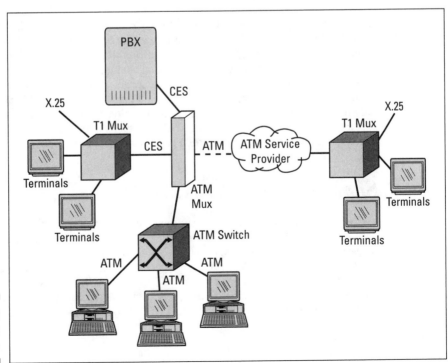

Figure 5-7:
Emulating
circuits.

Note: Circuit emulation uses a CBR connection, but it is not the same thing as CBR. Sometimes the two terms are used interchangeably, but such use is not accurate because the CBR service category can support applications other than circuit emulation, and in the future, circuit emulation may use service categories other than CBR.

Mixin' and matchin' frame relay

The Frame Relay Forum and the ATM Forum have developed implementor agreements to address the issue of interworking between ATM and frame relay technologies. Two types of interworking are defined:

✔ Network interworking targets service providers who want to use ATM technology as the underlying platform for a frame relay network. Frame relay enters and exits both sides of the network. Inside the network, the switches convert the frames to ATM for transport over the backbone, and then from ATM back to frame for delivery to the frame relay customer.

✔ Service interworking enables you to easily mix and match frame relay and ATM services within your WAN. You can choose the technology or service at each network location that best meets the application and speed needs of the site, while still enabling all locations to smoothly send information from one site to the other.

Several service providers in the U.S. already offer frame relay to ATM service interworking, typically without a surcharge. The most common use of this capability is to connect many remote locations that use low-speed frame relay connections to one or two central locations that need ATM. As frame relay networks grow to hundreds and even thousands of sites, the aggregation of this traffic back to a few central sites can in itself justify the use of ATM at these locations. In other cases, the primary site (or sites) may need the quality of service and multimedia support of ATM, as well as needing to aggregate traffic from remote locations. See Chapter 11 for more specifics about interworking.

Shakin' up IP over ATM

In Chapter 4, we introduce the methods for carrying Internet protocol (IP) datagrams over ATM. All methods carry IP in its native form using ATM only to transport the IP packets from one network endpoint to another. The IETF's RFC 1483 specification provides transparent encapsulation of the IP and other internetworking protocol packets into ATM cells. LANE provides transparent connectivity of LANs and, by default, any of the higher layer protocols, such as IP, that use the services of the LAN. RFC 1577 provides a way to map IP addresses into ATM addresses to carry IP and its applications directly over ATM within a single subnet — a *subnet* is an IP network which can be reached through a single IP address. And finally, Multiple Protocol Over ATM (MPOA), exists for carrying IP and other internetworking protocol between multiple subnets over an ATM network.

Using ATM to transport IP can offer benefits over other solutions. If you migrate existing private line based IP networks to ATM, you can eliminate backbone routers by using ATM's logical connectivity to provide direct connections between all of your edge routers. Direct connectivity can reduce your equipment costs as well as lower the transmission delay across the network. You can also depend upon the new ATM network to recover from physical network failures — saving your router network from rebuilding thousands of new route entries during a failure. Some network managers also choose to migrate to ATM from frame relay to support higher transmission speeds in their IP backbone networks.

If your routers are already high-end systems, the migration to ATM requires only activation of some router software and changes in the physical interface card. ATM cards are now available from most router vendors. If you're increasing the WAN port speeds, you'll also need to get a new access line.

Now that's a switch

Building a private ATM network or connecting to a public ATM service requires ATM premises equipment, which is usually a high-end router or an ATM switch. A class of ATM equipment called the access mux is also emerging. The *access mux* is basically a low-end switch that is capable of supporting multiple, different customer applications at the same time. Sometimes this equipment is also called an *access switch*.

Service providers offering ATM services are somewhat sensitive to the type of CPE connecting to their public networks as well as the supported user applications. An ATM switch is capable of aggregating a great deal of traffic over a single connection, increasing the average utilization of the connections and shifting some of the statistical multiplexing gains from the service provider to the user. Service providers are especially sensitive to this shift when the "customer" happens to be another service provider, such as an Internet service provider.

The buffering capabilities, number of supported logical connections, types of interfaces, and many other issues impact your decision about premises equipment. We discuss these issues in more detail in Chapter 15.

It'll cost ya

Upgrading to an ATM WAN is costly compared with low-speed solutions but saves money compared with using TDM technology over the same high-speed lines, so the actual cost of ATM is really a matter of perspective.

If you have been using lower-speed connections for a private network, such as T1s (E1s), then the upgrade to T3 (E3) ATM connections may shock you. However, if you are already accustomed to the price of high-speed circuits, then ATM may not only improve network utilization and performance but also lower costs. In a private network environment where T3 circuits are already in use, the only real upgrade cost for ATM is the equipment itself and the learning curve (plus any new maintenance and management hardware or software). If you are operating a private network that uses multiple lower-speed circuits, then the upgrade costs for ATM also include purchasing higher-speed access and network trunk lines (at least until inverse multiplexing over ATM is standardized — unless you use a proprietary solution).

If you are accustomed to public data services, then switching to ATM is a slightly different story. In general, the U.S. carriers claim that frame relay and ATM prices are about the same at the same speeds and that both cost less than a private line network. However, the actual comparison often depends on the pricing structures of the different services and providers and the individual deal you cut with your carrier.

The published comparisons against private lines are usually done for a partially meshed configuration — that is a configuration which falls somewhere in between a centralized star configuration and direct full connectivity between all sites. Of course, how many companies need a partial mesh of T3 circuits between multiple sites? This prohibitive cost is one of the major problems that everyone hopes ATM helps overcome. T3s are too expensive today to support a partially meshed configuration, so this comparison doesn't really hold water.

Point-to-point comparisons are more realistic, but the only way to make these comparisons is on a case-by-case basis, because private line costs are mileage sensitive and ATM, generally, is not. For the local environment in the U.S., ATM is frequently more cost-effective than T3 private lines greater than 30 miles. In the long-distance environment, ATM wins if the average mileage of the private lines exceeds 300 miles.

One situation in which ATM can save money, even for a low-mileage point-to-point circuit, is when a fractional increment of bandwidth (such as 10 Mbps) is needed. Buying a whole T3 (or E3) is overkill. ATM, in theory, lets you buy just what you need. With some services, you pay on a usage basis depending upon the number of cells you transmit, and with others, you pay a flat fee based on the port and PVC speeds.

REMEMBER

Right now, the best way to determine the price for a public ATM service is to ask for a price quote from a few service providers. The market is young enough that carriers handle pricing on a case-by-case basis, using general pricing guidelines. Of course, in regulated environments, such variable pricing is not the case, and you can just look up the tariff to get the price.

KIERAN TAYLOR

Inside ATM with Kieran Taylor
Broadband Consultant
TeleChoice, Inc., (Headquarters) Verona, NJ

Converting Copper: How xDSL Paves the Way For ATM

ATM's value in the backbone is understood and its use there is growing. But a key question remains: How can remote businesses and residences take advantage of high speeds when they are miles from fiber backbones? Traditional access links limit speeds to a small information trickle, but an emerging modem technology enables an information torrent over ordinary phone lines.

This new technology is known as xDSL, a catchall term that covers a number of similar, yet competing, forms of digital subscriber line (DSL) technologies.

Simply put, xDSL calls for the installation of special modems on each end of a copper wire. Through advanced modulation techniques, the modems can speed multimegabits of data over ordinary phone lines. Most maintain a separate channel to carry phone conversations. While multimegabit transmissions usually require fiber or coax, xDSL uses ordinary copper lines that wind their way from the CO into 98 percent of homes in America. Worldwide, there are nearly 700 million copper phone lines; an installed base that overshadows fiber and coaxial cable combined.

Each technology offers different speeds, ranges, and operating characteristics but all essentially create high-speed "dumb pipes." These pipes deliver the protocol of choice to the customer premises, including ATM. ATM is considered a good fit with xDSL because it handles low latency applications at high speeds.

While many are talking about xDSL's use in residential Internet access, the Internet is not where xDSL will have its debut. In fact, the bulk of the xDSL lines deployed in 1997 will go to businesses rather than residences. While xDSL is often mentioned in conjunction with Internet access, its high speeds also make it a good fit for remote offices, telecommuting, and transparent LAN services. Branch offices that rely on lower speed links might otherwise be excluded from high speed connectivity. xDSL offers a cost effective solution for the branch office. It's estimated that initial services will cost about $200-$400 a month.

But all those high speed links can mean major headaches for service providers and corporate network managers aggregating the traffic. ATM offers the high speed relief needed for xDSL backbones. Its ability to statistically multiplex traffic and assign qualities of service to each connection can ensure that everyone gets a connection without a bottleneck.

Eventually, all of the xDSL technologies may become the conduits for the delivery of high speed, ATM-based services. For that reason, it's important to understand what the various flavors of xDSL offer and where they best fit into the network.

The x in xDSL is actually filled in with other letters, depending on the technology. The major xDSL categories are as follows:

- High-bit-rate Digital Subscriber Line (HDSL)
- Asymmetric Digital Subscriber Line (ADSL)

(continued)

✔ Rate Adaptive Digital Subscriber Line (RADSL)

✔ Very-high-rate Digital Subscriber Line (VDSL)

HDSL

Of all the xDSL offerings, HDSL probably has the largest installed base because it was first on the scene. The technology arose from carriers' problems in extending T1 (1.544 Mbps) and E1 (2.048 Mbps) services over long copper loops. Because long copper loops distort signal quality, telcos must install repeaters or amplifiers on copper pairs at prescribed intervals to restore signal quality. Today's T1/E1 lines require repeaters every 3,000 to 4,000 feet — a time consuming and expensive process.

But HDSL eliminates the need for these repeaters when T1 or E1 is provisioned over two or three pairs of copper wire. Simply put, HDSL works by placing an HDSL compatible card at the central office and another card at the customer premises. Customers who utilize HDSL in this fashion don't realize it — to them its just T1 or E1. They use the same equipment they always have.

Mass consumer requirements for high bandwidth into the home and small office are driving new HDSL solutions. New HDSL broadband modems are able to operate over a single pair of wires rather than the two or three pairs required in traditional T1/E1 service. The penalty for operating over one pair is performance; current implementations top out at either 384 Kbps or 768 Kbps symmetrical speeds. Like all xDSL connections, these single pair HDSL solutions are nailed up and are not dial up like ISDN or an analog modem links. The connections are not structured into DS0 timeslots.

The chief difference between these single pair HDSL offerings and their ADSL and RADSL cousins is that they do not provide support for analog voice. Instead, they provide what is called "digital POTS" by stealing 64 Kbps of bandwidth for voice transmission. ADSL, RADSL, and VDSL offerings provide voice support on a separate frequency from data and as a result can provide voice connections without impact to data throughput.

Telcos will promote single pair HDSL for symmetric synchronous applications such as real time videoconferencing, and in the next year position it to provide Internet and corporate LAN access. Single pair HDSL has extremely low price points today and is very mature in its development. These advantages will keep the technology around for some time.

Sacrifice Symmetry For Speed

The real demand for multimegabit transport is likely to come from small business locations and consumers interested in applications like high speed Internet access and the ability to select video movies on demand. Both of these applications are asymmetric in nature. They demand a multimegabit downstream delivery to the consumer, but only a small upstream link into the network to transmit basic commands or the occasional e-mail. Since HDSL cannot provide high enough speeds for these applications, several vendors began work on alternatives to HDSL that can produce fast speeds, albeit in an asymmetric fashion. This is called ADSL, for Asymmetric Digital Subscriber Line.

These efforts produced two competing algorithms. Both offer downstream rates in excess of 6 Mbps and simultaneous upstream or duplex transmissions of 640 Kbps over single pair lines of 12,000 feet or less. One line coding, Discrete Multi-Tone (DMT), is established as the ANSI and ETSI standard; another, Carrierless Amplitude and Phase (CAP) modulation is widely implemented and is being pushed by certain proponents as a side-by-side standard with DMT. Which method the carriers will prefer remains to be seen, and most consumers will not ever know what their modems use.

ADSL does something else HDSL can't — through frequency division, it provides a single POTS connection over the same pair of wire without any impact to data throughput whatsoever. In contrast, HDSL offerings rely on "digital POTS" by reserving a 64 Kbps section of bandwidth for the transmission of a DS0 voice circuit. Depending on vendor implementation, both can support what is called "lifeline POTS" or the ability to connect voice circuits despite power failure in individual residences.

Either way, a telco can use the same pair of wires presently running into a home to provide both multimegabit data streams as well as the existing analog phone service.

ADSL approaches place a modem on each end of a twisted-pair telephone line, creating three information channels: a high speed downstream channel, a medium speed duplex channel, and a POTS (Plain Old Telephone Service) channel. Filters split off the POTS channel from the digital modem, thus isolating the voice circuit so the telco's central office can power it as a traditional phone line. This guarantees uninterrupted POTS connections, even if the ADSL connection or outside power fails. With most digital POTS solutions as provided over HDSL or ISDN, an external power supply is responsible for powering the digital POTS connection — so if the power goes out, so does the phone service.

The high speed downstream channel ranges from 1.5 to 8 Mbps depending on loop length, while duplex rates range from 16 to 640 Kbps. Each channel can be submultiplexed to form multiple, lower rate channels.

Several RBOCs have already penned an RFP for an xDSL concentrator called a Digital Subscriber Line Access Multiplexer (DSLAM), and several vendors including Alcatel, Amati and Westell have already announced availability of such a device early in 1997. This device will aggregate a large number of xDSL lines for connection to ATM backbones and, as such, is crucial to ensure that xDSL subscribers don't run into a bandwidth bottleneck at the CO.

While ATM's future in relation to ADSL still remains up in the air, several vendors (including Alcatel and Westell) believe that end-to-end ATM is the best protocol for deployment over ADSL and are designing DSLAMs that concentrate ADSL onto an ATM backbone.

Putting an R into DSL

ADSL developers will concede that ADSL isn't the end-all-be-all to network access, and some vendors have already announced the availability of CAP-based Rate Adaptive Digital Subscriber Line (RADSL) solutions. This technology will enable modems to adjust their line rate to become more symmetrical. While Internet access and video on demand applications are asymmetric in nature, other data services such as remote LAN access are not. For this reason, some vendors will offer RADSL modems in the first quarter of 1997.

In addition to altering upstream and downstream ratios, these modems also offer the benefit of connecting over phone lines of varying length and quality. The benefit for telcos is that they can reach customers that might otherwise be beyond the reach of xDSL offerings.

Value in VDSL

While ADSL can currently reach top downstream rates of more than 6 Mbps, several vendors have already identified the need for more speed over shorter distances. While Hybrid Fiber/Coax (HF/C) is the usual contender for offering very high speed services to the home, some telcos lacking installed coax are looking for solutions that run over installed copper. One solution being offered is Very-high-bit rate Digital Subscriber Line (VDSL).

In simple terms, VDSL transmits high-speed data over short reaches of twisted-pair copper telephone lines, with a range of speeds depending upon actual line length. The maximum downstream rate under consideration is between 51 and 55 Mbps over lines up to 1000 ft (300 meters) in length. When lengths go beyond 4000 ft (1500 meters), the rate averages 13 Mbps.

Like ADSL, early VDSL implementations are asymmetric and offer upstream speeds from 1.6 to 2.3 Mbps. Analog POTS support will also be possible since the frequency bands used for voice and digital transmission are separate. VDSL chip development is just beginning, and it will likely be the last of the xDSL technologies deployed on the local loop. VDSL deployment is expected to begin in 1999.

Chapter 6

Who Needs ATM? Do I?

*T*he U.S. and other governments worldwide were some of the strongest and earliest supporters and users of ATM. The governments, along with many leading universities and a few businesses, erected hundreds of test beds in cooperation with ATM equipment and service providers in order to figure out the costs, benefits, and idiosyncrasies of networking with ATM.

Many early ATM users were technology junkies who couldn't get enough of the latest and greatest networking toys, especially when someone else was footing the bill! These early users spent days and nights (yes, they thought it was fun) trying to make initial ATM implementations work, testing the technology, and discovering the early gotchas for the rest of us. Their experiences enable vendors and carriers to offer basic ATM equipment and services today that work and that are, for the most part, reliable.

Who Is Using ATM Today and Why?

Today, a few early adopters have joined the technology junkies and taken the plunge — they're trusting ATM to support day-to-day communications for their organizations. For these early adopters, ATM quickly emerged as the best, and sometimes only, solution. In some cases, one bandwidth-hungry, strategically important application drives the deployment of an ATM solution. A smaller number use ATM as an enterprise backbone to support a mix of applications and the aggregation of traffic for high-speed communications between two or three remote locations or on a campus backbone.

Most of these early users are from the financial, heavy manufacturing, computers and communications, and defense industries, or a few high-tech-dependent government departments and their associated university research groups. The split in ATM 1996 spending by government users compared to commercial users is approximately 70 percent to 30 percent.

ATM has been widely promoted in the government, particularly within the Department of Defense, because of its advanced capabilities and anticipated cost savings. Passage in 1991 of the $92 million High Performance Computing and Communications (HPCC) Act, sponsored by then-Senator Al Gore (you know — the Information Superhighway guy!), provided the high-tech agencies with much of the initial seed money to invest in ATM. The National Aeronautics and Space Administration, the Department of Education, the National Science Foundation, and multiple Department of Defense and security agencies all operate local and/or wide area networks. These government groups, along with various agencies for other countries' governments, substantially jump-started ATM development and continue to be the most important user group pushing for further enhancements.

Another group of early users are providers of Internet and frame relay data services. These providers are finding that an ATM backbone handles the growing traffic load of their networks more efficiently. ATM provides a switching core to fully interconnect service nodes and increase backbone bandwidth utilization. An ATM backbone may also enable the provider to add new features — features that set it apart from other frame relay and Internet services, such as quality of service or prioritization.

ATM and your tax dollars

If you research their roots, you find that many of ATM's earliest projects began with seed money from the U.S. government.

The earliest roots go back to the 1989 National Science Foundation's (NSF) funding of five gigabit test beds to research emerging high-speed computing and communications technologies. Carriers ponied up free bandwidth to the five test beds, providing high-speed connectivity among the participants of each individual group. Participants included the country's leading national and corporate labs, along with many university groups. In 1991, the Defense Advanced Research Projects Agency (DARPA) added its own test bed.

Some of the six gigabit research test beds are still in operation.

Another early ATM project was the Navy Research Lab's (NRL) exploration into local ATM. Over time, this project provided $12 million to FORE Systems, enabling that company to develop its initial switch and interface cards. Much of the money was received while the four FORE founders were still professors at Carnegie Mellon University.

Government jump-starting of telecommunications industries isn't unprecedented. The most widely known example is the Internet, now a booming market.

Do Commercial Users Need ATM?

Need may be too strong a word to use when discussing ATM for most commercial users, at least at this time. Our children *need* all those toys on their Christmas wish lists, but if they had to, they could survive without toys. Survival just wouldn't be as much fun. ATM is being implemented to address the changing network requirements of some businesses, but so are many other technologies.

At one time, conventional wisdom proclaimed that almost every business with at least two locations would adopt ATM in its campus backbone, its WAN, and its desktops . . . typically in this order. However, the emerging enhancements of switched LANs, frame relay, and IP have cast a shadow on this commonly held view. We discuss alternatives to ATM more in the next chapter and in Part III of the book. For now, look at the following situations in which businesses may want to *consider* ATM.

In large businesses, the demand for network capacity is rapidly outpacing the bandwidth of existing LANs and WANs. Capacity increases alone can't satisfy all the needs of evolving communications applications. Networks must be flexible enough to meet the unique service quality requirements of each application. ATM, and now a variety of other solutions, can meet these two needs with varying degrees of success today and in the future. We further explore your technology choices in various segments of the network in Chapter 10 and Chapter 11.

Commercial users are seriously considering ATM for today only when they have a particular networking situation that requires a great deal of bandwidth. Your free-spirited friend from college who has a summer lifeguard job at the beach and a winter job as a ski instructor may love change for the sake of change, but no self-respecting (employed) network manager lives by this adage.

A networking need of the business that is currently unmet but highly visible or a network crisis forecast for the near future is the typical motivation for further investigation into ATM. A company ends up choosing ATM because it values ATM's capability to solve an existing problem while strategically positioning the company network for future expansion and new applications. Early adopters of ATM used it in small pieces of their networks, and the experience they gained through that experiment positions them to take advantage of ATM's growing capabilities as it matures and price points decline in the future.

The issues that drive business users toward ATM can be grouped into the following three areas:

- ✔ A bandwidth bottleneck in either the campus or WAN data backbone

- ✔ A new end-user application that requires the support of high bandwidth or interactive multimedia

- ✔ An unacceptable cost for supporting multiple enterprise networks

These same needs also hold true for government users. However, government users may be more readily able to justify ATM because of the scale of their networks, a heavier preponderance of very unique high bandwidth and multimedia applications, and national security considerations, which tend to muffle the effects of the price versus performance ratios.

A few hundred companies use ATM today in production environments, in various parts of their networks, to solve real business problems. Each case is a unique study in itself, with a set of distinct circumstances that led to ATM being selected as the winner. We include four examples from commercial users in Chapter 16, so that you can see what motivated these particular users to migrate to ATM.

ATM for data bottlenecks

Are you finding that the aggregated bandwidth demand of your data applications is creating a networking bottleneck in your backbone? Do you expect your bandwidth requirements to continue increasing as you add, in both number and power, personal computers, workstations, LANs, and applications? Hint: If you don't expect this increase to happen, you may want to re-evaluate — everybody else has this problem!

If you manage a large network (especially one of the top five percent of networks, as measured by size), you may have already discovered that traditional LANs and T1 (1.544 Mbps) service solutions are becoming inadequate to meet the communications needs in your highest volume locations. Moving to ATM to meet growing bandwidth needs is the easiest way to justify the investment that ATM requires, because in this case, the change simply enables your business to continue doing what it already does. After your ATM network is in place to meet the current needs, you can consider how you can use it for other needs.

Uncork your campus backbone

The most common implementation of ATM today is to relieve a bandwidth constraint in the campus LAN backbone. ATM uncorks the data bottleneck, with higher speeds than possible with CDDI/FDDI or 100 BaseT Ethernet, while providing an infrastructure that can support future multimedia applications. Another big plus of an ATM backbone is high-speed connectivity for frequently accessed corporate servers. An ATM connection running at 155 Mbps or more allows many users to simultaneously download large files without delay.

In many of the existing commercial implementations, much of the fancy signaling and routing protocols defined for ATM are missing, and some believe that those protocols may never be implemented; ATM is just a speed demon for the campus backbone, and using ATM simply for its speed does greatly reduce the complexity of the implementation and the interoperability nightmares. Other people think that these advanced signaling and routing protocols are necessary

MULTIPLICITY

The growth of the intranet

While Internet technologies are revolutionizing the ways in which you can obtain information, order flowers, or register to vote, a fundamental change in how corporations internally distribute information is also building — using these same technologies.

The need for internal accessibility to information and resources has dictated the advent of the intranets. *Intranets* can be described as *private internets* — a company simply internalizes the technology used over the Net to provide an easy-to-use but secure communications environment.

With some estimates putting the number of internal Web servers being deployed as high as five times the number of external Web servers, intranets are fast becoming an important communications tool for business. Like their Internet siblings, these intranet servers are often providing very graphic and image-intensive content — in other words, lots of bits and bytes to push through the corporate network.

Intranets enable employees to publish work electronically and post schedules, meetings, and referendums. The internal network gives a large, branched company a "virtual meeting place" for all its employees, regardless of time zones or geographic locations. Corporations are using intranets for posting up-to-date product information for their sales department, giving ready access to human resource policies and forms, streamlining purchasing processes, communicating corporate objectives and performance, and supporting many other processes where information can become bulky and changes rapidly.

Just as the Internet ushered the public into a new era of communication, intranets are giving companies an economical and easy-to-use electronic haven for distributing information, facilitating the exchange of ideas, and supporting the development and distribution of goods and services.

for ATM to effectively address the campus network. We further discuss using ATM locally, along with the many alternatives, in Chapter 13.

Unplug your WAN

The second most common implementation is an ATM WAN to support a router infrastructure. For a few companies, a T1 frame relay or private line backbone is no longer sufficient to handle peak demand at the largest locations.

Public or private ATM are good options to meet this demand, but neither option is cheap. The higher cost stems from the increase in bandwidth that typically accompanies a move to ATM. Increasing network access from T1 to T3 is a costly proposition, regardless of the technology. However, the other benefits of ATM, such as the ability to eliminate backbone routers or consolidate disparate networks, may mean that your overall cost of network ownership decreases. A very few users have so much traffic on their data backbone that they find they have no choice but to consider ATM; other companies may get many of ATM's benefits from other technologies and solutions.

ATM lets you:

- ✔ Reduce access costs

- ✔ Increase reliability with automatic rerouting

- ✔ Offer the option to purchase bandwidth increments between T1/E1 (1.544 Mbps/2.048 Mbps) and OC3 (155 Mbps)

We discuss wide area ATM and its alternatives in Chapter 12.

ATM for new applications or new installations

A few users have adopted ATM to meet a network need created by a specific, new application that is critical to delivering their product or carrying out their business strategy. Examples include an entertainment company using high bandwidth ATM services to speed up their editing and several brokerages using ATM at the desktop to give their traders the best, most up-to-date market information on which to base decisions.

ATM proves necessary in the LAN or WAN to support high bandwidths and/or real-time video/imaging applications. Typically, these applications are custom built to help the business differentiate itself from its competitors. The applications speed up development between remote groups, distribution of content, or access to information.

The cost of implementing ATM for these advanced applications is generally difficult to justify, particularly in the WAN, but in a few cases, the new savings or revenue is sufficient to pay back the investment. Planning, evaluation, and implementation of these applications and networks generally take a year or more. Scoping out the initial set of capabilities of the new applications, agreeing to the best design, and convincing the Powers That Be of the project's worthiness takes a long time. For most corporations, ATM is first implemented to meet current business needs and later to enable multimedia. Multimedia isn't usually the initial driver for ATM.

A few early users have also selected ATM for a brand-new building or application where they have no existing equipment — and therefore, no interoperability challenges. Perhaps the best example of this is FORE Systems, a rapidly growing company that supplies ATM equipment for the desktop, LAN, and WAN. Founded in 1990 and having ready access to ATM equipment, FORE has built the majority of its underlying network infrastructure, supporting its more than 1,500 employees, using ATM. FORE has been able to implement the grand ATM vision of a unified network, supplementing it with advanced internetworking and voice features that use routers and PBXs. We just can't deny that ATM adoption is much easier when your network starts as an ATM core network and doesn't have loads of legacy technology from the '70s and '80s that has to be supported and accommodated.

ATM for enterprise networks

Very few implementations from the third driver group — consolidation of networks to save money — are in place. However, consolidation is one of the few applications for which ATM remains uniquely qualified, unless voice traffic makes a rapid migration to the LAN, which seems unlikely. Consolidation is also likely to emerge as the primary catalyst for ATM implementations within the next two years

ATM may enable your corporation to consolidate private and public networks for cost-efficiency, ease of management, and support of new applications. Your company fits this adopter profile if you have an extensive telecommunications infrastructure that is primarily private but also includes contracts for public voice and some public data services. Your internal user base probably ranges from headquarters to hundreds of remote sites. The applications that your network must support vary from simple voice services to advanced video and imaging.

The big economic factor that pushes ATM adoption for enterprise networks may turn out to be voice traffic. If you already have to deploy a T3/E3+ network for your data backbone, you can use ATM instead and add your voice traffic for very little additional cost. The old adage has flipped; instead of data riding for free, voice rides the network for free.

If you have made the T3/E3 ATM investment, you can support your voice calls on the same ATM infrastructure for as little as 1¢ per minute (in incremental costs) for long-distance, on-net calls. Unless you are the U.S. government, with its cut-rate pricing, putting your voice traffic on ATM can mean very substantial savings. If you can't justify your ATM wide area network with data only, the added voice savings may push you over the hump.

Early deployments are limited to private calling between the locations on your ATM network until the carriers provide connectivity between their public switched telephone and ATM network infrastructures. Deployments are also based upon proprietary voice-over-ATM schemes until the ATM Forum finishes its Voice and Telephony Over ATM (VTOA) standard in 1997.

For most of you, your VPN (virtual private network) services, combined with low-speed private or public data networks, will remain the best choice for voice for many more years. But for a few of you, ATM may be a path to lower monthly telecom bills!

Figure 6-1 shows an ATM implementation for an enterprise network. Large businesses will deploy ATM in their enterprise networks over time as effective migration strategies become available and obvious cost and performance benefits justify ATM solutions.

Before we close this section, we have to let you know that even the enterprise fortress is fast disappearing as the sole dominion of ATM. Frame relay equipment vendors are making a bold strike for the heart of the enterprise network with SNA and voice FRADs (frame relay access devices). Although only a few all-in-one-box solutions are available for enterprise networking (and these are expensive), frame vendors are working furiously toward the goal of a cost-effective, sufficiently capable solution. Frame relay may become the no-frills enterprise solution for lower speed sites (and possibly higher speed, too). Vendors have already shown that mixing traffic types on a frame relay access link is fairly easy, and by using an ATM backbone, frame service providers can ensure that each traffic type receives the needed quality of service in its backbone.

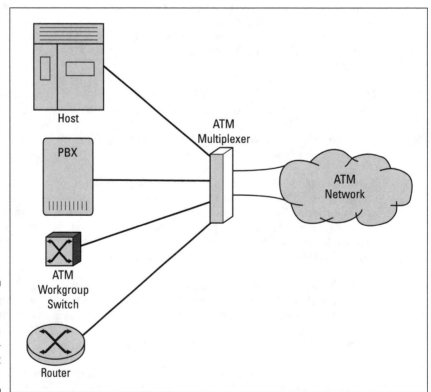

Figure 6-1:
ATM in the
enterprise
network —
the next
big thing!

Do Internet Providers Need ATM?

As we explain in the sidebar "The growth of the Internet," the Internet is one of the fastest growing groups of networks in the world. As traffic volumes increase at exponential rates, Internet providers need a new solution for carrying this immense traffic load efficiently and cost-effectively. ATM is already being installed by National Service Providers (NSPs) such as MCI, Sprint, and AGIS and by some of the largest Internet Service Providers (ISPs) to meet this demand.

Meeting demand

Figures 6-2 and 6-3 show before and after graphics for Internet providers that adopt ATM. Before adoption of ATM, the routers that make up the network have dedicated facilities connecting them (see Figure 6-2). The expense of dedicated network facilities makes full interconnection of all the routers impractical. Each router has a minimum of two connections so that a failure in one connection cannot completely isolate a site. If the network is very large, backbone routers serve as concentration points to maximize efficient use of the backbone bandwidth.

Any given message (that is, an IP packet) may have to traverse three or more routers. Each router represents more delay (unhappy customers), and each packet represents more required processing power (big bucks) in the router. Clearly, an economical method for fully interconnecting the routers in a meshed configuration could significantly improve networking performance and lower costs. Furthermore, a network that only has routers becomes very difficult to manage and optimize as it grows in size.

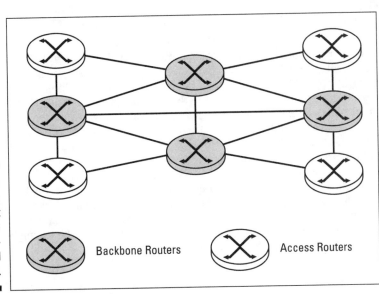

Figure 6-2: Providing Internet service the old-fashioned way.

Backbone Routers   Access Routers

Figure 6-3 shows the router network after the introduction of ATM switching. Virtual connections now interconnect each router with all other routers over one physical path. This configuration lowers the costs of the network by enabling more efficient use of bandwidth, eliminating the retransmission of a packet over multiple links, and eliminating the backbone routers in all but the very largest networks. Delay is also lessened, because each packet crosses a maximum of two routers. In addition to ATM, ISPs are also implementing frame relay to provide virtual networking on slower speed links.

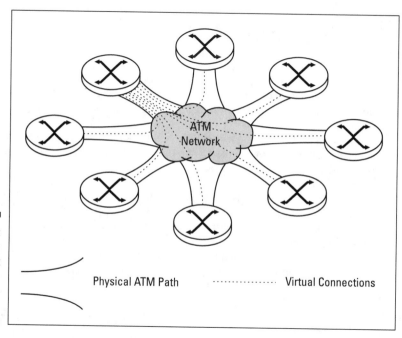

Figure 6-3:
Providing
Internet
service the
new way —
using ATM.

Physical ATM Path   Virtual Connections

Another benefit of the logical ATM network is its inherent stability. If the physical links fail (which will happen as long as we allow backhoes in the world), the ATM network automatically reroutes connections very quickly. Routers no longer need to reroute the thousands of sessions maintained in their tables. Rerouting with a router is very slow and processor intensive and can quickly bring a high-traffic IP network to its knees. On the other hand, the ATM switches can easily move the much fewer number of virtual connections to alternate physical links in just a few seconds.

We expect the increasing Internet load and consolidation of the IP market to result in very large NSP and ISP networks. These large networks will require 45 Mbps or greater backbone links within the next two years. The Internet providers will find ATM backbones for their router networks to be the highest performing, most cost-effective architecture.

Offering new services

Growing traffic volume and associated costs are not the only factors driving ISPs to use ATM; supporting new applications on the Internet is also a strong attraction. Historically, the only traffic on the Internet was e-mail or file transfers. These applications were almost entirely data dumps, and the tortoise pace of many Internet connections was acceptable for these uses. Today, the World Wide Web and Internet telephony are creating new problems, and opportunities, on the Internet.

The Web is the part of the Internet offering easy graphical retrieval of information. Companies and individuals can attach to the Internet computers (called *servers*) that contain information about different organizations and their products and services and that even enable potential customers to make purchases. The Web is the fastest growing sector of the Internet today.

As more companies launch Web sites and become familiar with Web technologies, the sophistication of the Web is increasing. Web sites offer more than just simple text-screens. Graphics and imaging are commonplace, and now video segments, sound bites, and complete multimedia presentations are being added as well. The most important objective of any Web page designer is for the site to be *cool,* and cool means more graphics. More graphics greatly increases the level of traffic, because video and voice files tend to be much larger than simple data files.

Additionally, the Internet is being used for new applications, including real-time voice and video. These applications are computer-based. Special equipment and software packetize the voice and video for transport over the Internet. The quality is typically not as good as using the public switched telephone network (PSTN) for voice or ISDN for video, but the quality is often adequate. The biggest plus? Using the Net for voice and video is very inexpensive, sometimes even free. This alluring attribute is spurring increasing use, especially for international applications.

Internet telephony, which makes your PC seem more like a telephone, is a relatively new market that has been limited to early adopters and computer geeks until now. Netscape, the largest provider of Internet browser software, is adding Internet telephony to its standard browser package, and so is Microsoft. At the same time, many of the limitations surrounding Internet telephony are being lifted as new solutions become available. For example, you can now hear your PC ring and then answer it. New capabilities to prioritize Internet traffic, using enhanced IP routing methods and ATM infrastructures, will help to significantly improve quality and reduce delay for real-time applications over the next two years, sparking added demand for Internet telephony.

The growth of the Internet

The Internet, despite widespread public misconception, is not the result of an overnight joy ride along the Information Superhighway. The origins of the Internet date back thirty years, to the Rand Corporation and the Department of Defense. What began as a communications instrument for Cold War government has evolved into a critical tool in our quest for knowledge and information.

Arpanet, the Internet precursor, was created in the 1960s to enable researchers and scientists to communicate and collaborate on projects immediately. The small "fishnet" connecting a handful of government agencies and universities provided instantaneous discourse. In 1971, this network consisted of 23 hosts (a *host,* in this case, is basically a computer connected to the network).

By 1981, Arpanet boasted 213 hosts, with a new addition surfacing every twenty days. The progression of this revolutionary network escalated to a rocketing speed in the 1980s. Individual networks, such as Bitnet and SPAN, jumped on the proverbial bandwagon, joining Arpanet to form the foundation of the Internet. By 1984, the Net served over 1,000 hosts; three short years later, the number of hosts exceeded 10,000. The Internet had truly emerged as a communications tool and expanded to over 100,000 hosts by 1989.

The Internet has grown quickly, and in the beginning, it was a radical departure from traditional networks. The reasons for this unique growth and status are that the Internet is based on an open infrastructure and the TCP/IP protocol stack is *free.* Until the advent of the Internet, protocols were highly proprietary, and purchasing the code, if possible at all, was extremely expensive (an example would be IBM's SNA

protocol suite). Making TCP/IP open and available to programmers meant that this protocol was used by many different companies in many different ways.

TCP/IP paved the way for advancement among all Internet developers. In 1991, a computer programmer at the University of Minnesota developed an Internet navigational tool, affectionately called "gopher," That same year, the programming language of the World Wide Web emerged from CERN in Switzerland, The National Science Foundation recorded that traffic on the network backbone exceeded 1 trillion bytes per month. By 1993, with the aid of the Web's first browser, Mosaic, and over one million hosts, Internet traffic was racing along.

Today, an estimated 9.5 million hosts and 40 million users are on the Internet. The Internet has emerged as a new marketplace for the 90s, supporting $436 million in a 1995 sales report, according to the July 10, 1996, compilation of The Internet Index. An earlier report from the Index cited that approximately $33 million were spent in advertising on the Net that year.

Clearly, the Net is developing into a large industry with plenty of territory still yet to chart. However, like the barrage of explorers racing to seize the New World centuries ago, industrial rivals are clamoring to chart and lay claim to the Internet. Local and long-distance carriers, cable providers, and new entrants are all enticed by the seductive, and lucrative, lure of the Net. As surely as the Internet has grown beyond the DOD's wildest ruminations, so, too, will the Internet eventually surpass what its 40 million current users imagine. The next 30 months, never mind 30 years, are going to be e-Net-trifying.

Do Carriers Need ATM?

ATM technology initially emerged as a solution to the carriers' need to build very large, scalable, efficient infrastructures cost-effectively, and this need is still the main reason for ATM adoption. ATM's attractiveness has been sought after by service providers worldwide because ATM promises a new and more cost-effective approach to building public networks and delivering services. All large local, long-distance, national, and international carriers have strategic network architecture plans outlining their migration to an ATM backbone in all or parts of their network, sometime in the future.

Backing up the data

ATM will probably become the backbone for carrier frame relay, Internet, and intranet services. Several large carriers have already made the transition. The largest carriers have the most to gain in bandwidth savings but also the most to lose if they inadvertently mess up their customer networks. They must transition their networks only after thorough modeling, design, and testing to ensure a smooth conversion to the new backbone. Such a conversion also requires an investment in new management systems, operations procedures, training, and customer support systems. And, everyone supporting the network has to understand his or her new role in the converted platform.

Many of the advantages ATM brings to carriers are the same as the advantages ATM brings to Internet providers. For example, ATM infrastructures give carriers a flexible backbone to support fully meshed connectivity between all network nodes while dynamically allocating network capacity by using statistical cell multiplexing. The combination of these attributes enables the carriers to use their existing bandwidth investment or recurring bandwidth lease expense more efficiently and effectively. In the past, service providers had to build a single, isolated physical network to support each of their different service offerings for different end-user needs. This approach is expensive and lowers the economies of scale that the service provider may achieve in a single network. ATM provides the single platform to support many different service offerings, fully sharing the network bandwidth and equipment, while still treating each application according to its needs.

Backing up the voice

Another parallel to Internet providers is the way in which ATM enables carriers to offer new services in their frame relay and intranet offerings. As frame relay networks support growing voice traffic, carriers have to find more efficient ways to engineer the backbone while still providing the quality of service now expected by voice frame users. Carriers are looking at providing quality of service options over frame relay services, much as we see in ATM services, to support a variety of applications such as voice, SNA, and LAN traffic on a single

Internet service provider case study

Several Internet service providers (ISPs) are already using ATM in their backbones. We asked AGIS, one of the fastest growing and fourth largest backbone provider of the Internet, to share their ATM story with us.

AGIS is a carrier's carrier. Many local and regional ISPs depend on AGIS for their backbone links in the US and to Europe and Asia. Considered in aggregate, the AGIS network transports over a gigabit of data in each second — that's a lot of data to keep moving across a net. The AGIS engineers have to keep up with a growth rate that is driving revenue increases of over 15% each month.

AGIS was perhaps the first Internet provider to recognize the merits of ATM. The company designed their network backbone with an ATM core from the start. For nearly three years, ATM switches and services have been helping to keep the AGIS network humming along smoothly. Although ATM experienced some rough water in its youth, AGIS remains as enthusiastic as ever about the benefits that ATM delivers.

Phil Lawlor, President and CEO of AGIS, shared five benefits of using an ATM core for the company's Internet backbone.

- **Scalability:** ATM allows AGIS to build an increasingly higher speed backbone. The network grows as they need it.

- **Bandwidth Flexibility:** The logical configurations of ATM allows AGIS to easily add bandwidth as they need it, where they need it. If a network route is becoming congested, a simple change in the PVC configuration sets everything right again. This was particularly important when AGIS was primarily using public ATM services priced based on subscribed bandwidth. Private lines are one size fits all, but ATM can be whatever you need.

- **Lower Delay:** ATM helps to significantly reduce delays and therefore get traffic on and off the AGIS network as quickly as possible. Moving information through an ATM switch can be ten times faster than a router with its processor intense routing lookups. And with ATM's logical connections providing a meshed backbone between routers, AGIS can keep its hop count to one. Low delay makes customers happy. It also allows AGIS to carry more traffic. Each packet spends less time using the network resources as it speeds along the backbone.

- **Quality of Service:** AGIS is delivering three different quality of service levels to its customers. ATM enables AGIS to more closely match the desired price/performance of different Internet applications. Phil believes, "The Internet is the next great communications media of the planet. ATM allows us to deliver the many different communications applications of the Internet with the right priority. No longer will the corporate video conference become blocked by the eight megabyte downloads of the latest doom file by all the teens home on early dismissal."

The three defined classes available from AGIS are the following

Store and Forward — Lowest priority service class for applications such as file transfers, x-mail (which we learned is a term referring to either e-mail, voice mail, or video mail), and USENET groups.

Interactive — Service class for Web searching and browsing.

Guaranteed — Highest priority service for Internet voice and video telephony.

AGIS and its ISP customers distinguish the different traffic types through the address screening capabilities of their routers.

Economics: All the above feed into improved economics for running the network. Scalability allows purchase of large chunks of bandwidth at a lower cost/bit. Bandwidth flexibility allows efficient load balancing of physical resources and incremental purchase of bandwidth (if you are using ATM services). Lower delay moves traffic on and off the network more quickly, allowing more packets to use the same networking resources. Quality of service enables price discrimination for those customers who value improved performance. And lastly, the full meshed connectivity of ATM reduces the number of required backbone routers, a very expensive networking component.

We also discussed some of the frequently cited downsides of ATM by Internet engineers. Phil viewed these as necessary aspects of the protocol required to deliver its many benefits. The 10 percent cell tax is small compared to the overall bandwidth efficiencies gained through ATM. And if you argue that the cell tax is actually higher due to partially filled packets, AGIS still strongly believes that the statistical gain achievable with ATM delivers the best overall use of the bandwidth. They may also question how many empty cells are actually running through the network.

AGIS is an Internet provider who has built a strong case for using ATM as a core for the Internet. After nearly three years of experience, they are beginning to now use ATM to differentiate their services with different priority classes. And, many AGIS customers agree with ATM's merits. AGIS says that more and more ISPs are connecting to their network with ATM equipment. (Others use frame relay, a closely related circuit-based technology, at T1 speeds and lower with AGIS providing the interworking between the customer's frame relay access and their ATM backbone.)

We closed the interview by discussing the lessons learned by AGIS in their long experience with ATM. Phil offered two tips to other Internet providers and any large IP network operator considering ATM.

---

frame relay network. Many frame relay users want the ability to consolidate separate networks but do not need the speeds or added complexities of ATM.

Voice applications are working for the initial adopters by prioritizing voice only at the ends of the network. Voice FRADs process voice traffic into tight formats, places the voice traffic into small frames (sounds like the ATM cell, doesn't it?), and prioritizes those frames above all other traffic types for transmission over the access line. After the voice frame reaches the network, it moves quickly from switch to switch. Most carriers have over-engineered their backbones to avoid any possible congestion, so a frame's movement at this stage of the journey is usually pretty fast. However, this engineering methodology doesn't economically scale for the frame networks that the largest providers are now building to meet demand. Significantly over-engineering the network wastes precious and costly bandwidth resources. Dropping an ATM core with its associated quality of service capabilities into the frame relay network can increase bandwidth use while maintaining the needed quality of service for the voice frames.

Several carriers are also considering an ATM backbone for the trunking in their public switched telephone network (PSTN). Silence suppression during the pauses in speech, voice compression, and ATM's statistical multiplexing of traffic can result in greatly reduced trunking requirements. Mixing voice traffic with other traffic types on a carrier backbone can also smooth the peak demands. Networks must be built to handle the peak demand, so any smoothing of this demand can help to reduce costs. Voice networks typically have the highest utilization in mid-morning and mid-afternoon, while Internet networks are busiest in the evening, a situation that enables the carrier to earn more revenue from the same bandwidth investment.

Bringing it all together

Figure 6-4 shows an ATM backbone supporting many different carrier services. The backbone typically has high-speed core switching that rapidly and efficiently moves ATM traffic across the network, with edge devices supporting native ATM services and/or conversion of other protocols to ATM. How quickly

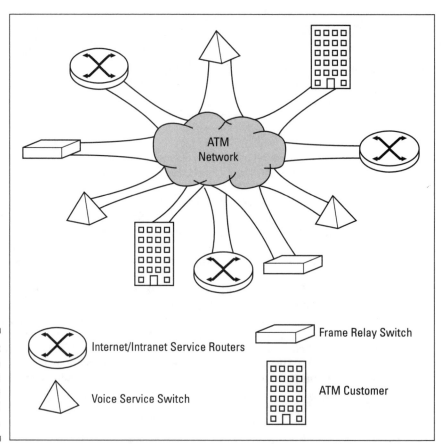

Figure 6-4: The endgame, a full service ATM network.

Internet/Intranet Service Routers

Voice Service Switch

Frame Relay Switch

ATM Customer

each carrier moves to this infrastructure depends on its size (small is not necessarily a delay indicator — some smaller carriers may find making the move easier than larger carriers do), ease of conversion in Information Systems (IS), engineering talent and resources, and cost of bandwidth.

A challenge for carriers is whether to focus their energy on implementing ATM as an infrastructure or as a revenue-generating service. Balancing investment and engineering resources in these two conflicting business needs can drive any network vice president to the spirits of the other world for some breath of insight. Backbone infrastructures need to be big and reliable — *really* big, *really* reliable — but they can also be fairly dumb. ATM services, competing to the death in the marketplace, require constant infusions of the new advanced features and functions that the technology-savvy early users demand. Understanding where your carrier fits on this spectrum helps you to discern how well it is able to meet your needs.

Inside ATM with John Fjeld
Vice President of Marketing
NetEdge, Research Triangle Park, NC

Benefits of ATM without the Complexity

With more and more people using the Internet and businesses relying more every day on data communications, the industry is discussing ATM as a vehicle for companies to get the high bandwidth service they need. Will it be useful or necessary to distribute raw ATM directly to every computer site? Might there instead evolve a distribution system between the ATM service producers and users, much like electricity?

Today, you wouldn't even think of generating your own electricity to turn on the toaster oven or of pulling raw wires out of the wall to heat your bread. You simply take the business end of the electric cord and insert it into an outlet. There are some specialized plugs for heavy-duty appliances like your washing machine or air conditioning, and sometimes you even have the electrician install a separate line with more power for the power-hungry machines. Most of you know that such things as Direct Current (DC) and Alternating Current (AC) exist, but you don't spend much time worrying about it when you plug in the toaster.

At the turn of the century, people who wanted to sell electricity and the inventors who wanted to sell electric bread burners, had to learn how electricity would best be delivered. Quickly, everyone realized that electricity would be cheaper if it could be produced in big batches and sold in small quantities when and where people needed it. Everyone who wanted electric lights didn't want to understand the complexities of producing their own power if someone else could do it for them less expensively. A generation after the electric light was born, electricity distribution grids and electric appliances were everywhere.

Today, computers in the form of individual, independent workstations are nearly everywhere. Increasingly, computer users are discovering that the information they want exists on other computers, which may be across the room or around the world. In the past ten years, people have been connecting their personal computer workstations within a building or a campus using local area networks, or LANs.

(continued)

Connecting to information

Users are connecting LANs over great distances to reach all the information they need to conduct business. Data communications groups and network service providers alike have struggled with a variety of technologies and wiring schemes to cross the gaps between LANs.

Both consumers and producers of computer communications services would like a single, simple scheme for delivering communications in the way that is most natural for computer users. Both would like a scheme for creating and distributing communications power as easily and simply as electricity is today.

Although the world of networking will likely never create a distribution scheme as simple as the power grid, one can envision significant improvements over today's services. Service providers could hide much of the complexity in their data communications offerings to end users. Instead of defining services in the technology terms familiar to the carriers, the carriers could choose to offer services defined in the context of the end user applications. Service providers could define services that were natural, 'plug and outlet' schemes defined for attaching different information appliances.

As an example, the dominance of LAN-based communications suggests that a LAN plug could improve the delivery of ATM-based services. In today's emerging Native LAN service offerings, users subscribe to Ethernet or Token Ring connectivity services that provide wide area transport for subscribers' LANs. These services mask the complexity of today's switching and routing protocols. Devices called Multiservice Access Platforms, or MAPs,

act like power transformers between the LAN plugs and the service provider's ATM network. The complexities of these devices are left to the domain of the carriers just as we leave most of the complexity of electricity to our power utility.

Letting ATM simplify the connection

ATM services can also support many different type of devices besides LANs, both old and new. Service providers could define plug and outlet services based on these communication applications as well. To consolidate access for both old and new services not yet migrated to the LAN, many vendors are providing ATM Access Multiplexors, which can adapt a combination of telephony voice, video, mainframe data, and LAN on to a single ATM connection.

Support for multiple communications requirements means ATM-based services provide both economies of scale and scope. Service providers can take advantage of economies of scale by offering multiple ATM-based services to many customers, providing you reasonably priced application-defined services. You receive the benefits of ATM without having to invest in ATM technology and without having to deal with the complexities of ATM. Economies of scope refers to the future potential of ATM-based services. ATM infrastructures can support existing communications requirements as well as emerging new services targeted to the increasingly functional LAN-attached desktop.

The same ATM infrastructure inside communications provider networks can support applications which are on the LAN, and those which are not on the LAN — yet. By the turn of the coming century, ATM could become much of the invisible core behind the sockets into the global information grid.

Chapter 7

When Should I Use ATM?

Determining whether and when ATM is right for your network requires a solid understanding of your application needs, assessment of your current network equipment and protocols, consideration of your internal communications resources, and knowledge of the potential solutions available to you. You want to evaluate both the advantages which ATM offers and the potential drawbacks. After you've gathered as much information as possible — despite your impossible schedule — you'll be in a good position to make the ATM decision for your network.

As with any relatively new technology, the ATM decision is not easy and very much depends on the unique situation of your organization — so we don't offer any hard and fast rules but hopefully some good considerations and guidelines to assist in your decision.

ATM.Com — Taking Advantage of ATM

As we've said dozens of times in many different ways throughout this book, ATM's developers designed it to deliver more information faster, better, and comparatively cheaper than previously designed telecommunication technologies. They built into ATM three unique characteristics that set it apart from other protocol technologies:

　✔ Scalability

　✔ Quality of service (QoS) integration

　✔ Commonality

Scalability: 0 to 600 in one nanosecond

ATM's developers want a networking solution that can keep up with transmission speed increases well into the future. No one knows the upper limit to ATM's scalability. Today's equipment is capable of transmission speeds of up to about 600 Mbps (Megabits per second), and ATM engineers think that speeds will scale up to at least the next two transmission steps: 2.4 Gbps (Gigabits per second) and 9.6 Gbps. The 9.6 Gbps transmission equipment is so leading-edge that as we write this book in 1996, it is only available in labs. A few researchers in the outer reaches of the technology stratosphere are considering methods for scaling ATM to the terabits-per-second range.

ATM can also scale down in size, with a low limit of 1.544 Mbps in use today and a lower limit of 64 Kbps defined by standards. Debate continues as to how useful ATM really is at 1.544 Mbps and below because of the overhead associated with the technology. *Overhead* is extra information that must be sent along with the user's information or data so that the network has the right directions for transmitting the data.

ATM is also available at speeds in between, including Nx1.544 Mbps, 25 Mbps, 45 Mbps, 50 Mbps, 100 Mbps, and 155 Mbps.

Another important aspect of scalability is the number of supported switches and users. Although the upper bounds of ATM remain the subject of theoretical research, the developers' intent is to support thousands of switches and millions of users on the largest networks — similar to the current public switched telephone networks (PSTNs) that support voice traffic today.

Quality of service integration: The estimated time and condition of arrival

ATM's developers also want a solution that can meet the different communications needs of many different types of information. ATM uses the concept of a *traffic contract* to meet these different needs. The traffic contract is simply the list of bandwidth and service quality parameters which the ATM connection will meet. Three of the more common measurements of a telecommunications exchange are

- ✔ **Traffic Rate:** The amount of traffic the user can send to the network. This includes it's predictabilty, that is, the traffic distribution function including the average, minimum, peak, and deviation values for the traffic — nah, too technical. Predictability is having a reasonable guess as to when traffic will arrive at the network.

- ✔ **Delay:** This one's a no-brainer: How long does the data take to get from point A to point B?

✔ **Loss:** How much of the data disappears into that great electron graveyard in the sky on its way from point A to point B.

Different kinds of communication exchanges require different QoS. For example, voice communication typically requires a fixed amount of transmission resource (bandwidth) that is constantly available to it. Voice calls are also very sensitive to delay. You know how annoying poor quality international connections can be, when the unpredictable amount of delay results in uncomfortably long periods of silence on both ends. Then you both start talking at once, and then both stop. (Nervous giggle.)

"You go first." "No, you go."

Imagine if every domestic call went this way!

Poor quality lines are no better. Static isn't the only problem; sometimes on long-distance connections you get that annoying echo where you say something and then hear yourself say it again. Hearing yourself is weird and actually kind of spooky. Or the transmission quality is so poor that you hear pops and crackles and the person's voice at the other end cuts in and out, so that **derstan**ng ***t's **ing sa** gets difficult. This same poor quality conversation can happen over an ATM network if cells are being dropped. Quality of service parameters were developed to help ensure that poor quality transmissions don't happen.

In contrast to the requirements of voice calls are the computer calls that we all know as *data communications*. Data communications are usually not very predictable because the typist can press the return key at any time. Furthermore, pressing the return key may trigger sending a single word, such as "Thanks," or millions and millions of words, like when we electronically transfer *ATM For Dummies* to our wonderful editors at IDG Books. (What — did you expect us to say that they're not wonderful?)

The good news is that data can often tolerate delay. Your boss is probably at a meeting anyway and won't read your message for a while — maybe not for days. Computers have no tolerance for information loss (imagine losing $1000 because of a dropped 0 bit), but they also don't mind asking each other to repeat messages when information is lost along the way. A check-and-balance process validates whether everything was sent and received accurately.

Actually, computers can't be stereotyped as having these communications requirements because they really have all kinds of communications requirements. Some transmissions are very predictable and others are very time-sensitive, depending upon what application the user is running.

Thus, having a telecommunications solution (like ATM) that can meet transmission requirements for voice, different types of computer applications, and video in one network is very useful. As the future of business telecommunications needs become more and more unsure in our fast-paced world, having something already in place that can handle whatever currently-unheard-of applications pop up later as critical-business-requirements-needed-right-now is kind of nice!

Commonality: Any road, anywhere

Previous transmission standards usually tied rates and transmission resources into one package, resulting in incompatibility among various networking solutions. The ATM standard describes a uniform electronic package (the *cell*) that is independent of rates or transmission resources. Thus, many different systems such as your desktop, office LAN, office backbone, metropolitan, national, and international networks can support ATM.

With ATM, a cell generated by a 155 Mbps LAN in a business office can be carried over a 45 Mbps circuit to a carrier switching center where it moves to a 2.4 Gbps carrier backbone. (We wish we had one of those running into the back end of our PC — don't you?) Each of these three systems is very different, but each carries the message in the same basic electronic package — rate-scaled and formatted to fit each network segment — without the need for complicated and expensive magic black boxes that translate between protocols (what a pain those things are!).

And the bottom line is . . .

In the past, each networking solution was designed to meet a unique (or a group of unique) telecommunication needs. Businesses had to build multiple networks to support their many different kinds of communication application. A single large business may have as many as 50 or more different networks for voice calls, electronic mail, Internet access, intranets, customer service, CAD/CAM engineering, video conferencing, payroll, and many other applications (we could list more, but you get the idea).

ATM's designers hope to give network managers a fighting chance to consider building, operating, and maintaining a single network solution. ATM has the potential to drastically reduce the cost of owning a network. The single platform of ATM uses the underlying transmission resources (for example, copper or fiber) more efficiently through unique multiplexing techniques. ATM limits the types of equipment needed (and the associated spares in the warehouse). The operations folks are happy, too. With ATM, they need to understand only one basic networking protocol and purchase only one kind of network test equipment. And if everyone purchases ATM equipment, volume and competition may drive the component costs very low. With all these benefits on its side, ATM presents the opportunity to drastically lower costs throughout the corporate network.

This grand vision does have a few hitches:

- ✔ Most organizations already have a substantial investment in other networking solutions, and they certainly can't convert their entire network to ATM in a single flash cut. No one has the money or people power to accomplish such a monstrous task.

- ✔ Having such a transition go smoothly is highly unlikely, resulting in hours and even days of intolerable outages for the business.

- ✔ ATM has not yet reached its full technical maturity, The new ATM network may not yet be able to support all the communications applications of the business. Although this is ATM's ultimate objective, the finishing touches to support the many different applications of the corporate network are not all done.

- ✔ Lastly, present day costs can be high compared to other solutions. Prices never seem to get as low as we'd like them.

Marrying a New Technology

Using any new technology, especially one as complex as ATM, requires an investment in time and resources. For some companies, ATM is a strategic technology well worth a little pain to gain early advantages and experience. For other companies, the costs are too high. Using a public ATM service or an ATM-based service can mean off-loading some or all of the complexities to the service provider, but even this strategy has its costs.

Building a private ATM network this early in the technology's life cycle usually means taking advantage of the proprietary features and capabilities of the equipment you choose in order to get the full benefit from your investment. The up side is that you get to profit from the capabilities of the equipment and new technology earlier than others do. The risk is that when the standards of the new technology are finalized, your solution, already in place, may or may not be in full compliance. As long as the network remains private, this noncompliance may not be a problem, but conforming to the standards later may require a new investment.

The other risk of embracing a new technology early in its life cycle is that you're sometimes faced with unpleasant firsts: You may be the first to encounter a particular problem or software bug; you may be the first to try and use a particular protocol, application, or combination of equipment. You are a pioneer, and the down side is that problems may take longer to identify and solve. Fix-it information may not be readily available. However, the advantage of being a pioneer is that equipment vendors and service providers are typically very willing to help support new applications or troubleshoot problems. Often you have the best and brightest minds, and the most experienced resources, available to assist you.

Implementing a technology early in its life cycle is something of an adventure. However, sometimes being first can translate into strategic or competitive business advantages — the hope of many pioneers. And with each passing day, more and more experience is collectively acquired.

Alt.ATM: Alternatives to ATM

Since ATM's birth in the mid 1980s, the developers and vendors of other networking technologies have been enhancing their capabilities to provide, at least in some form, many of the previously unique attributes of ATM. ATM has spurred improvements in its competitors. But technology improvements have made life even more difficult for network managers. (The job ought to come with a complimentary, industrial-size bottle of aspirin.) They must choose where and when to invest their networking dollars from among a variety of technologies and vendors, often with only subtle differences in flavors, and all with big promises for the future (which may or may not come true).

In many ways, network managers have to be fortune tellers, accurately predicting the technology winners and losers, with no friendly spirits to help along the way. Strange, mystic forces of the competitive marketplace determine the fate of new technologies. Pick the wrong technology, and you soon find that you're at a dead end with high prices, delayed or dropped enhancements, and zero technical support. Wait too long to implement a new technology, and you're soon far behind your competitors, playing a desperate game of catch up. Or you may pick the best technology, only to find that it fails in the marketplace (look at all those betamax owners).

We recognize that all these choice and options are causing sleepless nights for many network managers, so we cover the alternatives to ATM in Chapters 12, 13, and 22. In those chapters, we compare a few of the more popular alternatives with ATM and tell you which alternatives (like Ethernet, switched Ethernet, and FDDI) are options for the local area and which ones (like private lines, frame relay, and IP) are options for the wide area.

Skeletons in the ATM Closet

You may have heard some rumors about ATM, and unfortunately, ATM does have a few skeletons in the closet. We would be remiss if we didn't point out some of the questions, uncertainties, and competing viewpoints surrounding the implementation of ATM. When you read about these issues, your first inclination may be to close the book and forget about ATM for another year. However, any emerging networking technology placed under close scrutiny results in a similarly long and difficult list of issues. If you need to meet a new networking requirement, you may find that ATM is the best answer despite these challenges. Chapter 18 and the close of this chapter are among the parts of this book that provide you with a list of networking environments in which you should consider using ATM.

Management by committee is the underlying cause for many of the issues ATM faces today. Do you think that the U.S. Congress is effective at reaching optimal decisions on policy? Many people do not think so, and one primary reason is that so many conflicting opinions and agendas must not only be considered, but also be appeased. Additionally, egos sometimes play a role in decisions (not that this drawback applies to anyone we know in the telecom industry!).

The ATM Forum and other standards organizations develop by committee. The Forum is fast and furiously trying to make up the rules while the game goes on all around it. As if this task weren't difficult enough, the Forum is made up of a group of people who work for competing companies and who sometimes have very different ideas about the best way to implement the features and functions of ATM. Despite these difficulties, the group must come to a majority consensus in order to write an implementor's agreement.

Finally (and this is a complaint whose source must first be acknowledged, because it comes from the authors — we spend most of our time helping companies turn technology like ATM into marketable products and services that can make money and be useful to their customers), the ATM specifications are written by engineers who may not take customer requirements demand, market conditions, and business issues fully into consideration.

Moving forward, backward, onward

Standards organizations are developing new ATM specifications at a very rapid rate. The development process is split among several standards bodies and into many small working groups within those bodies because so many technical issues need to be addressed, and each issue requires a very specialized level of expertise. You can gain an appreciation of the many different organizations developing ATM standards by turning to Chapter 21. The division of labor needed to determine details and allow simultaneous development also results in compatibility questions and problems between old specifications and newer versions.

For example, at this writing, products based on UNI 3.1 may not be backward-compatible with products implementing UNI 3.0 due to incompatible signaling protocols. Now the Forum has released Signaling 4.0, which builds upon the 3.1 specification (and, therefore, is also incompatible with UNI 3.0). Signaling 4.0 requires backward-compatibility with UNI 3.1, meaning more coding and testing for vendors — in other words, more time and money.

Another common ailment of standards is the creation of options from which vendors can choose as they implement the specification. This fragmentation is typically done when the diverse interest groups of the standards committee can't agree to a single solution.

We can look again to the Signaling standard to find a critical example. The Signaling standard supports four addressing schemes, one designed for public networks and three for private networks. The carriers or managers of private networks determine the best addressing for their implementation. In the meantime, these undecided issues further strain interoperability.

The incompatible, unspecified standards aren't the only factors working against interoperability. If a company wants to provide functionality beyond the standard, it can (and many do) implement *proprietary extensions* — a nice euphemism for *nonstandard implementation*. Many very usable and marketable features result from nonstandard implementation, but at a cost — the advanced features only work with other equipment from the same vendor.

Recognizing that the rapid increase in incompatible standards is a major problem, the Forum took action and developed the Anchorage Accord in April 1996. The Forum specified foundation specifications in all the key areas of ATM. The Accord requires that new Forum work must build upon this foundation while maintaining backward compatibility. Furthermore, the foundation standards may only be altered to solve interoperability issues.

If you read between the lines of this accord, you probably see I-N-V-E-S-T-M-E-N-T P-R-O-T-E-C-T-I-O-N. Provided that the Forum sticks to its guns and vendors also mind their manners with their "proprietary extensions," this accord is good news for all of us.

Choosing which route to take

One issue that continues to plague ATM development is where and how to handle routing in an ATM network. In modern day public voice networks, which support some of the most complex and sophisticated call routing in the world, the connection routing and call processing is handled by specialized, centralized servers. This structure is very different from traditional data networks, in which routers form the basis of a distributed process for routing control.

A conventional router handles many functions, two of which include the calculation of routes and the forwarding of packets. The debate raging in the networking industry is whether these functions should be segregated for greater speed and efficiency and where they should be placed in the network. Therefore, the allocation of these functions within the network has a big impact on

- ✔ Performance
- ✔ Where routing decisions are made
- ✔ How quickly routing decisions occur
- ✔ How much routing and switching adds to the cost of ATM
- ✔ Which vendors find implementations easier or more aligned with their other networking strategies

What is the best implementation for ATM? The answer(s) have far-reaching implications. In the middle of this debate are several *competing* specifications and ideas, including LANE, MPOA, and switching of IP. We give you a brief introduction here; you can find out more about these techniques in Chapters 11 and 23.

The best implementation of ATM for your network depends on your application requirements, equipment investment, network traffic loads, number and location of endpoints, and many other internal network factors along with the success of each of these techniques in winning the market's attention during the next several years.

LANE

LAN Emulation (LANE) is a specification providing interoperability between traditional LANs, such as Ethernet and token ring, and ATM LANs and users. As LANE connects LAN technologies, LANE implementations can support any higher layer networking protocols used by the LANs includdling IP, IPX, and DECnet.

The fundamental connection versus connectionless differences of traditional LANs compared to ATM resulted in a long and complex standard. Functions necessary to connect these two environments include address resolution and conversion and broadcast over ATM's connection-oriented circuits.

LANE implementations provide virtual LANs in a single IP subnet of a network — a *subnet* is an IP network which can be reached through a single IP address. Virtual LANs logically include users in a LAN group based on their communications needs compared to physically including them in a LAN group based on their location. LANE is now the only defined virtual LAN standard, although others will follow for traditional LAN technologies in the next two years.

The Forum approved the current version of the specification as LANE 1.0 in 1995. Work continues to build LANE's functionality in the LANE 2.0 specification expected for 1997. This version requires a new frame format to support MPOA software, and hardware changes may potentially be necessary to move from the first specification to the second.

MPOA

Multiprotocol over ATM (MPOA) builds on LANE's functionality by supporting connectivity between the traditional routed network and ATM even across subnets. The MPOA specification is expected to be complete in 1997.

MPOA splits the functionality of *packet forwarding* (sending traffic into the WAN) from the other functions of a router. MPOA edge devices can provide direct connectivity between different endpoints of the ATM network, even if the endpoints are located on different subnets. Providing this direct connectivity is known as *cut-through routing*. Benefits include lower network delays and reduced layer 3 processing load. While proponents of MPOA point out that it simplifies the network edge devices (terminology that means *lower cost* to the rest of us), skeptics point to the extreme complexity of the MPOA routing protocol. Others believe that they have found a better way to provide routing across subnets, as you see in the following sections.

Switching of IP

A relatively small company, Ipsilon Networks, Inc., has said to heck with adding all the routing complexity with ATM and developed yet a third approach, called IP switching. Since Ipsilon's intial announcement, Cisco and now others have thrown their hats into the ring with a flavor of switching of IP called tag switching. All companies are now vying for support in standards and the market.

Switching of IP depends on IP protocols as opposed to ATM signaling and MPOA to move packets across ATM switches. Each ATM switch is enhanced with routing intelligence. Short messages use the traditional routing side of the switch to traverse the network without the delay and expense of setting up virtual connections for just a few small packets. Longer communications, such as real-time interactions or large file transfers, use the IP switching side of the switch over ATM PVCs. Switching of IP exploits ATM hardware performance while maintaining compatibility with existing routing equipment.

Switching of IP also has its skeptics who point out that the techniques are new and untested when compared to ATM — which has already solved many of the issues still requiring extensive work in switching of IP. These skeptics also question the scalability and performance of the new techniques compared to ATM. Because the switching of IP techniques are not yet complete (nor will they be for some time), these debates can only rage on paper (and not through real performance) for now.

Forecasting the amount of rain

Unless you're in a desert, or perhaps Boston in January, forecasting the weather is far from an exact science. In Kansas City, one weather man pays out money if he's off in his prediction of the day's high temperature by more than five degrees in either direction, but even he doesn't dare take any bets on his ability to forecast the rain. In Richmond and Tulsa, they tell you to expect weather conditions the opposite of what is predicted by the supposed experts.

At this stage in the game, predicting whether, when, and how ATM may be used in different parts of the network of the future is difficult. But the ATM standards expect very detailed forecasts of your network traffic. Forget that most network managers don't have much of a clue of the traffic patterns ebbing and flowing in their IP networks or even an accurate accounting of the level of utilization on their private lines. If you want to use ATM and optimize the network, you need a Doppler radar system for the bits, bytes, and broadcast storms on your network.

Network managers implementing ATM may be able to relate a bit better to the weather forecaster after their rite of passage through ATM performance parameters. For each and every virtual connection, the specifications demand that network managers forecast the peak, burst length, and, often, the average or minimum of the expected traffic. Discipline can be harsh for those who fail the test — cells can be assassinated on the spot!

Most of today's ATM implementations, especially in the local area, use the UBR (unspecified bit rate) service category to get around this difficulty — UBR does not require the specification of all these bandwidth rates. In fact, ATM interoperability standards for LANs and network subgroups such as LANE (LAN Emulation) and MPOA (Multiprotocol Over ATM) are currently defined only for UBR — newer versions will address multiple service categories. However, the UBR-only approach also negates the quality of service benefits of ATM.

Signaling is supposed to help by taking all these hard questions and answering them in software instead of the network manager's head. But someone still has to figure out how to program the software. The questions don't go away, they have to be answered at least once.

The mother of all solutions to these problems is the ATM Applications Programming Interface (API). The API creates an environment in which the applications are programmed to request a specific bandwidth for a specific time with a specific variation (in other words, they request a specific quality of service from the network). But that's another box of bones to dig up. Keep reading!

APIs, Winsock 2

An Application Program Interface (API) provides a way for an application to request and use the resources of a network. Popular APIs are X/sockets in Unix and Winsock in Windows. APIs mask the complexity of the network and give program developers an easier way to interface their application to the network.

ATM is far more sophisticated than today's networks, and none of the existing APIs provide access to the advanced networking functionality of ATM. Examples include specification of particular QoS or bandwidth from the network. Until new APIs are available on operating systems and are implemented by program developers, ATM remains an expensive luxury, locked behind a vault, that no one can get to. If applications can't take advantage of ATM's QoS benefits, then many people question the real benefit of switching to ATM.

To address this issue, the Winsock Forum, a coalition of several hundred vendors and developers, completed the Winsock 2 standard. Applications written to Winsock 2 are able to request point-to-point or point-to-multipoint connections of specified network bandwidth and performance. Microsoft is currently testing its early releases of Winsock in its new Windows versions for clients and servers. The task remains for software developers to incorporate these new capabilities within their applications. How quickly new applications include the new QoS options available in Winsock 2 and new UNIX APIs will greatly impact how quickly networks must support QoS.

Winsock 2 is not prejudicial in its support of protocols, extending network protocol independence to applications. As you find out in the next section, other network protocols are gaining the capability to support different qualities of services. Thus, Winsock 2 applications can use these alternatives as they become available, and some question the need for using ATM to provide the different qualities of services within the network. Others see the advancement of these protocols, especially IP, as good news — generating more traffic that is most effectively transported by an ATM network.

Getting graffiti on ATM's hallowed walls

The conventional wisdom and relative positioning of different technologies in the industry changes so fast that keeping pace is nearly impossible. If you recently blinked, you may not have realized that multimedia no longer belongs solely to ATM. The mix of text, image, audio, and video traffic in multimedia requires a different network performance for each traffic type — one of the primary advantages of ATM. But the hallmark of ATM, the idea of guaranteed network quality of service, is being adopted (some people may say stolen) by grassroots, upstart protocols like frame relay and IP. The nerve of them!

IP takes over the world

In the eyes of the IP fanatic, the idea of Internet Protocol as the foundation for all networking isn't unreasonable, and if the saying that "ownership is nine-tenths of the law" is true, this future scenario is possible. The Web is all IP, and multimedia applications are being supported today — albeit questionably offering the needed communications quality and ease-of-use to satisfy most users. So why introduce a whole new protocol like ATM when a few modifications to IP can do the job more quickly and more easily?

The Internet Engineering Task Force (IETF) is defining a suite of protocols for transferring IP packets across a routed network with specified QoS. These protocols don't provide guarantees but can limit delay and jitter while improving fairness in the network. The IETF expects to finish several of the protocols to support the many aspects of multimedia by 1998. Although early versions of some standards should be available in 1997, complete, mature implementations of these protocols will take years. Implementation requires new software and, potentially, firmware upgrades to ATM. (*Firmware* is programable microchips.) Adding further to the complexity of routing, these new protocols burn more processing power on already overburdened routers.

One of the new IP protocols for multimedia is the Resource Reservation Protocol (RSVP). RSVP is a draft standard for IP that enables an application to request bandwidth and prioritization for real-time information streams, all handled within the IP protocol stack. Performance may not be as good as in a connection-oriented environment, but it may be good enough to make the added complexities and cost of ATM unjustifiable, at least in some networks. RTP (real-time transport protocol) is another new protocol. It delivers real-time traffic by including timing information necessary for reconstruction at the far end.

Even if new protocols for multimedia are not the weapon that lets IP take over the world, at least they must now be recognized. *Recognition* most likely means yet another ATM standard that addresses how an application that uses RSVP and other new protocols is handled over an ATM network, and how the bandwidth reservation request is translated into the allocation of ATM network resources.

Frame Relay QoS

Frame relay is quietly waging its war for the almighty market share percentage as well, and doing so successfully. A good percentage of frame relay users are already putting voice, fax, and desktop video applications over their frame relay networks. The voice, fax, and video traffic is put into fixed-length frames and given priority over data traffic within the premises equipment.

The next step, in the minds of many frame relay advocates, is adding qualities of service within the network. Several frame relay switch vendors already support doing so, although as proprietary extensions — there they are again — to the standards. Adding qualities of service is a relatively easy step for service providers to take. When combined with high-speed frame relay service, the move may make ATM unnecessary in the wide area for many companies. This turn of events may even stall ATM in locations where it makes sense, because interworking with frame relay sites just got much tougher.

Will ATM Join the Skeletons?

When you dig into almost any data commmunications technology, you probably can find a few bones of contention; some just have more meat on them. ATM and its competitors are no different: In their exploration of new ways to overcome technical challenges, some of their developments turn out to be false starts, and you can find something to criticize about their efforts if you try hard enough.

Trying to design high-speed networks is difficult by itself; adding the challenge to support multiple classes of service really weighs down the efforts. Most people in the industry see multiple service class support as necessary to help justify the high-speed networks, so ATM and its competitors must try to meet the challenge. Developing new technology is just plain hard, regardless of how advanced the technology is already. Each of the alternative networking solutions is struggling with the same basic issues with varying degrees of research support and success.

Few, if any, pundits paint a picture of a future dominated by only one of these technologies. Cooperation between the technologies is essential. The real questions to be answered are

- What will be the relationship between the technologies?
- What will be the relative dominance of each technology in different segments of the network?
- How can a network manager time implementation to get the best price and performance?

Are You a Candidate for ATM?

Confused? Sorry. :+(

We really are trying to help you out. We want to give you as realistic a picture as possible of the benefits of ATM as well as the potential downsides, too. We know that making the choices for your business isn't easy. Your choices depend on a wide range of needs and situations that change as often as a toddler's temperament. In this section, we try to add a little perspective to the material covered in Part I of the book.

- ATM is still an easy winner to pick in the service provider backbone for both ISPs and carriers. (We like starting out with the obvious and the positive.)

- ATM will probably emerge as a widely implemented technology for campus backbones operating at speeds greater than 25 Mbps in both government and business. These backbones will include direct, high speed connections to servers. We think that ATM will prove to have strong price for the performance value, while still holding tightly to that strategic carrot of being able to position the enterprise for multimedia that may someday get here. ATM can be that highly-needed speed demon for the campus backbone.

- Over time, the largest enterprises will discover that adopting ATM for the wide area network can be very cost-effective. Other organizations will bring ATM to their doorsteps through a native LAN or managed service from their carrier. The carrier will use the ATM infrastructure because ATM provides a common platform for operating and maintaining the service. The customers may not even know that ATM is sitting on their doorsteps.

- ATM can be a good solution at the desktop for isolated, high-powered workgroups, especially if multimedia is a known future application. Prices for network interface cards will continue to tumble, closing the gap with other solutions. If you already have Ethernet cards on your desktop for a shared LAN, your best bet for a performance upgrade is probably Switched Ethernet, unless you need much more than 10 Mbps to each desk or are transporting real-time traffic now. If you do need more than 10 Mbps to each desk, then switching to fast Ethernet will probably require a wiring upgrade, just like ATM will, so you need to evaluate each option in the light of your current plans.

✔ The remaining organizations will continue to use traditional and switched LANs, frame relay, intranet services, Internet services, and public voice services to meet their networking needs. As ATM technology matures and bandwidth costs fall, the majority market may finally discover that a direct ATM connection to their carrier backbone makes more sense than getting to the backbone through another service type. After they're using ATM in the WAN, spreading ATM into other parts of the network may then make sense. At that time, ATM adoption may rise quickly.

The biggest hurdle to ATM's breakthrough is the cost of high-speed WAN bandwidth. Bandwidth is the most expensive component of high-speed networks, and networking budgets will not increase ten times just because information needs have increased ten times. Network budgets will continue to constrain communication growth, because the price of bandwidth isn't likely to go into a free-fall. Prices will probably continue their decrease over time, as we discuss in our editorial for Chapter 14. But don't expect a bandwidth glut that will reduce the cost of an ATM T3 to the current cost of a T1 frame relay connection in the next three years. Very, very low-cost bandwidth may be available sometime in your lifetime (depending on how long you plan to live), but the likelihood of dramatically reduced bandwidth costs allowing you to add over 20 times the bandwidth to every site at your current budget is low.

The special attributes of ATM do warrant further investigation for most large enterprises and for smaller organizations with rapidly growing or changing communications needs. Many businesses have chosen ATM as a strategic goal for all, or at least parts, of their network. We tell you more about some of these businesses in Chapter 16.

Inside ATM with Tony Rybczynski
Director of Strategic Marketing
Nortel Multimedia Networks, Ottawa, Ontario, Canada
tony.rybczynski@nt.com

ATM Enterprise WANs: Best Performance for the Buck

Since the early days of enterprise networking, the major parameter of concern has been bandwidth cost. In the 1970s and 1980s, users widely deployed T1 multiplexors in enterprise networks. T1 muxes provided a multimedia network consolidation vehicle in environments dominated by voice and sub-56Kbps mainframe data. Network managers set the network design objectives to minimize the cost to meet the required performance (that is, 3-second response time for mainframe data).

With the explosion of inter-LAN traffic, network managers had to change the design goal to be *to*

(continued)

maximize performance for a given bandwidth cost. In more recent times and with the objective of maximizing performance for a given bandwidth cost, many network managers have turned to public frame relay services for inter-LAN and SNA connectivity, public virtual private voice services for voice traffic, and to ISDN for video connectivity. If you are a network manager, your traditional T1 multiplexors are likely no longer a strategically important vehicle for network consolidation. Now, ATM has hit the scene. Will it change the focus back again to network consolidation?

A number of enterprise users in industries as diverse as finance, healthcare, and film have decided to consolidate, or perhaps to reconsolidate, their voice, data, and growing video networks onto an ATM-based infrastructure. They are discovering that ATM can establish new levels of price/performance to meet growing multimedia, intranet, and distributed computing applications.

In this chapter, you may have read about ATM's scalability in speed from 1.5 Mbps to 1000 Mbps and beyond. And there's also scalability in reach that will allow you to mix public and private facilities in the optimal manner using international standards. And ATM's multimedia capabilities means that it is scalable in application for your data, voice, video, image, and multimedia.

This feature gives you a look at three other key attributes of ATM: dynamic bandwidth, effective multimedia classes of services, and switched operation.

Dynamic Bandwidth

T1 muxes allow you to independently preassign expensive bandwidth for voice and data applications based on your peak requirements. While this method served well in the past when the mix of voice and data was in favor of voice, it is a conservative approach that keeps bandwidth locked away *just in case* the application needs it.

To understand the impact of such bandwidth management, assume that you must assign 60 percent of your T1 multiplexor network capacity for voice to meet a 15-minute traffic peak during the day and that the data traffic uses the remaining 40 percent. A file transfer of 50MB will take approximately 12 minutes. However, it is likely that your bandwidth requirement for voice is far below 60 percent during most of the day, and hence the file transfer could use much more of the T1 bandwidth. During the non-business hours of the day when there are no voice calls, your entire T1 bandwidth could be available for your file transfers, allowing these to complete in 5 minutes. This type of performance improvement is achievable with ATM, which offers all the available bandwidth to data *just in time* if voice does not need the bandwidth at that instant.

Effective Multimedia Classes of Service

T1 multiplexors support multiple traffic types by dedicating bandwidth channels in your network on a static basis. The boxes limit class of service support to offering you reconfiguration priorities under failure conditions.

ATM gives you broad control over the class of service offered to users and the ability to bill back the users appropriately. For example, you could guarantee performance offered to your real-time mission-critical applications, whether they be voice, video, or data, while offering a best-effort service for your lower priority Internet applications.

Two generic approaches support circuit-based, real-time traffic (such as PBX traffic and video) over your ATM network. Circuit emulation dedicates ATM bandwidth to the circuit (much as is done in a T1 multiplexor), though this incurs a 10 percent overhead as a result of ATM cellification.

A second approach takes advantage of the inherently bursty nature of video and voice sources and uses a special class of service called ATM variable bit rate (real-time). The voice or video application uses bandwidth only when there are meaningful bits to send, allowing you to exploit ATM's dynamic bandwidth capabilities.

The barriers to desktop multimedia applications defined to run on IP are rapidly coming down. Multimedia-ready PCs are increasingly becoming the norm, and you're probably already deploying switched Ethernet and token ring in your workgroups. However, the prospects of putting real-time sensitive traffic over your already overloaded router network may not be very appealing.

The good news is that by the time you are ready to deploy desktop multimedia applications on a wide scale, various techniques will be available to identify real-time IP flows and to map these flows to the appropriate ATM class of service. Given that ATM can guarantee the provided quality of service, this approach could emerge as the preferred method for many users.

Switched (SVC) Operation

While traditional T1 multiplexors operate on the basis of pre-assigned configuration of bandwidth, ATM operates on the basis of dynamic bandwidth. To manage multiple traffic classes, ATM defines the concept of virtual circuits. While early implementations use permanent virtual circuits, the standards also define switched virtual circuits (SVCs).

SVCs are a critical capability to extend the value of dynamic bandwidth in an ATM environment. Not only can end-user equipment specify class of service requirements at connection setup time, but the network can assign and prioritize resources to meet the application requirements. SVCs are inherent in various ATM standards for LAN connectivity including LAN Emulation (LANE) and Multiple Protocol over ATM (MPOA).

Another major use of SVCs is your intra-corporate voice traffic. ATM SVCs can simplify your voice network topology by eliminating the need for tandem PBX configurations. This is done by interpreting signaling from a PBX and routing the connection directly to the remote end via SVCs. This simplified topology has the added benefit of enhancing voice quality for a given voice compression rate. Ultimately, ATM service providers will route calls to offnet locations as well.

There is one catch: Most carriers have deployed permanent virtual circuits and are still busily developing operational support and billing systems needed to support SVCs. Before ATM SVCs are widely deployed by carriers, tunneling of SVCs on Permanent Virtual Paths can provide connectivity over the wide area.

Equipment to Build the Enterprise ATM Network

A number of vendors offer ATM switches with a rich set of interfaces providing value more appropriate to today's enterprise WAN environments than traditional T1 multiplexors. ATM muxes can meet the requirements in some cases. However, there is a new class of product, called ATM Enterprise Network Switches, that are optimized as multimedia network consolidation vehicles.

These boxes interface to public ATM services and sometimes can also interface to existing telco services (such as frame relay) at narrow and wideband speeds. Inside the building interfaces supporting circuit, frame networks, LANs, and native ATM interfaces are available. Support for variable bit rate voice and IP cell-based routing are additional features allowing you to exploit ATM SVC classes of service.

ATM enterprise networks are winning the hearts of WAN managers because they can provide better performance for existing applications at a lower cost. If you are a network manager responsible for one of the top 1000 networks in size, then you likely can build a business case today for an enterprise ATM network with a 12-month minimum payback. As an added incentive, an ATM enterprise network gives you a networking infrastructure that positions your corporation for the future. ATM can eliminate the network bottleneck giving you the network foundation you'll need when your end users approach you to launch new multimedia applications.

Part II
Finding Out How ATM Works

The 5th Wave   By Rich Tennant

"WELL, I NEVER THOUGHT I'D SEE THE DAY I COULD SAY I DIALED IN A MODEM VIA A STAT MUX INTO A DEDICATED PORT ON A COMMUNICATIONS PROCESSOR,... BY ACCIDENT."

In this part . . .

Part II presents you with a more detailed view of ATM. The four chapters in this part tell you about the basic structures, functions, and standards related to ATM. Find out everything you ever wanted to know about connection-oriented technology, but were afraid to ask. Also in this part, we give you more of the ATM technical scoop — specifications, service categories, protocols, bandwidth parameters . . . all with acronyms galore! And we tell you just how ATM gets along with other players in the telecommunications environment.

Chapter 8

Conquering the Basic
Bits and Bytes

. . . .

In This Chapter

▶ Looking at the ATM Protocol Model

▶ Understanding adaptation

▶ Reviewing the responsibilities of the ATM layer

▶ Finding out about the ATM physical layer

. . . .

*O*kay, here comes the fun. We are now introducing in this chapter — and the following three — the dreaded technical details of ATM. We recommend that you don't try to read these straight through, unless it's three in the morning and you're having a serious case of insomnia. We wrote these chapters so you have a place to turn if you're ever in a situation where you need to know what's really under ATM's hood. Trust us, you find more wires and gizmos than you ever thought possible in a network. On the other hand, have you ever looked under TCP/IP's hood?

The good news is that you really don't have to understand all the technical details to take advantage of ATM's benefits. Work with good vendors who can help lead you past the land mines and booby traps. Steve Glick from Dallas Community College found this to be the wisest choice, as we discuss in Chapter 16 . We strongly recommend this approach if you're a first-time ATM user. After all, how many of us can really rip apart a carburetor and get it all put back together again — still running smooth as silk? Besides, ATM is more like a sophisticated fuel injector than a carburetor anyway.

Acronyms Used in This Chapter	
Acronym	*What It Stands For*
AAL	ATM Adaptation Layer
ADM	Add/Drop Multiplexer
B-ISDN	Broadband - Integrated Services Digital Network
CES	Circuit Emulation Services
CPE	Customer Premises Equipment
CPI	Common Part Indication
CRC	Cyclic Redundancy Check
DSU	Data Service Unit
DXI	Data Exchange Interface
ESF	Extended Superframe
FDDI	Fiber Distributed Data Interface
HEC	Header Error Control
IAM	Inverse ATM Mux
IPX	Internet Protocol Exchange
ITU	International Telecommunication Union
PDU	Protocol Data Unit
PLCP	Physical Layer Convergence Protocol
SAR	Segmentation and Reassembly
SEAL	Simple and Efficient Adaptation Layer
SONET	Synchronous Optical Network
TCP/IP	Transmission Control Protocol/Internet Protocol
UNI	User-Network Interface
UTP	Unshielded Twisted Pair
UU	User-to-User
VT	Virtual Tributaries

Unpeeling the Protocol Model

To help guide you through the ATM technical maze, the ITU created the B-ISDN (Broadband - Integrated Services Digital Network) Protocol Model shown in Figure 8-1. B-ISDN is the service architecture defined by ITU for high-speed services. ATM happens to be the transport mode used by B-ISDN. Most folks use the terms B-ISDN services and ATM services interchangeably, with ATM being the more common. ITU defined B-ISDN specifically for SONET-based ATM public carrier services. (SONET stands for Synchronous Optical Network).

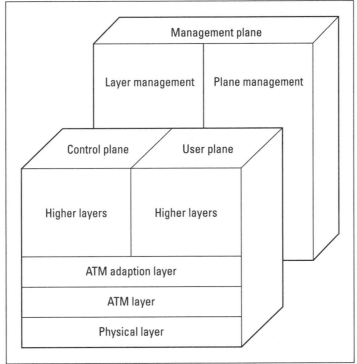

Figure 8-1:
The planes
and layers
of the
B-ISDN
Protocol
Model.

The model consists of both planes and layers. The user plane defines how ATM carries user information across the network. The control plane provides connection administration tasks through signaling for switched ATM services (examples of these tasks include call setup and teardown).

ITU broke the management plane into two sections:

- ✔ Plane management performs functions used by the whole system and provides coordination between the planes.
- ✔ Layer management performs functions specific to each layer, such as operations, administration, and management.

All layers of ATM cooperate to provide end-to-end transport. The higher layers of the B-ISDN model represent any information stream. The stream may be voice, data, or video, including any defined protocol format for data including TCP/IP, IPX, and others. The remaining layers are part of the ATM network.

The ATM adaptation layer is the top layer of ATM functionality in the model. The adaptation layer defines how user information streams are mapped into the payload of the ATM cells. The ATM layer (in the middle) defines how the network carries these cells between users. At the bottom, the physical layer defines the mapping of ATM cells onto the transmission system.

Standards groups have already defined several different specifications for both the ATM adaptation layer and the physical layer. The different adaptation layers allow ATM to transport various types of information flows. The different physical layers allow ATM networks to run on a variety of physical media and framing formats.

That's the basics on the protocol model. The ITU recommendation itself is only ten pages long. We provide more details on each of the ATM networking layers in the remainder of this chapter — if you aren't too bored yet.

ATM UNIs

Before we unlock any more of the deep mysteries of the layers, we have to provide you with a few reference points. The model makes sense only if you define the two entities exchanging information. Most existing ATM specifications define the communications process details (that is, the protocol) between a user and a network. A few specifications outline protocols for communicating between two different nodes of a network or two different networks. We discuss these protocols in Chapter 10.

The interface between the user and the network is known as the User-Network Interface, or UNI. UNIs come in two flavors: private and public, as shown in Figure 8-2. The private UNI defines the communication exchange protocol between an ATM user and a private ATM switch. A user in this case is any Customer Premises Equipment (CPE) packaging information into ATM. This CPE

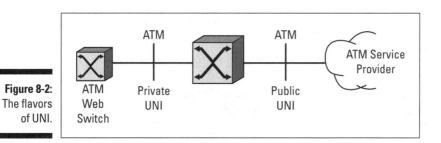

Figure 8-2:
The flavors
of UNI.

could be a desktop computer, a router, or a multiplexer. A private switch is owned by the user as opposed being owned by to a public carrier service. You can deploy private switches to build local and campus networks and as an alternative to subscribing to public services in the wide area. The public UNI defines the communication exchange protocol between an ATM user and a public carrier service.

Very little difference exists between these two UNIs. Private UNIs support physical-layer interfaces for short-distance links and reduce operations and management intricacies, whereas public UNIs support interfaces between a user and a carrier requiring longer distance performance and carrier management.

Adopting to Adaptation

Adaptation defines how higher-layer information such as voice, data, and video are prepared into the payload of the 53-byte ATM cells. Adaptation typically takes place only at the user endpoints of an ATM communications exchange.

In the beginning of the ATM days in the 1980s, ITU expected to define several adaption layer recommendations to meet the requirements of various multiple higher layers. Table 8-1 outlines the four anticipated types of ATM Adaptation Layers (AALs).

Table 8-1	The ATM Adaptation Layers
Layer	**Used for**
AAL1	Traditional voice
AAL2	Packet video
AAL3/4	Multiplexed data
AAL5	Data

In reality, only AAL5 is widely implemented right now. Providing unique services for each information type is now relegated to the service categories of the ATM layer.

Because AAL5 minimizes overhead, the ATM Forum originally defined AAL5 for very efficient transport of TCP/IP data. Also known as the Simple and Efficient Adaptation Layer (SEAL, AAL5's first given name), AAL5 is now favored by most service types as vendors strive to maximize available throughput of ATM connections. Unlike other AAL types, AAL5 uses just a tiny portion of the cell payload for its overhead. AAL5 also provides better error detection than other adaption types.

AAL3/4, the third layer listed in Table 8-1, was the adaption layer used in the very earliest implementations. It's called 3/4 (pronounced *three-four,* not *three fourths*) because ITU originally intended to define a unique adaption layer for connection-oriented (3) versus connectionless (4) services. When they got to the details of actually writing the recommendations, ITU realized the two could be merged. AAL 3/4 provides multiplexing of multiple data streams over a single ATM virtual connection. Because of its similarity to the adaption used by SMDS, originally it was the easiest of the adaptation layers to implement. (SMDS is a connectionless broadband service defined by Bellcore that also uses a 53-byte cell but has no provisions for supporting multiple-traffic types. You can find

More on AAL5

The figure in this sidebar shows defined fields for the variable-length AAL5 PDU (protocol data unit). The PDU consists of user data and a small trailer created by AAL5. The segmentation and reassembly (SAR) sublayer of AAL5 breaks down the PDU into 48-byte chunks for transport over the network.

User Data	PAD	UU	CPI	Length	CRC

The User Data consists of information requiring transport across the network. This field can be 1 to 65535 octets long.

PAD stands for padding to size the PDU to a multiple of 48 bytes. Its length ranges from 0 to 47 octets.

The User-to-User (UU) field allows one byte of information to be sent transparently between users. The Common Part Indication (CPI) byte is intended to identify subsequent fields but is not currently used.

The Length field stores the length of the transmitted user data using two bytes. This field is necessary to discriminate between user data and padding.

Closing the PDU is a 32-bit Cyclic Redundancy Check (CRC) performed over the entire contents of the PDU.

more on SMDS in Chapter 10.) AAL3/4 eventually fell into disfavor because it robs 4 bytes from the 48-byte user payload, further burdening the overhead tax of ATM.

ITU intended to use AAL2 to support packetized video but has never gotten around to writing the recommendation for that use. Today most packetized video implementations use AAL5. Besides, AAL5 supports packet data just fine.

AAL1 has actually been defined and has seen limited use in circuit emulation services. Circuit emulation services (CES) provide mapping of traditional TDM streams into ATM without any statistical gain. CES was originally intended to support voice services, but ATM vendors recognized the benefits of packetized voice. Packetized voice allows further compression, compared with traditional voice digitization, as well as silence suppression, which substantially lowers the total number of transferred bits. You can find out more about CES and packetized voice in Chapter 9. AAL1 steals one byte from the 48-byte user payload of the cell to support transport of sequencing information.

The ITU broke down the adaptation layer into two sublayers:

- ✔ **Convergence sublayer** is service-dependent and can provide message identification and clock recovery among other functions. As noted in the sidebar, AAL5 adds only a small trailer in this sublayer. This approach substantially minimizes overhead compared with other AALs. The other defined AALs add a header or trailer in both AAL sublayers.

- ✔ **Segmentation and reassembly (SAR) sublayer** acts like a Ronco slicer and dicer for ATM. It takes the longer protocol data units (PDUs) of the convergence sublayer and segments them into the appropriate cell payload size, adding any needed headers or trailers. For AAL5, SAR adds no additional overhead, and the PDU data fills all bytes of the 48-byte cell payload. At the destination, this same sublayer puts everything back together again as expected by the higher-layer protocols being served.

Whistling Dixie

To help facilitate adoption of ATM technology in the early 1990's, the ATM Forum defined a specification known as Data Exchange Interface (DXI). (Yes, the sidebar title is a clue —it's pronounced *dixie*.) DXI and ATM UNI v2.0 (no, we don't know why they started with the number 2 and we don't know why your TV channels are missing a 1) were the first in a long line of specifications defined by the ATM Forum. DXI split the functions of the adaptation layer between an existing router and a new external box known as an ATM DSU (Data Service Unit). This allowed the existing routers to use ATM transport through a software upgrade. Today, most router vendors provide a direct ATM interface without the help of external hardware. A few DXI implementations remain today, primarily to support NxT1 services (in 1997, the IAM specification will replace these few DXI holdouts).

Networking with Cells

The ATM layer is where most of the action is, so we decided to give it a chapter of its very own in our book. We're giving you a little background here, but you'll find most of the info on this subject in Chapter 9.

The ATM layer performs several very critical functions needed to support the end-to-end communications exchange:

- ✔ The ATM layer accepts the 48-byte package from the ATM Adaptation Layer (with both user data and AAL overhead) and adds a 5-byte addressing header to create a 53-byte cell.

- ✔ The ATM layer then multiplexes cells from various connections into a single-cell stream for the physical layer. This includes adding idle cells to fill the transmission path for synchronous transmission systems such as SONET.

- ✔ If the cell needs to switch from one physical connection to another, the ATM layer provides translation between the two virtual connections associated with the physical links.

- ✔ The ATM layer is also responsible for understanding the capabilities of the virtual connections carrying the cell and ensuring that the cell flow conforms to these capabilities, which vary according to allowed bandwidth, delay, delay variation, and cell loss of the connection.

The ATM layer and AAL layer communicate with each other using two messages:

- ✔ **The ATM-DATA.request:** An AAL to ATM layer message that requests transport over an existing connection and includes information to complete the ATM layer header fields

- ✔ **The ATM-DATA.indication:** An ATM layer to AAL message announcing the arrival of a cell and its associated header fields

Poetry in Motion: SONET and ATM

SONET is a standard optical interface for transmission systems and is rapidly becoming the physical infrastructure of choice for carrier ATM networks. SONET is the specified physical layer in ITU's B-ISDN (Broadband - Integrated Services Digital Network) definitions. It's also the physical layer for ATM LANs and LAN backbones operating over fiber at 155 Mbps and higher. Therefore, understanding a little about SONET adds to your understanding of ATM.

The initial objective of the SONET standards was to allow optical connection of two different pieces of transmission equipment, a connection often referred to as a *mid-span meet*. While defining the new standards, SONET's developers added a lot of desired capabilities not previously available in optical transmission systems.

SONET is an international transmission standard defined by the ITU. (The ITU refers to the standard as the *Synchronous Digital Hierarchy* [SDH]). SONET allows carriers to build high-speed international links without requiring conversion from one transmission protocol to another (for example, T1 <> E1 and T3 <> E3). The international hierarchy begins at 155.52 Mbps — which brings us to another benefit of SONET— its high speed. Defined SONET speeds begin at 51.84 Mbps and scale to an unknown limit. Implementations in 1996 topped off at 2.4 Gbps, but new solutions of 9.6 Gbps are available in 1997. This compares with the maximum 1.7 Gbps speed of previous optical transmission technologies. SONET has an easy method for determining the speed of any system. The lowest speed of 51.84 Mbps is known as an *OC-1*. All subsequent speeds are simply a multiple of this base number. The most common SONET implementations are OC-3 (155.52 Mbps), OC-12 (622.08 Mbps), OC-48 (2.4 Gbps), and OC-192 (9.6 Gbps).

SONET achieves its high speeds because it is a *synchronous* protocol, which provides a third benefit. Previously, transmission equipment used *asynchronous* protocols. Asynchronous systems use a technique called *bit stuffing* to construct larger transmission signals from smaller signals (for example, 28 T1s into a T3) and to accommodate timing differences between transmit and receive systems. Bit stuffing inserts bits into the transmission stream somewhat randomly, making it impossible to identify a smaller component (such as a T1 in a T3) without deconstructing the entire signal. Thus asynchronous systems require banks of *multiplexers* to

build up and break down the transmission signal at each intermediate point.

SONET overcomes the difficulties of bit stuffing by adding pointers to identify the starting bit of the payload (that is, the transmitted information). Hence we call it a synchronous protocol. In this way, SONET allows retrieval of a smaller signal in the bit stream without decomposing the entire transmission signal. For example, an OC-48 SONET system built to transmit and receive from New York to Washington, D.C., can use devices known as *add/drop multiplexers* (ADMs) to also deliver a few OC-3s to Philadelphia along the way. Such techniques significantly ease the job of network circuit *provisioners* who now have more assignment flexibility and allow a higher fill rate (the assigned capacity/total capacity) for each transmission system. SONET's component identification scheme can be extended to both T1/E1s and T3/E3s through *virtual tributaries* (VTs) defined to carry these smaller signals. Virtual tributaries are just a protocol packaging scheme defined in the SONET standards.

Another drawback of the older asynchronous systems is that they provide limited network control because the asynchronous stream embeds little management information. SONET, however, offers significant management control through overhead channels defined within the signal. These overhead channels ease management, repair, and provisioning. They also allow fast recovery from failure. Depending on their architecture, SONET systems configured in rings can recover from single fiber cuts or equipment failures in less than 250 ms. These recovery techniques use spare capacity waiting in the backside of a ring to reroute traffic around the failure. The fast recovery of many SONET systems makes them ideal candidates for transporting high-speed ATM connections carrying large amounts of mission-critical information.

Getting Physical with Interfaces

ATM operates on a variety of different physical medium such as wire, fiber, wireless, and satellite. It also uses various transmission protocols on the medium. The ATM Forum has defined 13 different physical interface specifications so far, with 9 more underway.

Specifications for the wide area include T1 (North American transmission protocol operating at 1.544 Mbps), E1 (European transmission protocol operating at 2.048 Mbps), T3 (North American transmission protocol operating at 45 Mbps), E3 (European transmission protocol operating at 34 Mbps), and SONET (optical transmission protocol operating above 50 Mbps).

The two most popular specifications for local area networks are 155 Mbps and 25 Mbps. 155 Mbps requires Category 5 UTP (unshielded twisted pair) or optical wiring (the ATM Forum has started working on a version for UTP3 wiring). 25 Mbps ATM can operate on Categories 3 or 5 UTP. 600 Mbps local interfaces are also now available for fiber. In its first specifications, the Forum defined a 100 Mbps TAXI interface. TAXI is the same physical interface defined for FDDI (Fiber Distributed Data Interface), and it enabled vendors to leverage existing designs and investments.

The physical layer provides a means for using the physical medium. The ITU model broke down the physical layer further into two sublayers known as

- ✔ The physical medium sublayer
- ✔ The transmission convergence sublayer

The physical medium sublayer provides functions specific to a particular medium including bit timing and line coding. The transmission convergence sublayer maps the cells of ATM into a bit stream carried by the transmission system.

Functions performed by the physical layer (specifically the transmission convergence sublayer) include

- ✔ **HEC generation and verification:** HEC stands for *Header Error Control* sequence. The HEC ensures the integrity of the header information of the cell, ensuring correction of single-bit errors or detection of multiple-bit errors. Typically, a switch provides correction for a single error, but drops into detection mode if consecutive cells show single-header errors. The switch drops any cell detected with multiple-header errors. HEC provides error checking only for the header bits of the cell. HEC uses the last byte of the 5-byte cell header.

- ✔ **Cell scrambling and descrambling:** Cell scrambling mixes up the cell payload to avoid long strings of ones or zeros and other bit patterns that may confuse underlying transmission equipment such as fiber-optic terminals (the boxes generating optical signals for the fiber). Cell scrambling was a source of trouble in early implementations because not all switches supported scrambling. Scrambling serves a useful purpose and generally remains turned on in most implementations. The key is to make sure that scrambling stays either consistently off or on; otherwise, you see errors on the ATM line.

✔ **Cell mapping:** Defines how the ATM node loads the cell bits into the transmission frame.

✔ **Cell delineation:** Identifies the cell boundaries within the transmission frame using the HEC field in the cell header.

Debate continues over the usefulness of some of the defined physical interfaces. No one uses TAXI anymore; it was just an easy way for LAN ATM vendors to introduce a wire interface for ATM. We already questioned the usefulness of 25 Mbps ATM in the previous chapter. (Many wonder if 25 Mbps ATM investment is justifiable (although it is the least expensive LAN ATM interface because it provides a very small incremental gain in speed). Conversion to switched Ethernet or token ring seems to be the current upgrade path of choice.

On the WAN side, T1's doubting Thomases cite the overhead introduced by ATM cellification. The effective AAL throughput on a T1 ATM connection is 1.39 Mbps, allowing transport of only 21 traditional voice channels. Others argue that T1 ATM makes a lot of sense. It provides a service interface that can support multiple traffic types (more effectively using the costly dedicated-access connection from the carrier) while offering commonality in the subscribed service at both large- and medium-sized sites. T1 ATM could become more popular if carriers interconnect their ATM and voice networks. Frame relay will probably remain the clear winner of this lower-speed horse race for a long time, if carriers widely implement frame relay class-of-service. We hope that they'll think to provide seamless frame-to-ATM interworking across multiple service types.

T3 interfaces are now available in two versions:

✔ PLCP, which provides a maximum AAL throughput of 36.1 Mbps

✔ Direct Mapping, which bumps the AAL speed over 40 Mbps

The original definition of the T3 interface used a mapping scheme known as Physical Layer Convergence Protocol (PLCP). Because it emulates many services provided by SONET overhead, PLCP uses substantial overhead from the T3 bit stream. These services aren't terribly exciting to the end user and not really worth the bits lost on a T3 facility for the service provider. More and more equipment has an optional Direct Mapping scheme for the T3 interfaces.

T3 ports offered by carriers expect transmission facilities supporting C-bit parity. C-bit parity provides management functions on T3 facilities similar to those provided by Extended Superframe (ESF) on T1. If your facilities carrier cannot support this capability, ATM can run without C-bit parity, but make sure C-bit is off on all your switches.

Keep an eye out for the Inverse ATM Mux (AMI, also called AIMUX and IMA) implementations, an upcoming physical interface generating a lot of interest. The ATM Forum plans to complete this specification in 1997. IMA defines a standard method for carrying ATM cells across multiple T1s, typically two through eight. Proprietary solutions are available from vendors right now. IMA allows you to move from T1 frame relay or private line services to higher-speed ATM interfaces without the expense of a dedicated T3 facility. A potential catch lies in the expense of the IMA equipment required both at the customer's premises and in the network. In the meantime, wait and see if the new option provides sufficient cost benefit over T3 to justify deployment. One more thing to watch: The Frame Relay Forum is also defining a NxT1 standard solution for frame relay services.

Inside ATM with
Claire Lewis, Senior Manager for Broadband Cell Services and
**   MCI representative to the ATM Forum's Marketing Committee**
Tim Dwight, Senior Engineer — ATM Engineering and
**   MCI representative to the ATM Forum's Technical Committee**
MCI Telecommunications, Inc., Richardson, TX

Pilgrims' Progress: Exploring the ATM Forum

Sometimes users of leading-edge telecommunications technologies can feel like modern-day Pilgrims, exploring telecom boundaries, not knowing what lies ahead. Since its founding in 1991, the ATM Forum's charter has been to make the New World of ATM a place of abundant opportunity for both users and suppliers.

The ATM Forum is an international not-for-profit organization, working to accelerate the worldwide use of ATM products and services through market-driven development of interoperability specifications. Two concepts are important here: market-driven development and interoperability specifications.

The ATM Forum is a unique experiment in the telecommunications industry. More than 700 user and vendor organizations work together, developing the specifications they need to use ATM in real-world, production environments. Over 200 are principal members who vote on the text of each specification in this majority-rule organization.

This is in contrast to traditional, consensus-oriented standard setting bodies, which are usually scientific or academic in nature. These groups develop technical standards which they then present to users and vendors to implement.

A Pilgrim in the Standards World

The ATM Forum was one of the first telecommunications organizations to mix the perspectives of both users and vendors. The Forum, in effect, puts itself in the middle — between implementers and traditional standards bodies. It is not an officially-sanctioned standards organization; instead, it applies influence towards both these organizations and users.

The second difference to note is that the ATM Forum focuses on establishing interoperability specifications instead of de jure standards. ATM happily coexists with many other internetworking technologies including Frame Relay and Switched Multimegabit Digital Service (SMDS), and the ATM Forum wants to keep it that way. So instead of declaring ATM technical standards in a vacuum, a strategy that could lead to telecom incompatibilities, the ATM Forum works to promote industry cooperation and awareness.

In doing so, the Forum collaborates with a number of other specification- and standards-setting organizations, including the International Telecommunication Union (ITU), the Internet Engineering Task Force (IETF), the Frame Relay Forum, and the SMDS Interest Group.

Agents of Change

So what exactly does the ATM Forum do? Reviewing the organizational structure is a good place to start.

The ATM Forum consists of a worldwide Technical Committee; one Marketing Committee each for North America, Europe, and Asia-Pacific; and an Enterprise Network Roundtable, through which ATM end-users participate.

The Technical Committee comprises working groups that address specific issues, such as the Physical Layer, LAN Emulation, Multiprotocol Over ATM (MPOA), Security, and others.

The Marketing Committees also have their own subgroups, which focus on user issues specific to various countries and regions around the world. The Marketing Committees and subgroups also promote awareness of ATM technology, hosting user conferences at which users share testimonials and experiences.

Issues and Answers

An issue can become the subject of a technical working group in one of two ways: The issue can surface as a user issue through the Marketing Committees, or it can arise in a working group. Those interested in the new issue can then request (from the Technical Committee) a new working group to explore the issue. The Marketing Committees and the Technical Committee work closely to ensure that users' and vendors' requirements are being fulfilled through the Technical Committee's developments.

The ATM Forum has not yet perfected its snapshot understandings of the real marketplace and has recently gone through some growing pains to improve its picture quality.

The ATM Forum does strive to meet its objectives of offering specifications that are useful and practical to users. Users and vendors don't simply comply with decreed standards; they are part of the decision-making process.

After Technical Committee working groups develop technical specifications that are agreed upon users, the ATM Forum works routinely with other user-vendor associations (such as the Frame Relay Forum and the SMDS Interest Group) to help ensure interoperability. The ATM Forum may also collaborate with other, more formal standards bodies if the specification will affect greater portions of the global telecommunications infrastructure.

Part of the Global Standards Movement

The ATM Forum works with two of the larger global standards bodies: the Internet Engineering Task Force (IETF) and the International Telecommunication Union (ITU).

The IETF is a self-organized group of people that makes technical and other contributions to the engineering and evolution of the Internet and related technologies. The IETF is the principal body engaged in the development of new Internet standard specifications, including protocol and architecture recommendations.

Significant collaboration takes place between the ATM Forum and the IETF; the ATM Forum has working groups that deal with IP Traffic Over ATM, LAN Emulation and Multiprotocol Over ATM (MPOA). The Forum and IETF make a strong effort to build solutions — and set standards — that satisfy mutual or complementary needs.

Founded in Paris in 1865 as the International Telegraph Union, the International Telecommunication Union took its current name in 1934 and became a specialized agency of the United Nations in 1947.

The ITU is a consensus-driven, intergovernmental organization. Through the ITU, public and private sector organizations cooperate on the development of earth-bound and satellite telecommunications. The ITU also develops standards to facilitate worldwide telecommunications interconnections, regardless of the type of technology used.

In the past, some specifications established by the ATM Forum were designated international standards by the ITU. The ATM Forum

(continued)

collaborated with the American National Standards Institute (ANSI) to accomplish this international designation. (ANSI is an officially-sanctioned standards body that has been the United States' traditional liaison with the ITU.) More recently, the ATM Forum has worked directly with the ITU, thereby simplifying the information-sharing process between the two groups.

Market-Driven Results

As ATM evolves from a nascent technology into one being implemented around the world, keeping in mind how *slowly* the traditional standards world has moved and how *quickly* the ATM Forum has made an impact in the marketplace is important.

One key example of that impact is the Anchorage Accord, reached in July 1996. The Anchorage Accord is a set of mission-critical specifications that the ATM Forum identified as forming a cohesive, stable ATM framework for product and service development.

The ATM Forum will continue meeting every other month as it has for the past five years. The Forum strives to recognize user requirements and incorporate technological developments to churn out the key standards required to implement ATM.

You can find out more about the ATM Forum in Appendix A of this book.

Chapter 9
Getting Inside the ATM Layer

· ·

In This Chapter

▶ Looking at virtual connections in ATM

▶ Recognizing ATM's five service categories

▶ Knowing the rules for well-behaved network traffic

· ·

*T*his chapter explores the many, many details of the ATM Layer introduced in Chapter 8. And, believe us, we lost count on the number of details. So hang on, dig in, discover, and enjoy (well, at least try to do the first three).

Acronyms Used in This Chapter	
Acronym	*What It Stands For*
ABR	Available Bit Rate
CBR	Constant Bit Rate
CDV	Cell Delay Variation
CDVT	Cell Delay Variation Tolerance
CLP	Cell Loss Priority
CLR	Cell Loss Ratio
CPE	Customer Premises Equipment
CTD	Cell Transfer Delay
EFCI	Explicit Forward Congestion Indication
GCRA	Generic Cell Rate Algorithm
GFC	Generic Flow Control
HEC	Header Error Control
MCR	Minimum Cell Rate
NNI	Network-Network Interface
NPC	Network Parameter Control
PCR	Peak Cell Rate

(continued)

Acronyms Used in This Chapter *(continued)*	
Acronym	*What It Stands For*
PTI	Payload Type Indicator
PVC	Permanent Virtual Connections
QoS	Quality of Service
RM	Resource Management
SCR	Sustained Cell Rate
SNA	Systems Network Architecture
SVC	Switched Virtual Connection
TCP/IP	Transmission Control Protocol/Internet Protocol
UBR	Unspecified Bit Rate
UNI	User-Network Interface
UPC	Usage Parameter Control
VBR-NRT	Variable Bit Rate–Non-Real-Time
VBR-RT	Variable Bit Rate–Real-Time
VCC	Virtual Channel Connection
VCI	Virtual Channel Identifier
VPC	Virtual Path Connection
VPI	Virtual Path Identifier
VS/VD	Virtual Source/Virtual Destination

Virtually Everything about ATM Connections

The ATM layer's primary responsibilities are to establish connections across the ATM network by fairly sharing the resources of the physical layer. The ATM layer does this through logical connections between communicating ATM users. Logical connections allow many end-to-end circuits to share the same physical resource — each circuit uses the resource when it has traffic to send.

The ATM layer must ensure that each connection receives its fair share of the physical resources and that connections requiring special treatment receive priority handling. The shared physical resources in an ATM network are the buffer capacity in the ATM switches and the bandwidth capacity of the trunks between the switches. Buffers hold cells until those cells take their turns riding the ATM trunks.

The ATM layer uses cells to move traffic through the network. The cell carries 48 bytes of payload plus a 5-byte header which contains all the information that the ATM layer needs to get the cell safely from the source to the destination. Every cell header contains an address identifier used by the ATM switches to track how cells move from one physical link to the next.

Because address identifiers are unique to each physical link, they enable an ATM network to support millions of connections. If a single connection hogged an address across the entire network, a much larger addressing space would be necessary to track all the unique connections. The switches assign the needed address identifiers locally. The connectivity information is stored in the memory of the switching tables only and, of course, their management systems. Thus we have the name *logical connections,* also commonly called *virtual connections.*

An ATM switch reads the address identifier of an incoming cell and then looks to its switching tables for the appropriate outgoing link. It changes the cell's address identifier to the assigned logical address on the new link and then moves it to the output buffer of the proper outgoing link. Before any communication exchanges take place, the connectivity information stored in the switches must be loaded. The switches receive this information through either manual connection setup or signaled connection setup.

Permanent virtual connections

Connections loaded manually into the ATM switches are known as *permanent virtual connections* (PVCs). Network operators must load all the connection information into the switching tables before an ATM network can carry any cells. Entering and tracking PVCs can quickly get unwieldy for very large networks. If the users require *fully meshed* connectivity, the number of connections needed adds up to $N*(N-1)/2$, where N is the number of connected users. If the users also require more than one service category between them, this number multiplies. In reality, very few networks exist today that need a fully meshed configuration.

Today's intelligent management systems allow an operator to select the endpoints desiring connectivity to setup PVCs. These systems are a great improvement over older management systems that required operators to load each of the local address assignments of the connections in each switch. Current systems must know the full network topology, how to load balance connections across multiple links, and how to make the necessary address assignments in each of the switching tables. The management systems must then accurately track and organize this information for the network operator.

Switched virtual connections

Alternatively, ATM virtual connections may be set up on a call-by-call basis. Known as *switched virtual connections* (SVCs), these connections use signaling messages between the user and the network to exchange information about the type of connection required whenever it is needed. SVCs eliminate the headache of PVC management but also introduce their own set of complexities (one of the most critical being how the network determines the best route to the requested destination). SVC users include the desired connection destination in a call setup message using a global address. SVC networks use various address types.

In very large ATM networks connecting thousands of users, SVCs eventually will be the only practical implementation of virtual connections. Many more details on SVCs and how they work are in the next chapter.

Virtual paths and virtual channels

The preceding two sections give you most of the highlights of ATM's virtual connections. But we want to clear up one last thing. The address identifier in the cell header actually consists of two parts:

- ✔ The virtual channel identifier (VCI), typically a 12-bit field
- ✔ The virtual path identifier (VPI), typically an 8-bit field

VCIs identify virtual channels carried by an ATM link. VPIs identify virtual paths carried by an ATM link. The VPI is the higher order address, and a virtual path can contain multiple virtual channels. Each direction of the virtual path or virtual channel requires an address assignment.

ATM connections relying on both the VPI and VCI addresses for switching are known as *virtual channel connections* (VCCs). These connections are a joined series of virtual channels from individual physical links. The switch provides the intelligence to join one virtual channel to the next along the connection route. The VPI provides a way to group virtual channels for transport across the network. Connections relying solely on the VPI address for switching are called *virtual path connections* (VPCs). VPCs are a joined series of virtual paths from individual physical links. The switch provides the intelligence to join one virtual path to the next along the connection route.

Figure 9-1 provides a graphical representation of these different virtual connection types.

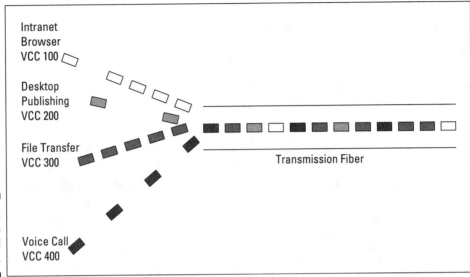

Figure 9-1:
ATM's
virtual
connections.

VPCs simplify connection management for the network operator by grouping channel connections together. VPCs also give users a way to subscribe to carrier PVC services while allowing management of individual channels (typically through signaling).

If by the time you've reach this point you're totally confused by all these virtual terms, you're normal. If you've somehow managed to keep it all straight in your head, please, please e-mail us your secrets.

The most-common terms you need to recognize for virtual connections are the following:

- ✔ **PVC (permanent virtual connection):** The general term for an ATM virtual connection which is always present in the network.

- ✔ **SVC (switched virtual connection):** The ATM virtual connection set up through signaling by the user on an as needed basis.

- ✔ **VPC (virtual path connection):** The group of connections switched as one unit and known as a path.

- ✔ **VCC (virtual channel connection):** The single connection known as a channel.

The ATM cell header

The 5-byte ATM cell header shown here contains six fields.

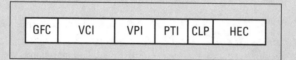

| GFC | VCI | VPI | PTI | CLP | HEC |

✔ The Generic Flow Control (GFC) provides 4 bits to locally share congestion information. Its use is not yet well defined.

✔ The Virtual Channel Identifier (VCI) typically provides 16 bits to identify the virtual channel address. The assignment of bits between the VCI and the VPI fields is actually an optional setting in ATM.

✔ The Virtual Path Identifier (VPI) typically provides 8 bits to identify the virtual path address. The number of assigned bits between the VCI and the VPI fields also is an optional setting in ATM.

✔ The Payload Type Indicator (PTI) uses 3 bits to distinguish the difference between user data and maintenance traffic such as management and congestion information.

✔ The Cell Loss Priority (CLP) bit indicates a high or low priority for the cell.

✔ The Header Error Control (HEC) provides 8 bits used by the physical layer to correct single errors or detect multiple errors in the cell header.

Multipoint connections

ATM supports both point-to-point and point-to-multipoint connections. Point-to-point connections are *duplex*, which means that traffic simultaneously moves in either direction. Each direction may have a different associated bandwidth assigned to it through the bandwidth parameters discussed in the next section.

A multipoint connection provides *simplex* connectivity from one site to many sites. A simplex connection can pass traffic in only one direction. Good implementations of multipoint should duplicate traffic only at the last possible point in the network. Figure 9-2 shows a multipoint simplex connection. In the case of multipoint ATM connections, the direction is from the single source to the many destinations.

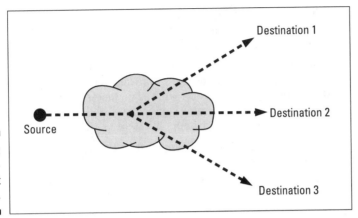

Service Parameters

Each connection defined within the network features a unique quality of service (QoS). Quality of service determines how the network treats the cells riding the connection. Because the ATM network can carry a variety of traffic types, such as as voice, data, and video, different connections require a different quality of service. The user and network exchange information about the needed quality of service through a set of defined QoS parameters. In PVCs, the QoS parameters are typically shared through a paper order. In SVCs, the user shares requirements in the call setup message of signaling.

The ATM Forum defined a variety of QoS parameters. We're going to give you just their definitions here. How to use these parameters is the subject of service categories. Each service category uses a subset of the QoS parameters to deliver an expected service quality. We cover service categories in the next section.

The seven QoS parameters defined by the ATM Forum are the following:

- **Peak cell rate (PCR):** The maximum number of cells per second the connection can transfer into the network. Typically, but not always, the peak cell rate is set to the maximum number possible for the given line rate.

- **Cell delay variation (CDV):** The change in interarrival times of each cell. Cell multiplexing can introduce variable delays in the cell stream in both the CPE and network, making this QoS measurement necessary. Cell delay variation tolerance (CDVT) represents the maximum allowed value for CDV on a connection.

- **Sustained cell rate (SCR):** The average number of cells per second that the connection can transfer into the network. The burst tolerance determines the length of time over which the network measures this average.

- **Burst tolerance:** The maximum length of time that the user can transfer at peak cell rate. If a user sends traffic for the full burst tolerance, cell rate must drop until the connection once again meets the requirements of the SCR parameter. Burst tolerance can be measured in number of cells, a measurement known as maximum burst size (MBS).

- **Minimum cell rate (MCR):** The smallest cell transfer rate that the connection must always support.

- **Cell transfer delay (CTD):** The time delay experienced by cells using the connection as measured on an end-to-end basis.

- **Cell loss ratio (CLR):** The allowed percentage of cells that the connection can lose in the network as measured on an end-to-end basis.

Service Categories

Way back in the previous chapter, we promised to give you information on ATM's service categories. If for some reason you've been waiting with bated breath, you have now arrived at the "Service Categories" section.

So don your togs (that's an Aussie saying for put on your swimsuit) and jump in. But remember, still waters run deep. The ATM Forum provides a list of service categories and associated parameters in their Traffic Management 4.0 document. You can order a copy of this and other Forum documents from their Web site at www.atmforum.com

If you're not terribly good at swimming through a bunch of technical muck that wraps around your ankles and drags you under until you feel like you're drowning in engineering goo (wow, that was really visual!), you can simply move on to our more user-friendly descriptions of service categories:

- **Constant bit rate (CBR):** Supports connections requiring a steady, predictable throughput with minimal delay and very low loss. Applications suited to CBR connections include traditional real-time voice and video, in which a form of pulse code modulation (PCM) digitizes the traffic stream. Circuit emulation of private lines or other TDM circuits are other candidates for CBR service. For CBR connections, the user must specify the PCR, CDVT, CTD, CDV, and CLR. Most public providers of native ATM services allow users to establish the PCR with all other parameters at a default setting.

- **Variable bit rate–real-time (VBR-RT):** Supports somewhat bursty connections requiring a strictly bounded delay. VBR-RT connections expect to carry fairly predictable traffic that is sensitive to delay and loss. Applications using VBR-RT include packetized voice or video and IBM Systems

Network Architecture (SNA) links. In VBR-RT, the user specifies PCR, CDVT, SCR, MBS, CTD, and CLR. Most public providers of native ATM services allow users to set the SCR and possibly MBS and PCR. The other parameters generally have default values.

✔ **Variable bit rate–non-real-time (VBR-NRT):** Supports somewhat bursty connections having less-stringent delay requirements but still requiring low loss. Examples might include an SNA network in which local spoofing minimizes the strict delay requirements. (In *spoofing,* a local networking device responds to the polling inquiries of hosts instead of waiting for the response from the actual end device located far across the network.) The parameter specifications are the same as in VBR-RT.

✔ **Unspecified bit rate (UBR):** Supports connections that have no performance requirements. UBR service is equivalent to the services provided by general Internet offerings, which have no objectives for delay or loss. In the UBR service category, no performance parameters are set except the PCR which generally equals the line rate.

✔ **Available bit rate (ABR):** Is the newest service category (the final definition was just completed in 1996). It supports high throughput at low loss of very bursty traffic through network congestion control mechanisms. ABR works for non-real-time traffic with no commitments for delay. The control mechanisms can occur within the network or on an end-to-end basis where the network expects users to modify the flow of traffic based on a provided congestion feedback mechanism. ABR's primary application is LAN interconnect. The user specifies the PCR, CDVT, MCR, and CLR. Public ABR services should be available in 1997 and probably will allow users to specify the minimum cell rate (MCR) with values of the other parameters set to default. Find out more on ABR in the next section.

Table 9-1 gives a tabular view of service categories.

Table 9-1	**Service Categories Unplugged**			
Service Category	*Network Priority*	*Cell Delay and Delay Variation*	*Cell Loss*	*Burst Tolerance*
CBR	1	low	low	none
VBR-RT	2	low	medium	some
VBR-NRT	3	high	medium	some
ABR	4	high	medium	high
UBR	5	high	high	high

Managing Your Connections

Assignment of QoS to each connection is critical to the network not only for providing each application with the required service quality but also for optimizing network use. The network expects each user to behave according to the rules (that is, the QoS parameters) set up for each virtual connection. Well-behaved, predictable traffic, or at least knowledge of the worst-case traffic flow, lets network designers optimize capacity assignment without worrying about wide fluctuations from the expected traffic load.

ATM networks define two functions to make sure users follow connection rules:

- ✔ Traffic shaping in the CPE smooths out the transported traffic.
- ✔ Traffic policing by the network ensures that the application follows the expected rules, providing fairness across all connections. Traffic policing also goes by the terms usage parameter control (UPC) at the UNI and network parameter control (NPC) at the NNI.

Getting in shape

Traffic shaping allows a source to modify the stream of cells sent over the virtual connection. Shaping smooths traffic so that it conforms with the bandwidth parameters (PCR/CDVT, SCR/MBS, and MCR) of the connection and does not exceed the expected flow into the network. It temporarily hold cells in buffers and then respaces them onto the outgoing connection. Shaping accommodates only minor changes in the cell flow due to the limited practical size of buffers. Appropriately enough, traffic shaping is also called traffic smoothing.

Traffic shaping is not yet available on all premises' equipment, so find out how strictly your network provider polices your traffic.

Calling the police

The network polices traffic to ensure that connections conform to their established bandwidth parameters (PCR/CDVT, SCR/MBS, and MCR). Policing improves the overall performance of the network by limiting the negative impact of a poorly behaving connection to just that connection. Depending on the implementation, the policing mechanism employs various recourses for connections in violation of their traffic contract. The contract is, simply, the set of established QoS parameters for the connection.

Most switches discard any traffic exceeding the peak cell rate (PCR). If the traffic exceeds the sustained cell rate (SCR) of a VBR connection for longer than the allowed maximum burst size (MBS), the switch may either discard or tag the cell. Tagged (also known as marked) cells are the first cells dropped if switch buffers overflow from network congestion. The policer tags the cell by flipping the cell header's cell loss priority (CLP) bit from 0 to 1. This bit is sometimes called the *clip* bit. The ATM end station can also choose to set the CLP bit to 1 for lower priority traffic. The traffic policer monitors either the VPC grouped connection or the VCC individual connection but cannot simultaneously monitor both a VPC and one of its associated VCCs.

How well your carrier treats nonconformant traffic is a measure of its service quality. As we've mentioned repeatedly, existing applications weren't designed for ATM. Therefore, they have no way to monitor their traffic output by the definitions provided in ATM. A carrier may choose to discard all nonconformant traffic or pass it as tagged cells. Typically, no performance objectives for cell loss, delay, or delay variation exist for tagged traffic.

The ATM Forum defined the relationship between each QoS parameter in something called the generic cell rate algorithm (GCRA). The GCRA defines the permitted cell flow on a connection. Think of GCRA as the function for shaping and policing traffic.

The policer monitors connections using a mechanism affectionately known as the *dual leaky bucket* to the ATM faithful. If you can understand the dual leaky bucket mechanism, you've earned your black belt in ATM. We've taken a crack at trying to explain it to you in the nearby sidebar, "You've got holes in your buckets." Don't feel bad if you still feel clueless. Dual leaky bucket is one of the most nonintuitive technical concepts we've found in all of telecommunications, and the subtleties of how it works really aren't that important. All you need to know is that *dual leaky bucket* is a method to explain how an ATM switch measures the bandwidth conformance of each CBR and VBR connection.

Admitting all calls

Connection admission control (CAC) is another traffic management function that makes sure the network doesn't accept new ATM connections when it can't provide the requested QoS. CAC is associated primarily with signaled connections. During CAC, the network determines whether it has the resources for the requested connection at the requested QoS. The network rejects calls if it can't meet the requested QoS and still maintain the QoS of previously accepted connections. How frequently the network rejects calls is a key performance measurement of signaled networks. For more about CAC and signaling, see the next chapter.

Following all traffic signs

The outcome of these traffic management approaches is this: Applications deviating too far from the assigned bandwidth values risk information loss in the network. Asking applications to behave by ATM's rules isn't always easy.

Many applications never had to live by this kind of strict behavior. Most applications use networks without any strict QoS parameters to follow and therefore haven't been receiving commitments to service quality.

In traditional networks, higher-layer protocols or the engineering design of the network itself ensures service quality. For example, TCP provides guarantees of no data loss in an end-to-end TCP/IP information exchange, although individual IP links may experience substantial loss. All SNA network designers consider timing and delay factors in the number and lengths of network links. Existing applications typically assume a given quality of service inherent in the unique network designed for them. In general, they can't adapt or change to fit the capabilities of the network.

These inconsistencies between what the network expects and how applications actually behave create special challenges for designers of both ATM networks and their supported applications. The ATM industry still has a lot to learn about the practical, day-to-day implementation of ATM for corporate networks.

Removing Gridlock

An exception to the inflexibility of applications in adapting to changes in the network is TCP/IP's windowing mechanism. TCP/IP applications adjust their information flow to the network based on acknowledgments received from their remote ends. The number of outstanding packets (those without acknowledgments) that the application can send on the network is the *window*. If acknowledgments from the remote end arrive too slowly due to limited network resources, the window quickly gets used up and the transmitted data flow slows down. Window size is one of the parameters that network managers adjust in TCP/IP networks to optimize throughput across a given network. TCP/IP's mechanism for monitoring the amount of transmitted information provides *implicit flow control*.

Available bit rate (ABR) service takes advantage of TCP/IP's implicit flow control to maximize throughput and optimize engineering of available capacity. If the network is lightly loaded, applications send at full-speed-ahead line rate. During busy periods, the network expects applications to slow down or risk traffic loss. The network informs the user location of network congestion through various feedback mechanisms, depending on the type of ABR implemented.

The bandwidth available to the virtual ABR connection must fall between the minimum cell rate (MCR, which may be set to zero) and peak cell rate (PCR). The network informs the user of the available bandwidth to the connection through one of four feedback mechanisms. Cells transmitted at a rate below the network's offered available bandwidth rate are conforming and experience minimal cell loss.

TECHNICAL STUFF

More about ABR

The ATM Forum defined four types of feedback mechanisms in available bit rate (ABR) service, each designed with an increasing degree of complexity. In each method, individual switches can modify feedback to indicate new or dissipated congestion. The effectiveness of ABR to control congestion and maximize user throughput depends on the type of ABR used in the network. Compatibility between different ABR implementations is an issue of these services.

✔ The simplest ABR service uses the explicit forward congestion indication (EFCI) bit in the cell header. Network switches in a congested state flip this bit from 0 to 1. The flipped bit occurs in the direction of cells heading to the destination.

✔ The next level of ABR service routinely inserts resource management (RM) cells within the connection's information cell stream. After receiving the RM cells, the destination returns the cells to the source in the backwards direction. The congestion feedback has thus formed a closed loop. The network alters these RM cells to indicate congestion. This ABR type has two weaknesses. First, the rate of increase or decrease in cell traffic is not explicit — the only possible states are no network congestion or network congestion experienced. The endpoints step up or step down their offered traffic based on this feedback in a predetermined increment. Thus, this feedback mechanism is sometimes call *binary mode*. The second weakness is that the feedback loop can be very long for large networks. In long feedback loops, the user reacts to network states that may have changed during the time it took to notify users of the condition.

✔ The third level of ABR service also uses RM cells, but in this case, the cells provide the exact rate to which the ABR connection is supposed to modify its traffic. The explicit rate reduces overreaction by the cell source to congestion, allowing for quicker available bandwidth use.

✔ The fourth level of ABR service addresses the second issue in the RM method by adding a technique called *virtual source/virtual destination* (VS/VD). In VS/VD, ABR's feedback mechanisms operate in only a subset of the end-to-end network. This allows implementation of ABR in just a portion of the network without requiring all users or nodes to have ABR awareness. VS/VD also shortens the length of the feedback loop, allowing for nearly instantaneous reaction to transient states in the network. For example, a network provider could implement ABR solely within its network to more quickly dissipate congestion. In this example, the information exchange for flow control occurs between the originating and terminating switches of the network. The originating switch reacts to network feedback by buffering traffic until congestion passes. Cell loss may occur if the buffers fill before the network provides a green light. Despite that, VS/VD's developers say that the loss is less than it would be without VS/VD.

Available bandwidth changes over the life of the connection due to transient states in the network. Increasing VBR or CBR connections with committed bandwidth values mean less capacity for ABR connections. ABR bandwidth also fluctuates if a number of ABR users are trying to send traffic at the same time. The method each switch uses to fairly allocate bandwidth among all ABR users depends on each vendor's implementation.

ABR service is valuable in meeting two very critical design objectives: It helps soften the network's peak traffic load as it increases average network utilization. Sharp utilization peaks result in high networking costs. Meeting peak bandwidth demand leaves significant excess capacity during unloaded times. To a service provider, the implications of this are not good. The carrier must spend big dollars to buy more switches and more bandwidth to handle peak demand and, because the network is usually lightly loaded, little extra money comes in the door to help pay for this extra equipment. There is some relief: ABR allows carriers to more highly optimize their networks, which should result in lower service costs.

However, because ABR has yet to be implemented in large networks, its promised capabilities remain untested. More time will pass before ATM end stations are capable of adjusting their traffic flow according to the feedback of the network, and different levels of ABR service present compatibility issues, as explored in the nearby sidebar, "More about ABR."

The Performing Network

A network's capacity to carry an excessive number of marked cells, or limit the frequency of congestion and associated ABR-service feedback, depends largely on the engineering of the network. Good switch and network design can substantially increase the goodput of the network. *Goodput* is a measure of useful throughput. The use of large buffers, per VC queuing, fair-weighted queuing, and packet discard methods, all improve network performance and reduce susceptibility to congestion.

- *Large buffers* is an obvious descriptor of desired capability. Large buffers allow switches to hold traffic without loss until transient congestion passes. Determining the best buffer size is a balance between large buffers that reduce cell loss and small buffers which lower cell delay and equipment costs.

- *Per VC queuing* allows a switch to independently hold the cells of a connection without impacting other connections.

- *Fair-weighted queuing* is a mechanism for fairly servicing all virtual-connection queues destined to a particular outgoing link while providing each with the requested QoS. The term *weighted* refers to a switch's capability to give a higher priority to certain service categories requiring low loss and low delay.

✔ *Packet discarding* drops whole packets in the network, not just specific random cells, to relieve congestion. Packets are actually the larger-information pieces that higher-layer applications (such as TCP/IP) use to communicate. A packet with a small chunk missing due to intermittent cell loss is worthless to the higher layer that must request retransmission. With packet discarding, the network destroys only one of the higher-layer packets during congestion instead of corrupting multiple packets with occasional cell loss which only exasperates congestion causing multiple retransmission requests a situation.

Choose equipment and services vendors who are adept at all the different aspects of the engineering puzzle. A good network design minimizes the occurrence of congestion and also effectively limits its length and impact when congestion does occur. You can learn more about engineering considerations for switches and networks in Chapter 15.

Oh, by the way, CONGRATULATIONS are in order if you've actually made it to the end of this second highly technical chapter (the first was Chapter 8). You now know the basics of ATM technology. Understanding a few of the support functions and interoperability specifications completes the ATM picture. We describe these in the next two chapters of this book.

If you didn't take a break earlier, it's time now for a hot-fudge sundae (or a beer). If you already indulged in ice cream at our earlier suggestion, have another! We did.

Inside ATM with Christopher Baldwin
ATM Business Manager
Cascade Communications, Inc., Westford, MA

The Importance of QoS

Introduction

Wide Area Networks (WANs) carry traffic with widely differing economic and performance characteristics. The traffic can range from thousands of simultaneous financial transactions generated by the largest banks to bursty Internet-surfing traffic generated by unemployed teenagers. To date, most WANs consist of independent overlay networks, one for each traffic type. As the volume of network traffic and the number of different network applications grows, WAN service providers and customers alike require a common infrastructure to achieve economies of scale and cross-application integration.

ATM exists precisely to build this infrastructure. To succeed in this role, ATM switches must, however, deliver a technical feature termed Quality of Service (QoS). QoS can be understood as the control knob on the statistical multiplexing gain in the network. With the knob turned up, precious bandwidth is amortized over multiple users allowing lower price services; with the knob turned down, the network delivers premium private-line equivalent service. ATM's QoS guarantees the successful deployment of different price economies on the common infrastructure.

QoS and Network Engineering

QoS is a term used to differentiate the technical characteristics of information streams in

(continued)

the WAN. QoS categorizes these streams based on the burstiness of the traffic, on their tolerance for delay variation, and on their tolerance for transmission loss. Circuit and SNA traffic is highly intolerant of delay variation and loss. (SNA is an IBM communications protocol between mainframes and between mainframes and terminals.) Bursty computer traffic admirably tolerates delay variation and loss but generally requires much higher throughput than SNA and circuit traffic.

Four general classes of QoS have been defined:

- **Constant Bit Rate (CBR):** Offers no statistical gain and is for leased-line emulation.

- **Variable Bit Rate-real-time (VBR-rt):** Offers some statistical gain, and delay variation is controlled.

- **Variable Bit Rate non-real-time (VBR-nrt):** Offers more statistical gain; delay variation is not controlled, but cell loss is controlled.

- **Unspecified Bit Rate/Available Bit Rate (ABR/UBR):** Offers the most statistical gain with no guarantees of throughput. ABR, however, includes congestion control features to make the service class fair.

Even within a particular class of traffic, prioritization distinctions can arise for economic reasons. For example, corporate-LAN transport will require and pay for a higher quality of transport than will home Internet surfers on the Internet, even though from traffic characteristic perspectives, their traffic may be identical.

A well-designed ATM switch manages the information streams with close regard to QoS parameters so that a bursty file transfer does not disrupt a SNA session. Mapping application traffic to QoS classes defines the art of ATM network design, as network economics are directly proportional to QoS traffic engineering. If all traffic uses the CBR QoS class, the ATM network economics can actually be worse than a pure private-line network — with no statistical multiplexing gain.

ATM has been described as splitting the problem of moving traffic into *brains* and *brawn* components. Hardware-based ATM cell switching provides the *brawn* to move cells while software-based routing technology provides the topology *brains* that steer the ATM traffic in the greater network. So as to not confuse anyone with the term *routing*, in this context, ATM network routing refers to the process of finding the best set of links over which to establish a new switched circuit in the ATM network. Route establishment is an important step in any circuit-based network, including the large voice carrier networks which can handle thousands of calls a minute.

ATM switch brawn also includes cell buffer queues to absorb traffic bursts from simultaneous transmissions destined for the same output port. Buffers are, in effect, the repositories of statistical gain. The management of traffic in switch buffers constitutes the art of implementing QoS support. Switches must schedule cell traffic with a queue serving discipline that prioritizes traffic according to its QoS and priority levels. This queue scheduler must be QoS aware and must reallocate priorities as the traffic mix changes. In the case of congestion (too much traffic into the switch compared to the exit capacity), the scheduler must be fair in discarding cell traffic both within and across QoS classes. Ideally, the scheduler uses a congestion notification algorithm to talk to all of the other switches on the network.

Implementing QoS Support

It is a common misconception that just by using ATM cells, any ATM switch inherently has QoS support for data, video and voice. For cost reasons, some switch designs may dispense with sophisticated traffic policing and traffic management functions to get a low cost switch optimized for LAN data applications. Existing computer and LAN operating systems historically have no need for QoS support because these systems generate only a single QoS class of traffic.

So what does it take to support QoS? At the highest level, ATM brawn must be QoS-aware so that predefined streams get higher priority than other lower-priority streams in the queue serving discipline. Similarly, the ATM brains of dynamic SVC networks must not only understand the physical topology of the network, but must understand routes in terms of their QoS capabilities. Links have QoS characteristics that alone can determine their appropriateness for carrying a particular ATM connection. Changes in traffic alters the QoS carrying capacity of a link, and thus, QoS capacity is a very important but very dynamic link attribute in a network topology map. I will examine QoS-capable ATM in more detail in the following sections.

Implementing QoS: Policing the Input

Traffic enters an ATM switch from user ports. Connections on these ports are provisioned as Permanent Virtual Circuits (PVCs) or initiated by an end station as Switched Virtual Circuits (SVCs). The switch and the user/end-device negotiate the traffic characteristics for the established connections. But what prevents the user from sending in more traffic than negotiated? The answer: Usage Parameter Contract (UPC). UPC enforcement is clearly a very important checkpoint into an ATM switch. WAN service providers generally perform extremely thorough testing of the function as UPC is critical to managing the traffic load and thereby the financial viability of their network. UPC is also the first step to guaranteeing the QoS performance of all connections because traffic violators can destroy the QoS of good network citizens.

Implementing QoS: Connection Admission Control

Many ATM switches support only hop-by-hop PVC establishment. The network administrator must hand craft both the route and the QoS delivery on each hop to the destination. QoS delivery is completely dependent on the skill of the operator — not a pleasant job.

ATM switches supporting SVCs and or operations-friendly PVC establishment provide an automatic facility for connection establishment. When users request a connection, the switch's brain determines the best route and whether the switches along the path have the resources to support the desired QoS. This automatic facility must also feed into the buffer queue serving discipline of a switch if the network is to guarantee QoS. A fundamental algorithm in the operation of this connection establishment facility is Connection Admission Control (CAC).

CAC effectively compresses the many dimensions of QoS into a single metric to provide a per QoS-class accounting of traffic. The switches use this accounting to route calls and drive the queue serving discipline. Most commonly, CAC computes an *equivalent bandwidth* for the connection. ATM switches typically sum this equivalent bandwidth hop-wise across the network to determine whether each link can support the newly requested connection. The switches must also determine equivalent bandwidth totals on a QoS class basis to facilitate queue management within the switching ports.

Conclusion

WANs must scale to meet the burgeoning demand of today's LAN interconnect, SNA, and Internet traffic. The price sensitivity and transport characteristics of these WAN applications differ wildly, yet carriers and private enterprises are discovering that they can most cost effectively deliver the many services if they use a common infrastructure. ATM's QoS is an essential characteristic that drives its success in the WAN, while paradoxically, it is this same feature that may make ATM incongruous with the current single-QoS LAN. Even if the initial usage of the planned ATM network will fall into a single QoS, network planners evaluating an ATM solution would be wise to consider QoS operation as a primary factor in their choice of ATM technology, not just as an afterthought consideration.

Chapter 10

Looking at ATM's Support Functions

. . . .

In This Chapter

▶ Bolstering support for signaling signal

▶ Connecting ATM networks

▶ Defending your secrets: Security in ATM networks

▶ Defining network management

. . . .

*1*n this chapter, we introduce you to some of ATM's support functions. We give you a brief explanation of a function's purpose and how the function works. Many of these support functions are very complex, requiring pages and pages of details to cover all potential situations. The ATM Forum's specification for connecting ATM switches known as *PNNI* (Private Network-Network Interface), for example, is 365 pages long. The committee was kind enough to give you a page to read every night, to help you sleep better, for a whole year.

If you really need to know all the details of ATM's support functions, you're probably getting paid big bucks as an ATM software developer, so you have to wade through the original specifications for the full scoop. For the rest of you, the information we provide gives you sufficient background and understanding to do whatever tasks you must do every day in order to earn your paycheck. (If you're reading our book, we assume that your paycheck somehow depends upon your understanding these basics of ATM's support technology.)

Acronyms Used in This Chapter

Acronym	What It Stands For
ABR	Available Bit Rate
AIS	Alarm Indication Signal
AMON	ATM Monitoring
CAC	Connection Admission Control
CBR	Constant Bit Rate
CDVT	Cell Delay Variation Tolerance

(continued)

Acronyms Used in This Chapter *(continued)*	
Acronym	*What It Stands For*
CLR	Cell Loss Ratio
DDC	Data Country Codes
FERF	Far End Reporting Failure
GUI	Graphical User Interface
ICD	International Code Designator
IETF	Internet Engineering Task Force
IISP	Interim Inter-Switch Protocol
ILMI	Integrated Layer Management Interface
IP	Internet Protocol
ISDN and B-ISDN	(Broadband) Integrated Services Digital Network
ISO	International Standards Organization
ITU	International Telecommunications Union
LAN	Local Area Network
LANE	LAN Emulation
LECS	LAN Emulation Configuration Server
MAC	Media Access Control
MBS	Maximum Burst Size
MCR	Minimum Cell Rate
MPOA	Multiprotocol over ATM
NSAP	Network Service Access Point
OAM	Operations, Administration, and Maintenance
OSPF	Open Shortest Path First
PBX	Private Branch Exchange
PCR	Peak Cell Rate
PICS	Protocol Implementation Conformance Statements
PNNI	Private Network-Network Interface
PSTN	Public Switched Telephone Network
PVC	Private Virtual Connection
QoS	Quality of Service

Acronym	What It Stands For
RMON	Remote Monitoring
SCR	Sustained Cell Rate
SNMP	Simple Network Management Protocol
SSCOP	Service Specific Convergence Protocol
SVC	Switched Virtual Connection
UBR	Unspecified Bit Rate
UNI	User-Network Interface
VBR	Variable Bit Rate
VPI/VCI	Virtual Path Identifier/Virtual Channel Identifier
VPN	Virtual Private Network
VC	Virtual Connection

Signaling 101

As we describe in Chapter 9, ATM networks can use two types of logical connections to transfer information through the network. Permanent virtual connections (PVCs) are set up on a long-term basis by the network operator. Switched virtual connections (SVCs) are set up on a call-by-call basis through a signaling exchange between the end-user and the network equipment. This signaling exchange occurs over a UNI (User-to-Network Interface). The SVC remains in place as long as the users have information to send or receive. The end-user of the UNI may be a LAN adapter card connecting to an ATM workgroup switch, a router connecting to an ATM backbone switch, an ATM access multiplexer connecting to a public ATM service, or any other user connecting to an ATM network combination.

Benefits from SVCs

Using a signaled connection offers the following benefits over a PVC:

- ✔ Eases network management
- ✔ Supports any-to-any connectivity
- ✔ Conserves network bandwidth
- ✔ Supports LAN and IP interoperability
- ✔ Tracks call-by-call usage
- ✔ Automates QoS setup

Eases network management

SVCs, unlike their PVC cousins, don't require network operators to establish and maintain many logical connections to build the network. Even a modestly sized ATM network needs hundreds of PVCs to support connectivity from each location to every other location. You can determine the number of PVCs you need for full meshed, any-to-any connectivity through a simple formula:

```
N * (N-1)/2
```

where N is the number of locations.

Using this formula, ten locations require 45 PVCs, and 20 locations makes the number of PVCs jump to 190. Each PVC is a new element to establish, track, and troubleshoot. If you're going to support multiple service categories over the ATM network, then the number of PVCs geometrically increases as you add each new service category.

Every time you add a new network location, you must meticulously plan the new PVC connections required. You have to load each circuit into your backbone switches or request the new connectivity from your carrier. After you have the new VPI/VCI numbering associated with the PVC endpoints, you must also load the information into your endpoint equipment. Each step takes considerable time and care and opens your network to easy human errors. SVCs can quickly become very handy if you have the job title of *network operator*.

Supports any-to-any connectivity

In very large networks, setting up all the PVCs necessary for every end-point to reach every other end-point isn't even possible. Just consider the implications if every person in the US had a logical connection to every other person in the US, ready and waiting just in case any two people meet some day and want to talk over the phone. Even establishing such functionality for your hometown is probably unreasonable (unless you're from one of those *really* small towns).

SVCs expand the reach of the ATM network. Any site connected on the network can communicate with any other site, as long as it has the correct address. Users don't have to wait for network operators to go through the time-consuming process of establishing a new PVC; their end equipment can instantly set up the direct connection through a signaling exchange. SVCs are commonly seen as the only practical way to set up connections between different organizations.

Such a capability probably sends shivers up the spine of all conscientious network managers, raising many security concerns in their minds. Public SVC offerings, therefore, must include capabilities to minimize security risks. As a fundamental capability, ATM networks always require end-user equipment to accept the call from the requesting device before establishing the connection — a beneficial but insufficient fix. SVC ATM services will probably mature to include many of the advanced feature offerings of voice-based virtual private networks (VPNs), including closed user groups, account code screening, and billing flexibility. This chapter has more on security if you keep reading (or skip ahead).

Conserves network bandwidth

Most switches reserve at least some bandwidth for each PVC established over any physical link. To ensure the guaranteed performance required from most service categories, the switch often reserves the amount of bandwidth needed in a worst-case scenario. Such a conservative approach may not really be necessary. Perhaps the connection only supports traffic once a month for a system back up or peak bursts occur only a few times a day. Nevertheless, the switches follow the rules of ATM programmed into their software and are ready for any rainy day.

A common switch algorithm for reserving bandwidth is known as *equivalent capacity*. Equivalent capacity takes all the bandwidth parameters (such as PCR, SCR, MBS, and MCR) of the requested connection and consolidates them into a single number, that is, an equivalent capacity. Equivalent capacity reserves the peak bandwidth for CBR connections. For a VBR connection, the reserved bandwidth depends on the vendor implementation but generally is nearly equal to the peak (remember the rainy-day preparedness of ATM networks). ABR connections need the minimum cell rate (MCR) reserved. UBR connections have no bandwidth reservations. Many switches do allow some oversubscription of the port — *oversubscription* exists where the sum of the bandwidths of the logical connections exceeds the actual physical throughput. (Refer to Chapter 9 for more information about bandwidth parameters.)

SVCs eliminate all the guesswork and tinkering required in PVC bandwidth reservations. On a call-by-call basis, the network switches determine whether they have sufficient capacity to support the requested connection. This process is known as *connection admission control* or CAC. The equivalent capacity or a similar algorithm provides the metrics for making this decision. However, unlike many PVCs, signaled connections reserving bandwidth are likely to use that bandwidth soon. After the user equipment finishes exchanging all traffic, the connection is released, and the bandwidth is available to establish another SVC (we are, of course, assuming that the user equipment is set up to release connections after a short, predetermined time-out period of no traffic). Also, all connections are direct so traffic does not have to pass back and forth through a central site further tying up bandwidth as is common with PVCs.

Thus, a network made up of SVCs probably has higher average utilization than a network of PVCs. If the network doesn't have sufficient capacity to fulfill an SVC request when the request comes in, it simply rejects the call. Determining the right amount of backbone bandwidth for an ATM network to maximize utilization while minimizing call blocking is a special blend of science and art that will differentiate the different switch vendors and service providers. As operators gain more experience in ATM networks, they will probably depend more and more on the science of the decision. Until then, building more backbone than necessary will be a common approach, because network managers know that rainy days always come.

Supports LAN and multiprotocols interoperability

Specifications defined by the ATM Forum to support interoperability with existing LAN and various internetworking protocols (IP, for example) depend heavily on SVCs. The LANE (LAN Emulation) and MPOA (Multiprotocol over ATM) specifications don't work without SVCs. LANE supports connectivity of ATM with LAN networks (such as Ethernet and Token Ring) at the MAC (Media Access Control) Layer (also known as Layer 2). MPOA enhances ATM's support of Layer 3 protocols. You can find out much more about these two specifications in the next chapter. These specifications are extremely important in enabling a smooth integration of ATM into existing networks, an absolute key to success for ATM. In the next chapter's discussions, you see how much these two specifications depend upon ATM SVCs.

Tracks call-by-call usage

SVCs enable network operators to gather detailed statistics on the usage of the network. This information can be very useful for sizing backbone links and other resources in the network. Good usage statistics help build the knowledge needed to base decisions about network design more on science than on art. Tracking the length and bandwidth of each call also enables the network operator to bill users only for the time that they use.

Many users claim that they *want* their operators to bill them only for what they use. Such an accounting approach is the standard for voice networks, where you pay on a per minute basis for each call. However, many data users have become very comfortable with receiving a flat rate bill. The most popular data services, private lines and frame relay, typically charge one monthly fee based on the subscribed bandwidth regardless of how much traffic the network circuits carry. Network managers appreciate receiving their very predictable bills, for which they can budget each year (voice bills are also generally very predictable, despite their metered rates, because voice traffic patterns are usually well understood). Seeing whether network managers really want the bandwidth-on-demand benefits (and payments) frequently touted as an advantage to SVCs will be interesting. Perhaps usage-based billing will become more important as bigger and bigger pipes become the conduit into the network.

Automates QoS setup

SVCs automate the determination of the QoS parameters for each call. This automation offers a welcomed relief for network managers who are currently struggling to determine the proper QoS settings for each one of their PVCs. No longer do network managers have to consider cryptic, secret, technical details such as SCR, CDVT, and CLR when setting up their service. All the service category and QoS stuff covered in Chapter 9 becomes transparent to the user. The switch just knows what to ask for from the network in each SVC setup based on the source and application.

Where the switch gets all this intelligence is a nontrivial detail for the vendors to figure out. You may want to ask your vendors about their game plan, including what programming you need to do for their switch. Today, most SVC implementations (excluding those few supporting voice traffic) just use the UBR service category, which has no associated QoS parameters. The current versions of LANE and MPOA that depend on SVCs cannot yet distinguish between service categories. Some time will pass before vendors really can deliver on the promised vision of users being able to setup calls whenever they need with the switches handling all the hard work of determining the proper QoS values.

It's for you!

To explain how SVCs work, we are first going to explore the operation of a well-known signaled network, the public switched telephone network (PSTN). When you want to place a telephone call, you pick up the handset. The network gives you a dial tone that tells you that it's ready to receive dialed digits. You dial in the digits, and then the originating switch establishes a path through the network by using internal routing tables.

If the call is using the public dial plan in North America, the switch (or an adjunct database) uses the first six digits (the area code and exchange) of the ten-digit number to determine the next switch in the connection chain (or perhaps the entire route, depending upon the type of database the network is using for call routing). If the caller is using a private dial plan or an 800/888 number, the switch first converts the dialed number to a ten-digit number associated with the specific area code, exchange, and extension of the terminating location (using its built-in knowledge of the incoming circuit and special network databases) before routing the call. The switch-to-switch routing process can be quite complicated, especially for long-distance calls passing though multiple switches and carriers. The last switch on the route alerts the called party by sending a ringing current over the connecting wire loop. The call is set up when the called party accepts the call by picking up the ringing handset. When the parties finish their conversation, they hang up, and the network quickly tears down the circuit that had carried the call.

The entire PSTN process can be broken into four basic steps:

- ✔ Call request
- ✔ Call routing
- ✔ Call accept
- ✔ Call teardown

ATM's signals

The ATM-signaled connection process can be broken into the same four basic steps as the PSTN process: call request, call routing, call accept, and call teardown. (We repeat the four steps in case you were sleeping a minute ago or you are using a funky, chaotic process to read the text, which caused you to miss the last sentence.)

The signaling protocols for ATM have to handle all the potential scenarios of a voice network, including *called party busy, network congestion* (a fast busy in the phone network), and *misdialed digits*. ATM gets to add even more possibilities to its list because of its unique characteristics, including service categories and flexible bandwidth.

A setup request for an ATM connection contains, at a minimum, the destination address, the requested category of service, and requested cell rate. The setup may also include specific QoS parameters associated with the service category. Recent signaling definitions also introduce the concept of negotiation. *Negotiation* enables a source to request alternative service parameters if the network is unable to meet the initial service request.

Because signaling only occurs between the end-user and the network, call routing is not a part of the signaling specifications. The signaling protocols only define the messages that are exchanged between the end-user and the network in order to manage different types of connections. The specifications optimistically assume that the network is able to handle the internal communication necessary to set up, manage, and tear down connections. Call routing is an exhaustive study in itself (remember the 365-page PNNI specification we mention in this chapter's opening). We cover call routing in the next major section.

Standard signals

The ATM Forum has developed three successive documents, UNI 3.0, 3.1 and 4.0 (4.0 is really a collection of documents) to describe the signaling exchange messages and procedures of ATM. These documents draw heavily from ITU recommendations that cover signaling in a B-ISDN (ATM) network. The ITU signaling version is known as Q.2931, and you're likely to hear reference to these specifications in any technical signaling discussion. In fact, you can't read the UNI signaling specifications without the ITU signaling specs because of the frequent references to Q.2931.

The differences in the UNIs are important, at least through 1997. UNI 3.0 signaling is not compatible with UNI 3.1. The ATM Forum completed its 3.0 spec before ITU competed its work, so the Forum guessed at the outcome of ITU's work. However, the Forum guessed wrong and had to revise the defined signaling to match ITU in the 3.1 version.

The most popular implementation in late 1996 was 3.0. Very few devices support both UNIs 3.0 and 3.1, making interoperability impossible when your vendors have each selected a different standard. Manufacturers are now focusing on moving as quickly as possible to UNI 4.0, which is becoming the common implementation for signaling. Signaling 4.0 is part of the Anchorage Accord, and the ATM Forum has promised that all future signaling versions (none are currently planned) will be backwards compatible with 4.0.

Let's make a call

The best place to begin explaining the details of how ATM works is to look at the exchanges required in a normal point-to-point call. The user and the network exchange all signaling messages across the UNI over a predefined connection: VPI=0, VCI=5. The messages contain a variety of information elements that are defined based on the message type. The signaling protocol runs on top of Service Specific Convergence Protocol (SSCOP). The SSCOP protocol guarantees message delivery through windowing and retransmission.

The message exchange required to connect a normal call is shown in Figure 10-1. We explain the different messages of this exchange in the sidebar, "Normal call exchange." The messages must traverse the network as quickly as possible to minimize delays from call setup. The result of the signaling exchange is the assignment of a series of linked VPI/VCIs to support the requested communication. The resulting connection is *duplex*.

Deviations from the typical call exchange can arise. Examples that require special message fields and/or messages include destination call reject, insufficient network resources, or an unknown address.

Who are you?

In the preceding discussion, we skip an important first step, before any call processing can begin — address assignment. All end devices on the ATM network must have a unique address to support SVCs. The ATM Forum has defined addressing schemes for both private and public networks.

Public network addressing includes support of 15-digit E.164 addresses, which are similar to the telephone numbers of the voice network. E.164 is the addressing defined for ISDN and B-ISDN by ITU. This addressing scheme enables interoperability between public ATM networks and the public switched telephone network (PSTN) and is a key requirement for any network manager hoping to provide off-net access from and to the corporate ATM network. Unique E.164 address assignment should come from a third party that has knowledge of all the assigned addresses of different carrier customers. Bellcore administers the current PSTN area code and exchange assignment in North America, with the local exchange provider assigning the remaining four digits. What organization may fill this role for ATM is unclear at this time.

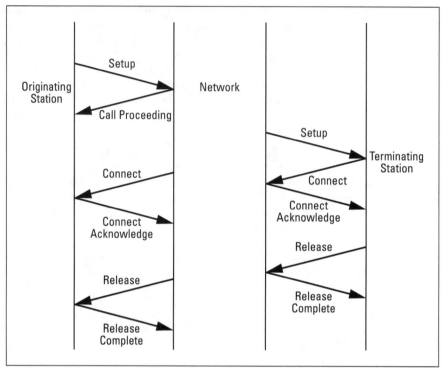

Figure 10-1:
A typical
ATM call
exchange.

Public networks may also choose to support the private addressing scheme that we define in the next few paragraphs. As the carriers roll out their ATM SVC services, they must determine the supported addressing in their offerings.

Because E.164 addresses are public and assignment may be difficult for private networks, the ATM Forum also defined special addressing for private networks. The Private ATM addresses are 20 bytes in length. The address form is modeled from OSI's Network Service Access Point and is, therefore, called *NSAP address-ing*. Despite the commonly used name, the ATM address is not an NSAP.

The definition of an NSAP address is based on both host switch information and end station identifiers. Thus, every end station's address includes its host routing information. The commonly used end station identifier part of the address is the end system MAC (Media Access Control) address; that is, the Layer 2 LAN address. MAC addresses are generally hardwired into adapters and other LAN equipment.

The signaling specifications actually define three acceptable addressing formats for private ATM networks. These formats vary by the address administration authority used. Each of the formats is very similar and has the same defined general fields. To comply with ATM Forum specifications, all private networks must be capable of supporting call setup with any of the following ATM address types:

MULTIPLICITY

Normal call exchange

The call exchange is made up of six messages, as shown in Figure 10-1. Here's a brief explanation of the messages:

✔ **Setup:** Sent by the source to the switch to initiate a connection.

✔ **Call Proceeding:** Sent from the originating switch to the source acknowledging the start of the process to establish a call. Also may be sent from the destination to the terminating switch.

✔ **Connect:** Sent by the destination to the terminating switch, passed through the network, and then from the originating switch to the source to accept the call.

✔ **Connect Acknowledge:** Sent by the source to the originating switch and then passed on from the terminating switch to the destination to complete the call setup process.

✔ **Release:** Sent by either the source or destination to terminate the call. The destination can also use the release message with proper error codes to reject a call during setup.

✔ **Release Complete:** Sent by the source, destination, or network switches to complete the call teardown process and acknowledge release of the network resources.

Other common messages include the following.

✔ **Status Inquiry:** Sent by the source, destination, or network switches at any time to request a status message regarding the connection.

✔ **Status:** Sent in response to a status inquiry message or at any time to report an error condition.

✔ **DCC Addressing:** DDC stands for Data Country Codes. The address administrator is the ISO National Member Body in each country.

✔ **ICD Addressing:** ICD stands for International Code Designator. The address administrator is the British Standards Institute. ICD codes identify particular international organizations.

✔ **E.164 Addressing:** Private networks may use an assigned E.164 address from a public service provider and identify local nodes by the lower order bits. This format is similar to large corporate locations receiving a thousand group (such as 624-6000), which can then be assigned to individual handsets within that location. The network knows to route all called numbers associated with the thousand group to the corporate PBX.

To ease network administration, the ATM Forum has defined a method for automated address registration in its ILMI (Interim Link Management Interface) specification. Any device joining the network immediately exchanges address information with its host switch to determine its complete ATM address.

All these different public and private addressing schemes provide flexibility, but they may cause confusion down the road. Network managers must determine the best approach for the private networks they manage. Carriers must determine what addressing schemes they want to support in their public switched offering and how they can accomplish address assignment. Difficulties will probably emerge when users on two previously segregated networks (such as two different regional ATM services) now want to communicate but are using different addressing schemes.

Reach out and touch everyone

ATM networks must also support the establishment of point-to-multipoint (typically shortened to just *multipoint*) connections — a more complicated process. UNI 3.0/3.1 addresses can only identify single endpoints, but Signaling 4.0 adds group addressing capabilities. Group addressing provides a much more efficient means to set up multipoint connections.

The originating point of a multipoint communication is known as the *root*. Receivers are called the *leaves* of the connection. UNI 3.0/3.1 supports the configuration of a multipoint connection only through incremental requests by the root to add each leaf. In 4.0, the root may initiate the connection with a group address that establishes the entire connection at once. 4.0 also includes procedures for a leaf to initiate its own connection to a multipoint conference. Such a utility is handy for end devices that want to join a videoconference or a distribution list.

Signaling 4.0 also includes *anycast addressing*. The anycast address is a well known address used to route a call to a node providing a particular service. An example is a LAN Emulation Configuration Server (LECs). The network routes calls to an anycast address to the nearest end station registered with the network to provide the specified service.

ATM Network Meetpoints

The ATM Forum has defined two meetpoints within the network. The first meetpoint is known as the Private Network-Network Interface (or Private Node-Node Interface, if you prefer). PNNI defines a protocol for interconnecting private switches and will probably be the preferred method for interconnecting switches within a single carrier network. The second meetpoint is known as the B-ISDN Inter-Carrier Interface (B-ICI). The B-ICI defines an interface for interconnecting different carrier networks. Figure 10-2 shows where these two interfaces may occur within the network.

Meeting points between switches

Upon receiving a signaling request, the network needs some way to establish the new connection. The ATM Forum's PNNI specification defines the methodologies for sharing routing information and establishing a connection with the requested QoS. ATM routing is similar to the routing used by routers in the Internet and corporate networks, with the added challenge of supporting multiple service categories.

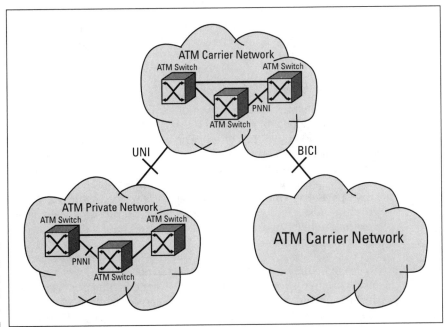

Figure 10-2:
ATM's network meetpoints.

PNNI consists of two protocols enabling call management by the ATM network:

- ✔ **A routing protocol** is defined for distributing network topology information between switches and groups of switches.
- ✔ **A signaling protocol** facilitates communication between the network switches to propagate UNI and other signaling messages throughout the network.

PNNI uses a distributed routing scheme based on the IETF's OSPF (Open Shortest Path First) protocol. This routing scheme is much more complex than any existing routing protocol and will take time before being fully implemented into ATM switching equipment. PNNI's structure supports phasing of the capabilities. Phased implementations will ease implementation and interoperability testing in existing ATM networks. Be sure to understand your vendor's PNNI implementation plans. Pay close attention to the new processing power needed at each step to maintain reasonable call setup times as networks grow larger and larger.

OSPF is a *link state* routing technology. Link state protocols employ a distributed map database model. Each switch describes its local environment and propagates this information throughout the network. In ATM, the information includes *reachability* and *QoS metrics* (measurements). Reachability information is basically the list of addresses accessible through a switch. QoS metrics include the bandwidth, guaranteed cell delay, jitter, and other performance options available for a new ATM connection. Each switch builds a local database describing the known network. The switch must frequently update its understanding as new traffic enters the network.

Organizing a network hierarchy

PNNI allows hierarchical organization of the network. Although introducing many complexities, hierarchical routing is necessary to build large networks (those with 1000 switches or so). The bottom of the hierarchy organizes switches into small groups known as *peer groups.* All the switches of a peer group have complete knowledge of each other's reachability and QoS metrics. The bottom peer group is analogous to a single area in the OSPF protocol. A single peer group may support a couple of hundred switches. The bottom groups represented by a single peer leader are then organized as groups at the next hierarchical level. The process continues until only one group exists at the top of the hierarchy.

To calculate the best path for a requested connection, the connection request must pass to the lowest level hierarchy that contains both the source and the destination address. Hierarchical routing scales because each switch only has to know how to route to destinations in its own local group. Be sure to note that hierarchical routing does not necessarily imply hierarchical switching. The objective of the routing process is to simply discover the best sequence of switches to submit the call request for establishing the requested connection.

The result of the PNNI routing process is a source route that lists the combination of ATM switches and links through which a particular connection can reach its destination. The originating switch inserts this information into a signaling request and forwards it through the network to the destination. The signaling messages for exchanging call management information among the network switches is also a part of PNNI. Of course, the information gathered by the routing information may not be perfect and completely up-to-date. The connection request may traverse a switch with no remaining resources to support the new connection. A process called crankback sends the message to the preceding node to try alternate rerouting.

We want to take a minute to remind you that this entire section is only in reference to the routing of signaling messages in the ATM network for call setup. The result of ATM call setup is an end-to-end connection following the switches and links identified by the routing process. All subsequent communication takes place over this connection as long as the source and destination have traffic to share (without requiring any additional routing). This process is significantly different from IP routing, in which each individual packet must bear the burden of finding its own route in the network (although various planned enhancements to IP allow establishment of flows which provide the same capabilities as connections — more on that in Chapter 11). Refer to the highway system analogy in Chapter 3. As part of this analogy, we describe getting instructions for finding your way from a gas station attendant (routing) versus following predefined structures like traffic circles (switching). (Did we take more than a minute?)

Setting up specifications for switching

Recognizing that PNNI would take time to both define and implement, the ATM Forum defined the IISP (Interim Inter-Switch Protocol) as an interim step in 1995. IISP allows interoperability of vendor switches through a standard routing functionality, but its capabilities are very limited. IISP only provides static routing and associated switch-to-switch signaling (based on a slight variant of the UNI 3.1 signaling specification). Switches cannot dynamically share routing information but must depend upon static routing tables loaded into their memories. Because the switches do not share real-time information, IISP cannot guarantee QoS for circuits.

For your sake, we're going to hope that you aren't implementing ATM networks of hundreds of switches requiring your having detailed knowledge of PNNI — so we end our explanation here. The PNNI documentation from the ATM Forum is actually somewhat understandable, especially the introductory descriptions of the routing and signaling protocols. If you need more information, we suggest you go straight to that source (the Forum's documentation, that is). If you're planning to deploy a very large network, you want to have this understanding.

The PNNI specification is just that, a specification that can flexibly support many different implementations. Your call management performance and acceptable network resource utilization level vary depending upon how well your vendor has implemented PNNI. Vendors still have a lot to learn about building fast, scalable ATM networks that can deliver on the promised quality of service of ATM. The small ATM networks supporting several hundred UNI's today are from the grand visions of mature ATM networks supporting multiple traditional services and thousands of native ATM customers.

Meeting points between carriers

The ATM Forum has defined the B-ISDN-InterCarrier Interface (B-ICI) to define the interface between two carriers. The initial versions of the B-ICI were very similar to the UNI providing PVC services with limited additional functionality. These versions of the B-ICI were never really developed or implemented. The few carrier-to-carrier connections in place today are primarily for testing and pilots. All such connections that we know of are based on the UNI specification. The B-ICI working group of the ATM Forum recently passed v2.0 to support SVCs and is now working on a 3.0 version to tackle PNNI aspects. Time will tell whether carriers have interest in interconnecting and what the preferred interface specification may be.

Security

Security is a relatively new area of interest for ATM vendors (although it has been a subject for ATM researchers for some time). All parties (except the most sensitive of organizations such as certain government departments and agencies) have few fears with the security in a private or PVC-based ATM network. Those more sensitive organizations, however, are only satisfied by security in their direct control. A few of these groups have purchased the proprietary ATM encrypters that are available on the market to interface their network access links.

However, the pending arrival of public SVC services raises security concerns for even the less paranoid among us. The ATM Forum has, therefore, established a new working group on security. The working group is exploring ways to add security to a signaled connection. The group hopes to develop a mechanism for negotiating the security requirements of the connection at call setup. This mechanism would support many different security services, algorithms, and key lengths to meet the variety of security implementations adopted by various organizations worldwide.

Network Management

As in any large network, network management is an absolutely essential support function of an ATM network. Network management provides network managers with a window into the operations and performance of their new ATM networks. Most ATM switches include a Simple Network Management Protocol (SNMP) interface for integration with other network management systems, although a few carrier-class switches come only with a proprietary interface to a proprietary management system (which, as you can imagine, lowers their popularity in the eyes of most carriers).

Management by vendor

Many vendors also provide the option to purchase a management system developed specifically for their switch. Such systems can offer many enhanced features that greatly improve the manageability of the network. These features include sophisticated GUIs (graphical user interfaces), point-and-click PVC configuration, and advanced LAN management (for ATM workgroup switches). The drawback to most (but not all) of these ATM management systems is that they provide visibility into only the ATM elements of the selected vendor and not the many other ATM and non-ATM pieces of equipment making up the network.

The tested standards

Now if you've faithfully read through the maze of new ATM terms, capabilities, and standards (and you may have other, more technical chapters to read yet), you may be curious about whether the ATM Forum has done anything to keep all these ATM elements straight. And indeed, the resourceful Forum (which you can read about in Appendix A) recognizes the need for having a way of testing all the varied, defined capabilities of ATM. In fact, the ATM Forum has established a special working group just for testing.

The Testing Working Group creates three different types of documents. Each testing document refers to a single standard created by the ATM Forum.

✔ **Conformance Test Suites:** Check that the tested equipment meets all the mandatory requirements of the written specification. A test suite includes many different test cases, each of which test a single requirement or option. Two conforming pieces of equipment have a high probability of interoperating.

✔ **Interoperability Test Suites:** Are similar to conformance test suites, but they test interoperability between two pieces of equipment. Interoperable equipment may or may not conform to the entire set of mandatory requirements in a specification.

✔ **Protocol Implementation Conformance Statements (PICS):** A checklist of all the requirements, conditional requirements, and options of a specification. A PICS performa provides questions to determine whether a vendor complies to the standard. Some customers are beginning to demand that their equipment providers respond to the PICS performa of a given specification.

The test suites are available in abstract or executable form. Abstract test suites are similar to uncompiled source code. Sometimes a single specification can result in more than one abstract test suite. As an example, any UNI specification has both a user and a network abstract. Test equipment vendors use the abstract form to create an executable test suite for their product.

Management by ATM model

To facilitate integration of the many potential elements in a large ATM network spanning from the LAN to the WAN and across private and public networks, the ATM Forum is defining a family of network management specifications. Defining these specifications is a long, tedious process requiring cooperation with other standards-setting organizations, including the Network Management Forum and the IETF (Internet Engineering Task Force).

Figure 10-3 shows the five defined interfaces of the ATM Network Management Model (we fully introduce these in Chapter 2, in case you've been skipping around). These interfaces cover the spectrum of the ATM networking environment, including the LAN and WAN as well as both public and private networks. The first versions of the M3 and M4 management interfaces from the Forum are now complete. Additional work to these and an initial M5 specification is underway as we write in late 1996.

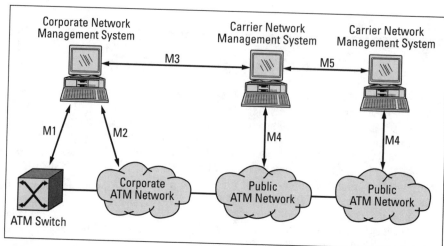

Figure 10-3:
ATM
Network
Management
Model.

The specifications include defined interface requirements and logical MIBs with primarily fault, performance, and configuration objects. The M3 interface is SNMP-based, while the M4 specifications include both SNMP and CMIP for carrier management.

To provide early functionality, the ATM Forum has also defined the Interim Link Management Interface (ILMI) as part of the UNI specifications (UNIs 2.0, 3.0, and 3.1 and ILMI 4.0). ILMI is a protocol for sharing management information between the user and the network based on a limited subset of SNMP capabilities. ILMI can automate the discovery of new interswitch connections and new users and supports the exchange of addressing information during switch initiation.

Management by cells

ATM network elements share management information over preassigned virtual channels through specifically defined Operations, Administration, and Maintenance (OAM) cells. Eventually, OAM cells will enable ATM network devices to gather end-to-end statistics, reducing the number of needed MIBs.

Two of the defined OAM cells are Alarm Indication Signal (AIS) cells and Far End Reporting Failure (FERF) cells. Network switches generate AIS cells to communicate failures of switches or virtual connections. FERF cells communicate failure of one-half of a full-duplex ATM connection. The Forum also defined a special OAM loopback cell, which is handy for testing new installation and troubleshooting the network.

Management by monitoring

Additionally, the ATM Forum is considering standards for ATM Monitoring (AMON) and Remote Monitoring (RMON). AMON supports duplication of a virtual ATM stream through a nonintrusive, real-time external monitoring device. RMON provides embedded probes in ATM equipment for capturing real-time information on the operation of the network.

That wraps up our discussion of ATM support functions. You're all set, at least until the next time someone has a great idea and adds more capabilities and makes a few changes. In the next chapter, we cover interoperability and adaptation. If you're curious about a few techniques for keeping track of all these capabilities, read our sidebar, "The tested standards."

Inside ATM with Martin Taylor
Vice President, Network Architecture
Madge Networks, Stoke Poges, England

Telephony Is the Real Killer ATM Application

While networked multimedia and video-conferencing get most of the headlines, the application that proves the superiority of ATM — the mythical *killer app* — is likely to be telephony: specifically, the integration of voice and data through a single desktop connection and over a single network infrastructure.

The frame-based LAN technologies that dominate today's networks — Ethernet, Token Ring, FDDI, linked with bridges, routers or switches — don't provide us today with a solution for voice integration. One reason for this is that these technologies treat all packets with the same priority. When voice packets are queued up behind bursts of file transfer data in the buffers of a congested router port, we can say good-bye to any hope of a toll-quality voice connection across the LAN. And even with the enhancements being proposed as new standards for Quality of Service in the LAN, such as priority tagging of Ethernet packets and the Resource ReSerVation Protocol (RSVP) which reserves bandwidth for multimedia IP streams, it isn't obvious that we are going to be able to meet the exacting standards for quality and end-to-end delay set by existing PBX-based voice solutions.

But ATM excels at exactly what telephony requires: delivering the real-time response and bandwidth-on-demand necessary for running telephony-quality voice transmissions. ATM excels, too, at providing the right blend of scalability, resilience and performance needed to meet growing data traffic loads for intranet Web access, client/server transaction processing and workflow applications. So as large organizations move to address the question of bringing together voice and data networks, they inevitably start off down the path to ATM.

Today's desktops have separate connections for PCs and phones. However solutions will soon be available to deliver telephone-quality voice over the LAN, and leverage the processing power of the desktop PC to help with the process of placing and receiving phone calls. In these solutions the PC has become the phone — and the LAN has become the PBX. We can choose to retain the phone handset as our physical interface for telephony, but it now connects to the PC as just another peripheral device, alongside the keyboard and the mouse.

(continued)

Of course, it would be somewhat rash — and probably career-threatening—to simply dump the PBX without putting an equally reliable system in its place. The PBX has been among the most bullet-proof pieces of communications hardware for decades. But in an era of severe cost control and directives to economize, MIS and telecom managers are finding it increasingly difficult to justify the price of buying, installing and maintaining separate and incompatible information systems: one for the computer and another for the telephone. And the reliability issue is fading fast: today's switched LANs are built for fault tolerance and reflect the up-time rates of the most trustworthy mainframes and PBXs. For example, you can deploy ATM in a redundant mesh of interconnected switches that renders the failure of any one device undetectable to users.

But before putting all our electronic eggs in a single basket, careful attention must be paid to building an infrastructure capable of supporting the very different demands of data and real-time voice traffic. This means creating a true multiservice architecture.

And that's where an ATM network demonstrates its unique advantages. ATM is designed to accommodate markedly different kinds of network traffic, while assigning each the bandwidth and quality of service needed for optimum efficiency. Data networking protocols such as TCP/IP are quite tolerant of network delay, and users would not notice if the network took, say, 200 milliseconds to get a data packet from server to client. *So ATM delivers data traffic as fast as it can, but with no guarantees about end-to-end delay.* On the other hand, a telephone conversation suffers substantially from a 200 millisecond delay, as anyone who's experienced the annoying satellite bounce on international calls can attest. Therefore, ATM assigns priority to voice transmissions and guarantees their end-to-end delivery within the time required to conduct a coherent conversation.

But there's more to the PBX than simple telephony switching. The PBX also adds a sophisticated array of call control functions that the multiservice, ATM-based network must replicate or exceed. These include routing unanswered calls to voice mail or to a secondary contact; assigning security policies to control

unauthorized use of the phone system; transferring or diverting calls; and adding or dropping parties from conference calls.

Some of the call control functions we need can be implemented in the desktop PC, which is now acting as an intelligent phone. But many of the features provided by PBXs need centralized configuration and control — such as directory services, pick-up groups, call-barring policies and so on. The intelligence needed to support these can be housed in a "call control server" PC connected to the ATM backbone. Each telephony client PC takes its orders from the call control server. In effect, we have now reinvented telephony as a client/server application on the LAN.

All of this is well and good as long as we're talking about in-house telephony needs, but what about using PCs on ATM networks to connect calls with the outside world, a place where ATM will be the exception rather than the rule for some time to come? Here we are going to need some kind of gateway that links our voice-enabled ATM LAN to conventional phone systems — the public phone networks, and any existing PBX systems that may be in place.

A voice/LAN gateway can convert the 64 kilobits/second digital streams that carry voice in the public networks and in PBXs into cell streams that traverse the ATM network. Not only that, the gateway can provide a link between the conventional phone systems and the call control server for the telephony signaling protocols that manage the set-up and tear-down of voice connections. From the viewpoint of the public phone network, the combination of the voice/LAN gateway, the call control server, the PC phones and the ATM LAN that connects them all together looks just like a conventional PBX. In reality of course, what we have done is to create a virtual PBX.

As with any new kind of networking solution, standards are an issue when we are considering voice over ATM. And because this is a very new area of technology, not all the pieces are in place. The ATM Forum is developing a set of standards under the heading of "Voice Telephony Over ATM" which describe both the trunking of voice connections in the WAN and the use of ATM to bring voice to the desktop. But VTOA is not yet focused on the delivery of a full range of call control functions which would enable the ATM network to match the PBX for features. This part of the problem is most likely to be addressed by other bodies which have an interest in computer telephony, such as the Enterprise Computer Telephony Forum. Inevitably the early running is going to be made with proprietary solutions, with the advantage that the experience gained by vendors deploying those solutions can be harnessed to create practical and well-considered standards in the future.

So, in the space of a few hundred words, we've challenged conventional thinking about the separate-but-equal status of voice and data communications. We've created the possibility of a single wire to the desktop carrying both voice and data communications, and a network-based voice switching function which does not rely on a PBX. We've given phone users a graphical user interface to telephony services. We've also opened up the world of voice to server-based call routing and voice processing, bringing a whole new meaning to the phrase Computer Telephony Integration. And we're doing all this on an ATM LAN which also just happens to provide the most powerful possible solution to all our local data networking needs.

And, of course, you're thinking that it's just not that easy. There's a long way to go before ATM supplants conventional voice and data networks. Investment in legacy equipment is substantial, ATM costs a lot of money and nobody's willing to take that kind of financial hit.

But ATM-based solutions for telephony to the desktop will certainly find their place in new installations or network expansions, particularly where tight integration between voice and data is a must — such as in call centers, sales offices, telemarketing operations and help desks. And where ATM is being considered alongside alternative technologies as a scalable, high performance, fault tolerant solution for data networking, the knowledge that ATM can also be used to deliver a low cost, high functionality solution for telephony to the desktop may well be the factor that tips the balance in its favor.

Chapter 11

Playing Nicely with the Other Kids: ATM's Interoperability Functions

. . . .

In This Chapter

▶ Interoperating with existing wide area protocols

▶ Working within internetworks

▶ Operating with existing LANs

▶ Using ATM with existing voice and video traffic

. . . .

*P*rivate organizations and carriers have spent hundreds of billions of dollars building their existing networks (just check out the net worth of some of the largest vendors of networking equipment for a glimpse of the big money in this industry). No new technology can be successful unless network managers can integrate it easily into their current networks. Furthermore, network managers typically demand interoperability based on standards. Standards-based solutions enable these managers to mix and match vendors as their networks grow and change (somewhat randomly) in the different areas of their businesses.

Since its infancy, the ATM industry has well understood the requirement for solutions based on standards. The result has been a multitude of specifications developed for interoperability with a wide variety of the most popular networking protocols. Because vendors target ATM solutions for both the LAN and WAN, the industry has defined interoperability specifications for both domains, piling on the number of new terms and protocols you need to understand if you implement ATM. In a few situations, you have more than one specification to choose from. The best specification choice for you depends on your current and future networking environment, as well as your applications.

We close out Part II of our book — the part that really dives into the ATM technology — with this chapter on the most popular interoperability protocols. We tell you how each protocol works, where to use it in your network, and when to choose one option over another. We also discuss a few new interoperability protocols under development in the various industry standards organizations.

We try to give you just the key points and not drag you into all the details associated with the myriad of standards and specifications used in ATM networks. We stick to the aspects of the standardization work that we don't expect to change much as ATM matures. If you need to know the details, your best source is probably the standards themselves. In any case, we hope that the glimpse into ATM interoperability is helpful and understandable — at least it should be helpful in getting you to sleep a couple of nights.

Acronyms Used in This Chapter

Acronym	What It Stands For
AAL1	ATM Adaptation Layer 1
AAL5	ATM Adaptation Layer 5
ABR	Available Bit Rate
ARP	Address Resolution Protocol
BUS	Broadcast and Unknown Server
CBR	Constant Bit Rate
CLP	Cell Loss Priority
DE	Discard Eligible
DLCI	Data Link Connection Indicator
DSU	Data Service Unit
FDDI	Fiber Distributed Data Interface
FECN	Forward Explicit Congestion Notification
FRF	Frame Relay Forum
FTP	File Transfer Protocol
FUNI	Frame User Network Interface
IETF	Internet Engineering Task Force
IP	Internet Protocol
IPX	Internetwork Packet eXchange
ITU	International Telecommunications Union
LAN	Local Area Network
LANE	LAN Emulation
LECS	LAN Emulation Configuration Server
LES	LAN Emulation Server
LIS	Logical IP Subnet

Acronym	What It Stands For
LLC/SNAP	Logical Link Control/Sub-Network Access Protocol
LNNI (LENNI)	LAN Emulation Network-Network Interface
MPEG	Motion Picture Experts Group
MPOA	Multiprotocol Over ATM
NHRP	Next Hop Resolution Protocol
NLPID/SNAP	Network Layer Protocol Identifier/SubNetwork Access Protocol
OAM	Operations Administration and Maintenance
PT	Payload Type
PVC	Permanent Virtual Circuit
RFC	Request For Comment
SMDS	Switched Multi-Megabit Data Services
SNMP	Simple Network Management Protocol
SS7	Signaling System 7
SVC	Switched Virtual Circuit
TDM	Time Division Multiplexing
UBR	Unspecified Bit Rate
UNI	User-Network Interface
VBR	Variable Bit Rate
VBR-RT	Variable Bit Rate–Real-Time
VC	Virtual Circuit
VLAN	Virtual LAN
VPI/VCI	Virtual Path Identifier/Virtual Channel Identifier
VPN	Virtual Private Network
VTOA	Voice and Telephony Over ATM

Emulating a Circuit

The ATM Forum's Circuit Emulation standard provides the specification for interworking ATM and TDM circuits such as private lines. Circuit emulation doesn't provide compression or conversion of the TDM circuit. The standard simply outlines how to encapsulate a TDM circuit into ATM cells by using AAL1 adaptation. (You can find out about ATM adaptaion in Chapter 8.)

Circuit emulation results in a constant stream of bandwidth that's slightly greater than the adapted TDM stream (keep in mind that AAL1 and ATM's cells add approximately 6 bytes for every 47 bytes of information). A 1.5 Mbps T1 circuit actually requires 1.7 Mbps of ATM bandwidth. Circuit emulation continually encapsulates the incoming TDM stream, regardless of whether the stream is actively carrying traffic.

Circuit emulation is available in structured or unstructured forms. *Structured circuit emulation* preserves the individual channels of the TDM stream (such as DS0s in a T1). Depending on the implementation, the network may be able to deliver each of the channels to different destinations on the ATM network. Structured circuit emulation also supports transport of fractional T1 (or T3) channels. *Unstructured circuit emulation* doesn't preserve the individual channels, and the network delivers the entire emulated stream to a single destination.

Circuit emulation provides the migration step for private lines and an interim step for voice, which will ultimately use the Voice and Telephony Over ATM (VTOA) standards from the ATM Forum. Transporting voice traffic using circuit emulation is not very efficient, especially when no calls are active. The ATM Forum is developing a more efficient method for adapting voice into ATM in its VTOA specification. You can find out more about VTOA later in this chapter.

Most vendors currently support T1 circuit emulation with a few T3 solutions expected in the next year. Figure 11-1 shows a common configuration for private line interworking. With circuit emulation, you can preserve the existing private line even after adopting ATM at one of the endpoints.

The ATM network terminates the non-ATM site with its existing TDM equipment and access circuit. Thus, the non-ATM site requires no change in customer equipment or access. The ATM network provides adaptation of the TDM circuit for transport to the new ATM location. Typically, the network carries the emulated circuit by using the CBR service category. The ATM site converts the emulated circuit back to TDM by using an ATM access multiplexer or other device. The legacy T1 multiplexer then terminates the TDM circuit delivered from the ATM Mux.

Circuit emulation enables network managers to use ATM where its use makes sense without having to change the entire network. Customer circuits carrying legacy protocols (for example, X.25 or bysinc) can continue to use a TDM infrastructure, reducing the amount of change required in the ATM adoption. Over time, network managers can retire these circuits or terminate them directly into the ATM equipment, eliminating the need for the emulated circuit.

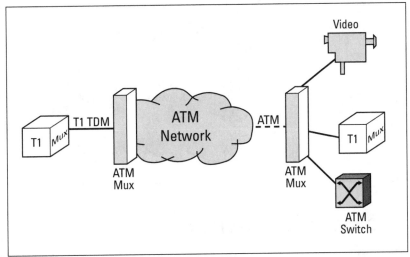

Figure 11-1:
Private line
interworking.

Interworking with Frame Relay

The Frame Relay Forum has defined the specifications for interworking frame relay and ATM in its FRF.5 and FRF.8 standards. The ATM Forum has endorsed these specifications. FRF.5 specifies network interworking; FRF.8 specifies service interworking.

Network interworking

Network interworking simply provides a standard way for an ATM network to carry frame relay PVCs. (Future standardization efforts will focus on interworking for SVCs.) Network interworking lets frame relay connections be transported through an ATM backbone, as shown in Figure 11-2. This movement is sometimes called *tunneling of the native protocol.* The ATM backbone is simply replacing the traditional TDM circuits that were used between the frame relay switches. The network interworking functions can take place in either the frame relay or ATM switches, depending upon the network's design. Each frame relay PVC may map to a single ATM PVC, or all the frame relay PVCs can be multiplexed onto one ATM PVC. The standard specifies AAL5 as the adaptation layer type. (You can find out about ATM adaptation in Chapter 8.)

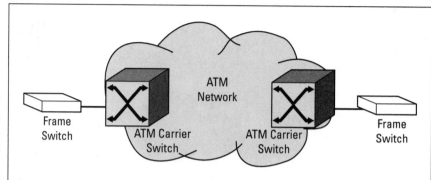

Figure 11-2:
Frame relay
network
interworking.

Service interworking

Service interworking supports communication between an ATM device and a frame relay device using PVCs. (Standardization of interworking for SVCs is in the future.) Service interworking provides conversion between the ATM and frame relay protocols. It eases a migration to ATM by allowing a staggered adoption of ATM in new sites as needed. Neither the ATM or frame relay sites recognize that they are communicating with a far end using a different technology. Figure 11-3 shows a typical configuration for frame relay to ATM service interworking.

The router at the frame relay site sends frames over a RS-449 or V.35 physical interface to a standard DSU (Data Service Unit). The DSU site transmits traffic to the frame relay network over a physical WAN interface (such as DS0 or T1). Service interworking between the frame relay and ATM networks maps the frame relay PVC to an ATM PVC using AAL5. Service interworking only provides for a one-to-one mapping. Conversion functions provided by service interworking include the following:

- ✔ Mapping the frame relay Data Link Connection Indicator (DLCI) address to the ATM VPI/VCI address.

- ✔ Mapping the discard eligible (DE) bit of frame relay to the cell loss priority (CLP) bit of ATM.

- ✔ Mapping the frame relay forward explicit congestion notification (FECN) bit to ATM's payload type (PT) indicator bit.

- ✔ Converting frame relay PVC status signaling to ATM operations administration and maintenance (OAM) cells. This conversion enables users to find out about failures on the other network.

- ✔ Converting frame relay's multiprotocol encapsulation procedures (RFC 1490 defined NLPID/SNAP [network layer protocol identifier/sub-network access protocol]) to ATM's multiprotocol encapsulation procedures (RFC 1483 defined LLC/SNAP). The procedures aren't identical, so conversion

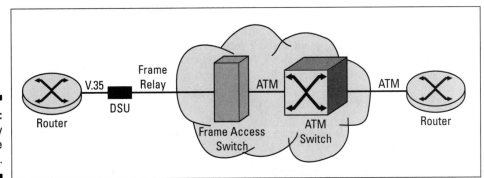

Figure 11-3:
Frame relay
service
interworking.

between the two procedures is necessary. When the service interworking function provides the conversion, it is said to be *operating in translation mode*. In older implementations of ATM equipment using DXI (Data Exchange Interface), before RFC 1483 was defined, routers used RFC 1490. In these configurations, conversion wasn't necessary, and the service interworking function was said to operate in *transparent mode*.

At the ATM site, the traffic terminates in a router with a direct ATM interface. The router is unaware that it is actually communicating with a remote router using the frame relay protocol.

Working at Lower Speeds: FUNI

FUNI (Frame User Network Interface) is actually an ATM protocol defined by the ATM Forum. It provides frame-based access to ATM networks by using the same frame structure as frame relay (and ATM DXI). However, all the management and control functions are the same as cell-based interfaces to ATM networks. FUNI also uses ATM's RFC 1483 for encapsulation of higher layer protocols. The purpose of FUNI is to provide a more efficient access method for lower speeds such as T1 and fractional T1. FUNI gains this efficiency by exploiting the lower overhead of frames (as compared to cells).

FUNI's developers chose the frame relay format to simplify implementation. The only difference in the two formats are a few of the bits in the header fields. Also, similarly to frame relay, FUNI specifies the AAL5 adaptation type to map its frames into ATM cells. FUNI requires software in both the user equipment and the ATM network. The ATM network is responsible for mapping the logical frame address of FUNI into an ATM VPI/VCI address.

FUNI's similarity to frame relay has enabled many vendors to implement FUNI on the frame relay cards in routers and the frame relay service interworking cards in ATM switches. FUNI is just an alternative protocol option of the cards, so adopting FUNI can be very cost-effective.

Despite being a defined standard since early 1995, FUNI has not yet been widely implemented. The popularity of frame relay has slowed the rollout of FUNI in most equipment and carrier services. For today's implementations, most network managers see frame relay to ATM service interworking as the preferred method of integrating lower speed sites into an ATM network.

FUNI has its technical merits:

- ✔ FUNI *is* ATM, except that frames replace cells in the user-to-network interface.
- ✔ ATM's signaling and VBR service categories are readily extendible to FUNI sites.

Using a common signaling protocol and service definition in both frame-based and cell-based connections into the wide area network makes good sense, except for the overwhelming fact that frame relay has gained widespread deployment in customer networks.

The migration from frame relay to FUNI can be fairly simple for the user, requiring only a change in the selected software option and, of course, an understanding of ATM networking. However, the merits of shared signaling and service category support with ATM may not be sufficient to drive a conversion. Furthermore, the Frame Relay Forum is also working on a frame relay to ATM service interworking standard that also supports these functions. So the fate of FUNI remains in question.

IP and Its Siblings

Transport of the Internet Protocol (IP) has been the primary focus of ATM implementations thus far. Ninety percent of the traffic on existing ATM networks is IP. The early IP over ATM implementations use RFC 1483 for encapsulation of packets, and RFC 1577 defines a method for address resolution between IP and ATM addresses.

LANE (LAN Emulation) is now another available option defined by the ATM Forum. LANE, which supports interoperability between ATM and legacy LANs such as Ethernet, presents an alternative to the IETF RFCs.

Various players in the industry have presented several different future alternatives for increasing the efficiency of carrying IP over ATM. These options include MPOA (Multiprotocol Over ATM), IP switching, and tag switching, with each alternative reflecting the perspective of its advocate organizations. MPOA is from the ATM Forum; IP switching and tag switching are from equipment vendors who are each vying for its solution to become accepted RFCs of the IETF. We provide information on MPOA in this chapter and tell you a little bit about IP switching and tag switching in Chapter 23.

The best IP over ATM solution depends on your networking environment, applications, and the outcome of the battles taking place in the standards organizations. In this section, we provide you with background on these different technologies including their advantages and disadvantages. We begin with the standards from the IETF and then move to standards from the ATM Forum.

IETF standards

In the following sections, we introduce the applicable interoperability specifications from the Internet Engineering Task Force (IETF): RFC 1483 and RFC 1577.

RFC 1483

RFC 1483 actually outlines methods for multiprotocol encapsulation, not just IP packets, over ATM. The title of RFC 1483 is *Multiprotocol Encapsulation over ATM Adaptation Layer 5*. The title tells you just about all you need to know. RFC 1483 is essentially the encapsulation method used by all the specifications defining interoperability between ATM and other internetworking protocols (that is, RFC 1577, LANE, and MPOA).

RFC 1483 includes two multiplexing methods for carrying multiple packet types on the same connection. The protocol prefixes each packet with a multiplexing field to identify the packet type and application and then adds the appropriate AAL5 trailer.

- **LLC/SNAP** (Logical Link Control/Sub-Network Access Protocol) encapsulation is the multiplexing method most commonly implemented. LLC/SNAP enables a single connection to support multiple packet types.

- **VC multiplexing** is the second method. In VC multiplexing, the ATM connection carries only a single protocol. The packets, therefore, don't need to carry a multiplexing or packet type field, although the encapsulated packet may need a pad field. The VC multiplexing option isn't currently supported in the frame relay to ATM service interworking specifications (although you read more about it in the LANE section).

RFC 1577

RFC 1577 is titled *Classical IP and ARP Over ATM;* it provides a way to carry IP directly over ATM within a single logical IP subnet (LIS). (A *subnet* is an IP network that can be reached through a single IP address.) However, because ATM uses connections for communication, a single ATM end station can actually be a member of several different subnets spread across the network.

Connections between end users on different subnets must pass through a router; this is true even if physical ATM connectivity is available between the two locations. The router may connect to the ATM network through a single physical interface. This configuration is known as a *one-armed router*. Traffic requiring routing services must pass in and then out of this router before proceeding to its destination. MPOA provides an alternative configuration to the one-armed router and moves beyond classical IP, which requires all traffic leaving a subnet to pass through a router.

RFC 1577 is necessary to determine the ATM addresses of other routing devices. If the network is using PVCs, the addressing information is manually loaded into the ATM end station or router as a VPI/VCI value — a management nightmare for rapidly changing and growing networks. If the network is using SVCs, RFC 1577 defines an ARP (Address Resolution Protocol) mechanism to automate the discovery of ATM end device addresses.

RFC 1577 uses the LLC/SNAP encapsulation defined by RFC 1483 for carrying the IP packets over ATM. It adds to this functionality by providing mechanisms to map IP addresses into ATM addresses. If the ATM network uses SVCs, RFC 1577 also includes conventions for when to set up and tear down virtual connections and automated address resolution (that is, determing the address of an end device) through ARP.

An ATM *ARP server* is a resource within each LIS that maintains a database for mapping IP address to ATM addresses. End stations query the ARP server to determine needed ATM addresses, and the server frequently updates its databases through registration packets from the ATM end stations. After an ATM end stations receives the appropriate ATM address from the ARP server, it establishes an SVC to the destination indicated by this address.

If you have an IP only environment, you can consider implementing RFC 1577. Its advantages include the following:

- ✔ It may offer better performance for IP traffic
- ✔ It is better suited to PVC implementations
- ✔ It may offer easier implementation for IP-fluent network managers

RFC 1577 also has certain limitations:

- ✔ It does not include multicast traffic. An IETF working group is now developing a proposal for a *multicast address resolution server (MARS)* to provide this functionality. MARS will resolve IP addresses to a single ATM point-to-multipoint address that reaches an entire group of users.
- ✔ It can carry only IP and not the other popular internetworking protocols (like IPX and Appletalk) used in many corporate networks. Multiprotocol environments require implementation of LANE or in the future, MPOA.

A trip down ATM LANE

LAN Emulation (LANE) provides interoperability between devices on ATM LANs and traditional LANs (Ethernet and token ring) and also supports configurations connecting traditional LANs over an ATM backbone. Because LANE provides interoperability of LANs (that is, at layer 2 of the network), it enables interoperability between any higher networking layer (such as IP, IPX, or DECnet) that uses the services of the LANs. LANE is therefore an alternative to RFC 1577 for providing interoperability between IP and ATM.

LANE's existence allows you to introduce ATM into your local networking environment wherever it makes sense while still providing interoperability with the significant base of existing LAN users. With LAN Emulation, network managers can introduce ATM into their networks without modifying existing LAN equipment, networking protocols and operating systems, computing devices, and applications. The backbone ATM network appears as a traditional Ethernet or token ring LAN to these entities.

LANE does not support connectivity between two unlike traditional LANs; that is, it cannot support communication between a token ring and an Ethernet LAN. Ethernet users can communicate with only ATM users or other Ethernet users over the ATM network. The same holds true for token ring users who can communicate only with users on a token ring or ATM LAN network.

The broadcast environment of traditional LANs sharply contrasts with the connection environment of ATM. Higher layer networking protocols (like IP and IPX) running over traditional LANs leverage the broadcast capability of the LAN to perform many functions including address resolution (determining the address of an end device) and multicast (sending the same packet to a group of users, such as an e-mail group address). To overcome the inherent differences between ATM and traditional LANs, interoperability must support the following functions:

- Mapping between ATM and LAN addresses
- Discovering unknown addresses
- Broadcasting of packets
- Welcoming new users to the network

In an emulated ATM LAN, the end devices connected to the ATM network are known as the clients. *LANE clients* are either ATM end stations or proxies representing traditional LAN end stations on the ATM network. The proxies may be routers, LAN switches, or other ATM devices that connect traditional LAN users to the ATM network. Proxies pass packets between the attached traditional LANs and the ATM network in both directions; this process is known as *bridging*.

The needs of the LANE clients using the ATM network are met by the *LAN emulation services*. Communication between the LANE clients and the LAN emulation services occurs over the LANE Emulation User Network Interface (LUNI).

The LANE specification breaks the LAN emulation services into three different server functions:

- **LAN Emulation Server (LES):** Provides the address discovery and mapping function identified in the first two bullets above.

- **Broadcast and Unknown Server (BUS):** Provides broadcast of broadcast packets and packets for which the LES has not yet determined the destination address; the function required in bullet three above. LANE's developers viewed centralized distribution of these packets by the BUS as much more efficient than individual point-to-multipoint circuits from each client to all other clients. However, if a LANE is not well implemented, the BUS can become a bottleneck in the network.

- **LAN Emulation Configuration Server (LECS):** Provides the welcoming function identified in the last bullet above. Whenever a client first joins the network, a LECS dynamically assigns it to an emulated LAN on the network. Network managers can create various rules for this assignment based on physical addresses or some logical association as supported in each particular vendor's implementation.

The specific implementation of each server is vendor dependent, and you can find servers in stand-alone devices such as a workstation, or in networking devices such as routers or ATM switches.

To communicate with other clients or the LANE servers, a client sets up an SVC (switched virtual circuit) using UNI 3.0 signaling to define a UBR (unspecified bit rate) connection. Clients can cache (that is store) ATM/MAC address pairs associated with frequently contacted clients (the MAC address is simply the address used by the traditional LAN network; for more information on how traditional LANs work, flip to Chapter 13). If an ATM/MAC address pair is not in the client's memory, it must depend on the services of the LES to discover the desired address.

In addition to providing interoperability between LANs, an important benefit of LANE is the configuration of virtual LANs also sometimes called emulated LANs. A *virtual LAN* is a LAN defined logically instead of physically. Traditional LANs provide communication between physically attached end stations, regardless of whether these stations need to frequently communicate with each other. Alternatively, a virtual LAN provides communications between end users that are logically grouped because of a shared interest.

Consider this example of a logical grouping. Because of space limitations, your company may have to locate eight new members of the accounting department on a floor apart from all other accountants. (Maybe these new members got stuck with the lawyers, or worse yet, with the executives of the firm.) Traditional LANs require that the new accounting employees join the LAN used by the other employees on the floor, even if the accounting employees have little need to communicate with these other users. Using a virtual LAN avoids this problem by allowing network managers to logically define LANs regardless of end user location. If the company has implemented virtual LAN networking technology, the new accounting members can join the virtual LAN shared by all the other members of the accounting department. Chapter 13 gives you additional information about virtual LANs.

Other benefits of using virtual LANs include the following:

- ✔ Grouping LAN users logically instead of physically reduces the amount of LAN traffic because users receive broadcast messages only from other users with shared interests.

- ✔ Using virtual LANs creates secure workgroups among users that frequently communicate with each other.

- ✔ LANE simplifies physical moves, adds, and changes on the network. If an employee changes desks, he or she can still belong to the same LAN group, eliminating the need for the network manager to completely reconfigure the network and update addressing tables to accommodate the change.

- ✔ Joining an ATM end device to multiple VLANs for different applications gives the network additional flexibility.

Network managers typically define more than one virtual LAN on a single ATM physical network. Clients are assigned to virtual LANs based on the LES that they use. Only those clients assigned to the same LES (and belonging to the same virtual LAN) can learn about each other and can communicate directly over the ATM network. Traffic destined to devices outside of the virtual LAN must pass through a router. The router provides the needed addressing and route information to reach the desired device. MPOA (multiprotocol over ATM) is an alternative for supporting communications between virtual LANs or other defined subnets.

Since LANE implementations have become available, most users are choosing this approach over RFC 1577 to support interoperability between IP and ATM in the local network. LANE offers the following benefits over 1577:

- ✔ Support for all higher networking layer protocols

- ✔ Support for multicast communication

- ✔ Easier network management

- ✔ Foundation for a move towards MPOA

- ✔ Provision of virtual LAN services.

MPOA

MPOA (multiprotocol over ATM) allows end devices attached to an ATM network to communicate directly with each other instead of through a router, even when the end devices are on two different subnets. Such communication is sometimes called *cut-through routing*.

Standards for a walk down the LANE

The ATM Forum approved LANE version 1.0 in 1995. This version provides specifications for the interface between the client and servers but does not address communication between servers. The second version of LANE is now under development to standardize these communications, too, and to support server redundancy. (Communications between the different servers will occur over the LAN Emulation Network-Network Interface, LNNI, also known as LENNI.)

Until the approval of the second version of LANE, customers must buy all LAN emulation service functions from a single vendor. The interoperability of clients as specified in version 1.0 has been proven through various testing labs and customer implementations. Other enhancements planned for LANE include upgrading to UNI 4.0 signaling, support of multiple qualities of service, and improved handling of heavy broadcast traffic (such as that required for desktop videoconferencing).

MPOA adds to the capabilities of LANE (LAN Emulation) by supporting direct communication between ATM devices located on separate virtual LANs. The benefits of MPOA include shorter network delays and reduced processing load in the routers of the network. The ATM Forum expects to complete the MPOA specification in early 1997, and vendor implementations will probably arrive 6 to 12 months later. Questions still abound as to the ease of implementation and price of MPOA because of its dependence on switched virtual connections (SVCs). Time will tell if these concerns are valid.

We'd like to use an example to illustrate the benefits of MPOA. Suppose that you have a workgroup with certain remote members, for example, eight persons from the accounting department located on the legal floor. The eight people in the accounting work group are members of the accounting department virtual LAN. Perhaps one of the accountants is working with a corporate tax lawyer located across the aisle and needs to communicate electronically with the lawyer. The communication process goes like this:

> **Without MPOA,** the accountant's messages must travel to the LAN switch serving the small accounting group, to the router serving the accounting virtual LAN, to the router serving the legal department LAN, to the LAN switch serving the legal group.

> **With MPOA,** the accounting LAN switch knows that it can send the message directly from the accounting LAN switch to the legal LAN switch over the ATM backbone without passing through all the intermediary routing equipment.

This example shows that if MPOA standards are implemented by vendors, they can extend the life of existing routing equipment by off-loading some traffic and routing functions to lower-cost LAN switches. MPOA defines three functions within the network:

- ✔ **Hosts:** End devices directly attached to the ATM network.

- ✔ **Edge devices:** ATM end devices representing end stations that use traditional LANs. An example is a LAN switch. The edge device is responsible for forwarding (that is, sending) the user information into the ATM network.

- ✔ **Route servers:** Servers providing address resolution (discovering the proper ATM address) and multicast support to the hosts and edge devices. Route servers provide this functionality for destinations outside of the virtual LAN (or other subnet) and are therefore sometimes said to support layer 3 networking.

MPOA splits the traditional role of the router into two roles by off-loading packet forwarding from the router to the hosts and edge devices. The ability to separate packet forwarding from other router functions allows a more flexible implementation of the two components. Enabling packet forwarding in a separate device from the router is known as *cut-through routing*, a distinguishing characteristic of MPOA. The sidebar, "Cutting through the routing tape," tells you more about this process.

Looking at Video Traffic

The ATM Forum and other groups are busy defining standards for transporting video traffic over an ATM network. The working group focusing on video transport over ATM within the ATM Forum is known as the Service Aspects and Applications (SAA) group. Much work is ongoing to determine the best AALs

Cutting through the routing tape

Cut-through routing is possible in MPOA by using a newly defined protocol from the IETF called *next hop resolution protocol (NHRP)*. NHRP was defined specifically for nonbroadcast networks, which allow many users to directly attach to the network. ATM, frame relay, and X.25 are all examples of this type of network. NHRP defines methods for routers to communicate among each other to determine unknown IP-to-ATM address mappings regardless of the IP subnet of the end devices.

Edge devices and hosts discover the ATM address associated with an IP destination by sending a NHRP (next hop resolution protocol) query to their router server. The router servers also use NHRP to communicate among themselves. After learning the appropriate address, the edge device can then establish a cut-through route to the destination.

Alternatively, the route server can choose to forward shorter information flows that don't justify the setup of an SVC and a cut-through route across the ATM network. The route server determines which flows of information justify a cut-through route with a technique known as *flow analysis*. The algorithms for flow analysis will be vendor specific as the standards focus on the communications between the MPOA components.

(ATM adaptation layers), service categories, and processes to carry video traffic over an ATM network.

The primary area of focus targets carrying MPEG (Motion Picture Experts Group) video. Two MPEG standards are defined:

- ✔ MPEG-1 defines compression schemes to produce VHS-quality video and audio. Its primary use is in the playback of stored video.
- ✔ MPEG-2 defines compression schemes for high-quality, full-motion broadcast video and audio delivered in real time.

The resultant bandwidth depends on the compression scheme used, but typically ranges between 1 and 2 Mbps for MPEG-1 and 2-8 Mbps for MPEG-2. Both compression schemes result in a bursty traffic stream.

Desktop video is another aspect of carrying video traffic within an ATM network. Most desktop video streams are encoded into IP before being transported over the ATM network. Thus, desktop video depends on the specifications for carrying IP traffic over ATM, as well as, emerging standards from the IETF for carrying real-time traffic over IP. In Chapter 23, you can find out more about desktop video and new protocols to carry multimedia traffic in IP.

Listening to the Voice Traffic

The definition of standards to carry voice traffic over ATM has only recently begun. Only one method — circuit emulation — is final as of this writing. We began this chapter with a discussion of circuit emulation. Circuit emulation is not an ideal solution for carrying voice traffic because it requires a fixed amount of bandwidth to be continually dedicated within the ATM network.

Despite its slow start, carrying voice traffic over ATM has strong potential for drastically lowering the cost of voice calls, especially over the long distance network. Using the ATM infrastructure to reach the desktop for voice can present many benefits by offering a consolidated network to build and manage. The VTOA (Voice and Telephony Over ATM) working group of the ATM Forum, as well as several ITU groups, are now aggressively pushing forward to define a bunch of needed new standards.

The initial focus of the Forum VTOA working group has been in two areas:

- ✔ **Desktop voice:** Defines a way to deliver voice connections all the way to an ATM desktop. The Forum's work is focusing on the transport aspects of carrying voice over ATM LANs. You can find out more about using ATM to support voice to the desktop in the *Inside ATM* feature for Chapter 10, "Telephony Is the Real Killer ATM Application."

✔ **Voice trunking:** Defines a way to connect PBXs (private branch exchanges) over an ATM network. The standard includes processes to dynamically establish a switched virtual circuit for each call between the PBXs. Voice trunking offers two benefits. First, delay is reduced as each call can directly reach its destination without passing through tandem (that is intermediate) PBXs. Second, network bandwidth is conserved by reserving bandwidth only when the voice call is active.

Although these specifications add to the available functionality, the real benefits of carrying voice over ATM networks require moving beyond this initial standard set, which use the CBR service category and AAL1 (ATM adaptation layer 1). An ATM network can most efficiently carry voice by packetizing the voice and using the VBR-RT service category. The result of packetized voice is a bursty traffic stream which allows increased sharing of the ATM bandwidth.

Packetization converts the steady voice stream created by most phones into a bursty packet stream by using compression and silence suppression. *Compression* uses well-standardized techniques to reduce the amount of bandwidth necessary to carry a call. Many compression implementations can achieve a compression ration of 8-to-1 (that is, the required bandwidth of the compressed call is 1/8 that of the uncompressed call) and still provide an acceptable quality of service.

Silence suppression removes the pauses in speech as opposed to traditional implementations which carry both speech and silence on the circuit (the exception is international circuits, which have used silence suppression for many years to reduce the bandwidth required in overseas transmissions). The Forum is just beginning to look at the needed specifications to standardize these techniques and will probably define one or more new AALs (ATM adaptation layers) to carry voice.

Two key issues which must be resolved when migrating voice traffic to an ATM network are echo cancellation and call control. Echo cancellation is necessary to remove the echo introduced by telephone handsets and exaggerated by network delay. If you are using public VPN services, you are probably now depending on the carrier network to provide echo cancellation. If you're migrating to a private or public ATM network, you need to undertake this responsibility for the long distance networks yourself through your ATM equipment or external echo cancellation equipment.

Call control is a much more complex issues and its impact depends on the specific implementation. The most challenging implementations within the carrier network which uses a call control method known as SS7 (Signaling System 7) to route and control calls across networks. Voice implementations in corporate networks have to determine how to interpret or pass through call control including advanced features such as call forwarding or caller ID on the ATM network.

Although standards organizations still have a lot of work to do, proprietary solutions for efficiently carrying voice over VBR-RT connections are available now. You may find that implementing one of these solutions is beneficial for your network. You can find out more about the business case considerations of carrying voice traffic over ATM in Chapter 14.

**Inside ATM with
Martin McNealis, IP Product Manager
David Benham, ATM Product Manager
Cisco Systems, San Jose, CA**

IP version 6 and ATM — Friend or Foe?!

As global enterprise communications and the Internet continue to expand, the underlying networking infrastructure and protocols need to scale accordingly. However, one question has surfaced—will IP version 6 (IPv6) and ATM compete with each other, or will they work together to keep pace with these networking needs into the next millennium?

The question that should be asked is, "Can we afford for them not to be friends?" **No.** The following begins with a concise overview of IPv6 and ends with a discussion of how IPv6 and ATM can work together and leverage each other's strengths.

Actually, IPv6 and ATM each have different goals at which their designs are targeted. IPv6 is designed to be the replacement for the current version of the popular IPv4. IPv4 provides connectionless traffic forwarding over the Internet today and supports countless applications. ATM provides a new level of high-speed switching, and multi-service integration includes traffic from IP-based applications.

IPv6 originally evolved out of concerns over future IPv4 address depletion. However, in redefining the predominant networking protocol, the IETF's IP Next Generation Working Group took the opportunity to introduce enhancements. These enhancements offer certain optimizations based upon deployment experience and integrate support for emerging networking requirements and applications. The main enhancements made in IPv6 over IPv4 are

✔ Expanded Address Size: IPv6 quadruples IPv4's 4 bytes of address size to give 16 bytes of address space and to provision for increased scalability via greater addressing hierarchy.

✔ Packet Header Simplification: To expedite packet processing and bandwidth overhead, the IPv6 header is fixed length, eliminates IPv4's checksumming (a method for checking the integrity of transmitted data), and avoids hop-by-hop segmentation.

✔ Flow Labeling Support: This new capability enables packets to be identified as part of a *flow* (where a flow is simply a set of packets coming from the same source to the same destination). Consequently, packets are subject to special handling, such as that required by time-sensitive multimedia applications.

✔ Security Extensions: The IPv6 protocol incorporates authentication and encryption techniques to provide for secure internetworking.

There are already some completed, as well as emerging, standards for implementing IPv4 over ATM, and IPv6 will utilize or leverage these standards. The completed standards include; RFC 1483-style encapsulation (LLC/SNAP format or VC multiplexing with the IPv6 packet directly in an AAL5 wrapper) and RFC 1577 Classical IP over ATM.

IPv6 also utilizes the Next Hop Resolution Protocol (NHRP) and the Resource Reservation Protocol (RSVP), both of which are being integrated with ATM services. NHRP is a fundamental component of the ATM Forum's emerging Multiprotocol over ATM (MPOA) specification. MPOA defines a standard approach to forwarding layer 3 protocols, such as IP (version 4 or 6) and Novell's IPX, transparently over ATM backbones. MPOA clients will use NHRP to dynamically ask for direct "cut-through" ATM connections between clients on different IP subnets. When finished, MPOA will allow newer applications, such as a packetized video application using IP's Resource Reservation Protocol, to request a desired service guarantee. MPOA also will enable these applications to take advantage of ATM's quality-of-service and multi-service integration capabilities when they traverse an ATM backbone (see the following table).

RSVP to ATM Service Correlation

ATM Service Types	RSVP Flow Types
Unspecified Bit Rate (UBR) or Available Bit Rate (ABR)	Best Effort
Constant Bit Rate (CBR) Real-Time Variable Bit Rate (RT-VBR)	Guaranteed; peak = average Guaranteed; peak > average
RT-VBR	Controlled Delay
non RT-VBR	Controlled Load

However, NHRP, LAN Emulation, and the emerging MPOA can be very ATM signaling-intensive. They all rely on flow detection / classification, address resolution, and SVC call set-up utilizing CPU-intensive UNI and P-NNI protocols. Alternatives are therefore being considered for carrying IP traffic over an ATM wide area network where signaling concerns are greatest. Cisco is currently leading one of these efforts, termed tag switching. *Tag switching* uses a control plane of common routing protocols versus the defined ATM Forum / ITU control plane. Tag switching may offer improved performance and scalability advantages in some networking environments.

Both IPv6 and ATM are expected to play significant roles within the networking landscape going into the next millennium. Their success as technologies could in part depend on their ability to work together to meet the ever increasing networking requirements.

Part III

Investing In ATM: Decisions, Decisions!

"You know, I've really noticed a difference in attitude since operations began using that ATM technology."

In this part . . .

1f what you really want to know about ATM is how to get it into your network environment, then Part III is for you. In this part, we give you the straight story about the benefits, costs and/or cost savings, risks, and rewards of choosing ATM for your network. We point out the considerations for using ATM in local and wide area networks, and we give you practical ideas for justifying ATM in your business environment. Plus, you get case studies of real-world applications that tell about the trials and successes of current ATM users.

Chapter 12

Evaluating ATM for Wide Area Networks

*T*esting out ATM to discover more about how its benefits can be applied to the network and the organization is an entirely valid approach. But, how do you know when it's time to get serious about considering ATM as a new and better networking solution? As you find out in this chapter, a few signs of readiness may indicate a need for an ATM solution in your wide area network (WAN).

Acronyms Used in This Chapter

Acronym	What It Stands For
ABR	Available Bit Rate
AIMUX	ATM Inverse Multiplexing
CBR	Constant Bit Rate
FRAD	Frame Relay Access Device
FUNI	Frame User Network Interface
IETF	Internet Engineering Task Force
IP	Internet Protocol
ISP	Internet Service Provider
PBX	Private Branch Exchange
PVC	Permanent Virtual Connection
RSVP	Resource Reservation Protocol

(continued)

Acronyms Used in This Chapter *(continued)*	
Acronym	*What It Stands For*
SMDS	Switched Multi-Megabit Data Services
SNA	Systems Network Architecture
SVC	Switched Virtual Connection
TDM	Time Division Multiplexing
UBR	Unspecified Bit Rate
VBR	Variable Bit Rate
VTOA	Voice and Telephony Over ATM
VPN	Virtual Private Network

Is It Time for an ATM Cure?

Evaluating ATM services consumes time and resources. Simply comparing services from various carriers is difficult because of the lack of similarity in their definition and pricing. Before taking the ATM plunge, ask yourself these questions:

- ✔ Do I need network connectivity beyond 1.5 Mbps at more than one location?

- ✔ Do I have applications requiring the support of high bandwidth or end-to-end quality of service?

- ✔ Am I experiencing performance problems with single applications or parts of my corporate network?

- ✔ Is the backbone connecting my routers getting too expensive to grow and maintain?

- ✔ Would integrating my various voice and data networks into fewer back-bones to lower the overall networking costs be helpful?

- ✔ Do I plan to implement ATM in the campus or LAN?

If you answered "Yes" to one or more of these questions, you may be a good candidate for ATM services. Most users today move to an ATM wide area network (WAN) for the following reasons:

- ✔ To upgrade a congested data backbone to improve performance.

- ✔ To consolidate separate, parallel networks to save money.

- ✔ To support a single bandwidth-hungry application that's important to the business.

Help, ATM! Fix this congested high-speed data backbone

When network congestion negatively impacts employee productivity and wreaks havoc with important business applications, it may be time to look for a solution to that congestion.

Before jumping to any conclusions, first try to understand the nature of the network congestion, its causes, and timing. If congestion occurs intermittently, analyze the nature of applications using the network during peak traffic hours. You could discover that some applications contributing to the congestion don't need to be operational during these time periods.

You may find that changing the protocols used by the routers in your LAN network substantially reduces congestion at all times of the day. If you still have inter-company voice applications running over the private TDM backbone, splitting them out to a virtual private network service may free substantial capacity and be less costly than upgrading the data backbone.

Evaluating the characteristics of your network congestion can help you to discover other less-costly solutions to the problem before looking for a new WAN solution. But this analysis helps also if you do consider alternative WAN options.

If you do determine that a new WAN configuration is necessary, selecting a service providing *logical connectivity* (such as frame relay or ATM) can provide many benefits. Building direct connections between edge routers can eliminate the use of backbone routers in your network. No backbone routers means lower equipment costs and less network delay. The logical connectivity also provides a stable underlying network and avoids congestion-prone, route reconfigurations necessary during network failures.

Help, ATM! Pull these separate, parallel networks together

Operating several networks out of one location to support a variety of data, video, or voice applications means higher costs (for equipment, access, inter-exchange, operations, and administration) than if you were using a consolidated network. A new consolidated network may also increase performance for all applications because bandwidth can be dynamically allocated and shared.

ATM can be a good networking choice if you want to pull together large, separate, parallel networks. Currently, you are a candidate for this consolidation approach only if you are managing very large, parallel networks like those used in Fortune 500 businesses. Within the next year, advanced, low-cost ATM equipment supporting network consolidation at T1 rates may become available and open up this approach to other networks as well. You want to wait until you can get equipment with sophisticated management tools that do the following:

- ✔ Prioritize traffic and reserve bandwidth based on time-of-day, day-of-week, and other factors
- ✔ Allocate bandwidth dynamically, based on traffic load
- ✔ Intrepret PBX signaling for voice connections
- ✔ Use compression and silence supression to carry voice traffic
- ✔ Control echo in long distance voice trunks

These capabilities are also the desired attributes of higher speed devices.

If you're seriously considering network consolidation to reduce cost of ownership, an analysis of existing networks and an understanding of the applications using each network are required. This information helps you determine whether you can reach your goals by consolidating just the data applications in a high-speed frame relay network, or whether you need to consider consolidating many different data, voice, or video applications in a more sophisticated solution like ATM.

Planning migrating to and operating an ATM network presents many challenges (which we discuss throughout this book), especially if you are supporting multiple networks. You want to carefully consider the impacts and requirements of this change before moving forward.

Help, ATM! This high-bandwidth application needs taming

A single, high-bandwidth application considered critical to a business often cost-justifies the investment in ATM. *Scientific visualization* (that is, using computer-generated images to analyze problems) is just one example of a relatively new and bandwidth-hungry application that can translate into improved competitive positioning, lower production costs, or other benefits to an organization. Data transmission between hospitals of sizable X-rays and other medical images for analysis by highly paid (and highly scarce) medical experts is another high-bandwidth usage.

Gain a thorough understanding of the nature of each application to choose a solution that provides the best performance at the lowest price. Supporting a single high-bandwidth application now with ATM can mean other benefits for your organization down the road.

Seeing How ATM Stacks Up against Other Technologies

You know whether your network needs some sort of cure, but before making a commitment to ATM, take a look alternative technologies. Also, look at how ATM stacks up against the alternative technologies to determine the best solution for your environment.

Most enterprise networks deploy a combination of technologies and services based on applications being supported, user needs and other factors. For some applications and business environments, using a high-speed Internet service may be a good alternative to ATM, especially if such service offers substantial savings. For other companies, the reliability or throughput of this alternative may be totally unacceptable, given the nature of their applications and business goals. In short, the best choice of network technologies for each application or business location is largely situation dependent.

Private lines and TDM technology versus ATM

Private lines are available in speeds ranging from 56/64 Kbps and below on up to 45 Mbps and above. The most common increments of bandwidth for private lines are 56/64 Kbps (DS0), 1.5 Mbps (T1, also called DS1), 2 Mbps (E1), 32 Mbps (E3), 45 Mbps (T3, also called DS3), and even higher speeds delivered through SONET networking at 155 Mbps (OC3) or more. DS0 is available just about everywhere, but SONET, at the opposite side of the spectrum, has limited availability because of its very high speeds. T1s and T3s are available in North America, with E1s and E3s as the corresponding available option in Europe and other international locations.

Private lines use time division multiplexing (TDM) technology instead of the statistical multiplexing used by ATM. With TDM technology, bandwidth is not dynamically allocated among active applications as it is with statistical multiplexing. Instead, it's statically pre-allocated when the network is designed. If at any moment an application is not using the bandwidth assigned to it, that bandwidth is wasted. Unlike with statistical multiplexing, other active applications can't temporarily take advantage of the unused bandwidth. We compare and contrast the multiplexing technologies of TDM and ATM in the sidebar, "How did ATM get its name?" in Chapter 3.

Despite TDM's bandwidth-sharing limitations, building a private TDM network using private lines and advanced equipment called intelligent time division multiplexers provides many of the same advantages as a private ATM network or public ATM service. With the right equipment, the private TDM network can support allocation of network bandwidth based on the time of day and automatically route around network failures. However, this equipment does use proprietary solutions which vary from vendor to vendor.

The biggest differences between private networks built with TDM versus ATM equipment are in the type of equipment needed to terminate leased lines and ATM's ability to dynamically share bandwidth in real time. With either choice, you're still responsible for building, managing, and optimizing the network to ensure sufficient capacity and the network's survival. The differences are much greater between building a private TDM network using private lines and using a public ATM service. With the ATM service, the carrier assumes responsibility for building circuit redundancy between ATM switches, managing and optimizing capacity, and troubleshooting network problems.

Frame relay versus ATM

Frame relay services are widely available in the U.S., Japan, and Australia, but less likely to be found in other parts of the world. These services traditionally scale from 56 Kbps to 1.5/2 Mbps (depending on your location), but some service providers now make frame relay available at higher speeds of 3, 4, 6, 12, and 45 Mbps. Digital and analog dial access options into frame relay can support mobile users and small remote offices. Dial access also provides a backup to dedicated physical access facilities. Transparent protocol translation between X.25 and frame relay (that is, service interworking between the two different WAN protocols) is available for connectivity to locations in and out of the U.S. that are difficult to reach or have low-quality analog communications lines.

Frame relay shares some similarities with ATM:

- ✔ Reliance on statistical multiplexing to dynamically allocate capacity to active applications in real time
- ✔ The ability to support a mix of different applications including voice, packet video, and data
- ✔ Logical connections to provide end-to-end connectivity through a series of network switches

ATM and frame relay also differ in many ways:

- ✔ Frame relay uses a variable-length packet (a frame) whose size depends upon the amount of transmitted information or network equipment settings as opposed to ATM's use of a fixed length packet (a cell).
- ✔ Frame relay standards are much less complex than ATM's. This has its pros and cons— frame relay is much easier to learn and implement than ATM but doesn't deliver the sophisticated level of standardized service that ATM does.
- ✔ Frame relay cannot be used in the LAN unlike ATM which is at home in both the LAN and WAN.

Early in the life of both standards, many people thought there would be very little overlap in the target markets and applications for the two technologies. ATM was defined at speeds of 45 Mbps and above while frame relay was defined at speeds of 1.5 Mbps and below. ATM targeted multimedia environments that simultaneously support voice, data, and video applications, while frame relay targeted data applications only. This is no longer the case.

ATM lowered to a speed of 1.5 Mbps, and options like FUNI (Frame User Network Interface) allow connections to ATM networks at speeds even below that. Frame relay equipment vendors and service providers now support frame relay at speeds up to 45 Mbps and can provide special service quality for delay-sensitive applications such as SNA (Systems Network Architecture) and voice through vendor specific designs.

Frame relay has been deployed and accepted more quickly than ATM, especially in the U.S. market. A greater number of service and equipment choices is available, reflecting the more-mature market. Frame relay access device (FRAD) vendors offer customer equipment based on proprietary implementations to support multiple applications, including SNA, voice, fax, and video over a frame relay network in addition to the more common LAN and client-server traffic. Router and switch vendors are working to deliver the same capability, and the Frame Relay Forum (a standards group for frame relay) is moving towards standardizing support for different types of traffic.

All of this means more competition between frame relay and ATM than initially envisioned. ATM still offers higher performance in supporting different traffic types than frame relay in very large networks, unless the frame relay backbone network has been engineered with much excess capacity. For those companies with more-basic needs, or who subscribe to a carrier using an ATM backbone for its frame relay service, frame relay may provide a more cost-effective alternative than ATM in the WAN.

For companies that could go in either direction, economics plays a major role. ATM equipment tends to be more expensive than frame relay equipment, both because of the added complexity and also because the market is less mature. Over the next several years, however, ATM prices should drop. Most U.S. service providers have a strategy to price equivalent speeds and service classes of ATM and frame relay the same. However, actual relative pricing varies from customer to customer and carrier to carrier as most large customers subscribe to frame relay or ATM services under special contract. The goals of your carrier for each service and the desirability of your network along with its traffic and locations determines carrier aggressiveness in pricing each service.

Internet/IP versus ATM

The Internet and IP (Internet protocol) is developing into a competitor to ATM public network services and the ATM protocol, at least in IP-based networks. IP is a connectionless technology and IP services, as well as the public Internet, are available worldwide at speeds ranging from low-speed analog dial access of 14.4 Kbps to very high-speed dedicated connections of 45 Mbps. Many Internet service providers (ISP) already scale the backbone infrastructure to very high speeds and in some cases use ATM technology to do this.

The Internet now supports multimedia applications including voice and video traffic. Inexpensive hardware and software packages allow users to make phone calls and hold desktop videoconferences over the Internet, although not nearly with the ease of use and quality of traditional alternatives. These types of applications are expected to grow, unless the pricing policies for Internet services change.

What the Internet does not offer today are the following:

- ✔ Delivery of various qualities of services
- ✔ Specific support of delay-sensitive applications
- ✔ Guarantee of end-to-end service quality

However, many ISPs plan to offer such services in 1997 — a least for their business customers.

The Internet operates as a truly public network service, Frame relay, ATM, and X.25 services, on the other hand, exist as virtual private networks based on connection-oriented technologies. This means that while a shared infrastructure is available for all users, each individual company uses a partitioned segment of the network based on their defined PVCs that are as secure as what you'd find in a private-line environment. (SVCs will open new security challenges for both frame relay and ATM services.) Options are available to secure Internet transmissions and some service providers now offer secure intranet solutions that ride on a separate IP backbone or over the public Internet.

Connection-oriented services allow companies to purchase increments of bandwidth to provide predictability and guarantee throughput between locations. The Internet offers no such option at this time. It's a true free-for-all. In fact, one of the advantages of ATM lies in its ability to support both highly *deterministic* and *non-deterministic applications* (in other words, applications that need very predictable response times and delays and those that don't). The Internet is notorious for being unpredictable in its performance. The nature of its router-based backbone makes it unsuited to support applications requiring a high level of predictability in delay or promised availability of network throughput.

The Internet could become more competitive with ATM if more and more of the Internet backbone migrates to ATM. In theory, this could allow Internet-based offerings that support various qualities of service, levels of privacy and security, and possibly even levels of delay (and probably various levels of pricing, too). Even so, by its very nature, the Internet remains a single-protocol environment, that is, it supports IP traffic only. Environments requiring support of many protocols continue to examine ATM and other solutions.

Native LAN

Native LAN services are available from several local and a few interexchange service providers in the U.S. and other parts of the world. You can find these services primarily in larger cities offering more telecommunication service options. The interface to the customer is a LAN protocol including Ethernet, token ring, or FDDI. Carriers offering native LAN services typically do so at 4, 10, and 16 Mbps speeds and in some cases offer lower speed alternatives or higher speeds ranging to 100 Mbps. The underlying network infrastructure frequently is based on ATM.

Native LAN services relieve customers from the task of deploying wide area networking equipment or operating a wide area network. To transport LAN traffic over the WAN, the carrier takes care of installing, maintaining, and repairing all WAN equipment and protocols. Native LAN services price themselves very aggressively against equivalent private line and ATM alternatives. Yet, as the name suggests, these services are designed specifically to support LAN applications.

If you're driven to ATM by a single high-bandwidth application or network congestion on a LAN-to-LAN backbone, native LAN services could offer a very workable solution without moving to a native ATM service. Later in this chapter, the sidebar "Alternatives to ATM" tells you read about the experience of Booz-Allen & Hamilton, who made the native LAN choice. However, if your networking needs include support for many different types of applications, native LAN may not be a viable alternative.

X.25 versus ATM

In the U.S., *X.25* can't compete with ATM primarily because public X.25 services are typically limited to speeds of 56 Kbps and below. Outside the U.S., X.25 services offer higher speeds, wide availability, and economical alternatives to dedicated leased lines. In some countries, ATM and X.25 compete at the very lowest speed ATM and FUNI services.

X.25 and ATM include many similarities based on their connection-oriented technologies. They differ in their error detection and error correction capabilities. ATM only checks for errors in the cell header addressing information and cannot correct these errors beyond a problem with a single bit. If any part of an X.25 packet is damaged in the network, the damage is detected, and the network itself takes responsibility for correcting the error. The network makes copies of a packet as it moves from one switch to another. When a switch receives a damaged packet, that switch relays a message to the sending switch requesting a new undamaged copy — an important process when you have poor-quality underlying communication lines as found in some countries.

On the downside, this error-correction process is resource intensive and adds considerable time to the end-to-end transmission. In many parts of the world, the underlying network infrastructure has been upgraded to digital and fiber facilities, significantly reducing the likelihood of damage to a packet and making X.25's error correction unnecessary. ATM (and other broadband packet technologies such as frame relay and SMDS) expect high-quality underlying facilities and leave the process of error correction up to the intelligent end devices, such as the routers and the applications.

SMDS versus ATM

SMDS (Switched Multi-Megabit Data Services) never really took off in the U.S. except in a few geographic regions and within a few vertical industries. SMDS, unlike ATM but like IP, is a connectionless technology similar to a LAN environment. In some ways, it's surprising SMDS hasn't become more successful in the U.S. SMDS is much less complex than ATM, is priced aggressively, and offers speeds from 56 Kbps to 34 Mbps. Problems with SMDS center mostly around poor marketing and positioning, limited availability, and the tremendous success of frame relay.

SMDS enjoys greater success in other parts of the world, such as the United Kingdom, where it poses a competitive threat to ATM. Despite its advantages, SMDS is not by nature designed for deterministic, real-time applications and it does not include support for multiple qualities of service.

In a data-only environment, SMDS offers a viable solution to ATM, especially if most or all of the applications can handle variations in delay. For mixed-application environments, such as voice and data, SMDS does not offer a viable alternative at this time.

Populating the New World: Migrating to ATM

After you've made the decision to move to ATM, how do you get from where you are to where you want to be? The migration planning process begins by assembling a team of players that includes members of your IT staff, representatives from your service providers and equipment vendors, and possibly an applications user. Your available migration options obviously depend on what type of network equipment and services you already have in place. (If you lack an existing network solution for any applications, go ahead and install the ATM network and don't worry about a migration plan.)

Four general rules apply when developing a migration strategy:

- ✔ Have the end goal firmly in mind when the migration begins.
- ✔ Start with a single application or a small subsection of the network.
- ✔ Take small steps instead of replacing the entire network at once.
- ✔ Early in the process, purchase any tools necessary to operate or trouble-shoot the network.

Work with your vendors to script a migration plan that makes sense for your applications, equipment, goals, and network limitations.

Pick the sites and applications migrating first

Identify the first locations migrating to ATM. Pick sites with knowledgeable IT staff who can spend the time necessary to get the new network operational, help to optimize performance of applications on the network, and help with trouble-shooting when problems arise. If you have to fly or drive an expert to any locations in the event of a problem, those sites probably won't make good candidates for the first round of upgrades.

Applications migrating to the new network should be test copies of a production application or noncritical applications that can afford down time when problems arise. This avoids creating unhappy end users with problems that can't be fixed during the migration process. Keep a contingency plan in place at both the site level and application level that allows you to quickly switch back to the previously existing network if a major problem arises. This requires operating parallel networks for a few days or weeks as backup insurance.

Consider network costs and service availability early on

If your migration includes moving from T1/E1 circuits up to T3/E3 circuits, heed a few words of caution. In some parts of the U.S. a T3 local access loop or interexchange circuit can be difficult to procure and take several months to install, or is available but prohibitively expensive. The same situation applies for E3 circuits in other parts of the world.

You also want to consider the impacts of placing all the communications of a large location onto a single physical facility such as a fiber. Ask your provider about options for redundancy such as a standby T3/E3 alternatively routed to your provider's network (which can be very expensive) or facilities based on a ring configuration where the backside of the ring provides redundant capacity in event of a facility cut.

Early in your migration process, determine what the network requirements are and then their availability and cost. If you decide to move forward, place your orders early, involve the service provider in the migration planning, and make sure the service provider gives you regular updates once service installation begins.

Moving from private TDM to private ATM

If you're migrating a private line network, you probably are replacing TDM multiplexers with an ATM access mux or switch. This mux or switch connects multiple incoming customer ports supporting a variety of protocols (such as LAN, videoconferencing, and voice interfaces) to an outgoing ATM connection into the wide area network.

An explanation of one of the many ways to approach such a migration follows. Assume that the default configuration for each TDM device includes a connection to at least two other TDM devices; geographically diverse T1 private lines are used to ensure network survivability. The new configuration uses T3 private lines to connect the ATM equipment:

1. **Begin by connecting only the new applications directly to the ATM mux or switch.**

   After the network stabilizes, you can start migration of the TDM applications to the new ATM network. If a problem occurs during the migration, traffic can be routed back to the TDM configuration until you correct it.

2. **To migrate the TDM multiplexing traffic, redirect one of the TDM backbone trunk connections to a T1 circuit emulation port on the ATM device at each end.**

   Keep the connections to any other remote TDM switch in place until you are comfortable that your new network works. The redundant configuration of parallel networks provides a safety net for the applications.

3. **The traffic coming from the TDM device can be routed initially over an ATM constant bit rate (CBR) connection within the private ATM network.**

   If all DS0s are active, the emulated TDM circuit will use more than 1.544 Mbps of bandwidth because of the ATM overhead. After you have successfully completed this step, move on to consider your network applications.

4. **Directly terminate the applications of the TDM mux to the ATM device, through an application-by-application migration.**

If your existing network is composed of routers, instead of multiplexers, you can use the same migration plan. Redundant facilities between the routers are split to allow at least one non-ATM private line to carry traffic while the other WAN interfaces on the routers change to ATM.

Migrate applications on an individual basis and achieve stability before adding the next application to the mix.

Moving from private TDM to public ATM

After a private ATM network is operational, its enterprise switches or routers can make use of public ATM services, where cost effective, by using the same approach described in the preceding section. You need to operate parallel connections between ATM switches, one over a private leased line and the other over a public ATM service.

If connectivity to a public ATM service is your ultimate goal, skip the intermediate step of operating a private ATM network. Instead, migrate the original TDM network directly to a public ATM network using basically the same methods for migration to a private ATM network. The procedures and required equipment remain the same. The only difference is that instead of private leased lines a public service is used between your ATM switches.

A hybrid of public and private connections may achieve the best overall network price-to-performance ratio. This means that some of your enterprise ATM switches may use private line trunks, while others may be connected to a public ATM service, and still others may support both types of connections.

Moving from public frame relay to public ATM

If you've already deployed a frame relay network, migration to ATM can start with just a single site through frame relay to ATM service interworking. Use this approach if you have a location on the network, such as the primary data processing or headquarters site, with several T1 port connections on the frame relay network.

Service interworking provides all needed conversion between the frame relay and ATM protocols within the network. Permanent (or switched) virtual circuits (PVCs or SVCs) connect the sites together regardless of the protocol being used at each end. Different providers support the interoperability using different service classes in the frame relay and ATM networks. Frame relay to ATM service interworking is still relatively new and its users are now determining how to get the best overall throughput and performance.

If your service provider offers high-speed frame relay, this may be a better approach than service interworking unless you need native ATM services at other locations or you want to use the network to support different traffic types.

Migrating a frame relay site to ATM can be relatively simple. Typically the frame relay site currently uses routers. If your router is sufficiently large, the migration only requires a change in the interface card terminating the network traffic. Elsewise, you need to purchase a new router. Most users choose a direct ATM connection into their router. You also have to update or activate software and change your route mappings from frame relay logical connections to the new ATM logical connections. If you're also changing network speed, you have to coordinate a new local or access facility with your carrier.

Migrating voice to ATM

Most voice networks use a virtual private network service or leased private lines to connect private branch exchange (PBX) switches at major locations. In the 1980s, when many large corporations installed private multiplexer networks, they typically justified the cost with these voice applications. Moving voice traffic from the more expensive public switched telephone network to the private network provided substantial savings. This was before the lower-cost VPN services reduced the per-minute rates for voice traffic. At that time, any excess network bandwidth was used to support data applications. Because of this, data was said to *ride for free*.

Today, a similar approach can be used, only in reverse. The ATM network is usually cost justified because of the added performance and cost savings for data applications. Any excess bandwidth can then be used to let on-net voice traffic between your on-net sites ride for free.

Before migrating your voice traffic, you must determine where the network provides echo cancellation for long distance circuits. Echo cancellation is necessary to remove the echo introduced by telephone handsets and exaggerated by network delay. If you are using public VPN services, you are probably now depending on the carrier network to provide echo cancelation. If you're migrating to a private or public ATM network, you need to undertake this responsiblity yourself either through your ATM equipment or external echo cancellation equipment.

The safest migration plan of your voice traffic starts with a single T1 line routed over the ATM network while all others are left in place. This approach allows you to quickly switch all traffic to non-ATM paths if a problem occurs, and lets you reconfigure the network back to its original design if the problem can't be resolved. After this configuration stabilizes and performs as expected, you can begin to migrate other circuits.

The ATM network can carry the PBX traffic as emulated circuits using T1 circuit emulation and the CBR service category. You must configure the CBR connection at greater than T1 speed to support the higher bandwidths required by ATM's overhead. Better economies result from putting voice applications over VBR connections because ATM applies statistical multiplexing gains to the voice connections as well as to data. These gains come from supression of the silence during pauses in speech as well as voice compression. You'll need special equipment to support this approach until the VTOA (Voice and Telephony Over ATM) standards are complete, but the potential savings in your network may justify it.

What Kind of ATM Service Is Available?

As of this writing, ATM services are a buyer's market in that almost everything is negotiable. In the U.S., the interexchange ATM service pricing isn't publicized or tariffed; and that's also true for local services provided by nonregulated providers. A few of the RBOCs tariff this service in some or all of the states in their regions. In those states where the RBOCs have not filed tariffs, service can be provided through special assemblies for each individual case.

Service providers are doing less than they can to spur sales of ATM or make ATM easy to purchase and install. Providers define services in the complex terms of the technology instead of prepackaging them to offer solutions to specific applications and network problems. The price of high-speed access also remains a hurdle for most customers. Internationally, the picture isn't much different. Services are high-priced and limited in availability. This situation exists for three reasons — two related to technology and one to economics:

 ✔ ATM networks are in a state of transition as service providers ensure that the networks can deliver widely available high-performance service.

 ✔ ATM is very complex and prepackaging qualities of service for applications and protocols isn't an easy task.

 ✔ ATM poses a threat to the revenue base of lucrative installed services, such as virtual private networks and private line services (even though history tells us a rapid migration seems unlikely, even given the eventual savings and service advantages).

Bringing ATM successfully to the market mainstream requires a complete networking solution that predefines and prepackages the many complex options based on the applications being supported.

Basic service features

ATM services offer high-speed networking connectivity at speeds ranging from 1.5 Mbps to 155 Mbps. In the U.S., most carriers offer T3 (45 Mbps) and OC-3 (155 Mbps) port for connecting to the carrier's network, and a few offer T1 (1.5 Mbps) ports.

If you are connecting to an interexchange carrier in the U.S., the average T3 local loop providing access to the carrier network costs about $3,500 per month, and a T1 local loop costs about $300 per month. To help customers find a cost-effective solution for high-speed access, a few service providers are beginning to experiment with offering NxT1 access for ATM services using inverse multiplexers on each end of the access line. This may become more economically viable after the IAM (Inverse ATM Mux) standard is finished and implemented in central office and premises equipment.

ATM services are based primarily on PVCs (permanent virtual connections). Most service providers offer PVC bandwidths in 1 Mbps increments. In addition, some provide 64 Kbps for low-speed ports and the CBR (constant bit rate) service category. SVCs (switched virtual connections) may emerge on a limited basis during 1997. All service providers offer the VBR (variable bit rate) service class and most offer CBR (constant bit rate). Right now, only a few offer ABR (available bit rate) and UBR (unspecified bit rate) service categories on a controlled basis. Look at Chapter 9 for further discussion of service categories.

Carriers typically police the entrance to the ATM network to ensure that no connection exceeds its expected traffic rate. Despite this, carriers sometimes deliver cells in violation of the service contract, such as burst traffic above the expected bandwidth if the bandwidth is available on the network. Other carriers automatically drop violating cells, which means you'd better use CPE that shapes traffic. Traffic shaping ensures or at least minimizes the possibility of you violating the service contract.

Hiding ATM's complexities

Packaging equipment along with the public ATM network service would make ATM easier for many customers to buy and use. Only a few providers offer ATM-based services in which the underlying WAN data communications and CPE are hidden or transparent to the end user. The network configuration and design process, and its implementation, maintenance, and management, are relegated to the carrier. One such service is known as native LAN. ATM-based native LAN services are gaining in popularity. Providers offer these services primarily in metropolitan areas, although a small number of service providers offer native LAN services on on a regional or national basis. As of this writing, native LAN services can be purchased between the U.S. and a few other countries including the United Kingdom, France, Germany, and Sweden.

Alternatives to ATM

Booz-Allen & Hamilton is a global management and technology consulting firm that is utilizing an ATM network without experiencing the complexities of engineering, designing, and managing the network.

Booz-Allen & Hamilton went through the laborious process of learning a new technology when it deployed a frame relay network. The frame relay service required the company to invest time and money in new equipment, training, and testing. It also demanded continual maintenance to add and alter site configurations as networking needs changed — requiring a lot of network design and engineering for the BAH technical staff.

When the time came to move BAH's network to a platform capable of meeting increasing network performance and utilization demands, it skipped all the painstaking steps it went through to implement the frame relay network. BAH purchased a fully managed native LAN service that uses ATM in the backbone from MFS DataNet.

By purchasing a native LAN service the cost of ownership was minimal for BAH. Unlike the frame relay service, it did not have to invest heavily in telecommunications equipment. Daniel Gasparro, BAH's Chief Technologist, states that "technology product life cycles are so short that the equipment becomes obsolete before it fully depreciates. By purchasing a fully managed service we gain all the benefits of the ATM technology without investing the time and money into learning about the new equipment or all the details required to run a network ourselves. Since the service provider purchases all the hardware the return on investment is much quicker for BAH."

The native LAN service provides BAH with a leading technology WAN service while hiding all its complexities in the backbone. BAH does not have to determine the myriad of ATM PVC bandwidth rates or service categories to engineer the network for peak performance. BAH simply purchases a native LAN interface from MFS, and MFS installs, transports, monitors, manages and supports the service. The high speed interface to an ATM backbone increases BAH network performance and gives them a cost effective, scaleable network for a flat monthly rate. And the best news for users of the new BAH network — the staff now has more time to help them develop useful applications to meet their client needs.

Another example of a service using ATM but providing a much simpler interface to customers is a distance learning service in North Carolina. The distance learning service provides video communications between classrooms and remote teachers using an underlying ATM network. The service brings together video sessions from multiple locations so that students can learn advanced subjects such as foreign languages from teachers otherwise unavailable to them.

Over time we expect that other services masking the complexities of ATM's technologies to become available and increasingly popular. Most users would prefer not to have to read an entire book, such as *ATM For Dummies*, to figure out a new service option. If ATM does not become available through simpler packaging, many users may lack the patience to consider this option.

If The Network Ain't Broke, Don't Fix It

Ever notice how some people — male people mostly in our experience — always want to fix things that aren't broken? Like TV's Tim the Tool Man, these people are obsessed with making the fast faster and the big bigger. You won't find this type of behavior on the ideal personality attributes list for network managers, because tinkering with the network can have a major effect on the productivity of company employees and the performance of critical applications.

You probably don't need to consider implementing any new networking technology, ATM or otherwise, unless a network problem needs a solution now or in the very near future, or you believe your networking costs could be drastically (greater than 20%) reduced. Staying informed about the emerging technologies is good, and a few companies have even set up test labs to scratch that tinkering itch, a costly proposition for most firms. But the golden rule of networking — if the network ain't broke, don't fix it — continues to hold true.

Inside ATM with Mike Grubbs
ATM Group Manager, Product Marketing
Sprint, Kansas City, MO
`mike.grubbs@qm.sprintcorp.com`

ATM for the WAN: Evolution Not Revolution

At this point, readers should already be familiar with the many benefits of ATM, in both the LAN and the WAN. For many businesses, the benefits of ATM will be revolutionary, providing cost-effective high bandwidth and new capabilities that ultimately help businesses to do more business. Yet, despite the tremendous opportunities that ATM presents, implementation by businesses has been — and will continue to be — an evolutionary process.

ATM in the WAN will become a dominant carrier infrastructure in the next five years. In fact, the economics of wide-area ATM are so compelling that progressive carriers are already converting their narrowband, TDM, asynchronous networks into integrated, broadband networks by adopting ATM over SONET architectures. They realize that the efficiencies and enhanced service capabilities they will gain more than offset the cost of implementing ATM; thus, several are moving forward as fast as they can.

But the carriers' commercial customers aren't in the business of selling communications services and typically do not have sufficient budgets to do complete swap-outs of legacy equipment and management systems. Many enterprises still view ATM as too new to risk potential disruption of their production, mission-critical networks. Consequently, most companies are adopting ATM using gradual, cautious, and well-planned approaches.

A distinct pattern to ATM WAN adoption has emerged. The first phase of adoption is service and equipment testing/trials, which are usually limited to two or three sites. The next phase is conversion of key sites or applications to ATM, followed by the third conversion phase of entire production WANs at all large corporate locations. Phase four is

consolidation of multiple WANs (and LANs) into one seamless, efficiently managed network. Phase four is commonly referred to as "enterprise ATM." It is ATM's long term vision — a state achieved by only a handful of companies in the world today. Within a few years though, most large (and many medium-sized) enterprises will have reached phases three and four of ATM evolution.

Actually, there is a phase *0*, which is almost a prerequisite to success: a strategic vision of where the companies expect their networks to be in two to four years. Corporations are mapping out strategies that maximize preservation of existing infrastructure investment and minimize potential disruption and pain caused by change. As they gain more experience with ATM, they expand and often accelerate their deployment. But very few are jumping into the water without dipping their toes first.

The typical enterprise looking to ATM as a long-term solution already has multiple networks servicing multiple applications. Most large companies have voice, legacy data (i.e. mainframe), and LAN networks in place. Given the explosive growth in distributed computing, more powerful desktops, and complex software/multimedia, it is no surprise that LANs and LAN-to-LAN WANs are running into bandwidth bottlenecks. Enterprises are starting to understand that ATM can provide immediate, cost-effective relief of bandwidth bottlenecks while also providing an opportunity for long-term consolidation of networks.

Adding DS3 ATM cards to backbone routers is probably the most common approach used by businesses to implement ATM WAN service for their router network. All the leading router manufacturers now provide ATM cards

(continued)

for their backbone routers. The other popular approach is to add an ATM DSU between the router and the WAN, which then only requires a simple router software/port reconfiguration (ATM DXI and HSSI) to get up and running. These two approaches to overcoming router WAN bottlenecks are the least intrusive, least expensive, and most popular ways to implement ATM for the WAN. They preserve existing LAN investments and require only relatively small incremental investments. Of course, they are also the most limited approaches and do not address other networks (for example, voice and legacy data). Of the two, the router card approach provides the better long-term investment because it will survive most migration strategies.

For businesses envisioning using ATM as their single WAN transmission service, the ATM access multiplexer/concentrator solution is becoming increasingly popular. This equipment accepts non-ATM protocols and converts them into cells for transmission across an ATM WAN. It also accepts ATM cells and passes them on to the WAN. Thus, as with the ATM router card and DSU solutions, the access concentrator approach is minimally invasive and maximizes protection of existing infrastructure. It is an excellent migration vehicle, allowing companies to subscribe to a variety of ATM service categories to meet the requirements of the different applications.

For example, businesses might have a router connected to the mux and use a variable bit rate ATM carrier service for the data connections tied to that router. Then they might aggregate their legacy mainframe data to a mux port and buy constant bit rate ATM service to make the change transparent to the mainframe equipment. They can also connect their PBX for *on-to-on* connections via a CBR service to their PBXs at other sites.

To reach the phase four vision and consolidate multiple networks into one requires a significantly higher level of investment and change. It means converting all legacy voice and data into ATM. It means installing ATM switches at the premises. And if you want to extend the vision into the LAN, it means converting legacy LANs into ATM LANs. In exchange for that higher investment, the company dramatically lowers its management, training, and transmission service costs. Early ATM conversion projects of corporate networks are forecasting as much as a 40 percent savings in overall networking costs.

ATM is delivering real savings and performance improvements today. Businesses are rapidly recognizing the possibilities and accelerating their ATM WAN implementations. But adoption of ATM does not require wholesale change. You can implement it on a site-by-site, application-by-application basis. Businesses can — and are — making ATM investment commitments incrementally based on their business needs and comfort with the technology. All that is required is taking the first planning/evaluation step.

Chapter 13

Evaluating ATM for Local Area Networks

● ●

▶ Determining whether you need ATM in the local network

▶ Measuring ATM against other local networking technologies

▶ Finding out about routers

▶ Planning your migration to ATM LANs and campus backbones

● ●

*U*sing ATM in your LANs or LAN backbones gives you higher speeds and improved performance for real-time traffic, when compared to alternative solutions. Depending on your network and implementation, ATM can cost you more than other LAN alternatives and be similarly priced to other LAN backbone alternatives. Determining whether ATM makes sense in your local networks depends upon the requirements of your applications, your existing equipment and protocols, and your organization's tolerance for change.

Acronyms Used in This Chapter	
Acronym	*What It Stands For*
API	Applications Programming Interfaces
ARIS	Aggregate Route-based IP switching
CAD/CAM	Computer Aided Design/Computer Aided Manufacturing
CDDI	Copper Distributed Data Interface
CSMA/CD	Carrier-Sense Multiple Access/Collision Detection
DPAM	Demand Priority Access Method
FDDI	Fiber Distributed Data Interface
IEEE	Institute of Electrical and Electronics Engineers
IETF	Internet Engineering Task Force
IP	Internet Protocol
LAN	Local Area Network

(continued)

Acronyms Used in This Chapter *(continued)*	
Acronym	*What It Stands For*
LANE	LAN Emulation
MAC	Media Access Control
MPOA	Multiprotocol Over ATM
PBX	Private Branch Exchange
RFC	Request For Comment
RSVP	Resource Reservation Protocol
SNA	Systems Network Architechture
VLAN	Virtual LAN

Is It Time for an ATM Cure?

Before we jump into this chapter, knowing what types of networking environments can benefit from an ATM networking solution is essential. Your LAN or campus backbones connecting your LANs may benefit from ATM if you can answer "Yes" to any of these questions:

- ✔ Are users running applications, such as desktop conferencing, that require multimedia communication?

- ✔ Are users running applications requiring high-speed connectivity within a workgroup (for example, CAD/CAM, video editing, medical imaging, financial modeling, or parallel processing)?

- ✔ Are existing server connections causing congestion in the network?

- ✔ Is the LAN backbone network in the campus congested?

- ✔ Is the backbone connecting the routers getting too expensive to grow and maintain?

- ✔ Would integrating various voice and data networks into fewer local backbones to conserve existing bandwidth and wiring be helpful?

If you said "Yes" to one or more of these questions, that's still not enough evidence to immediately move from considering ATM to adopting it into your local environment. Many emerging networking technologies for the local environment can also satisfy your needs. To reach the best decision for your organization, conduct a thorough investigation of available solutions (like those we cover in this chapter) while understanding and focusing on your networking requirements.

Add the following points to the plus column when weighing the pros and cons of ATM:

✔ **ATM offers high speed with local connections standardized for 25, 100, 155, and 622 Mbps.** These speed measurements are duplex (simultaneous input/output) instead of the typical half-duplex (shared input/output) LAN speeds. This means that a quoted ATM bandwidth rate actually represents twice the capacity of the same quoted rate for a traditional LAN (unless you use a vendor-specific extension of the standard to support duplex connectivity to the LAN). High-speed connections are necessary in a few high-powered workgroups, for server connections, and in campus LAN backbones.

✔ **ATM can support multiple service qualities on the same network.** This capability becomes important as new Applications Programming Interfaces (APIs) such as Winsock 2 (and API for Windows) allow various applications to request different qualities of service. The most frequently cited example is desktop conferencing, which is subject to intermittent congestion in traditional LANs that offer only one service class. Desktop conferencing sessions can freeze if a large file transfer uses up all available bandwidth.

In contrast, an ATM network can make sure that some bandwidth is always reserved for carrying the conference traffic. Multiple service classes may not be a significant issue in dedicated desktop connections, but they're important to LAN backbone networks supporting hundreds or even thousands of users. Time-sensitive applications tend to be much more prone to congestion and poor performance in these shared backbones.

✔ **ATM allows integration of networks.** Within even a single building or campus, network managers find it simpler to integrate multiple networks (for example, PBX, video, SNA, and LAN) rather than undertake whole new wiring projects. New wiring requires ripping up walls, drilling concrete, and in general creating a big mess in the work environment, all of which mean added expense.

Leased building facilities introduce further complications. Wiring between buildings may be difficult, especially if the wiring must pass through public rights of way. Many times that's not even possible, especially for locations on busy, congested streets.

✔ **ATM uses layer 2 switching as opposed to layer 3 routing.** As we mention throughout this book, switching can significantly reduce network delays and save on expenses by decreasing the number of required routers and router termination ports. Replacing backbone routers with ATM switching allows full-meshed connectivity of the access routers on your campus network with a minimum delay using the one-hop connection.

The switches also provide a reliable underlying network lending stability to your routing tables. This saves the processing power of the router for other important tasks, such as *address resolution* (mapping between different address types) and *protocol conversion* (changing from one protocol to another). The potential benefits of switching versus routing in your campus backbone is covered in the Chapter 4.

✔ **Adopting ATM in your LAN now means greater integration with your WAN in the future.** (For higher speeds, ATM is the most popular choice in wide area networking.) In the long term, a shared protocol between your LAN and WAN can make management and operation of the network much easier.

✔ **Except for a few of the smallest start-up equipment vendors, the ATM standard is universally supported.** More than likely, your vendor of choice offers an ATM networking solution. Other emerging solutions' support of multiple priorities and qualities of service in existing LANs are available only as vendor-specific, proprietary solutions.

As we write this, vendors are promoting a variety of these solutions to differentiate their products. Some solutions may eventually become a networking standard, but most probably won't. Furthermore, unlike ATM, these solutions won't have defined standards for supporting interoperability with many other networking protocols — at least not for many years.

How Does ATM Stack Up against Other Technologies?

If the advantages of ATM make sense for the network environment you're evaluating, then migration to ATM may be your best option. Choosing the best technology for your network really comes down to how you prioritize the following evaluation factors:

✔ Your cost at the desktop level

✔ Available bandwidth at the desktop level

✔ Support for time-sensitive traffic

✔ Ease of operation and maintenance

✔ Ease of adoption into the existing network

✔ Interoperation with other vendors or technologies

✔ Future capabilities

Ethernet versus ATM

Right now, as we sit and type this text, Ethernet dominates the local area network scene with no signs of giving up its popularity. Ethernet is a mature, well-known, and low-cost networking solution. In fact, many new PCs come already packaged with Ethernet cards. This solution is by far the preferred choice for networking desktops and a strong choice for building LAN backbones.

In the 1970s, a handful of people got together and developed Ethernet to connect their computers. Originally designed as a 10 Mbps network with bandwidth shared among users, manufacturers later added creative innovations to enhance Ethernet's capabilities. A networking protocol designed by just a few folks involves a very different approach than that of the legions who devised ATM. Ethernet is hardly complex, but it gets the job done. Unlike ATM, which takes this whole book to explain, you can get up to speed on Ethernet by reading just a few paragraphs. If you do not already have a background in Ethernet networking, the following information will also be useful in understanding ATM LAN Emulation (LANE) technology, which supports interoperability between ATM and traditional LANs.

Ethernet basics

Ethernet was designed to allow multiple connected computers and printers to communicate over a single piece of coaxial cable known as the *bus*. The maximum distance of the bus is 500 meters and its speed is 10 Mbps. In a typical implementation, a single Ethernet LAN segment may be supporting 50 different computer users.

All computers connected to the bus through Ethernet cards broadcast bits onto the bus, and all cards listen to the transmitted bits. This means the 10 Mbps bus must support all the traffic moving among the connected computing devices. This sharing of limited bandwidth is Ethernet's greatest drawback.

Each Ethernet node listens to all packets on the bus but records only *broadcast packets* (messages needed by all end devices on the LAN) and those packets addressed specifically to the node's address. Broadcast functions in a significant way for Ethernet LANs sharing addresses and other status information and is an important element of higher-layer protocols using the Ethernet LAN. Ethernet uses MAC (Media Access Control) addresses to uniquely identify each host. The layer 2 MAC address is generally hard wired into the Ethernet card.

Each Ethernet card shares available bandwidth on the bus through the Carrier-Sense Multiple Access/Collision Detection (CSMA/CD) technique. Each card listens to the bus and as soon as it detects silence begins to send any waiting packets. Because several hosts may transmit simultaneously, each card must listen to detect any collisions in their packet. If one occurs, each card in effect backs off for a random time before listening and trying to transmit again. The resulting delays from sharing bandwidth negatively impacts the performance of time-sensitive traffic in large shared networks.

CSMA/CD performs very effectively until the network load reaches near 70 percent, at which point network performance degrades quickly. Repeated collisions result in less and less available bandwidth, and throughput can fall to less than 50 percent. Network managers must carefully monitor Ethernet networks to keep the load within acceptable levels. This isn't a difficult problem, however, because Ethernet has been a widely used networking protocol for more than ten years. Its behavior is well understood, its diagnostic tools are widely available, and the rules in network design are well known.

Over the years, improvements to Ethernet's original design broadened its capabilities:

- Repeaters extend the physical length of the coax cable.
- Bridges join two or more buses together, even over long distances.
- Routers join buses and use extra intelligence to filter packets and to convert packet formats among protocols.
- Hubs allow star-based wiring with the hubs in the star center and the end stations at the star points.
- 10BaseT allows Ethernet to use the twisted-pair wiring found in most buildings.

Even with these improvements, Ethernet remained a relatively low-speed networking technology good for data only. Recent developments now position Ethernet as a viable alternative to ATM in many local networking environments. The one remaining advantage ATM has over the Ethernet family of solutions is its multiple qualities of service for supporting real-time traffic. However, many vendors support this capability through proprietary solutions other than ATM; and a few standards bodies (IETF with RSVP and IEEE with 802.1p and 802.1q) hope to develop standards-based solutions within the few next years.

Switched Ethernet

Switched Ethernet provides a 10 Mbps dedicated Ethernet segment to each desktop. It improves upon the shared nature of the network topology by providing each desktop full use of the 10 Mbps connection. You gain higher speed for a very small upgrade cost.

Network managers can simply replace their Ethernet wiring hub with a switched Ethernet box and continue to use all of the existing adapters and wiring. Its ability to let you re-use adapters strongly positions switched Ethernet against ATM. As far as cost goes, switched Ethernet moves closer in price to a 25 Mbps ATM solution if the network requires total system replacement.

Switched Ethernet is probably the migration solution you need if your networking environment has the following characteristics (that probably describe the majority of current networking environments):

✔ Ethernet is the existing LAN solution.

✔ Network users need more bandwidth than you'd get with traditional Ethernet.

✔ User applications don't require multiple qualities of service.

Switched Ethernet is designed to be a desktop solution. It's not intended to work as a high-speed campus backbone technology.

Fast Ethernet

Fast Ethernet is a standard defined for LAN speeds of 100 Mbps. It uses technology very similar to Ethernet, only faster.

Fast Ethernet appeals to network managers who don't have the time to learn a whole new technology. For example, 100 Mbps and 10 Mbps Ethernet LAN segments can be connected relatively easily. However, fast Ethernet does require new testing equipment and additional training. It uses a shared bus architecture and can't dedicate bandwidth to individual workstations; but *switched* fast Ethernet solutions that do provide dedicated options are in the works.

Right now, fast Ethernet is the favorite high-speed solution for desktop connections. A number of vendors make fast Ethernet solutions available at a very competitive cost. Many network managers purchase Ethernet cards capable of supporting 10 or 100 Mbps Ethernet in their LAN switches for easier migration to 100 Mbps adapters later.

Although fast Ethernet is not the ideal campus backbone technology for scalability above 100 Mbps, fast Ethernet is often more practical than ATM in the campus backbone. Some manufacturers are also now introducing fast Ethernet implementations that allow duplex connections to support a higher-speed backbone.

Gigabit Ethernet

Gigabit Ethernet is an emerging technology that debuted in late 1996. It provides a gigabit of bandwidth (1000 Mbps) in a switched star topology. Standardized solutions probably won't be available until late 1997 or early 1998.

Gigabit Ethernet combines the standard Ethernet technology with a new physical layer known as *fiber channel*. This technology currently requires fiber optic connectivity, although some vendors are working on a copper wiring solution. If gigabit Ethernet works and offers adequate performance at a lower price, it will likely compete with ATM for use in backbone networks. As with fast Ethernet, gigabit Ethernet requires an investment in new equipment for testing and additional training.

Token ring versus ATM

The second most popular LAN technology is token ring. Token ring is popular in networks with a large number of mainframes because it was one of the first LAN interfaces available on IBM equipment.

Token ring connects computing devices on its LAN through a continuous ring. The bandwidth of the ring can be 4 Mbps or16 Mbps. To share bandwidth, the LAN passes a token among the end stations connected to the ring. End stations wishing to broadcast to the ring must wait until they receive the token. They hold on to the token as long as they have traffic to send. Only one station may have the token at a time.

Similar to Ethernet, token ring has received many enhancements over the years including, repeaters, bridging, routing, star wiring and switching. Switched token ring is a popular upgrade option for token ring LANs because it allows reuse of the exising LAN adapter cards.

Token ring is more expensive than Ethernet and therefore ATM can better compete against it. In fact, 25 Mbps ATM uses a physical interface similar to token ring, so ATM 25 Mbps solutions are often cost competitive with new switched token ring LAN installations that include new adapter cards. The benefits of token ring are its familiarity and the maturity of the technology. On the other hand, if you need new adapter cards anyway, changing to a 25 Mbps ATM solution offers guaranteed qualities of service for real-time traffic and seamless interoperability with other ATM networks.

FDDI and FDDI-II versus ATM

As of this writing, Fiber Distributed Data Interface (FDDI) may be the most widely deployed high-speed LAN backbone technology, at least in the U.S. Because it's been available for more than seven years, many vendors offer mature FDDI products. But it appears FDDI's popularity is waning as new alternatives recently made available for LAN backbones slowly diminish its status in new equipment purchases.

FDDI uses a variable length packet and includes a method to fairly allocate and share fiber optic bandwidth. A twisted-pair solution known as Copper Distributed Data Interface (CDDI) is now also available. FDDI shares bandwidth through its token passing contention algorithm and offers a widely available and highly reliable solution. FDDI topology typically features two counter-rotating rings to protect against network failure and provide a path over which to automatically reroute traffic.

FDDI isn't as scalable as ATM; it's defined to operate at 100 Mbps (200 Mbps in duplex mode). Nor does it offer the ability to designate different qualities of service or guarantee bandwidth to different applications. Like ATM, implementing FDDI for the first time means acquiring new protocol expertise.

The FDDI-II standard enhances FDDI with the option to run on twisted-pair copper wiring and support real-time information. It doesn't seem to be gaining the market support necessary to be a long-term solution. Other emerging alternatives are much more popular.

100VG-AnyLAN versus ATM

Hewlett-Packard developed a new high-speed, shared LAN protocol to support delay-sensitive applications and environments (such as multimedia and server farms). It's called Demand Priority Access Method, or DPAM, and goes under the brand name 100VG-AnyLAN. The VG stands for voice grade, indicating the protocol is compatible with four pairs of category 3 wiring. It operates at speeds of 100 Mbps, as the name also suggests, but has support from only a handful of vendors.

Routers and stuff

Routers are devices that join LAN segments. They provide needed connectivity including any required protocol conversions among defined networks, filtering to limit broadcast traffic and security. Routers are needed to build large, scalable networks supporting multiple protocols and users. Common tasks of a router include *address resolution* (mapping between different address types), *packet filtering* (identifying which packets need to go where), *route resolution* (finding the best path in the router network), *packet forwarding* (moving packets between routers), and *protocol conversion* (changing from one protocol to another).

A drawback to routers is the enormous maintenance and equipment costs required to accommodate a business's changing needs and locations. Some of the more time-consuming activities of managing routers include administering addresses and packet filtering selections, and maintaining firewalls (to secure the network).

ATM may offer a way to reduce the number of required routers by off-loading the packet forwarding tasks of the router. Although ATM can't replace all of your routers, fewer routers simplify your network and lower costs. The next time you need to purchase a new backbone router, consider introducing ATM switches into your network. You may find they can increase capacity, improve performance, simplify network operations and maintenance, and lower your costs. Chapter 14 offers more information on the potential benefits of switching versus routing in your campus backbone.

Other IP alternatives

New alternatives to pure routing and switching are emerging for carrying IP and other internetworking protocols over an ATM backbone. These alternatives use ATM cells for network transport but replace ATM's signaling and management functions with well-known routing protocols. Providing switching of IP packets, the alternatives tout keeping ATM's low cost hardware while dropping its high cost software. Proprietary solutions such as Ipsilon's IP Switching, Cisco's Tag Switching, IBM's Aggregate Route-based IP Switching (ARIS), and others are proposed but unproven as of late 1996.

The IETF is now working on standardizing these switching IP techniques. Many folks in the industry would like to see a single standard emerge, but a stable solution and mature software with demonstrated reliable performance and scalable networks are several years off. Nevertheless, each of the current alternatives merits watching over the next several years. More information on these future alternatives and their relationship to ATM is in Chapter 23.

Populating the New World: Migrating to ATM

Introducing ATM into a networking environment usually begins with one or more of the projects we describe in this section. (For a vendor's perspective on migrating to ATM, see the "Inside ATM" feature at the end of Chapter 4.)

ATM workgroups

Many companies begin small by implementing an ATM LAN for a single high-powered *workgroup*. Most large corporations maintain at least one workgroup that requires either ATM's high speed or its multiple service categories. The users in such workgroups typically keep a workstation at their desktops for running high-performance computing and visualization applications, so it makes sense to maximize the productivity of these highly skilled and well-compensated employees.

The ATM implementation for a single workgroup is straightforward. It requires one or more ATM switches (depending upon the number of users and your vendor's number of ports per switch) and an ATM adapter card for each workstation. Users are connected to the rest of the network through a router or LAN emulation software. (You can find information on LAN emulation in Chapter 11.) Of the two connection options, LAN emulation is probably less expensive and it introduces capabilities for expanding the network over time, although you may already have routers in place. You should initially configure the workgroup as a single broadcast domain (for example, with one IP subnet or one virtual LAN in LAN emulation).

After installing ATM for the first group of users, you may find it's practical for other workgroups. As you install more workgroups, you'll likely want to connect them over an ATM backbone on the campus or perhaps over your wide area network.

ATM virtual workgroups

ATM's LAN Emulation (LANE) standard allows establishment of logical as opposed to physical LANs. LANE is currently the only standardized option for establishing virtual LANs. The Institute of Electrical and Electronics Engineers (IEEE) is developing its own standard known as IEEE 802 1q for virtual workgroups, but it won't be complete and implemented for a couple more years. In addition, vendor-specific solutions are available from many traditional LAN technology vendors.

Virtual LANs (VLANs) maximize bandwidth use by allowing network managers to logically group users by their function, as opposed to by their physical locations. VLANs also offer many advanced functions that simplify the never-ending task of managing moves, adds, and changes of users.

Figure 13-1 shows the before and after of a network migrating to virtual LANs. In this case, one-half of the accounting department is on one floor and the other half on another, and the engineering department frequently communicates with many individuals in the marketing department. In traditional LANs, network managers group users by their physical LAN segment, regardless of which areas they communicate with most frequently. Virtual LANS allow logical groupings that can change from project to project, like you see in Figure 13-1.

Virtual LANs improve performance by eliminating the routing that causes transmission delays between users who communicate frequently while helping to limit broadcast traffic to only those users who commonly share information. Traffic moving between two emulated LANs must still pass through a router, however. This type of configuration is usually known as a *one-armed router*. Sometime in the future, the ATM multiprotocol over ATM (MPOA) standard will eliminate the need for one-armed routers and provide direct connectivity over the ATM network of the two virtual LANs.

If you choose to implement ATM in a small number of workgroups and implement LANE, you can set up virtual workgroups between ATM and non-ATM clients. You may find this capability to be a benefit in your networking environment. See Chapter 11 for more about LAN emulation and MPOA.

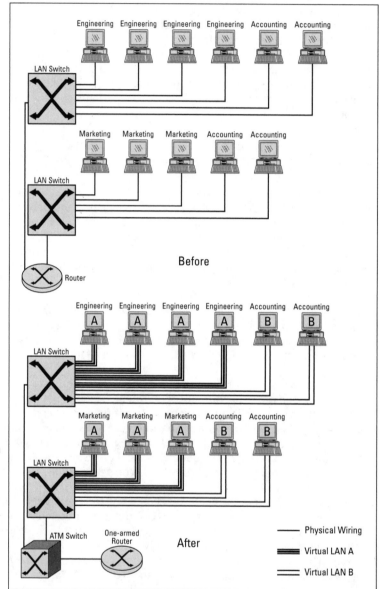

Figure 13-1:
ATM virtual
workgroups
allow
changing
groups from
project to
project.

ATM LAN backbone

LAN backbones are generally the strongest candidates for early ATM implementation in your network. ATM now supports speeds greater than 100 Mbps and offers the advantage of dedicated solutions. Replacing a LAN backbone with ATM (as shown in Figure 13-2) reduces potential congestion between clients and their centralized servers.

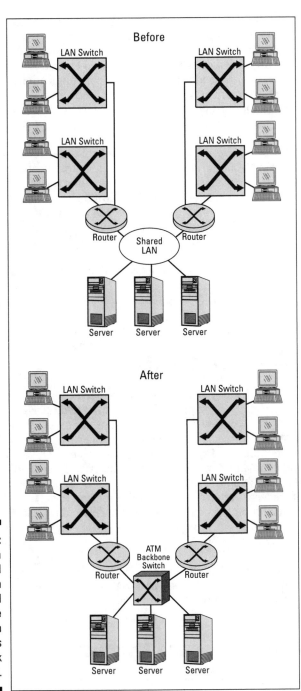

Figure 13-2:
Replacing a shared LAN with an ATM backbone switch relieves network congestion.

With the introduction of intranet web pages and other capabilities for user collaboration, client-to-client communication is on the rise. Internal web pages are increasingly popular allowing users to easily report on their projects, answer FAQ (frequently asked questions), and post up-to-date product information. While these tools improve internal corporate communications and employee teamwork, they add network load where it never was never expected to be. The backbones supporting these networks can become congested very quickly.

In Figure 13-2, before the introduction of ATM, all client-to-server communications shared the same FDDI ring, and client-to-client communication across routers had to traverse the ring as well. After the introduction of ATM, all servers have dedicated connections to the ATM switch, as do routers, providing higher bandwidth to their attached users. The new ATM backbone of this configuration greatly increases performance for both the client-server and client-client applications.

The configuration, connecting traditional LAN users over an ATM backbone and linking them to ATM servers, requires running LAN emulation or one of the other interoperability protocols (like RFC 1577 or MPOA) that we discuss in Chapter 11.

ATM campus data backbone

The ATM backbone switch may also provide high-speed connectivity to another portion of the corporate network, perhaps in another building. Figure 13-3 shows how this works. Two ATM backbone switches communicate with each other over an ATM link. As usual, two benefits of using ATM in this configuration are higher speed and improved support for real-time traffic. The ATM devices can prioritize traffic moving between them by using ATM's quality-of-service capabilities. This means applications such as desktop conferencing that require real-time support receive preferential bandwidth assignment. The ATM campus data backbone can also support direct connections from the backbone switches to ATM-attached LAN switches supporting Ethernet or token ring users (not shown in Figure 13-3).

Implementations combining traditional LAN clients with ATM backbones or ATM clients commonly require deployment of LAN emulation or other interoperability protocol to support communications.

ATM campus enterprise backbone

The same backbone supporting your corporate data traffic can also carry other traffic types such as voice and video, as shown in Figure 13-4. Nowadays, ATM backbone switches transport not only data, but also can interconnect two small PBXs and video conferencing rooms. By using the same backbone to aggregate

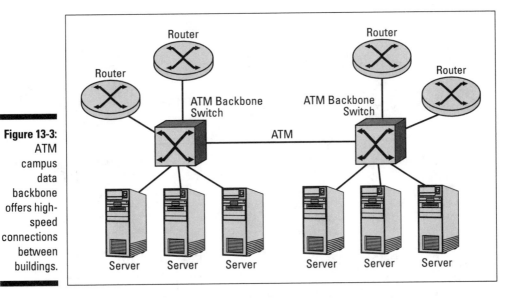

Figure 13-3:
ATM
campus
data
backbone
offers high-
speed
connections
between
buildings.

many traffic types, network managers may be able to avoid expensive or even impossible wiring projects. That same backbone may also provide access to the wide area network.

If The Network Ain't Broke, Don't Fix It

If your local networks are operating just fine and your applications won't be changing much in the next year, then you have no need to change your current solution. Unlike the wide area, where network managers must sometimes change solutions to lower costs even in well-operating networks, no such motivation exists for local networks where new projects just mean new investments without the benefit of ongoing service savings. Staying informed about the emerging capabilities for the day is important in order to see a good idea emerging. But embarking on expensive upgrades for perfectly performing networks (just to get some new technology) doesn't make much sense — and we don't know any network managers who would suggest it!

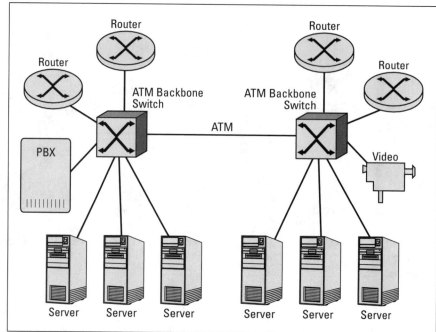

Figure 13-4:
ATM
campus
enterprise
backbone
supports a
variety of
network
traffic.

Inside ATM with Tim Hale
ATM Program Manager
Cabletron Systems, Rochester, NH
`support.ctron.com`

Implementing LANE

ATM is not a fad but a serious technology that is designed for specific purposes. It may not be a technology for everyone, but ATM has some built-in features that make it very suitable for certain applications.

Until such time that we have native ATM applications and operating systems, you need to use some form of integration to connect your existing (legacy) LANs into an ATM environment. LAN Emulation (LANE) is a technique specified by the ATM Forum that describes the interfaces and protocols needed to allow legacy LANs to interoperate with an ATM environment. Interoperability requires LANE because ATM and shared-access LANs are different technologies: ATM is connection-oriented, and LANs are usually connectionless.

The LANE 1.0 specification calls for the formation of Emulated LANs, or ELANs as they are known. An ELAN is a virtual Ethernet or token ring segment. An ELAN can also be referred to as a virtual broadcast domain. You can configure several ELANs within the same ATM network, and an end-station can belong to multiple emulated LANs. However, traffic originating from one emulated LAN cannot normally cross the boundaries of that LAN. This is similar to the way subnets work in traditional LANs.

Thus, a major issue in the LANE 1.0 specification has been left open to interpretation. That is, how do devices on one ELAN communicate with devices on another?

The role of the traditional router

Once you begin to implement ATM LANE, you have certain options in selecting the flavor of routing you want to use.

You can, for example, use traditional routing, which requires the use of a one-armed, ATM-attached router. Such a configuration is also known as a one-armed bandit because it sits in the middle of a data stream and robs you of system performance. Performance degradation results from two primary sources:

✔ overhead required for the router to segment and reassemble packets and cells,

and

✔ time required to look up layer-3 addresses in the router's tables.

In this configuration, a LAN Emulation Client (LEC), or user, on one ELAN communicating with a LEC on another ELAN must send every ATM cell to the router. Within the router determination of the destination address of the second LEC is a time consuming process. The router must reassemble ATM cells into LAN packets and then open up every packet and examine the layer-3 address.

The trip out of the router requires segmenting the packets back into cells before finally sending them on to their intended destination.

Smarten up your ATM network

An alternative to the one-armed bandit described above is cut-through routing, a new capability under discussion by the ATM Forum. Cut-through routing is one of several intelligent LANE services emerging in the marketplace to enhance LANE 1.0. Other capabilities include global directory services and automatic broadcast limiting. These services go beyond the basic capabilities of LANE 1.0 yet comply fully with the ATM Forum specification.

(continued)

The intelligence of the services provides major advantages over and above ordinary LANE implementations and includes the LAN Emulation Configuration Server (LECS), as well as intelligent LAN Emulation Server (LES) and Broadcast and Unknown Server (BUS) functions.

Cut-through routing eliminates the need for a one-armed router and the performance-degrading latency going along with it. Cut-through routing allows LECs of one ELAN to talk directly with LECs of another ELAN. No longer does the router sit in the middle of your data-stream examining every cell passing through it. By eliminating the router, you improve your ATM network's performance dramatically.

Cut-through routing works with the assistance of a global directory service. The global directory automatically discovers members of every ELAN. This allows the intelligent LESs to resolve MAC-to-ATM addresses not only within their own emulated LAN but also across ELANs.

An LEC on one ELAN needing to communicate with an LEC on another goes via the LES to the global directory service mechanism to determine the destination address. The directory service completes address resolution and provides the originating LEC with the destination address. The LEC can then "cut through" the switch fabric directly to the destination. The switch establishes a data-direct virtual circuit (VC) from source to destination, and data flows at wire speed.

This cut-through routing feature is the essence of multi-protocol over ATM (MPOA). MPOA, when it is complete, will allow path routing decisions to be made regardless of LAN protocol. It will also provide much faster performance when compared to traditional routers because only the first packet is routed to determine the path while the remaining packets follow through the resultant switched connection.

Automatic broadcast limiting is another advanced feature that can improve LANE 1.0 performance. This feature prevents nuisance packets from flooding all LECs in the network. An intelligent BUS uses an integrated layer-3 call processor to resolve and reduce these broadcasts. The intelligent BUS can answer broadcasted address requests with individual, unicast ARP responses. This contrasts to other LANE implementations, which forward all broadcasts to all LECs regardless of their need to know. With automatic broadcast limiting, each LEC receives many fewer performance-impacting broadcasts to process.

LANE 1.0 and its newest manifestation intelligent LANE services are furthering the acceptance of ATM. Advanced features, such as cut-through routing, global directory services, and automatic broadcast limiting, greatly improve performance. Intelligent LANE integrates legacy LANs and ATM in such a way that the entire infrastructure appears seamless to the user.

Chapter 14

Considering the ATM Business Case

- -

In This Chapter
▶ Devising your networking strategy
▶ Including potential sources of savings in your case
▶ Recognizing the new costs from using ATM
▶ Understanding the impact of timing on your ATM investment

- -

*F*unding the first ATM project can be a challenge, especially if you follow our recommendation: Keep the initial project small! Chapter 17 contains this advice and other tips you may find useful for managing a successful ATM project. In this chapter, we offer a few considerations for convincing the boss to approve your project.

Making a Case for Improving Your Network

Before you make a great case for new network equipment, services, and technologies (like ATM!), approach the process of preparing that case logically and with specific goals. Then, the networking proposal that you present to your boss is assured a firm foundation. We include the following list for your consideration when putting together your case:

- ✔ Evaluate your network's current information load.
- ✔ Identify your network's potential for growth (like new applications that need network support).
- ✔ Understand the benefits and costs of different networking options (including keeping the status quo) that you have for meeting the changing needs.
- ✔ Outline the potential benefits and cost savings of using ATM technology in your network.
- ✔ Delineate the added challenges and new costs associated with implementing ATM technology.
- ✔ Describe the ongoing management and operational issues that accompany ATM in your network.

> ✔ Evaluate ATM's role in the overall strategic plan for your business network.
>
> ✔ Define a realistic time frame for planning, designing, installing, and implementing your ATM network.

Networks on Wheaties

ATM is easiest to justify in a rapidly growing network. Sometimes ATM is the only choice to meet the bandwidth requirement. In other situations, ATM can be a more economical solution when compared with other alternatives (particularly, maintaining the status quo).

An important point that you need to evaluate during your analysis and business case preparation is exactly how fast the network is growing. This evaluation is often a difficult task. You probably have a good understanding of your network's voice traffic and mainframe growth from years and years of experience, and you may have statistics to back you up. However, if you are like many network managers, you don't have the right tools to measure your LAN-to-LAN traffic in great detail. You may just know that it's growing — and growing fast.

Although difficult to determine, the network's growth factor is key to making the right networking decisions. If you set the growth factor too low, you'll be going back for more incremental dollars to augment your networking project in just a few months. If you set the growth factor too high, you may buy equipment and services before your organization really needs them.

In our general experience, we find that network managers tend to underestimate the growth deluging their LANs and WANs. In one project, a business contacted its carrier in January, 1995, to begin planning the migration of a few core sites from two frame relay T1s to T3 ATM in mid 1996. By June, the migration date had moved to early 1996. By August, the cry was for the carrier to complete the upgrade as soon as possible. The large service business had not anticipated the phenomenal inter-router traffic growth that it had to support on its wide area network.

Another important but difficult evaluation during the planning period is identifying what new applications may be using the network. You can help identify some pending changes by taking a user survey, but many times the users cannot anticipate their networking needs. The survey is most likely to miss projects that individual users or departments can implement in a short time period, like a few months. Such projects include internal Web sites, new client-server applications for individual workgroups, and new desktop conferencing applications.

The following are two known facts about networks:

- ✔ Network traffic grows.
- ✔ Network user requirements change.

And these facts are sometimes sufficient justification for harried network managers to go with the ATM choice. They like the terms of the ATM insurance policy. The network managers believe that ATM can enable them to deliver whatever network requirements that their organization asks. ATM also gives the added flexibility of being an open networking scheme that supports at least some level of interoperability between networking devices.

Of course, a good insurance policy is not easy to sell in most businesses where executives carefully guard precious funding dollars. The preferred investment is to finance new product development, distribution channels, and other projects that help the business to grow and compete in the tough global market. Spending dollars on support functions takes away funding from other business opportunities.

Therefore, the easiest network improvement projects to justify demonstrate that a change in the networking investment direction can cost less than continuing investment in the current direction over the planning period — this cost factor largely depends upon the projected network growth. The difference between retaining the status quo and funding the ATM alternative should be greater than 20 percent to be convincing and worth the change effort.

You also want to understand how ATM stacks up against other alternatives available to you. We discuss these alternatives in Chapters 12, 13, and 22. Typically, network evaluation projects consider a minimum of three alternatives — two new directions and the status quo. If you understand your requirements, how well each alternative meets the requirements, and the associated costs, you can make a good networking decision for your business.

Looking on the Plus Side of ATM

If your network evaluation leads you to a decision to choose ATM, your next step is to convince everyone else. In developing your business case for ATM, you may use one or more of the following benefits to justify your decision:

- ✔ Potential savings on network costs
- ✔ New network capabilities
- ✔ Strategic fit with the overall business networking goals

Because convincing your business to fund an ATM implementation is easiest if you can demonstrate real dollars returned, we begin by looking at the potential savings benefits.

Potential savings from using ATM

You can investigate four potential areas for network savings with ATM technology:

- ✔ Wiring
- ✔ Local access costs
- ✔ Wide area bandwidth
- ✔ Equipment

You may also want to add simplified management and operations savings to the list. But we think that you may find these expenses actually increasing, at least initially, until everyone is on board with the new ATM networking solution. Most likely, you are augmenting your network with ATM and not completely replacing any existing protocols or equipment. So unfortunately, management and operations expenses probably belong in the *minus* side of your business case.

Saving on wiring

We discuss, in our opening feature for Chapter 1, that adding new wiring can be extremely expensive and sometimes impossible. In existing buildings, adding wiring can require ripping apart ceilings, floors, and walls. If you're leasing facilities, you have the added headache of convincing the building owners to support the wiring project. Adding lines between buildings may require digging up sidewalks and streets, and often you just cannot get the easement that you need.

If the ATM project is going to save you substantial rewiring costs by extending the life of your existing infrastructure, then you may have hit the paydirt you need to convince the boss.

Saving on access costs

Access costs may be another source of substantial savings if you are designing a wide area ATM network. ATM allows you to consolidate multiple access links into one. That is, an ATM network can support connections to many different sites through ATM's logical circuits, whereas private lines require a separate physical link for each connection. Figure 14-1 demonstrates the potential savings. In the before-ATM picture, the host site requires four different access connections to reach each of the remote locations over private lines. In the after ATM picture, the host site must subscribe to only one access link for the ATM connection, thereby substantially reducing access costs.

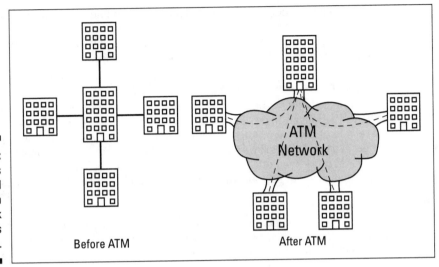

Figure 14-1:
ATM offers
potential
savings on
network
access
connections.

Before ATM   After ATM

Saving on bandwidth costs

Using ATM equipment and/or services can drive wide area bandwidth savings
in three ways:

- ✓ By allowing consolidation of multiple networks
- ✓ By using lower cost public ATM services
- ✓ By supporting voice compression and silence suppression

Of course, enjoying the wonderful bandwidth savings potential of ATM assumes
that you need a lot of bandwidth. If you are running a relatively low speed
network (such as 56 Kbps frame relay) today, you are probably at least a couple
of years away from needing the high bandwidth of a T1 or T3 ATM network,
which can deliver from 20 to over 500 times the current bandwidth.

Although the potential bandwidth savings of an ATM WAN may be substantial
for large networks, it may also be difficult to quantify. Obstacles to determining
cost savings that you may run into include the following:

- ✓ Carriers offer a convoluted web of discounts and incentives as traffic
  volumes and term commitments increase on existing services — not to
  mention the varying rates offered by the many different carriers from
  whom you can subscribe services.

- ✓ Actual ATM service pricing may be difficult to obtain, although private-line
  pricing for a private ATM network is more straightforward.

Determining an accurate before-and-after bottom line may take some time, but don't let the difficulty discourage you and cause you to drop the ATM project altogether. If you have a large corporate network, you may be able to mine some gold from ATM's efficient use of your bandwidth reserve.

Consolidation of multiple networks

We predict that your business runs multiple parallel networks to support different applications within your organization. Most companies have a separate network for their voice communications, SNA, LANs, and video applications. If a company grows from the consolidation of multiple businesses, you may find more than one network for each of these traffic types. When you add the networks that support unique, specific applications of the business, you are well on your way to 20 or more networks.

In the past, organizations developed a uniquely designed network for each new application implemented. With this type of network development, the average utilization of most links may be less than 20 percent. Furthermore, the peak traffic for each may occur at different times of the day. For example, voice traffic tends to peak at 10 a.m. and 2 p.m., your LAN traffic may be heaviest in the morning and late afternoon when everyone checks e-mail, while mainframe backups are driving network traffic peaks during the night.

ATM allows all the different applications to pool their networking bandwidth. ATM ensures that each receives the bandwidth required, when it is required. The excess bandwidth that results from this pooling is now available to support added network growth. Bandwidth pooling also benefits *bursty* LAN applications, which can use a large percentage of the pooled bandwidth when the other applications have no traffic to send.

In network configurations that consolidate many large, multiple networks, you can find 40 percent *plus* savings with ATM solutions. (Your mileage may vary.) The amount of potential savings depends very much on the behavior of your applications. Good network traffic statistics that pinpoint traffic peaks are invaluable in determining your bandwidth savings. You need to make some assumptions as to how much gain ATM can really give you. For example, if you are just combining your LAN and SNA networks, then you may experience little gain compared to the gain realized from adding voice communications to the mix.

When determining the required backbone bandwidth of the new ATM network, be sure to understand how your ATM equipment reserves connection bandwidth. Many ATM switches use an algorithm called *equivalent capacity* which tends to reserve the peak bandwidth required and allows little oversubscription of the link. (*Oversubscription* is a term describing a port whose virtual connection bandwidths total more than the physical speed of the port.) These ATM switches rely on subscriptions to the UBR service category for statistical gain because they reserve very little bandwidth for connections using this service category. We discuss equivalent capacity and bandwidth reservation in more depth in Chapter 10.

Despite the potential consolidation savings you might gain, we still stick by our advice to keep your initial ATM project small. We suggest that you begin consolidation with just three or four of your largest locations and consolidate only the largest two or three applications. Such an approach can keep the initial project sufficiently small to manage and move from the drawing board into an actual implementation. You also learn from your initial implementation, and you can apply your improved knowledge and skill when you migrate other sites to ATM in the future. You can find additional information on using ATM to consolidate multiple networks in the *Inside ATM* feature at the end of Chapter 7.

Lower cost public ATM services

If you are leasing private line services over long distances, you may find that converting to public ATM services is another source of bandwidth savings. Public ATM services typically have distance insensitive pricing. They are generally lower cost for local point-to-point T1 and T3 connections more than 30 miles and long distance point-to-point connections more than 300 miles. Networks consisting of a larger number of sites will have a lower mileage cross-over.

If you are not ready to convert to public ATM services, you can add this as possible future benefit in your business case documentation.

Voice compression and silence suppression

The third source of bandwidth savings is not a direct benefit of using ATM technology. However, some vendors are including advanced voice compression and silence suppression in their new ATM boxes. You may find that you can migrate your corporate voice traffic onto the ATM network for only the cost of the interface card on your ATM box. The incremental bandwidth required may be essentially free. The industry has flipped the old adage "data rides with voice for free" into "voice rides with data for free."

You still need to use public VPNs for traffic destined off-net until carriers interconnect their ATM and voice networks. However, the initial steps you can take today may save you significant bandwidth dollars.

Saving on equipment costs

Although ATM equipment in general can be expensive, adding such equipment may save overall network equipment costs. The greatest potential for equipment savings is in reducing requirements for future router purchases. High-end routers required for large backbone networks can be quite expensive. Even individual port cards cost a substantial sum of money.

ATM can reduce the number of routers and port cards required in campus and WAN backbones, by replacing high-cost, delay-inducing routing with low-cost, higher-performing switching. You still need your routers for address resolution, protocol conversion, and dividing your network into manageable subsets (or subnets as a fluent conversant in TCP/IP would say).

By adding ATM switches, you move your routers to the edges of your network where you need their address resolution capabilities. Your network backbone can then use a fast, efficient ATM core. Without ATM, the network requires backbone routers to support full connectivity. These transient routers add expense, processing delays, and potential network bottlenecks. But lower-cost ATM switches can replace the backbone routers and open up the networking express ways for all your applications. Each router connects to another through ATM's logical connectivity in one hop. You can also depend on your ATM network for more simple route recovery of a few virtual connections versus the thousands of end-to-end routes maintained by your routing tables. The constant stability of your routing tables (which is assured by the ATM logical connectivity) can also boost performance, leaving the processing power of your router to focus where you need it, on address resolution.

Looking at new network capabilities with ATM

Your primary motivation for an ATM network may be the new capabilities supported by ATM. Perhaps you need ATM's high bandwidth or multimedia support for a new application. If you fit this description, you need to justify your ATM project based on the business benefits of the new application, often a difficult proposition. Quantifying the potential business cost savings or the worth of reduced development and production cycles can be challenging. You also have to include the total cost of the new application, not just the ATM network. Projects requiring investment in only local ATM may be more fundable than projects requiring justification of high speed wide area bandwidth, especially nationwide networks. Often, these narrower types of projects are funded because an executive thinks that the project is important enough to do, and a detailed financial analysis is not necessary. We hope you have such a fairy godmother.

Fitting the BIG strategic vision with ATM

A few network managers fund their first ATM projects by showing how the projects fit into the network strategic plan. Their first step is to write the plan along with a high-level migration path for achieving the depicted vision. The strategic plan includes broad versus detailed financial analyses to support the merits of the selected ATM architecture. Perhaps the plan includes financial savings from one application area or demonstrated potential benefits given specific (but not necessarily proven) assumptions.

The approved strategic direction may lay the groundwork for starting a few early, limited ATM projects without full financial justification. In turn, these early projects may provide additional information to gain approval for more ambitious ATM projects.

Recognizing the Minus Side of ATM

Although you probably want to spend the majority of your business case describing the benefits and showing the plus side of the justification, you also want to show the new challenges. After all, you are probably going to need extra dollars or human resources to overcome these challenges. Two items that you may want to include on the minus side of your business case are the new costs associated with ATM and the challenge of network conversion.

New costs

As you prepare your business proposal, be sure to consider the following most common new costs associated with an ATM project:

- ✔ **Equipment:** Although some ATM networking configurations result in lower equipment costs, others require additional investments. As an example, if you are adding ATM equipment to build an enterprise WAN justified by bandwidth savings, then equipment costs may show up on the minus side of your balance sheet.

- ✔ **Test gear:** ATM test equipment can be very expensive, sometimes more than the price of a switch. Although you may not need the top of the line gear, you probably need some tools for monitoring the performance on your network and trouble shooting problems. Make sure you get an estimate of these costs before submitting your final funding request. We doubt that you'll be able to sneak your purchases into some other category after funding approval. These test boxes just cost too darn much. Don't forget them!

- ✔ **Management systems:** Similar to test equipment, management systems can be another overlooked category. Understand the new requirements for computing platforms and networking (especially if you'll be using out-of-band management circuits). Consider how your ATM management system can integrate into your existing systems (perhaps you can rely on the vast computing resources of the human operators for integration). As ATM hardware costs continue to fall, network management and other miscellaneous expenses become a larger percentage of the total outlay.

- ✔ **Operations expense:** Although you may prove us wrong, we expect operations expenses to end up at the minus side of your business case. ATM may require your hiring new talent into your organization due to resource or skill constraints. You may find that outsourcing these new tasks with your equipment or carrier providers is the best approach.

- ✔ **Training expense:** If you are going to support the new ATM equipment internally, then the networking staff will require training which also takes time and money. Hands-on training is most helpful for those who must support the network. Hold your training close to the time of conversion so that everyone soon has a chance to apply and reinforce what they learned in class.

✔ **Pretesting:** You may want to fund a small lab to pretest the performance of your applications over an ATM network. The lab gives you a flexible environment to work out all the details of your implementation before actually having to make it all come together in the production network. Most users don't have much patience waiting for their network connectivity while you try *this and that* to see what works best. The lab also provides a valuable benchmark to assist in trouble resolution and for considering the merits of future changes in the network.

Conversion

Conversion is always a dreaded word. Good network conversions take careful planning and extra time, and they also add risk that something may go wrong in the network. The probability that the network will work the first time out, even with lots of pre-testing, is probably low — Murphy's law and all of that.

Converting to an ATM implementation is no exception. In your ATM business case, be sure to include some extra resources for help during network conversion. Think about each step of your conversion and what equipment and activities are necessary. Identify any downtime that network users may experience. Most organizations hold conversions over the weekend, so you are probably looking at some extra overtime for you and your team. If possible, you also want to run your existing and ATM networks in parallel for at least a month to work through any glitches that don't turn up in the first couple days of testing. Often your service providers can give you the extra facilities during the conversion period for free as a perk for trying out their new services.

A Question of Time

Misunderstanding the impacts of timing can skew even the most accurate determinations of the factors in the plus and minus sides of the business case. The consideration of these timing parameters in your ATM business case is also very critical:

✔ **Planning period:** We recommend a planning period of three years. If you consider a shorter time frame, you are probably missing some real chances to get beyond the support fire drills and crises all too common in many network managers' lives. A longer time frame is probably beyond the unclouded vision of even the most gifted futurists, considering the many changes impacting telecommunications in the mid 1990s. We believe that a three year-time frame is a good balance between these two perspectives.

✔ **Depreciation cycles:** You also need to provide a recommendation to your accounting department on a practical depreciation cycle. Depending on the particular piece of equipment, 36 or 60 months seems to be a reasonable, conservative estimate. If your ATM equipment serves you longer through upgrades, card expansions, and redeployment in your network, the added life is a bonus.

✔ **Payback time:** The *payback time* is the point in the future at which your total expenses are recovered by your profits (or savings) from the project. All ATM projects initially require an outlay of capital and expense, but new savings resulting from implementation can chip away at the negative balance until it reaches zero. This zero point is the payback period. We would expect most ATM projects to begin providing a payback within 18 to 30 months. The uncertainties of the future probably do not warrant any longer payback. If your payback is even shorter, you further improve the chances that you're doing the right thing by implementing ATM.

Liza Henderson
Broadband Consultant
TeleChoice, Inc., (Headquarters) Verona, NJ

Justifying ATM: Not Always by the Numbers

If you've ever had the horrific experience of developing a business case to justify new networks or changes to network implementations, you know it's not a fun job. You usually can get through the executive summary, all the hated problems of the current implementation, the proposed solution, and the benefits of the solution sections of the business case unscathed.

Then you falter and hit a brick wall when it comes to the money part. This is where the big bosses want you to discuss how much money you're spending now, how much money the company will save with the new implementation, and how much it will lose if it decides to stick with the current network. Of course, the business case needs to include that dreaded financial spreadsheet with all the nitty gritties. We generally try to hide it in some appendix; but those smart execs know where to find it and often flip to that page first, past all our long hours of work. The first question usually is "Where or how did you get these numbers?" Perhaps if your exec would have read through your write-up first, then there would be no need to ask. A familiar situation, isn't it?

Unfortunately, justifying ATM implementations can be no different. Because ATM is a new technology or service, it will likely raise lots of questions and issues from some management person higher up your corporate stack. Hard facts may be hard for you to find. And if you're implementing ATM in the next two years, you may be the first on your block, so you will likely find little conventional wisdom or common assumptions.

We know of some companies that just chose to implement ATM in only a small segment of the network to avoid some of the justification nightmare (not to mention that implementation was easier). These users started with the most obvious piece of their network, generally some overloaded backbone. Sometimes they were able to expand ATM implementation from this birthplace to other parts of the network without further formal justification.

On the other hand, maybe you can find a shortcut that avoids the business case altogether. We like shortcuts. After all, how do things really get done in a corporation? Business cases? Yeah, sometimes. But we've seen other approaches as well.

(continued)

- Somebody doesn't care about the boss and is motivated by the Nike commercial to Just Do It. Not always the best approach if you want to keep your job or your boss is slightly more intelligent than Dilbert's.

- Somebody who just doesn't know any better starts down a path to solve a problem, and before anyone has time to review their work or ask questions, ATM is in the network.

- Visionary executives — rare.

- A part of the network crashes — a crisis that must be fixed NOW! We hate those days :+(.

- Giving users a taste test that whets their appetite for more.

If getting financial approval to implement ATM is one of your biggest hurdles, you might want to try one of the more unconventional but effective approaches to the situation.

One of our favorite examples comes from Bill Brasuell, who is a Network Technologist at Tandem Computers. Bill told us, "Trials are a very good way to show management what the business improvement is, and trials get the end users to state the benefits. It's a hard sell when it's all theory."

Tandem Computers signed up for a trial of LDDS WorldCom's ATM service back in 1994. Although carrier-provided ATM services have been around for a while, the services are still maturing. The carriers are craving to learn more about the practical application of ATM with the help of end users. As an end user, you have good leverage with carriers, either your incumbent or a hungry competitor. Most services are not tariffed, and carriers are willing to tailor their services to meet the unique needs of each end user. A lot of things are negotiable — service features, service guarantees, pricing structures, and even rates.

Tandem's ATM trial network connected its Cupertino, California, headquarters and its Integrity Systems Division in Austin, Texas. During the trial, Tandem engineers used the network for collaborative computing applications to design "next generation" computers for its customers. Tandem's objective was to provide the equivalent of having the staff co-located without requiring extensive travel or physical moves. Two weeks into the trial, the carrier had to take the network down to perform a network upgrade with the permission of Tandem. The network was sorely missed by the Tandem engineers, and requests to get the network back up as soon as possible flooded Bill Brasuell's office. Bill soon found out that although it was only a trial network, the engineers were already using it in a production mode. The engineers were relying on the network to meet their project deadlines. According to Bill, "the engineers could not live without it."

The engineers' testimonials, increase in productivity, and tangible cost savings proved to be extremely powerful reasons for Bill to justify keeping the ATM network. He was able to spend more of his time implementing the network rather than crunching numbers. Tandem is very satisfied with the ATM service. As a matter of fact, it plans to add its Reston, Virginia; Itasca, Illinois; Atlanta, Georgia; and Stockley Park, United Kingdom offices to the network. Bill also added that the network now carries "dozens and dozens of different applications ranging from Internet Web access to internal e-mail to engineering computer-aided design (CAD) to software development to manufacturing testing."

What Bill has done is take the bull by the horns and run with it. Time is of the essence to a network manager, and there often isn't much time for bull — taming.

Chapter 15

Implementing ATM

. . . .

In This Chapter

▶ Evaluating equipment and service providers

▶ Considering interoperability in your network

▶ Designing and engineering the network

. . . .

*N*ow that you've reached the decision to use ATM in a specific part of your LAN and/or WAN and have secured funding to put your plan into action, your next step is to actually do it — implement your ATM network.

The flood of evaluation information provided in this chapter may convince you that you've made the wrong choice by considering ATM. Don't let all the information overwhelm you. We want to give you as many insights and considerations as possible to help you weed out the weak versus the strong ATM providers. Use the information in this chapter to ask these providers some hard questions (and watch them squirm). After you find the right providers for you, they can help assure that your ATM project is a success, and you don't have to worry over all the technical details. You can leave those worries to the ATM provider's designers and engineers.

Acronyms Used in This Chapter	
Acronym	*What It Stands For*
ABR	Available Bit Rate
ASIC	Application Specific Integrated Circuit
BUS	Broadcast and Unknown Server
CAC	Call Admission Control
CAP	Competitive Access Providers
CBR	Constant Bit Rate
CIR	Committed Information Rate
CPE	Customer Premises Equipment

(continued)

Acronyms Used in This Chapter *(continued)*

Acronym	What It Stands For
FDDI	Fiber Distributed Data Interchange
IAM	Inverse ATM Mux
IETF	Internet Engineering Task Force
IP	Internet Protocol
ISDN	Integrated Services Digital Network
LANE	LAN Emulation
LATA	Local Access Transport Area
LEC	Local Exchange Carrier
MIB	Management Information Base
MPOA	Multiprotocol over ATM
NIC	Network Interface Card
PNNI	Private Network-Network Interface
PVC	Permanent Virtual Circuit
RBOC	Regional Bell Operating Companies
RFI	Request for Information
SMDS	Switched Multimegabit Data Service
SNA	System Network Architecture
SNMP	Simple Network Management Protocol
SONET	Synchronous Optical Network
SVC	Switched Virtual Circuit
TCP/IP	Transmission Control Protocol/Internet Protocol
TDM	Time Digital Multiplexing
UBR	Unspecified Bit Rate
VBR	Variable Bit Rate
VBR-RT	Variable Bit Rate–Real-Time
VC	Virtual Channel
VLAN	Virtual LAN
VP	Virtual Path

Selecting Your ATM Providers

Selecting your equipment and service providers for ATM can be a very daunting process. The ATM market is still very young, and a wealth of potential ATM providers are all competing for a limited number of pioneer ATM adopters. The market has yet to shake out, and you can probably find more than ten equipment vendors and at least five carriers who claim to meet your needs. All are aggressively seeking early flagship customers with whom they can work to understand emerging market needs. Many leading-edge ATM customers have found enthusiastic vendors who spend a great deal of time helping to plan and then implement their customer network.

As we discuss in the previous chapters, the best initial ATM project is small. Trying to implement the grand vision of ATM all at once only paralyzes your efforts because you find too many different considerations and activities necessary to complete such a large project. Nevertheless, over the long term, ATM can represent a significant change in your network, so take some time and shop around for providers and equipment options. You may be surprised at the choices that are available. Go to your existing provider and three or four alternatives in your initial investigations. You may want to include a dark horse candidate that present a unique networking perspective; the least likely candidate may have some ideas worth considering.

The Web is a great place to start your selection process. In the industry trade rags are lab tests and evaluation studies of most ATM networking elements. You can also find articles discussing the latest capabilities and issues of ATM specifications. Vendor sites contain a wealth of product and positioning information, and these sites often have tips for evaluating and integrating ATM into your network. We include a few of our favorite sites and starting points in Chapter 20.

In addition to the information we provide in this text, you can turn to the ATM Forum's mock RFI (request for information) for additional guidelines. The User Group of the ATM Forum, the Enterprise Networking Roundtable, wrote the mock RFI as a template for evaluating ATM equipment and services. The mock RFI is now over a year old but still contains valuable information of what functionality to consider in seeking high-performing, interoperable ATM equipment and services. The current RFI focuses on evaluation criteria for equipment, as opposed to services, so not all questions are applicable if you're investigating public ATM services. You can find the mock RFI on the Forum's Web site at http://www.atmforum.com

Equipment vendor considerations

ATM has received mind-boggling investments by both existing equipment vendors and aggressive upstarts throughout the world. All the leading equipment vendors are active participants in the ATM Forum, and most of these vendors now have working products of one type or another.

Many network managers go to their existing equipment vendors to discuss potential changes in their network or to find new and improved solutions. This approach can be good, but don't forget to visit some of the newer companies as well. If you simply accept the suggestions of your existing provider without looking around, you may implement the best solution for your provider rather than the best solution for your network.

New companies typically focus on a strong differentiator for their product line, such as lower cost, ease of use, interoperability, advanced capabilities, or even ATM technology. Alternative vendors often broaden your perspective of what's available, how to improve network performance and cost, and how to introduce new solutions into your network. Many of the alternatives have survived in the marketplace for several years because of their strong focus on particular issues. So if a prospective vendor has good, solid products, you don't have to be overly concerned about the vendor disappearing; it will probably survive, either independently or as part of another organization.

So take a few afternoons to learn about what's out there. Talk to a few router, LAN switching, hub, and ATM vendors for suggestions on alternative solutions for your network. Even the younger networking vendors understand the importance of preserving your existing investment and have worked hard to achieve interoperability with single vendor solutions. Most of their solutions focus on *integrating* ATM with the existing network wherever integration makes sense rather than *replacing* your embedded equipment.

When you talk with vendors, discuss the topics outlined in the following sections.

Corporate success and positioning

You want to work with a vendor who has a vision for its product line; commitment, knowledge, and skill to execute the vision; and previous success stories. The more ATM experience that the folks at your vendor have, the farther they are up the learning curve, and the more ready and able they are to assist you with your network design and implementation. Ask what version of their software they are currently offering. What other versions have been generally available?

Past experience in environments very similar to yours helps everything go more smoothly. Ask your vendor about the largest network it has supported. How many networks have its people installed? Insist on talking to other customers with application and network environments similar to your own. You can discover a lot from their missteps and mistakes and receive a wealth of knowledge to smooth your implementation.

Product Vision

Understand the intended networking environment for each product you consider. The developers of most equipment had a particular use in mind as they laid out their design; you want equipment that is intended for an environment similar to yours. The broadest breakout of ATM equipment categories is

- ✔ Private Network
- ✔ Public Carrier

Private networking solutions generally have significantly lower costs but lack some of the key redundancy, speed, environmental, and management features demanded by carriers. These two equipment categories may be further broken down.

Private networking equipment includes the following:

- ✔ **Legacy-to-ATM Devices:** Smaller devices supporting hubbing or switching of legacy LANs (such as Ethernet, Token Ring, and FDDI) and providing an ATM uplink to the campus backbone. One aspect to consider on these devices is how they support LANE: Some include all LANE elements and can connect back-to-back through an ATM connection; others require an intermediate ATM switch to support LANE and provide connectivity.

- ✔ **ATM Network Interface Cards (NICs):** Adapter cards for workstations and personal computers connected via an ATM LAN. Work with a NIC vendor who can support the personal computer and workstation architectures, buses, and drivers running in your enterprise. Pay close attention to how much processing power the card drains from the host machine. Some cards come with their own independent processors, while others slow down the desktop machine. You also want to know the buffering and shaping capabilities of your cards and whether they are capable of supporting SVCs.

- ✔ **ATM Workgroup Switches:** ATM LAN switches for workgroups of less than 24 users requiring high networking performance. These workgroup switches may also include a few interfaces for connectivity to legacy LANs. Port configurations and types, costs, performance, and features are key considerations in evaluating this equipment.

- ✔ **ATM Backbone Switches:** ATM switches for building corporate LAN backbones on a campus. Again, port configurations, costs, performance, and features are important, with particular focus on performance. Get switches that can meet the demands of your backbone to support a large number of virtual connections and fast SVC call setups, minimize delay, and maximize throughput.

✔ **ATM Access Switches, Concentrators, and Muxes:** These switches vary greatly in their functionality. Some advanced features available in this equipment class may have value to you, and others may not. Spend some time thinking about what features you require for your network. If you need support for many different data and voice interfaces, as well as sophisticated bandwidth management and priority, then one of these higher-end devices may be best for you. Otherwise, a more basic solution may be the right fit, and you pay much less.

Public carrier equipment generally includes the following:

✔ **Adaptation Devices:** Smaller devices providing adaptation of non-ATM traffic types into ATM. Carriers are placing adaptation devices as close to the customer premises as possible, even going all the way to the premises in larger multi-tenant buildings. Typical adaptation devices today can convert frame relay, SMDS, and IP into ATM. Future versions may add ISDN, voice, and dial-up data to the mix. A class of adaptation devices also supports native LAN services.

✔ **ATM Edge Switches:** Medium-sized switches for delivering ATM services (and perhaps trunking adaptation devices, depending on the carrier architecture). Edge switches enable a carrier to deliver a cost-effective, fully featured, high-performing ATM service to customers.

✔ **ATM Core Switches:** Large machines that deliver 20 Gbps of switching today, with expansion plans to 160 Gbps and beyond. Core switching enables carriers to concentrate traffic into a few large, highly utilized backbone trunks for their longest and most expensive links. The best core switches maintain traffic quality at very high switching and transport speeds.

If you deviate from the intended use of equipment, trouble may be on the path ahead. Equipment upgrades and enhancements will probably focus on the intended use, leaving you in a dead end with your special implementation. Also, beware of any equipment vendor that is trying to be all things to all people, feeling around in the dark for a useful implementation of its product. Such a vendor is likely to have missed the mark everywhere. Choose a vendor who clearly understands how customers use its products and what benefits motivate the purchase of their equipment.

Oh, the horror stories we could tell . . . such as ATM switches designed for private networking environments being sold as public solutions with only one working VP addressing space or gathering performance data on the input as opposed to the output side of the switch. But we don't want to scare you. Most of the equipment available performs as expected and is fairly stable and mature, at least for basic cell transport functionality and support. Just keep your eyes open!

Product architecture and features

Spend quite a bit of time understanding the equipment architectures and features of each prospective vendor. Ask the vendor to trace a cell through its switch. Is buffering appropriate at each point? Does a risk of head-of-line blocking exist anywhere? (*Head-of-line blocking* detains cells behind another cell that is waiting to enter a congested output port, even if the detained cells' destination port is free and clear.) How does the switch service the different port and service category queues? Is the switch servicing fair? What congestion management techniques are available on the switch? What type of switching matrix do the switches use, and what are the benefits of that switching matrix? What functions of the switch have the designers burned into ASICs (application specific integrated circuits)?

Pick a vendor who is aggressive in adopting ATM standards and features into its equipment, because ATM is a rapidly evolving technology. Ask your vendor when some of the existing standards (for example, traffic shaping, UNI 3.0 signaling, LANE, and various physical interfaces) were generally available in its devices. What are the vendor's plans to add newly emerging capabilities? Find out what the vendor is doing to meet its schedules. Have enough resources been assigned? Is the schedule sufficiently detailed and thought out? Our experience is that vendors are overly aggressive with their delivery schedules by as much as six months. Also ask about pre-standard capabilities that enhance the performance and management of the switch.

Table 15-1 outlines a few specific criteria you may want to use in evaluating the architecture and features of your prospective equipment vendors. More thoughts on architecture, specific to performance, availability, interoperability, upgradability, and scalability, are in the next sections.

Table 15-1   Equipment Vendor Architecture and Feature Criteria

Architecture/Feature	Questions to Ask
Port Types and Counts	What ATM and non-ATM interfaces are available? What physical medium do these interfaces support? What is the port density of the cards? How flexibly can you mix and match port cards? What is the maximum configuration for different card types? Can you use the cards in other pieces of equipment from the vendor?
Switching Fabric and Size	How fast is the switching fabric? How is capacity measured? Is the switching fabric expandable? What type of switching fabric does the switch use? What are the merits of this fabric? Is it nonblocking (that is, on a fully loaded switch, every port can communicate at line speed with any other port)? Are the switching fabric and processors redundant?

(continued)

Table 15-1 *(continued)*

Architecture/Feature	Questions to Ask
Buffering Sizes and Locations	Are input and/or output buffers included? What are their sizes? Is the buffer location helping to reduce congestion or just adding delay? How many different ports or service categories share a buffer? Are the buffers FIFO (first-in first-out) or shared memory?
Queue Serving Methods	What service categories are available? Does the switch queue traffic on a per-circuit basis? In what priority are the queues served? What is the fairness mechanism to assure some bandwidth for all resources?
Congestion Management	Can the device provide traffic shaping and policing? What are the vendor's implementation plans for the four types of ABR? Can the switch support early and partial packet discard (intelligently discarding whole or partial packets that remain rather than individual cells)? Does a LAN switch use forward pressure to increase frame throughput during congestion (by reducing the back-off time of Ethernet)?
Virtual Circuits	How many simultaneous virtual circuits can the switch support? Does the switch support both virtual paths (VPs) and virtual channels (VCs)? What is the available addressing space? What multicast support is available? Does the switch support oversubscription and alternate routing of PVCs?
SVC Call Handling	What signaling specification does the switch use? What call admission control (CAC) algorithms are available? How does the switch load balance connections? How many calls per second can the switch support? What is the call setup time? What is the switch-to-switch signaling method? Is the number of switches configurable in a single network limited? How do switches learn about new nodes on the network? How quickly can the switch re-establish connections after link or node failure?

Architecture/Feature	Questions to Ask
Feature support	Do you support the following: RFC 1483/1577 Frame Service Interworking ABR LANE MPOA VTOA?
VLAN/LANE Support	Can you organize virtual LANs around a mix of physical layer, link layer, and network layer criteria? Can a single port support multiple VLANs? How easy is creating and administering VLANs? What LAN types does the switch support? How many nodes can the VLAN support? How much in-depth understanding of ATM is necessary? What equipment do you need for LAN emulation? How closely does the LANE implementation follow the ATM Forum standards? How are the LANE servers backed up?
Environmental	What is the switch footprint? What type of powering does the device require? Do multiple power supplies load-share? What certifications does the equipment meet? What environmental monitoring is available? What clocking options are available?

Product availability and performance

The architecture of the ATM equipment determines its availability and performance. The processor and other networking elements should offer optional redundancy to increase network availability. *Optional redundancy* enables you to pick and choose the appropriate redundancy for the different elements in your network. Ask your vendors how quickly the switches recover from different failures and test a few scenarios. Most switches take several minutes to rebuild their connection tables. Look at the vendor's internal tests and outside tests that benchmark equipment performance, including the following:

✔ Equipment switching delay

✔ Variations in cell interarrival times

✔ Sustained quality of service support for voice and video with loaded data connections

✔ Fairness in allocation of network resources in congested conditions

✔ Congestion isolation

✔ Call set-up times

✔ Calls per second

✔ BUS broadcast speed (for LANE implementations)

✔ Throughput in packets per second of both small and large packets, transmitted in intermittent bursts for both lightly loaded and overloaded conditions

Interoperability options

Your ATM equipment needs to interoperate with a wide variety of your embedded equipment base, at least someday. Ideal ATM solutions extend the life of your existing NICs, hubs, switches, and routers, perhaps by using those items in a new way in the network. Ask your vendor to show you a step-by-step migration plan of how to implement ATM in your network where you need it as you need it.

When you check compliance, don't just check those from the ATM Forum; include other networking standards (such as the standards from IETF) as well. Remember that not all compliance is alike. Ask your vendors which specific elements and options they are supporting in the standards.

The best way to confirm interoperability is to ask for a testimonial or demonstration. Your prospective ATM vendors probably have proven interoperability with leading equipment solutions in other customer networks. Field-proven interoperability is best, but your vendor may also be working in different labs and interoperability groups that can provide some validation of interoperability with your existing equipment.

Although ATM is proving interoperable with existing networks, interoperability between ATM devices is typically not practical yet except in the simplest cell-transport configurations. Equipment supporting advanced ATM functions, such as LANE, MPOA, and even congestion management and signaling, have their own proprietary extensions that increase reliability, manageability, and ease-of-use. Discovering these potential interoperability trouble spots is usually easy, because vendors typically flaunt them as differentiators over their competitors. To avoid some of the hassles and to take advantage of pre-standard capabilities, consider working with just one ATM vendor, at least for each equipment category, for the next several years.

Upgradability and scalability options

Vendors design their products with the expectation of adding new enhancements every six to twelve months. New ATM standards will continue to emerge to support new capabilities for several more years, and vendors will continue adding bells and whistles that improve network performance and ease operation. Furthermore, as your network grows, you want the flexibility to easily add to your existing equipment and options without throwing away your initial purchases. You may even want to redeploy your switches in a new role as your network changes. For example, many campus switches can be retrofitted to become workgroup switches with a few minor card changes.

Equipment built with modular software and partitioned, hot-swappable hardware can provide a smooth upgrade path as your network changes. The equipment processor, switching fabric, power supplies, cooling system, and card interfaces ought to all be independently field-upgradeable.

Find out the details of your vendor's upgrade plans, including how much advance planning you need to do, the location, the required downtime, and how often downtime is needed. Be aggressive in negotiating for upgrades in your maintenance contracts, including new hardware, software, and associated support. If you're reading this book in 1997, find out your vendor's specific plans and costs for supporting explicit-rate ABR and new physical interfaces such as IAM (NxT1) and OC-12c/OC-48c (typically hardware changeouts of the port card) and Signaling 4.0, PNNI, and MPOA (typically software extensions). If you're reading this book a little later and the vendors have already crossed these hurdles, ask about the next set of features.

Network management

Ask for demonstrations of the vendor's network management system in your networking environment. If you use only one vendor's system, then the capabilities should be fairly straightforward. However, if you integrate the management stream into another system, you may discover that some of the functionality is limited.

If you plan to use ATM in a LAN or WAN backbone, determine how well the management solution integrates with the existing network. For example, if ATM is supporting multiple Ethernet LAN segments, can you trace logical channels between communicating end-points?

The best systems provide graphical interfaces, with network-level views and point-and-click zoom to the smallest components in each piece of equipment. Solutions that support remote configuration, trouble resolution, and software downloads enable central management. You also want visibility into the logical aspects of your network. If you use PVCs, get a point-and-click configuration that requires you to identify only the end points and the associated QoS parameters in order to set up the end-to-end circuit. If you're going to depend on SVCs, look for good call tracing and debugging tools.

Familiarize yourself with the debugging tools and MIBs. What local and remote equipment troubleshooting, fault isolation, and performance monitoring is available? What self-diagnostics can you run on the switch? What loopback tests are available? What alarms and thresholds can you set? What features can you turn on and off on a switch, card, port, and connection basis? How much flexibility is available in setting connection parameters? What are the tracked performance statistics of the equipment, including update intervals? Is this information correlated from the multiple switches traversed by a PVC? Network management statistics let you measure network performance and utilization and provide call accounting if needed.

Lastly, and yet very importantly, ask about error recovery. How is the management system backed up? How long does the management system take to recover from various failures?

Customer care

Ask about the technical support available to you and your staff. What are the equipment repair and sparing plans? Does the vendor provide readily available field support for on-site trouble resolution? Are the field engineers assigned to your account knowledgeable and helpful? Does your vendor provide easy access to corporate staff for more challenging issues? Is regular equipment maintenance necessary, and what is the support policy for upgrading software and hardware? How willing is the vendor to work with you to tune your network for your applications and to achieve full interoperability with your existing equipment? What documentation and training is available to you?

Overall costs

Consider not only price per port and total equipment costs, but also the other costs impacted by your equipment choice. Are the network management system and networking costs significant? What kind of test equipment do you need to purchase? (Sometimes test equipment can cost nearly as much as a switch.) Does the equipment choice increase or decrease the number of required operations staff?

If you are building a WAN backbone, make sure that you don't run into design limitations down the road based on the available physical ports. Also consider how effectively your equipment uses the precious bandwidth that you are purchasing. In WAN configurations, good congestion management and intelligent bandwidth management can help to reduce overall costs, whether you are building a private network solution or subscribing to public services.

Carrier considerations

Many of the considerations addressed in the preceding sections apply in carrier evaluations as well. After all, you depend on these providers for day-in, day-out performance, and your carrier had to choose vendor equipment on which to build their services. Fundamentally, your carrier can only offer you capabilities supported on its selected networking platform.

ATM network services are very young. The carriers are still trying to understand how customers can use their services, what features are wanted, and how to best package and price their services. Most carriers are very flexible in working with you — that is, if you are a serious buyer. Carriers are looking for a few flagship customers in different industry segments. Early adopters with valid ATM networking needs provide carriers with an invaluable understanding of the market, experience, and a credible reference base — all key elements to successfully building a large, broad base of ATM customers. You find a description of carrier services that are typically available in Chapter 12.

Many carriers can offer you capabilities beyond the standard offerings — if you demand them. Carriers hesitate to include these options until they work through all their internal system and process developments, but you can probably get the carrier to use your network as a guinea pig. Sometimes this approach can backfire because the carrier is not really ready to support the new capability, even for a few customers. However, in general, you probably can receive good service and extra attention while getting the capabilities you want, simply by asking.

An easy place to begin your evaluation is with your geographic requirements. Most carriers today still have some geographic limitations on service availability. RBOCs (Regional Bell Operating Companies) and other LECs (Local Exchange Carriers) cannot yet carry traffic between LATAs (Local Access Transport Area). CAPs (Competitive Access Providers) and other alternative providers serve a limited number of cities. Long-distance carriers provide broad national and even international coverage but can be very expensive for metropolitan connections. If your network spans both local and long-distance connections in a wide variety of cities and towns, you may need to work with more than one carrier.

In addition to the applicable criteria from the preceding vendor section (some of which we repeat in this section as a reminder), discuss the following topics with prospective carriers.

Corporate success and service strategy

Choose a carrier who has a vision for its service offering; commitment, knowledge, and skill to execute the vision; and previous success stories. How does your carrier position its service offerings and manage cross product conflicts between frame relay, SMDS, IP, and native LAN? Does the carrier limit functionality in one service line in favor of another? How does the carrier recommend that you use each of its services in your network? What migration steps do the people at the carrier talk about? Does what they say match up with what you want to do, and does their positioning make sense? Do you believe that they have sufficient resources and talent to carry out their plans? Can you get them to commit to their plans in a written contract?

The more experience your carrier's people have in ATM, the farther they are up the learning curve, and the more ready and able they are to assist you with your network design and implementation. Past experience in environments very similar to yours helps everything go more smoothly. Ask your carrier about the largest network it has supported. How many customer networks have their employees installed? What references are available?

Service packaging and features

Determining the right service packaging is still a difficult challenge for carriers. They want their services to be easy-to-use, but basing service offerings on ATM Forum standards results in a service appropriate for the PhDs who wrote the specifications. A few carriers are experimenting with application-based services such as native LAN. Some may introduce application-oriented service categories such as LAN Interworking, SNA, and voice. However, the carriers still have much to learn in offering these packages as well.

If you want to subscribe to native ATM services, you probably need to understand much of the ins and outs of the technology, especially in regard to categories of service (good thing you have our book to help get you through some of the details!). We've asked one of our consultants at TeleChoice, Beth Gage, to share some of her thoughts on service and feature considerations for evaluating carrier services. Her suggestions are in the *Inside ATM* feature at the end of this chapter.

Service availability and performance

Service availability depends on the reliability of both the physical and ATM network layers. Fast recovery of physical layers through SONET or DACs-based solutions enables the ATM network to quickly recover from failed links without tons of complex rerouting. Fast recovery also preserves access connections that the carrier network cannot protect through rerouting. Reliability of the ATM elements is also critical. Your carrier needs to use equipment with built-in redundancy for switching fabrics, processors, and power supplies. Line card redundancy provides added protection against card failures, which can be particularly troubling in unmanned offices. Alternate routing of PVCs protects against physical link or tandem switching failures (if an alternate path with sufficient capacity is available).

Take the time to visit in person or on the phone with the carrier's operations staff. A knowledgeable, experienced operations staff is indispensable in maintaining high service availability. Find out whether your carrier provides 24-hour-a-day, 7-day-a-week coverage in its operations center.

The number, type, and size of switches and backbone trunks determine the performance of the carrier network. Ask your vendor for a list of its engineering objectives for performance. Try to get service guarantees in writing, with strict penalties for the carrier when your network doesn't get the service it needs. Specific performance and availability information to request from your carrier includes the following:

- ✔ CBR cell loss
- ✔ VBR cell loss
- ✔ ABR cell loss
- ✔ CBR end-to-end transport delay
- ✔ VBR end-to-end transport delay
- ✔ CBR cell delay variation
- ✔ VBR-RT cell delay variation

    ✔ Network availability

    ✔ Mean time to repair

    ✔ Mean time between outages

    ✔ Port and PVC installation intervals

Interworking and interoperability options

Today many carriers offer interworking between their ATM and frame relay services. Make sure that your carrier provides service (rather than network) interworking. Ask about the network configuration, because service interworking performance has not yet been proven on a large scale. Also ask about the category of service used to support the interconnection. Some carriers also support ATM connectivity to the Internet, although perhaps not at full bandwidth.

We suggest that you ask your carrier about its plans for future interworking with other services, especially voice. An ATM benefit commonly touted by carriers is integrated access to many types of services. Long-distance carriers promised that ATM would provide one access connection into many different service types, thus lowering access costs. However, ATM won't be a widely applicable solution for corporate voice traffic until the carriers connect their ATM and voice networks. You need these connections to support the bulk of your voice traffic, which requires connectivity off your corporate network.

No carriers support commercial interconnection to other carrier ATM networks today. A lack of robust interoperability standards and the carriers' reluctance to share their customers is slowing this interconnection effort. Interconnection between long-distance providers and local providers may emerge in 1997 in order to reduce the significant costs of dedicated access to long-distance carriers and to expand the reach of local providers. Many CAPs are providing ATM services locally, nationally, and even internationally, but availability is limited to the cities which the CAPs serve.

Network management

A few carriers can offer you a network management system or SNMP interface to track fault, performance, and configuration information. These offerings include firewalls based on IP addressing, community strings, and password protection so that you can view only your portion of the network. A few systems enable you to enter trouble tickets and PVC change requests. However, all network management interfaces still provide just read-only capability (as opposed to real-time configuration control) for customers. The carriers are not yet comfortable with the idea of users setting their own configurations and parameters, probably with good cause.

Ask for a demonstration of the vendor's network management system in your networking environment. If you use only one vendor's system, then the capabilities should be fairly straightforward. However, if you integrate the management stream into another system, you may discover that some of the functionality is limited.

A simpler option is monthly performance reports. These reports typically provide monthly statistics on total number of offered cells, cell loss, and, perhaps, availability for each PVC direction. The report also includes summary numbers for each port.

Customer care

Ask about the sales and technical support available to you and your staff. If you already use the carrier for a few other services, you probably know what to expect. How responsive is the team assigned to you from the carrier? Are the field engineers assigned to your account knowledgeable and helpful? Does your vendor provide easy access to corporate staff for more challenging issues? Is the vendor willing to work with you to tune your network for your applications and to achieve full interoperability with your existing equipment? What documentation and training is available to you? What are the trouble-reporting processes and response time objectives?

Pricing

Pricing is one of the most difficult criteria in evaluating ATM services. Sometimes the elements of pricing aren't enough alike to do a straightforward comparison. Build a few sample scenarios of both small and large networks to compare the carrier pricing you receive. You aren't likely to get the best pricing quote the first time, unless you insist upon a best and final offer.

Typical pricing structures include access (for long-distance services), port connection, and PVC charges. Different carriers choose to weight more or less of the cost in the port connection instead of PVC charges. A low-priced port connection enables you to build a less expensive initial network but probably results in more rapidly rising prices as you increase your network size, compared to higher port pricing. PVC fees generally depend upon the service categories and subscribed bandwidth. Carriers choose different plans for accumulating and discounting these charges. As an example, some carriers choose to price the bandwidth on a per-PVC basis, while others use the aggregate PVC bandwidth on each port. PVC discounts may be available for the total port bandwidth, number of PVCs, or oversubscription rate.

Ask for a network trial. Most carriers see short trials as a necessary step to win business for early-market services. If you do run a trial, use it only to test the performance of your applications as well as the carrier's network. Remember that most carriers give trial customers dead-last priority in the event of network trouble. You don't want to be caught in this kind of situation if you are already running production traffic.

Engineering Your Network

Unfortunately, not much conventional wisdom is available for engineering your network. Most existing networks are over-engineered and will be tuned as the networks grow in size and network managers get more hands-on experience. Beginning your ATM implementation with a small section of either your LAN or WAN helps you build your knowledge and experience before undertaking a large ATM integration project. Your vendors can offer help, too, especially in regard to network design. Ask for suggestions on the best way to configure their equipment individually and within a network.

Engineering ATM WANs

If you're building an ATM WAN based on PVCs, your primary design concerns are determining the needed PVCs and setting their associated category of service and bandwidths. The two extremes of PVC-based configurations are stars and full meshes.

Star configurations hub all traffic into one central point and are popular in router networks that use private lines. The advantage of this configuration is the limited number of PVCs to manage and purchase (especially if your carrier is using PVC-centric pricing). If you're using a router to connect your ATM locations, you may find that stars can support only 15 PVCs feasibly. *Full mesh* configurations provide any-to-any connectivity among all site. Full meshes reduce delays, congestion, and single points of failure.

A third design option mixes these two configurations. A *tiered star* uses any-to-any connectivity among a few backbone sites, each of which, in turn, serves as the center of a star for a few small locations, as shown in Figure 15-1. The tiered star configuration provides high bandwidth and increased reliability for heavy backbone sites while still limiting the overall number of required network PVCs. ATM's logical connectivity means that you need to purchase only a single access connection at each location.

One last thought for those implementing private networks: Carefully consider the number and placement of your ATM switches, because the balance of your switch costs compared to transmission costs depends upon how you split up the work to each switch. Lightly loaded switches concentrating traffic at each of a few remote sites located near one another may actually be more cost-effective than backhauling all the traffic to a central site.

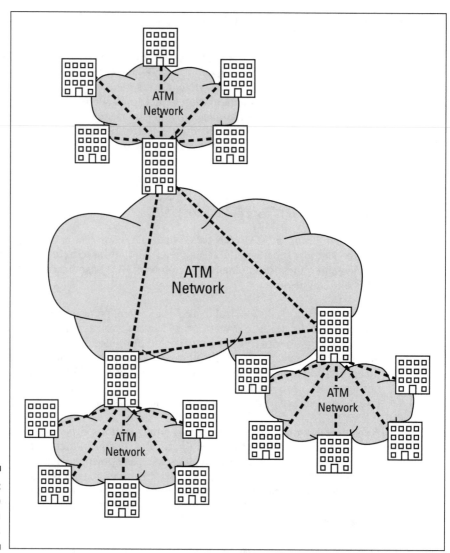

Figure 15-1:
Mixing it up
with a
tiered star.

Categories of service

A new consideration in designing ATM WANs is category of service. ATM is the only wide area service to provide this option (at this time). We discuss categories of service (ABR, CBR, UBR, VBR-RT, and VBR-NRT) in several chapters of this book, with the most in-depth coverage in Chapter 9.

Many early ATM WANs are transporting only TCP/IP and other LAN-based traffic. These networks are, therefore, relying primarily upon VBR, because VBR is the only suitable category of service for data which is available from most carriers today. Allen Robel at Indiana University recommends using one PVC per LAN protocol if your carrier's pricing structure is not too prohibitive. He uses different PVCs for IP, IPX, and AppleTalk. For the first time, he is able to track the usage of all these different protocols in his network. This capability provided an unexpected benefit of using ATM.

Private WANs also use the UBR service class. Many of these private WANs are using SVCs to provide connectivity. If you're an early adopter of carrier SVC services, then your network also probably uses primarily UBR, because existing implementations of LANE and MPOA only support one service category. A few vendors are developing SVC capabilities for trunking PBXs through their ATM switches. Such connections will use the VBR-RT category of service when it becomes available from carriers. Until then, such connections use CBR.

Sizing your connections

Determining the category of service for your PVC is not the only decision you face in establishing each connection. You must also determine the bandwidth size. You probably have an idea of how much traffic your current network generates (for example, not more than 1.544 Mbps or not more than 10 Mbps, which is Ethernet's maximum limit). This estimate can be a good starting point for gauging the required CIR of your connection. Most network managers prefer to set the peak bandwidth rate equal to the line rate to give their users maximum bursting capabilities. You can size CBR connection bandwidths by using various techniques for determining the number of DS0 or voice circuits in traditional TDM networks.

Most carriers today are fairly flexible in carrying traffic that exceeds the traffic contract, but a few are hard-nosed, so ask to be sure. As networks become more fully loaded, excessive traffic has a greater risk of loss. Many people are hopeful that ABR provides better throughput for carrying bursty data traffic over limited networking resources by giving users a dynamic bandwidth flow. We may all know whether ABR can live up to its promises by late 1997.

Until then, we suggest that you set your bandwidth parameters slightly higher than you think you need. Usage reports from your carrier or your ATM equipment can help to determine when to change these values. Understanding the intermittent peak loads is most helpful. Unfortunately, most equipment provides traffic measurements only in 15-minute increments, which is not very useful in tracking intermittent peaks. If you use ATM equipment that can shape your outgoing traffic, then you're always in compliance with your contract. Your CPE buffers can store small excessive bursts from your applications, but traffic loss occurs in the CPE if you're off the mark by too much.

Engineering ATM LANs and backbones

Many of the same considerations in engineering your WAN are appropriate for the LAN. However, SVCs are more common in the LAN and LAN backbone. If you choose to use SVCs, you can avoid many of the dreaded category of service and bandwidth decisions of PVCs in the WAN. Many current LAN implementations set up UBR SVCs at the line rate of the physical connection. The UBR category of service makes sense in the LAN when used with applications designed for non-deterministic networks. As we mention earlier, the current implementations of both LANE and MPOA do not allow specification of category of service.

Vendor equipment for the LAN is often self-configuring. Connect the physical links between your local switches, and they soon find each other and begin exchanging traffic. In fact, one equipment vendor told us that ATM frustrated its earliest users because it was so simple to set up. They set aside a whole weekend to configure and bring up the network and then were done by Saturday afternoon. That's when the calls started. They wanted to know what else they needed to do. We can't promise that your ATM implementation goes that smoothly, but if you follow our rule of keeping the first project simple, setting up ATM really isn't too bad.

If you're using ATM LANE, you have some special design considerations. LANE performance depends upon where you place your servers, how your equipment caches addresses, how well your equipment handles SVCs, and how you set up your virtual LANs. As an example, randomly assigning users with little common interest to virtual LANs substantially increases BUS traffic load because a high percentage of broadband packets must cross the BUS. Alternatively, well designed virtual LANs substantially limit this traffic.

Tuning your TCP/IP network

The subject of tuning your TCP/IP network can fill a whole book itself. Maximizing throughput of TCP/IP networks over ATM has been the subject of intense research by universities, testbeds, universities, and other organizations for several years. In ATM's earliest days, naysayers said that TCP/IP would never work with ATM, but early ATM adopters have proven them wrong. TCP/IP can run just fine (after a few tweaks in the protocol).

Optimization of TCP/IP throughput rates on ATM typically focuses on setting these host parameters:

- Packet size
- Window size
- Internal write buffer size

Your vendor probably has specific suggestions on what works best for its switch and your network. Talk to them for specific suggestions for your particular implementation.

Testing the network

After your network is up and going, run a few tests before christening it into production use. If you've used PVCs, start by checking the end-to-end connectivity of each one. Misloading addressing information is easy, especially if you had to do a manual setup in each switch, so check that the addressing is correct.

Ping tests to measure delay and network loading tests to measure throughput are the two most common tests. Back-to-back configurations of your ATM gear establish a baseline for ping tests. Run several iterations, and then introduce the network and measure the new round-trip ping time. Again, run several iterations. Use the following formula to determine your one-way delay in each network test.

```
one-way delay = (network ping time - baseline ping time) / 2
```

The loading tests require some type of traffic generator, which may be a test set or a specially programmed workstation. Run the tests, using the different protocols, packet sizes, and loads that may occur in your production network. If you do decide to invest in an ATM test set, be prepared to open your wallet wide. High-end test sets can cost more than your switch.

Don't run only network level tests, but also test the intended applications. Make sure that the network supports these applications as expected. This testing also provides you with some baselines for troubleshooting. Distinguishing the source of trouble in an ATM network is often difficult, because problems at the ATM layer, physical layer, and application layer can all contribute and affect one another in strange and non-intuitive ways.

A pat on the back

All that's left to do is giving you several brawny pats on the back and warm congratulations. You're now an ATM user! (And perhaps you're ready for a well-deserved week of vacation!)

We hope that the information we provide in this book proves useful and never leads you astray. Drop us a note and let us know how your ATM implementation went. We like hearing about the many experiences of ATM users, and maybe we can share your story with other readers in the next edition of our book. The more conventional wisdom we can all share on ATM, the easier future implementations are for all of us!

Inside ATM with Beth Gage
Broadband Consultant
TeleChoice, Inc.

How to Choose a Provider

If you're facing the daunting task of choosing an ATM service provider, the choices may leave you scratching your head at first. On the surface, most services seem identical. But, to use an old phrase, the proof is in the pudding. Getting the service providers to share the secret recipe may be the challenging part.

Go through the rigmarole of an RFP process, unless you have a close relationship with your current data service provider and plenty of confidence in their people. If you're a big account, they are probably very flexible in meeting your needs. An RFP is a great deal of work to put together and organize, but is worthwhile because, during the process, you clearly define your specific requirements for network support and you find out about the available capabilities and costs of different providers.

If, for example, you don't have a person who can be dedicated full-time to managing an ATM WAN, then you may opt for an application-based ATM service (such as a native LAN service) that includes equipment, design, maintenance, and management options. The applications-based route enables you to avoid much of the techno-muck for which ATM is famous.

On the other hand, if you have people who can be dedicated to the new network and can ramp up a technology learning curve fairly quickly and you have the budget to purchase your own ATM equipment, then the ATM transmission services that are commonly available from carriers may be the route you choose.

If you go the native services route, ask your RFP candidates about how their service supports the following areas. Although most of these questions are fairly technical, understanding how the ATM network is engineered and how your applications are affected by the

engineering is important, so that you have reasonable expectations of the service.

Service Category Offered: In 1996, most service providers offer a constant bit rate (CBR) and variable bit rate (VBR) service category as standard service options. However, available bit rate (ABR) and unspecified bit rate (UBR) are also offered by some service providers on an individual case basis. Ask what service category is recommended for your specific applications, and why. If a choice is available between VBR and either ABR or UBR service categories, be sure that you understand the reasoning for the recommendation, because any of these services can be used for data applications. If your carrier is suggesting ABR, understand the requirements of the user equipment. Many ABR implementations require that the user equipment follow flow control feedback from the network.

Policing and Traffic Management: The policing and traffic management of ATM networks is highly dependent upon the capabilities of the network platform and the operations policy of the service. Some service providers discard violating cells regardless of the availability of network resources, while other services let violating cells through if capacity is available. If you're looking at doing service interworking with frame relay, have the service provider explain how the ATM network handles a DE-marked frame relay frame, and how the frame relay network handles CLP-marked ATM cells.

Quality of Service (QoS) Objectives: In addition to the service category, several QoS parameters control certain aspects about the service quality. Knowing what error rate is set may not mean much initially, but if you have trouble with an application later (for example, you experience a great deal of jitter on desktop videoconferencing), then the QoS parameters may indicate why performance is not up to snuff.

Oversubscription: Oversubscription enables you to take advantage of the intermittent nature of your data applications and assign more connections to a port than can be assigned with dedicated bandwidth for each application. Most service providers allow some oversubscription for VBR and ABR traffic, but the level is often determined on a case by case basis. Ask what determining factors are used to set the oversubscription level for each port.

Automatic Rerouting: Although *self-healing* and *automatic rerouting* are presumed to be inherent ATM capabilities, they really depend on the network switches and engineering. Have your service provider map exactly what happens in different failure scenarios — local access failures, equipment failure on the ATM network, and physical failures in the fiber network.

Frame Relay-to-ATM Service Interworking: If you are operating a hybrid network (which occurs when you add ATM to a portion of your existing network), you need to understand your service provider's overall networking vision and service interworking strategy. In addition to asking what platforms are supported, ask how the translation between frame and ATM occurs and what limitations and service implications are the result of service interworking.

Automatic Rerouting with Service Interworking: At the network level, service interworking can be either graceful or clumsy. Be sure that you understand what happens in failure scenarios for connections that travel both the frame relay and ATM networks.

Service Category for Service Interworking: The service category question also applies specifically to service interworking connections. Either VBR-NRT, ABR, or UBR service categories can support frame relay to ATM service interworking. Make sure that you understand the implications of each option. Your service provider's network platform and engineering policies determines which service category supports interworking.

Service Level Agreeements: To encourage your service providers to always give the expected level of performance, you should set up service level agreements. The agreements can cover aspects of service availability such as allowed downtime per year, mean-time-to-repair (MTTR), and mean-time-between-failure (MTBF); service performance such as cell loss; and service installation such as installation intervals for new ports and PVCs. Effective agreements carry a sufficient penalty for the carrier and an easy way to identify missed service levels.

Customer Network Management Capabilities: If you want to negotiate service level guarantees with your service provider, then you need tools to monitor the WAN performance. Customer network management (CNM) provides performance information, along with network configuration information. You can also investigate the possibility of electronically submitting additional circuit orders and/or trouble tickets.

Performance Reports: Even if your service provider doesn't have a comprehensive CNM solution, it can provide you with performance reports for your ATM connections and port utilization statistics. This information is necessary to monitor any service level agreements that you negotiate for your service contract.

Chapter 16

It Works! ATM Case Studies

*T*hrough persistent diligence (we're thinking about going into sales after this experience!), we found some organizations willing to share their ATM stories with us. During the course of our asking around, we got a variety of feedback.

Many companies are now braving a limited introduction of ATM into their networks. These initial projects typically target one or two large network sites or key applications. Most of these users offered little information, except to say, "It works! Now we're looking at more broadly expanding our implementation."

A few companies that have already taken a deep dive into ATM say it's worth the risk. They figure the improved networking performance, lower costs, and new capabilities for advanced applications gives them a strategic advantage over their competitors. However, these companies were reluctant to talk because they would really rather that their competitors never find out about ATM's benefits.

We had one user tell us he didn't want to talk about his company's ATM implementation because he was afraid management would read a report about the firm being on the "bleeding edge" of technology. He didn't want to invite any hassles when the new network worked fine and he was preparing to increase the number of network sites.

In addition to the organizations who did share information with us about their ATM projects, a few other companies have 'fessed up during industry conferences and in publications to being ATM users. A list of the more well-known organizations implementing ATM follows. A list containing all the known businesses and university groups across the world would fill at least two more pages. Carriers and ISPs implementing ATM could fill at least another page. Maybe you know a few of them and can call them for advice:

- Home Depot
- Circus Circus of Las Vegas
- Kaiser Permanente
- Ashland Inc.
- Florida Power and Light
- Allegheny Hospital
- Fuji Bank of Japan
- Westinghouse Electric Corporation
- Basset Healthcare
- Amoco Corporation

- Texaco
- Tandem Computer Inc.
- Carnival Cruise Lines
- Bayer AG
- Educational Testing Services
- Schlumberger Geco-Prakla
- World Health Organization
- French National Library
- Chrysler Corporation
- Bear Sterns

To give you a few specifics on some of these implementations:

- The ATM Forum reports that Chrysler Corporation installed a 3000 node network in the Detroit area interconnecting PCs, workstations, server farms, and supercomputers — all based on ATM — that includes both 25 Mbps and 155 Mbps connections to desktop terminals, PCs, and workstations.

  The Forum also reports that McDonalds has implemented a backbone network providing 150 subnets. It uses ATM to transparently serve existing applications while adding new capacity and functions.

- FORE Systems recently announced two large European networks. The World Health Organization is installing a 2000 seat desktop ATM network in Geneva, Switzerland. The network consists of backbone ATM switches connecting LAN switches and directly attached PCs using 25 Mbps ATM, and servers using 155 Mbps ATM. The French National Library is installing 300 ATM switches to build a network connecting high performance servers and 3500 workstations. The library will use its ATM network for many new applications, including multimedia retrieval of library archives and digitized documents.

- Byte magazine reports that Educational Testing Services (the organization that has caused countless sleepless nights for millions of teenagers over the years with their SAT tests) has contracted Bell Atlantic Network Integration to manage a $1 million ATM backbone to support voice, data, and someday video traffic.

- 3Com told this tale about one of its customers in a recent news release: Home Depot deployed an ATM campus backbone with LAN emulation to connect users on LAN switches to a variety of mission critical applications. These include mainframe-based financial, inventory management and purchasing programs, and server-based e-mail, groupware, human resource, and sales and marketing applications.

✔ In Asia, Fuji Bank plans to use twelve ATM access switches to connect different computing centers. The currently under-construction network will soon be carrying teller transactions, automatic banking machine traffic, interbank traffic, and stock/bond transactions.

✔ Tandem's early experience can be found in our feature for Chapter 14.

We asked our four case study organizations lots of questions and they gave us plenty of answers. We hope you find their stories interesting and beneficial. Maybe by the time we're ready for our next edition, you'll be willing to share your success story with us.

Royal Bank of Canada: Taking a Risk That Worked

Royal Bank of Canada is Canada's largest bank with clients in more than 140 countries, $29 billion (Canadian dollars) in assets, and 1,600 branch locations across the country. The bank is now in the process of implementing hundreds of sites on an ATM network. An ATM network is widely regarded as a risky proposition and banks are supposed to shy away from risky ventures. So what's a prominent institution like the Royal Bank of Canada doing with ATM? The three-year project promises overall system cost savings and strategically positions the bank for the future.

They say you want an evolution

Alex Tashayod, a senior communications analyst for Royal Bank, and a team of seven technologists specializing in advanced emerging technologies together with its vendors have designed and implemented ATM in the WAN, metropolitan, and campus environment over the past three years. The decision to implement an ATM network at the bank evolved during talks about network alternatives, says Alex.

The discussions grew slowly from initial plans, to choose between a private line network versus a frame relay network, and finally leading to the design of an ATM network. ATM was chosen because of its ability to handle multiple traffic patterns, especially in multimedia applications. The technology gives Royal Bank the opportunity to enhance the performance of its existing networks and consolidate multiple networks. Since implementing ATM, Royal Bank has been able to add even more multimedia applications to its suite of services.

Testing 1-2-3

The up-front network design, system engineering, and network testing were critical to the success of the project. The network design sprung from a team effort between Royal Bank and its vendors; Bell Advance Communications, Rogers Network Services, and IBM. Royal Bank tested many applications and protocols over ATM, including the following:

- SNA/LLC2-based online banking
- SNA/SDLC-based personal touch banking
- IP-based distance learning and intranets
- NetBIOS-based check imaging applications and server consolidation
- IPX servers
- Routing protocols, RIP (routing information protocol) and OSPF (open shortest path first), over ATM
- Token ring switching with ATM uplink

"Extensive lab tests allowed us to more easily resolve network implementation problems," Tashayod says. Royal Bank remains committed to continually testing applications and protocols.

Royal Bank discovered many software bugs during the testing stage. For example, while using the *source route bridging* (a protocol supporting auto discovery among computers in a bridged network) on ATM, the router improperly handled a piece of the protocol that resulted in a total system failure. A new software upgrade fixed the bug. Another problem found and resolved during testing was the failure of an ATM switch to transport large frames sent by the routers at the network's edge. Royal Bank technologists discovered that the router needed the VBR service category and the ATM switch in question supported only CBR. As a result, the router dropped many cells — causing retransmission and finally, a system time-out.

It's a go

Before using ATM, each branch location connected to three large host locations on the bank's network through multiple, low-speed dedicated connections (4Kbps). The bank's network ran various applications over these disparate, parallel networks.

The decision to implement an ATM network was driven by the desire to support new multimedia applications, to consolidate the existing networks, and to realize the costs savings from the overall system and network engineering. Another driver of the ATM technology was the ability to receive reliable response times from the token ring networks, which were running mission-critical applications such as Royal Bank's online banking system, personal touch banking system, and IP-based transactions for credit and debit cards. Royal Bank also anticipated using the ATM network for new business opportunities that allow its business units to become even more competitive.

The Royal Bank network uses ATM services from its metropolitan provider, Rogers Network Services, and its long distance provider, Bell Advanced Communications. Rogers Network Services provides ATM branch access to an ATM uplink (OC3, 155 Mbps) using an *edge-router* from Crosscomm. The edge-router features two 16-Mbps token-ring ports and four serial ports. One of the serial ports is used for 56 Kbps to 128 Kbps ISDN basic-rate dial backup of the ATM network. Two PVCs carry traffic on this OC3 to two central-edge routers capable of load-sharing (based on source route bridging path determination). The sustained bit rate for the OC3 circuit is defined at 2 Mbps per PVC. The network is totally redundant. If a major edge-router failure occurs, another router takes over. For transmitting long distances, the Bell Advanced Communications DS3 network offers several interfaces including token-ring, T1, ethernet, DS3 UNI 3.0, and others. The planned interconnection between Rogers Network Services and Bell Advanced Communications (the system managers) is a DS3 defined with PVCs for the VBR service category following the ATM Forum's UNI 3.0 specification.

Royal Bank owns no piece of the ATM network except the campus ATM. It turned over implementation and management of the network to Bell Advanced Communications and Rogers Network Services. Bell manages the WAN, while Rogers manages the metropolitan area network. (Royal Bank will support the campus ATM network after it's implemented). Outsourcing the ATM network eliminates the need for extensive in-house training in network operations and leaves network management personnel free to work on core business applications.

You ought to be in pictures

Many of Royal Bank's departments take advantage of multimedia applications over the ATM network. The network will make Royal Bank's mutual fund group more competitive by allowing group members to share information every morning via videoconferencing and whiteboarding. The videoconferencing application can also enables employees to conduct training through distance learning programs. Other important applications planned to run over the ATM network include intranet and Internet applications, check and document imaging, and server consolidation.

During the past three years, Royal Bank has found its ventures with ATM to be challenging yet worthwhile. Alex Tashayod says that despite how strange it may sound, he has no regrets about anything done during the implementation and would do it the same way again.

DCCCD: Replacing an Outmoded System

Dallas County Community College District (DCCCD) installed a Texas-sized metropolitan area ATM network connecting seven colleges and three administrative sites throughout Dallas County. The college network supports approximately 45,000 full-time students, 45,000 continuing education students, and 2,000 faculty members.

DCCCD was running a private T1 microwave network prior to installing an ATM network. When network utilization reached 70 percent, the microwave network was struggling. It had very slow response times and regularly lost connections. DCCCD planned to replace the private T1 microwave system with a private T3 microwave system until Teleport Communications Group (TCG) introduced the college district to ATM technology. DCCCD knew very little about the technology at the time, and leaned heavily on Teleport to educate them about ATM's capabilities.

The first time Teleport discussed the technology, DCCCD assumed it would be too expensive to implement. DCCCD knew about ATM, its questionable reputation, and the expensive equipment required for an ATM network. It figured ATM would be implemented in the year 2000 or so, not in 1996. But after four months of continuous discussion between DCCCD and Teleport, pricing fell to an attractive level and Teleport had built such a strong relationship with DCCCD that it was providing fiber access at all DCCCD locations for unlimited bandwidth growth.

Cost-saving tactics

DCCCD chose a public ATM network for various tactical reasons. First, ATM provided DCCCD the bandwidth it needed to relieve network congestion. Second, the ATM network was less expensive (albeit after much negotiation with Teleport) than leasing a T3 private line or microwave system (microwave licensing and rental space alone cost the college district $75,000 a year).

DCCCD also avoided the high servicing cost including parts and labor associated with microwave systems. "It's hard to put a price on the amount of resources we saved," says Jim Hill, a retired DCCCD vice chancellor who was instrumental in the decision to move to an ATM network. DCCCD examined ATM network use versus microwave network use projected over a five year period. They concluded the ATM network can save DCCCD close to $300,000.

The DCCCD network connects Ethernet networks to a FDDI backbone using switches from network peripherals. The FDDI networks connect to Cisco 4500 routers and out to the ATM network. The network has 45 Mbps at each location and an OC3 connection at the host site. DCCCD manages the ethernet network, while Teleport manages the ATM network from the router. DCCCD leases the routers from Teleport; and Teleport is responsible for network management reporting and all router moves, additions, and changes.

Teleport converted the microwave network to the ATM network in a single weekend with only one glitch. The Windows NT server failed to hand out user addresses to the Cisco routers. The routers requested the addresses from the server but received no results. After discussions involving Teleport, Microsoft, and DCCCD, the problem was solved when Microsoft sent documentation on how to configure the Cisco routers.

Future strategies

Installing an ATM network strategically positions DCCCD for the future. "We installed ATM primarily for its future capabilities, but the service works great for our current needs," Hill says. Amazingly, the district signed a ten-year contract with Teleport to provide fully managed ATM service.

DCCCD anticipates using ATM technology to its full potential. "We plan to eventually move our T1 voice network to ATM, and we now have bandwidth for video conferencing," say Steve Glick, DCCCD manager of networking and distributed computing. The district plans to provide phone service over its ATM network once ATM PBX interfaces are developed. Currently, DCCCD runs various data applications including mainframe, Internet, e-mail, the CD-ROM library, and groupware on the ATM network.

University of Southern California: Taking ATM to the Next Level

The University of Southern California's Advanced Biotechnical Consortium (USC-ABC) has members from the medical community, academia, the medical industry, and federal laboratories. The USC-ABC develops state-of-the-art biomedical applications that, though telemedicine, expand the boundaries of health care. (Telemedicine provides medical care with the assistance of telecommunications.) The USC-ABC works to improve health care delivery through advanced telecommunications and high-performance computing. The consortium evaluates, experiments with, and implements various high-tech biomedical applications and advanced diagnosis systems that speed delivery and reduce medical costs.

In one of its projects, USC-ABC developed a system to expedite the diagnosis of retinal conditions.The consortium teamed with Doheny Eye Institution to install the network for remote consultation. An ATM network transmits patient records — including real-time color video, color images and graphics, and 3-D images. Using enhanced digitized images, ophthalmologists can diagnose a patient's retinal condition from a remote site.

Saving time with telemedicine

The network is one of the most advanced in the country. It enables physicians to provide more timely and convenient health care while reducing costs and improving patient access and treatment outcomes. "This telemedicine network allows us to create and share 3-D images and use them for better, faster diagnoses and treatment — saving time, dollars, and most importantly, lives," says Frederick W. George III, USC-ABC's executive director and professor of radiology in the USC School of Medicine.

The real-time system is invaluable for rapid diagnostics. "It's now possible to move the images, and not the patients or the doctors. That alone markedly enhances access," George says. "The system speeds diagnosis for more timely admissions, rather than waiting until an emergency admission situation arises," George adds. "This reduces the lengths of stay and also saves money."

Improving diagnoses with digital imagery

The most incredible feature of this system is its ability to enhance the accuracy of a diagnosis. Digitized images on a computer screen can be easily manipulated to enlarge or emphasize a certain area on a photo or video. By manipulating the image, doctors pinpoint problems that would not necessarily be visible during a physical examination. Digital technology enhances the details of an image for more precise diagnoses.

ATM technology is the catalyst that makes telemedicine, teleconsulting, and distant-learning applications possible, and that's just one example of ATM's impact on the future of health care. Look for ATM to also change the way we do work in almost every sector of society, including education, business, government, and in the home.

You can find out more about the retinal project and USC-ABC's many other efforts in exploring new ways that advanced computing and telecommunications technologies can improve the healthcare for us all. A visit to their Web site at www-abc.hsc.usc.edu gives you a glimpse at the many possibilities yet to come through the application of ATM and other advanced technologies.

Looking at All Aspects of ATM

Like the organizations that shared their ATM stories in this chapter, you may have any number of applications for ATM in your network. The goal behind employing ATM (and most any networking technology) is the efficient and reliable transfer of information. When you're considering ATM and investigating its usefulness for you, remember ATM's nature. That is, ATM has multiple personalities, as demonstrated by its many descriptions. (You can see Chapter 1 for a more thorough description of these aspects of ATM.):

- ✔ ATM is a set of rules
- ✔ ATM is a communications process
- ✔ ATM is a communications protocol
- ✔ ATM is a replacement technology for local area networks
- ✔ ATM is a replacement technology for campus networks
- ✔ ATM is a high bandwidth service of public carriers
- ✔ ATM is a transfer mode
- ✔ ATM is a telecommunications concept

Check out Chapters 12 and 13 for information specific to evaluating ATM for a LAN or WAN environment. And be sure to heed the expert advice that you find in Chapter 24.

Participating with a cells-in-frames ally

The Cells In Frames (CIF) Alliance is a loosely organized group defining standards for carrying ATM cells inside Ethernet frames. The first version of the CIF specification was completed in 1996. You can find out more this specification at the CIF Alliance Web site:

http://cif.cornell.edu/

CIF allows Ethernet devices to participate in the protocols of an ATM network instead of requiring the intermediary services of a directly attached ATM device such as a LAN switch. CIF thereby extends the ATM network and ATM QoS (quality of service) benefits all the way to the existing Ethernet device.

Because the Ethernet device is actually a node on the ATM network, it can directly specify the QoS of connections, respond to ABR (available bit rate) flow control messages, and otherwise participate in the ATM protocols.

To use ATM in existing Ethernet desktops, CIF requires some extra driver software in the Ethernet device and CIF-capable LAN switches. Several leading internetworking vendors are participating in the CIF Alliance, and time will tell whether the technology ever finds a market. The number of Ethernet devices really needing to participate in the sophistication of ATM protocols is uncertain.

Inside ATM with David Beering
Senior Staff Telecommunications Analyst
Amoco Corporation, Chicago, IL

How Will ATM's Role Change in the Future?

Reviews of the success of Asynchronous Transfer Mode technology in the telecommunications marketplace are mixed. Amid a great deal of hype and hope, ATM made its debut in the first part of this decade. ATM was touted as the end-all technology which would eventually tie systems together, spanning differing media, data rates, and geographic locality.

While many companies were achieving great success with ATM solutions, other technologies were vying for our attention — and our dollars. FDDI, 100 Mbps Ethernet and various switched versions of those technologies have experienced dramatic decreases in price. While ATM remains one of the best options for very high performance desktops, the clear choice for desktop connectivity has not become apparent. This is a situation that is, perhaps, exacerbated by the emergence of gigabit Ethernet — yet another high-speed desktop and LAN backbone technology which will doubtless capture mindshare among network architects and end users.

The wide area network still poses great challenges for cost effective high speed networks, however. More applications are being developed which allow (and encourage!) end-users to eliminate time and distance. Global enterprises are challenged to provide a uniform availabity of applications to employees in remote reaches of the world. This is perhaps where ATM shows the most promise.

Prior to the development of the Synchronous Optical Network (SONET) standard for wide-area network connectivity, network and applications were artificially limited to operate at

45 megabits per second. This was due to the fact that the fastest link speed in the WAN was DS3. It took ATM to unlock the bandwidth beyond DS3, effectively exploiting SONET's potential, and leveraging the carriers' investment in the technology. This capability will become even more important as more use is made of wave-division multiplexing technologies which allow carriers to further exploit the capacity of in-place fiber optic cable.

Therefore, the most important impact of ATM has yet to be realized and its future role is clear. ATM is the only technology which will allow digital information to be carried independent of speed, distance or physical media. This flexibility will place ATM in the role of unifying networks across the globe — regardless of which technology wins the desktop. ATM is more flexible than TDM at lower speeds and it provides the ability to scale rates up to gigabits per second — even over satellite systems.

The carrier community has always intended to base networks on ATM. Carriers will be able to carry a multitude of different services over a uniform architecture using ATM. Most importantly, carriers and large end-users will be able to lower their cost of operation and ownership due to the implementation of a uniform, scalable architecture throughout their networks. This will result in a wealth of services and lower cost to enterprises and end-users — and that's ATM's real bottom line — the potential to unify the world's communications systems and provide a broader choice of services, all at a lower unit cost than current technologies.

Part IV

The Part of Tens

"The department mascot seems to be having a bit of trouble with adaptation to the ATM environment."

In this part . . .

Part IV, The Part of Tens, actually contains only eight elements (chapters, that is). And each of the eight chapters may or may not contain ten elements. But regardless of the actual numbers, this part gives you quick, to-the-point, no-nonsense information related to ATM. You can find out the reason to use ATM (or the reasons not to use it, if you prefer). You can find tips for successful ATM projects, a discussion of alternative technologies, information about standards, influencers, and supporters of ATM, and a listing of sources for even more stuff about ATM. Have fun!

Chapter 17

Ten Tips for a Successful ATM Project

*B*y the time ATM projects reach the implementation stage they're usually successful in meeting or exceeding user expectations. That's the good news. The bad news is that many projects come to a standstill before ever reaching that stage. Migration to ATM stalls for a number of good reasons but mostly because ATM just isn't a good fit for the networking problems at hand.

Having participated in several ATM user start-ups, we want to pass along some tips for successful projects based on our experience. We hope you find this information useful in your own endeavors to move to ATM.

Keep the Initial ATM Project Small

We've put this tip first because it's the most important guideline to keep in mind. Projects expected to leap in one giant step to an ATM network reaching from your desktop to the wide area network for voice, data, and video never get off the drawing board. They end up much too large to budget, let alone approve, and much too complex to implement or manage. For most organizations, even three or four major ATM migration steps are probably too few.

Projects tend to balloon in size when users try to justify implementing an ATM network. Some users think

- ✔ That the network has to aggregate all the corporate traffic including voice calls.
- ✔ That ATM should be used throughout the network backbone infrastructure.
- ✔ That their businesses waste money unless they move to this broad ATM configuration as quickly as possible.

The reality is that projects of this scope, while offering many compelling benefits to justify implementation, are just too big to handle. ATM users need time to scale all the learning curves from planning and engineering to actual operation. Although ATM's capabilities offer a wide range of benefits, they present many more options and require much more decision-making than do other networking solutions.

A small, initial ATM project helps you get your feet wet. It leaves room for a few of those inevitable mistakes and gives you fresh information for planning and justifying new ATM projects. The best initial project focuses on one demanding desktop application, on a few congested campus backbones, or on a few large WAN networking sites. Although a small project may prove difficult to justify, you can still get it past management. After all, if a large project may be easy to justify but difficult to budget, then the steps of finalizing a design, selecting vendors, and determining a practical implementation plan could prove too unwieldy and complex to finish.

Have Good Reasons Why ATM Beats Any Alternative

If you don't heed the advice in the preceding heading, you may be sent right back to the project's beginning at some point. You should be able to clearly and convincingly state how an ATM solution benefits your organization. (And we sincerely doubt "Because it will look good on my resume," is going to sell the big boss on your idea.)

ATM is a great choice for many different networking environments. It's also a lousy choice for many other environments. In Chapters 18 and 19 of this book, we list reasons for and against implementing ATM.

If you believe ATM is the right fit for your network, your organization is likely to receive solid benefits. Identify a few of the most compelling reasons why you want to sell an ATM solution to your organization. Be prepared to defend your solution against other alternatives. A change in the status quo is always the most challenging (but we think the most fun) solution to sell.

We just don't want you to wind up among those poor folks who cling to ATM too long for the wrong reasons. Too many times we've seen the evaluation process last longer than it should because of all the ATM hype. Traveling too far down a dead-end ATM road ends up wasting the time and resources of both your networking staff and vendors. If ATM is the wrong fit for now, don't give up on it. You may find that the next networking challenge presents the right opportunity to begin your ATM journey.

Establish Clear Objectives for Your ATM Project

Nailing down the objectives for your ATM project helps you make the right decisions more quickly. While you're at it, consider prioritizing or weighting your objectives according to their importance. A clear picture of what's most important to change or achieve in your network helps you wade through the myriad vendor and configuration choices.

Some of your objectives may be very tactical:

- ✔ Supporting a new application
- ✔ Improving backbone networking throughput
- ✔ Saving on networking costs

Other objectives may be very strategic:

- ✔ Testing ATM's performance and benefits
- ✔ Gaining ATM networking knowledge
- ✔ Benchmarking various ATM configurations

Figure Out Your Long-term Networking Goals

A well-developed sketch of how you want your network to look in three years can also help you to make better decisions in your current ATM project. As you consider each alternative, ask yourself whether that altenative moves you closer to or farther away from your goal.

For example, a proprietary workgroup LAN may be the best choice for a networking problem you have now, but could be a future headache when you try to integrate it with a larger ATM backbone configuration. As another example, one vendor's switch mechanism may be ideal for the OC3 campus backbone that you're currently building, but the port density of the T3 cards that you eventually use to terminate ATM uplinks from LAN switches is dismal—a situation which can significantly increase your overall costs.

Develop some vision of how your network will change in the next three years, and find equipment and service providers to help you grow into that vision. We realize it may be next to impossible to project your future networking requirements and configuration, but you should develop some general directions to help guide you. Your early ATM project should also keep as many doors open to change as possible.

If you're completely uncertain of your future plans, your ATM project can simply smooth the path for future change. Let everyone know that the first objectives of the project are testing and benchmarking. If your project reaches payback in just 18 months (or less) and you use sufficiently short depreciation schedules for the equipment involved, whether the project provides the correct long-term solution is not as important.

Do Some Comparison Shopping

You may find that the high cost of one or more elements of the network knocks the ATM alternative out of the competition early. Although ATM is dropping in price, many of its elements are priced for sticker shock. On the other hand, don't assume ATM is too expensive until you've checked around. The current price points may surprise you, but don't expect to get that T3 ATM carrier connection for the same price as your T1 frame relay pipe. Get out there and ask about pricing early in your project.

Pick Vendors with Good Customer Support

Vendors willing to commit the time and resources necessary to make your project successful are invaluable. Choose providers with strong corporate and local customer support. A good account team is a powerful internal voice for your cause if you run into problems—a not-uncommon situation in any networking project. Equipment may not work quite as expected, or perhaps you lack sufficient understanding of your application requirements or traffic patterns. In these cases, you need a proactive vendor flexible enough to fix any problems that may arise.

A good provider also offers tips and suggestions learned from other projects similar to yours. Such advice can help you run your project more smoothly and avoid common mistakes. Your vendor should be able to offer recommendations on network configurations, performance optimization, and achieving interoperability with other networking elements and applications.

But don't limit yourself to ATM providers who've been in the marketplace a long time. Your best solution may come from a newer equipment vendor or carrier. Newer providers generally don't have mixed agendas to protect their existing product lines while easing into new markets. For established vendors, new markets represent customer dollars that are open again to competitors.

Newer firms typically have lots of good ideas for saving money by augmenting your current network rather than building a complete change out. They generally employ the latest, lowest-cost technology, and offer the time, resources, expertise, and inclination to help you along. The talented people in newer organizations often come from more-established firms where they learned what worked and what didn't. Having experienced employees gives a company a strong background, even though they may be new to the market.

It pays to broaden your horizons and invite a few new players in for the afternoon. Be as open as possible, at least in your early search. Whether you opt for a new or a traditional vendor, find a company with the right networking solution for your unique situation and the time and willingness to give you individual attention.

Assemble a Motivated ATM Project Team

Tackling an ATM project means some increased overtime and a few extra headaches for your staff. Therefore, enlisting team members who are eager to learn new technologies and build their networking skill sets is essential. A successful project depends on proactive interest and suggestions from everyone on your team, including the ATM users, designers, and operations support.

Allow Sufficient Implementation Time

Understanding and evaluating all your alternatives requires a significant time investment. ATM introduces new networking concepts that take some getting used to. Its capabilities present opportunities (and challenges) that you've probably never encountered before. We've participated in several ATM projects that took more than three years to move from initial planning, evaluation, and design through justification and provider selection to completed engineering and implementation. While we hope you never experience a project of this duration, don't expect a 30-day, quick-hit job that you do in your spare time.

ATM has matured greatly in just a few years, and the store of conventional wisdom about ATM has grown along with it. But it's still a young technology with many different suppliers and implementation alternatives. The recent rash of new, alternative technologies adds yet another dimension to decision-making. Take some time to make the right decisions for your organization.

Test, Test, and Test Some More

Before christening your network and sending it into production, make sure that you first test it for any bugs. Try out a number of expected configurations. Include your target applications in some of the tests. Pre-testing helps uncover potential problems and gives you some early experience in managing and operating the network. After your first implementation is in place, it can serve as a field test to prepare your group for other larger ATM projects.

Read Part III of This Book

If you have any questions along the path of your ATM project, check out Part III of this book. There we elaborate on the criteria for a successful implementation and provide many other helpful tips and suggestions. We compare and contrast ATM to other available technologies in both the WAN (Chapter 12) and LAN (Chapter 13) and discuss signs of the need for ATM and migration options. We offer ideas for justifying ATM in your network in Chapter 14 and provide ways to evaluate your equipment and carrier providers and to engineer and test your network in Chapter 15. We hope that you use these chapters as a sort of guidebook to completing your ATM project.

Chapter 18

Top Reasons to Consider ATM

In This Chapter

▶ Relieving network congestion with ATM

▶ Gaining strategic advantages for your business

▶ Eliminating extra elements from the network

▶ Combining networking functionality

▶ Lowering networking costs

▶ Providing high-speed network connectivity

▶ Building a new network

▶ Getting experience with ATM technology

*A*TM is a useful networking technology — when you need its capabilities. But implementing ATM can be expensive, involved, and time consuming. This chapter tells you about situations in which you want to consider using ATM.

Relieving congestion on the campus backbone

Of all the reasons that companies are deploying production ATM networks today, relieving congestion on the campus backbone may be the most common. LAN segment sizes are smaller, so more LANs are needed to support the same number of workers than were needed in the past. And all the LANs feed into the same high-speed campus backbone. LAN switching makes matters worse by increasing the availability of dedicated capacity to each desktop. As a result, the total aggregate bandwidth flooding into the shared campus backbone is driving the need for solutions of 100 Mbps and greater. In situations where several LAN segments operate at 100 Mbps, the shared campus backbone supporting these LANs must be greater than 100 Mbps to ensure throughput and availability.

The free-for-all nature of shared media solutions, such as fast Ethernet and FDDI, may not deliver high quality performance over the campus backbone to critical applications and users. ATM's scalability, guaranteed quality of service, and its connection-oriented environment make ATM better suited to controlling the level of performance when compared to a shared network architecture. ATM's scalability is currently unmatched by any other LAN backbone technology, and ATM can support speeds up to 622 Mbps today.

Relieving congestion on the WAN backbone

If you have locations on your wide area network that are linked together by several T1 (E1) private lines or frame relay links, and network congestion is slowing your data applications down to a crawl, then ATM may be a better solution. You can increase the speed of your WAN backbone by using ATM NxT1 or T3 services to relieve the WAN bottleneck. Depending upon when you are reading this book, you may have to wait for widespread availability of NxT1 services until carrier implementation of the IAM (Inverse ATM Mux) standard — probably not before 1998.

The higher speed ATM services may be a better choice over their frame relay counterparts, depending upon your present and future applications as well as services availability and costs. Deploying ATM now, to relieve the data network congestion, positions you to expand your ATM network to other applications in the future.

You can purchase ATM services in smaller bandwidth increments than you can with your dedicated private lines. This incremental purchase feature applies to the individual virtual circuits connecting remote sites and (in the future) to the port connections. With this incremental feature, you do not need to purchase more capacity on a point-to-point basis than what is needed by the application. The incremental ATM bandwidth purchase between T1 and T3 can result in savings as compared to the more traditional private-line network solution.

Eliminating backbone routers

With ATM, you may be able to eliminate some of the routers in your backbone router network. ATM's logical connections can provide direct connectivity between all your edge router sites, allowing you to get rid of the backbone routers previously needed to achieve full connectivity. Adding an ATM core to your router network is like building an expressway across town so that you can avoid all the side streets with their many traffic lights.

The ATM core can decrease costs by reducing the number of needed routers while improving your network performance. The direct connections of ATM are much faster than the delay-inducing backbone routers, which increase the number of network links and add processing delays. The ATM core also lends stability to your routing tables by providing a self-healing infrastructure. Congestion-inducing reroutes due to network failure no longer occur.

Gaining strategic advantage or lower business costs

New strategic business applications with very high-speed bandwidth or stringent quality of service (QoS) requirements may need the scalability or QoS support of ATM. The application itself must be important enough to translate into real business benefits such as competitive market advantage or lower operations costs that justify the ATM investment. The high speed nature or performance demands of the application must also place uncommon stress on the existing LAN or corporate backbone network, necessitating a separate network. If these conditions exist, then ATM may be the best solution.

After you put the ATM network in place to satisfy the requirements of the new application, you can expand its reach to support other applications.

Lowering network costs by mixing real-time and non-real-time applications

Operating separate networks for LAN, SNA, voice, video, and other applications increases the cost of network ownership. Consolidating these applications can significantly reduce equipment, wiring, access, wide area network, administration, and operation costs — but only if each application can be guaranteed a level of performance equal to or better than what is achieved in a dedicated environment. ATM's qualities of service allow end-to-end network connections to be designed with latency, throughput, and error measurements specific to the needs of real-time and non-real-time applications.

When many different applications use statistical multiplexing to share a pool of bandwidth, the total amount of network capacity needed to support the applications is often less than if each application had dedicated bandwidth. ATM uses statistical multiplexing to dynamically allocate bandwidth to active applications as each requires, improving overall network price/performance.

Only a few companies are using ATM for this type of consolidated enterprise network solution today. However, this enterprise vision can be achieved by starting with a single data application and then growing the ATM network.

Lowering network costs for highly intermittent, high-speed WAN applications

Some applications require very high speed transmission but only at certain times of the day or night, the week, or the month. And a few ATM WAN service providers price their services so that you pay an amount commensurate with usage, instead of paying for 100 percent of the bandwidth 100 percent of the time, as with leased lines. Users achieve this flexible pricing either through usage-based billing or through individually negotiated contracts. Pricing is based on the expected or actual network utilization.

For example, an application that requires 10 Mbps of bandwidth for four hours, two nights a week may be perfectly suited to an ATM network. A DS3 dedicated leased line may be too expensive, especially if the network locations are a long distance apart. Many companies faced with the (too expensive) situation today use the next best alternative — like putting the information on magnetic tape and sending it in overnight mail. If these companies can reduce the price of network solution (perhaps with ATM services), they can handle the application electronically instead.

Provide high speed server connectivity

Popular servers supporting many users or bandwidth-intensive applications may require the high speed connectivity provided by ATM. ATM local connections at 155 or 622 Mbps can handle even the most demanding traffic and give your users the throughput they need to reach their servers. ATM may also be a good choice if the server is supporting real-time traffic such as the playback of video clips. *Server farms* made up of a group of servers may also be good candidates for the higher speeds of ATM connections. If the users are non-ATM locations, then you must also implement LAN emulation to provide interoperability with the ATM connected server.

Building a new network

If you need to build a new network for a new workgroup or building location, then ATM may make a good choice. With no existing equipment investment to consider, you may find that ATM is as cost effective (or nearly so) as the alternative solutions. An ATM implementation can meet your networking needs today while providing you a networking platform to build upon for future applications.

Gaining experience with ATM

If you operate a high-speed LAN, campus, and/or wide area network and you are fairly certain that ATM is strategically important for your network in the future, then installing an ATM pilot network now can help you gain valuable experience. With this experience, you understand the benefits, problems, opportunities, and applications of ATM within your network environment. Gaining this experience is a primary reason for the deployment of ATM pilot networks today.

Many users are uncertain about the benefits that ATM can provide their companies and their networks. Finding out about these benefits and their associated costs is a highly valid reason to deploy a small ATM network.

Chapter 19

Some Reasons Not to Use ATM

*U*sing ATM isn't always the best option for your networking needs. Read this chapter to find out some reasons not to choose ATM.

Another technology meets your current needs

If your networking requirements are best met using another technology (such as frame relay, native LAN services, or switched Ethernet) and you don't expect these needs to change significantly over the next 18 to 24 months, you're probably better off not installing ATM for a while. ATM is in enough of a state of flux that if you wait a year or two, you'll find continued growth in its capabilities as well as lower costs.

Using another technology in the short term doesn't prevent you from taking advantage of ATM later. In fact, some technologies provide both a migration path to ATM and valuable experience with virtual networking. For example, in local and campus networks, a migration to LAN switching provides a first step toward ATM. In wide-area networks, using frame relay gives you experience with permanent virtual circuits and use of a public data network service. If the time comes when you need the increased speed and service quality ATM offers, you'll be in a good position to deploy ATM.

Information technology resources are scarce

If time is at a premium or you have a shortage of people in your information technology department, migrating to ATM may not be a great idea unless

✔ You use a service that hides all the underlying technology (such as an ATM-based native LAN service).

✔ Another company (such as a systems integrator) deploys and manages the network for you.

Both options spare you the pain of learning and implementing a new technology, never a simple task.

Implementation of ATM, and the ongoing management and operation of the network, requires a significant amount of time and expertise. Unless you can make this investment, you're better off putting the plans on hold. More harm than good is done by diving partway into an ATM implementation only to eventually discover you lack the skilled resources to complete the task. Reduce the scope of the ATM project or use another technology in the short term. Move to ATM when implementation can be done well and done right. You'll want your first project to be a clear success.

If nothing's broken, an ATM fix isn't needed

If your network works, the best strategy may be to leave well enough alone. If you don't have any problems with performance, cost, supporting a new application, or scaling to meet aggregate bandwidth needs, then stick with what you have. If these problems do crop up or are expected to occur within a year's time, consider switching to ATM or seeking some other solution.

Wide-area network requirements don't exceed 1.5 Mbps

If few or none of the locations on your network require aggregate bandwidth in excess of 1.5 Mbps, you probably don't need to worry about ATM for a while. Use another option such as private lines or frame relay. Look to ATM as a solution when several locations eat up a DS-1 (E1) or more of private line, frame relay, or X.25 bandwidth.

Campus network requirements don't exceed 100 Mbps

If the campus backbone supports only a few 10 Mbps LANs, and 100 Mbps or less of bandwidth is needed to provide acceptable performance, don't move to ATM unless you expect this situation to change dramatically in the short term. If possible, continue to use mature technologies that are familiar to your staff and widely available. If necessary, begin preparing the way for ATM by installing the proper wiring. Hold off on an actual ATM investment until a bandwidth problem arises.

Chapter 20

Ten ATM Web Sites and Information Sources

● ●

In This Chapter

▶ Recognizing the primary information sources — the standards

▶ Picking up inside information from telecommunications trade publications

▶ Scouting out hot online sources of ATM information

● ●

*W*hile we hope that you find this book to be a great source of information about ATM, we realize that you may want to find out more about particular aspects of the technology — not to mention the latest and greatest breaking news and developments in the industry.

We need to keep up on this sort of thing, and here's a list of Web sites and publications that we keep an eye on. If you want to stay informed, we recommend that you keep your eyes on them, too!

ATM Forum Web site

We won't spend much time belaboring this point, especially since we have an appendix dedicated to the Forum and its workings, but beginning the discussion of ATM information sources with the ATM Forum's Web site address makes sense! You can get the lastest Forum scoop at

```
http://www.atmforum.com
```

As you may have already found out, unless you randomly skipped right back to this chapter to begin reading this book (perhaps you've spent a few too many hours on the Web in hypertext land?), the ATM Forum is an organization dedicated to establishment of standards and education to promote the growth of ATM as a technology.

The Forum's Web page is as good a place as any to begin your journey into ATM resources. The Web site has information about the Forum and its members, tutorials and educational material, and listings of all sorts of standards and terminology.

IETF Web site

This offering may be a case of too much information being a bad thing, at least for some readers, but if you have an interest (or need) to find out a bit more about ATM and how it fits in with the Internet (there, we used the magic word, somebody quote us quick!), you should visit the Internet Engineering Task Force (IETF) Web site. It's easy to find — just go to

```
http://www.ietf.org
```

When you arrive at the IETF Web site, you can get more information about this organization (which helps establish a lot of the standards that make the Net work), and you find links to search through a huge number of RFCs (or Request for Comments).

International Telecommunications Union Web site

What the IETF is to the Internet, the ITU (International Telecommunications Union) is to the whole telecommunications world — and more! To boil it down to its essence, the ITU is an international organization that promulgates standards for telecommunications throughout the world by coordinating with governments and private sector telecommunications organizations (like the ATM Forum).

So if you want to find out more about the standards (and we're not talking about those old songs that every cabaret singer should be able to belt out), here's your one-stop shopping source:

```
http://www.itu.ch
```

By the way, that .ch part of the Web address indicates Switzerland, specifically Geneva, which is home to a bunch of international organizations (and some pretty good chocolate, too).

This Web site, which offers you a mix of free and pay content, lets you browse through lists of standards and recommendations, press releases, organizational information — basically everything about the ITU.

Network World magazine

As one of the leading trade publications for communications professionals, *Network World* is a good resource for news and information about all types of networking and data communications technologies. Like most trade publications, *Network World* isn't really designed to be sent to the homes of every interested party — in fact, subscriptions are kind of expensive — but if you qualify as the right kind of *professional,* you can usually get a subscription for free. Chances are, if you're reading this book, you qualify. If you can't get your hands on the print edition, check out *Network World*'s Web site at

```
http://www.nwfusion.com
```

You need to register online (which doesn't cost you anything), and you get access to a whole bunch of information, including searchable back issues. *Network World* primarily covers weekly news flashes in the telecom industry but also includes some in-depth articles on various networking topics. You may find the buyer's guides for networking equipment and services useful in finding the latest features and capabilities from vendors.

Data Communications and BYTE magazines

Data Communications and *BYTE* magazines are two monthlies that regularly cover ATM developments. *Data Communications* is an informative monthly that focuses on the happenings and technology of the data communications industry (oddly enough). Each issue includes in-depth tutorials that help to keep you up-to-date in a variety of different data technologies. *Data Communications* also conducts lab tests that scrutinize the capabilities of a particular class of networking gear from those vendors willing to meet the challenge. ATM LANE (local area network emulation) products were the spirited ensemble of a recent test.

BYTE magazine is perhaps a bit more of a general-interest publication than the others we list here, but it's no less valuable for keeping yourself up-to-date. Straddling the line between user-friendly computer magazine and hard-core geek publication, *BYTE* provides a wealth of information about computers, networking and communications — including lots of coverage of ATM and its applications within these fields. We thumbed through a few of the most recent issues and found coverage of the ATM LANE standard, articles about ATM in the LAN and an editorial about future ATM full-service networks (and we didn't even look very hard).

To find out more about *Data Communications* or *BYTE* and to view the online versions of these magazines, fire up your Web browser and head to

```
http://www.data.com
```
or
```
http://www.byte.com
```

Business Communications Review (BCR)

Another informative monthly is *Business Communications Review (BCR)*. *BCR* provides analyses and opinions in well-written, detailed articles covering all aspects of planning and managing the network including voice, data, and video; equipment and services; and LANs and WANs. Each *BCR* publication typically includes at least one ATM-related article and a broadband column from Dr. John McQuillan. McQuillan is also the chair of large yearly, ritualistic gatherings of ATM faithful, where those gathered discuss the latest and greatest ATM developments.

To receive a copy of *BCR*, you need to pay your $45 yearly subscription fee or get on someone's routing list, because *BCR* is not available on-line. This magazine is probably worth having your own copy.

A whole bunch of CMP publications

Another major publisher of telecommunications trade and technical periodicals, CMP offers a handy, all-in-one Web site with access to their many publications:

```
http://www.techweb.com
```

On the TechWeb site (which offers free membership), you can keep up to date on the latest technology news — the publishers call it a *technology super site,* and indeed, you can find a lot of information from varied sources.

In addition to the news and opinions available on TechWeb, you can also search through back issues of all the publications if you have a specific query. Or you can link to the home pages of the publications (a list that includes *Communications Week, Electronic Engineering Times, Information Week,* and *Interactive Age*). The publications cover many bases, and the site's search engine certainly comes in handy.

IEEE magazines and journals

If you're really interested in all the gory details of ATM technology, including the many, many unresolved issues in scaling ATM networks while still supporting QoS, you may want to turn to a few IEEE (Institute of Electrical and Electronic Engineers) Communications Society publications. Nothing like these magazines can keep you up-to-date on the most recent ATM technical developments and ongoing research, that is if you're really interested in the issues of the equipment and service provider engineers. We warn you ahead of time that these magazines can be very dry and dull, unless of course you're a committed propellerhead getting paid to figure this stuff out.

If you are a student or researcher in telecommunications, you may already be familiar with the broader technical coverage in *IEEE Communications Magazine* and *IEEE Network* along with the detailed technical papers from *IEEE Transactions on Communications, IEEE Journal on Selected Areas of Communications,* and *IEEE/ACM Transactions on Networking.* If you didn't know about these magazines before reading this text, the reason is probably simple — you don't need or want to know all those techno details!

You can find more information on the IEEE Communications Society and their publications at their home page

```
http://www.ieee.org/comsoc/comsochome.html
```

Cell Relay at Indiana University

As you may have divined from your investigation, ATM can get kind of esoteric and — dare we say — complicated. So, we find it refreshing that a good down-to-earth site, with lots of ATM information can be found on a university Web site. Specifically, we are talking about the Cell Relay site at Indiana University (not too far from our publisher's offices).

Home of the archives for some ATM newsgroups, the Cell Relay site also offers a host of other good ATM information, including some great stuff for beginners (FAQs, dictionaries, and Acronyms Lists, among other items), lots of documents, an events calendar, job listings (!), and links to other resources.

To visit the Cell Relay site, point your Web browser of choice to

```
http://cell-relay.indiana.edu
```

And sometime drop a note to thank Allen Robel, the author of this book's Foreword, for his great work in maintaining this site.

Institute of Computer Science, Greece

We recently stumbled on a very interesting site that we've not seen mentioned anywhere else. This site has more hotlinks to more ATM web pages all across the world than we even imagined existed. Take a visit to

```
http://www.ics.forth.gr/netgroup/index.html
```

The Telecommunications and Networks Group at the Institute of Computer Science – Foundation for Research and Technology – Hellas maintains the page. At this site, you find hotlinks to standards organizations, ATM tutorials, over a hundred different university research groups, and various high speed government projects and testbeds across the globe.

Vendors ho!

Depending upon your perspective, ATM vendors' Web sites can be great resources. Why the caveat? Well, vendors usually have an agenda — selling their product — that may keep them from being completely unbiased. Understanding that, and keeping that proverbial grain of salt handy, you can find lots of interesting stuff on the Web sites of ATM equipment manufacturers and service providers.

We're hesitant to just give you a big listing of vendors, for fear of leaving someone out, but you can find a good listing on the ATM Forum Web site and on the Cell Relay site (you can find the URLs for these sites in this chapter). You may also want to visit your favorite Internet search engine and snoop around there.

General Telecommunications Web sites

We are beginning to creep further beyond our allotted ten recommendations and realize that a top ten list is really only useful if it sticks fairly close to the number ten. These URLs lead you to Web sites with hotlinks to a wealth of other telecommunications sites.

Visit the University of Michigan's Telecommunications Information Resources page at the following URL. On this Wolverine page, you find telecom headlines, technical information and FAQs, standards bodies, research groups, and newsgroups.

```
http://www.spp.umich.edu/telecom
```

The page from Keith O'Brien has compiled several long lists including carriers/ PTTs (Post Telephone and Telegraph), vendors, trade magazines, and other organizations. See Keith O'Brien's Telecommunications Directory at

```
http://www.castle/net/~kobrien/telecom.html
```

The Australian carrier Telstra provides this home page with many international links to telecommunications companies, government and telecommunication authorities, and university and educational institutions. Telstra's {Tele}Communications Information Sources at

```
http://www.telstra.com.au
```

Chapter 21

More Than Ten Important ATM Standards

*S*tandards are a good thing. Moreover, standards are vital to the continued development and deployment of ATM networks (in all sorts of different places). Therefore, if you're interested in ATM networks, knowing what's what in the realm of standards and knowing where to go to find out more about the standards is important.

Selecting the top ten standards for ATM is really quite impossible, although the idea does make for a good chapter title. But we can limit the number of key organizations working on ATM standards to less than ten. You can find out more about how all these different groups work together in the "Inside ATM" feature at the end of Chapter 8.

ATM Forum

The Forum (as the ATM Forum is known to those in the ATM industry) is the most important and influential standards organization relevant to ATM. Over 700 organizations belong to the ATM Forum. Over 600 participants attend the six yearly meetings of the Forum. Each meeting is actually a collection of multiple, overlapping meetings of the different working groups — with sessions running all day and often well into the night.

And much work goes on between meetings. In 1995 alone, the Forum received 1701 contributions from its members. *Contributions* present alternatives, research, and arguments for various standard features and serve as the source documents for the completed specifications. The total of contributions in 1996 will be even higher. We provide you with more fun facts and ATM Forum contact information in Appendix A of this book. Each specification follows the same approval process:

- ✔ The Forum distributes the straw ballot document to their over 200 principal members for comment and a test vote.

- ✔ From the straw ballot and received comments, the appropriate Forum working group writes a final letter ballot document (or another straw ballot if necessary). Each of the principal members receives one vote, and a majority of *yeas* results in a finished specification (approval!).

Vendors often begin implementations after the straw ballot is written, depending on the known controversy of the specification. You generally see implementations of new standards in vendor equipment within 6–12 months of final approval, depending on the specification's complexity and the perceived market interest.

We describe the purpose and work of each ATM Forum working group in the following sections:

Broadband InterCarrier Interface (B-ICI)

The B-ICI group defines specifications for interconnecting carriers. You can find out more about the B-ICI in Chapter 10.

Data Exchange Interface (DXI)

The DXI specification provides a protocol for distributing the ATM UNI (user-to-network interface) functions between a router and an external ATM DSU (data service unit). The DXI working group is no longer active, and the specification is rarely used in new implementations. You can find out more about the DXI specification in Chapter 8.

Integrated Layer Management Interface (ILMI)

ILMI is a specification for exchanging management information over the UNI. UNI v.2.0, 3.0, and 3.1 included the ILMI as a part of their documentation. The breakout of UNI 4.0 into multiple documents resulted in a separate specification for ILMI. You can find out more about the ILMI specification in Chapter 10.

LAN Emulation (LANE)

LANE is a critically important working group of the ATM Forum. LANE defines an architecture and protocols for interconnecting legacy LANs (like Ethernet and token ring) with an ATM LAN or ATM LAN backbone. You can find out more about the LANE specifications in Chapter 11.

Multiprotocol over ATM (MPOA)

The MPOA working group is defining an important new standard to enhance ATM's support of Layer 3 protocols. MPOA will define a way for ATM to provide multiprotocol routing as part of the ATM network function. You can find out more about the MPOA specification in Chapter 11.

Network Management

Standard network management MIBs (management information bases) and interfaces are the subject of this working group. You can find out more about the working group's many efforts in Chapter 10.

Physical Layer

The abundant number of physical layers (of network protocols) supported by ATM is a credit to the Physical Layer working group. The initial physical specifications were included in the early UNI documents. Subsequent definitions have been separate specifications. You can find out more about all the different physical layer specifications in Chapter 8.

Private Network-Network Interface (PNNI)

PNNI provides a standard interface for interconnecting ATM switches. PNNI includes the most complex routing protocol ever defined. You can find out more about the PNNI specification in Chapter 10.

Residential Broadband (RBB)

The residential broadband working group is defining a reference model and specifications for carrying ATM into the residence. You can find out more about the RBB specification in Chapter 5.

Security

The security working group develops requirements and information flow specifications for ATM security. The group covers all aspects of security for ATM applied to user information, signaling messaging, and management information. You can find out a little more about the work of the Security group in Chapter 10.

Service Aspects and Applications (SAA)

SAA is responsible for specifications that enable existing and new applications to run on ATM networks. You can find out about some of the different efforts of the SAA working group in Chapter 11.

Signaling

The Signaling working group defines the messages exchanged across the UNI for call management. Signaling was a part of the UNI v. 3.0 and 3.1 before becoming a separate document in 4.0. You can find out more about the signaling specification in Chapter 10.

Testing

Testing has generated the greatest number of specifications. The specifications define conformance test suites, interoperability test suites, and protocol implementation conformance statements (PICSs) for the various ATM standards. You can find out more about the testing specifications in Chapter 8.

Traffic Management

Traffic Management defines ATM's quality of service parameters and network control mechanisms for delivering the requested performance. Traffic management text was also a part of the UNI specification before 4.0. You can find out more about traffic management in Chapter 9.

User-Network Interface (UNI)

The UNI was the primary specification for ATM prior to the 1996 release of the various v. 4.0 documents. The UNI included all functions operating over the User-to-Network Interface. The UNI was not actually a working group, but the result of all the working group's efforts. The Forum does not plan to release any more integrated UNI documents so that the various working groups retain more flexibility. UNI 3.0 remains the most common implementation of ATM in late 1996. You can find out more about the UNI specifications in Chapters 8, 9, and 10.

Voice and Telephony over ATM (VTOA)

VTOA is defining standard methods of carrying voice traffic over ATM. You can find out more about the VTOA in Chapter 11.

Wireless ATM

The Wireless working group is defining standard ways of carrying ATM cells in wireless media. Most of the work is very new, and this is probably the one ATM topic that we don't cover any further in our book.

International Telecommunication Union (ITU)

The ITU is the international organization defining standards for the technologies and operations of global telecom networks and services. It is actually a United Nations treaty organization, and members are international governments. The State Department coordinates the US representation. You can find the ITU Web site at

```
http://www.itu.ch/
```

The ITU refers to its standards as *recommendations* which are not generally as tight as the implementation agreements created by the ATM Forum. The objectives of the recommendations are to achieve end-to-end compatibility of international telecommunications connections. ITU was the first standards organization to begin writing specifications for ATM. The ATM specifications were part of the B-ISDN (Broadband-Integrated Services Digital Network) recommendations first released in the 1988 version of ITU documentation. B-ISDN is a defined group of capabilities for transporting broadband public services. The primary technologies of B-ISDN are SONET and ATM.

The ITU has remained a very influential organization defining ATM specifications, especially for public networking. The ATM Forum works very closely to keep its specifications in alignment with the ITU. Depending on the standard, either organization may be the source of original content. As an example, the ITU was actually the birthplace of many of the signaling and VTOA details.

Internet Engineering Task Force (IETF)

The IETF is the standards organization for the Internet. The primary communications technology of the Internet is IP (Internet Protocol). The IETF has broad responsibility for developing this protocol and the transport and routing and forwarding protocols which move the IP packets around the network. Because IP has evolved as an open standard, IP has also become the most popular choice for data communications within corporate networks. The primary traffic type carried by ATM networks today is therefore IP. Knowledge of IP networking and its many specifications is absolutely critical to understanding ATM.

In this book, we focus on the specific IETF documents for carrying IP traffic on an ATM network. The IETF is now developing specifications to enhance IP and its routing protocols to support multiple classes of service and priorities. These enhancements will allow IP based applications to use the QoS (Quality of Service) capabilities of ATM. However, they also present a new alternative to ATM networking, which we discuss in several sections of the book (such as in Chapter 22).

The IETF has an IP-over-ATM working group which develops standards for routing and forwarding IP packets over ATM subnetworks. We've taken our descriptions of this working group's documents from the IETF's own RFC 1932 text. The two most widely implemented specifications are the following:

- **RFC 1483:** Multiprotocol Encapsulation over ATM Adaption Layer 5 (AAL5). This memo describes two encapsulation methods for carrying multiple packet/frame-based protocols multiplexed over ATM AAL5.

- **RFC 1577:** Classical IP and ARP over ATM. This memo provides a model for transporting IP and ARP over ATM AAL5 in an IP subnet.

Other defined specifications include these:

✔ **RFC 1626:** Default IP MTU for use over ATM AAL5. This memo specifies the default IP MTU (Maximum Transmission Unit) size to be used with ATM AAL5.

✔ **RFC 1755:** ATM Signaling Support for IP over ATM. This memo defines how implementations of IP over ATM should use ATM call control signaling procedures.

✔ **RFC 1932:** IP over ATM: A Framework Document. The intent of the framework is to help clarify the differences between proposals and identify common features of IP and ATM.

You can find out more about the IETF specifications in Chapter 11. You find the specifications of the IP-over-ATM working group and meeting minutes at

```
http://www.com21.com/pages/ietf.html#B5
```

Frame Relay Forum

The Frame Relay Forum has defined two specifications for ATM.

✔ **Frame Relay/ATM Network Interworking Implementation Agreement (FRF.5):** Defines a standard way to carry frame relay traffic across an ATM backbone. This specification depends on encapsulation of the frames carried by the frame relay network.

✔ **Frame Relay / ATM PVC Service Interworking Implementation Agreement (FRF.8):** Defines a standard way for a frame relay site to communicate with an ATM site; it depends on conversion of the frames into ATM cells.

Much of the original content for these specifications came from several ITU documents. The ATM Forum has endorsed the Frame Relay Forum standards. You can find out more about both specifications in Chapter 11 and at the frame relay Web site:

```
http://frame-relay.indiana.edu/
```

Switched Multimegabit Data Services (SMDS) Interest Group

Similar to the Frame Relay Forum, the SMDS Interest Group has penned a specification for using ATM as a backbone for SMDS networks. The ATM Forum has endorsed the standard. An internetworking specification that allows an SMDS site to communicate with an ATM site is yet to be written. You can find out more about the SMDS Interest Group at their Web site:

```
http://www.cerf.net/smds/sig/index.html
```

Chapter 22

Ten Alternatives to ATM

*W*e cover many alternatives to ATM elsewhere in the book, but we want to give you one succinct listing of the services and technologies that can be used instead of ATM in local, campus, and wide area networks. If you are a user considering ATM for one of these networking environments, you should be aware of these alternatives and their unique advantages and disadvantages compared to ATM.

ATM Alternatives in the WAN

For more details on the alternatives to ATM in the wide area network and the practical trade-offs between the options, see Chapter 12.

Private lines and time division multiplexing

High-speed dedicated leased lines, primarily DS-3s (E3) that operate at 45 Mbps (34 Mbps for E3), are the most commonly used alternative to high-speed ATM services today. The private line uses time division multiplexing (TDM) to statically allocate pre-assigned chunks of bandwidth to individual applications. High-speed private lines are often prohibitively expensive, especially because the pricing is mileage-sensitive. ATM, with its dynamic bandwidth allocations based on statistical multiplexing, offers a cost-effective alternative to dedicated leased lines for multiple site networks or point-to-point connections greater than 300 miles for U.S. long-distance networks and 30 miles for local loops. However, the technology with private lines and TDM is well understood and many companies have made a sizable investment in TDM equipment at lower speeds, raising the barriers for displacement of this technology.

Frame relay

Frame relay services share many similarities with ATM, which is why frame relay can compete against ATM in some network environments. Both technologies use statistical multiplexing to dynamically allocate bandwidth, but frame relay uses a variable length packet, which means that overhead is much lower than with the fixed-length ATM cell.

Frame relay premises equipment is now capable of supporting a mixture of voice, data, and video traffic over integrated frame relay access circuits. Eventually, service providers may even offer a choice of service classes on public frame relay services, and many providers already offer high-speed port connections ranging from 1.5 to 45 Mbps. Frame relay equipment services are more mature and are well understood by many users. Cost of equipment is lower for frame relay, and cost of service is generally similar to ATM.

SMDS

Switched Multimegabit Data Service (SMDS) is a connectionless public network offering that operates much like a LAN throughout a metropolitan or wide area network. SMDS is much less complex than ATM. Each location connecting to the network needs only one E.164 address. Unlike ATM, SMDS is a connectionless network, so individual connections and their associated classes and qualities of service don't need to be designed and predefined between locations.

SMDS services are offered at speeds ranging from 56/64 Kbps to 34 Mbps, with several options in between. SMDS pricing, at least in the U.S., is often highly aggressive, compared to private lines, frame relay, and ATM services. However, poor marketing, lack of nationwide availability, and the inability to support highly deterministic applications (such as voice, real-time video, and possibly SNA) limit the use of SMDS as an enterprise network solution for many companies.

SONET

Some service providers offer Synchronous Optical Network (SONET) point-to-point connections or ring configurations as a solution to connectivity needs that exceed standard private line speeds. SONET services typically start at 155 Mbps (OC3) and go as high as 2.4 Gbps in 1996, with 9.6 Gbps in the lab (a gigabit is 1,000,000,000 bits per second). Carriers often deploy SONET in a self-healing ring configuration that offers restoration speeds much faster than the recovery speed of an ATM network (unless that ATM network uses a SONET infrastructure).

For network applications requiring very high-speed connectivity between two or more locations, especially within a city, SONET can be a viable alternative (or complementary physical infrastructure) to ATM. In the U.S., many large corporations lease or own SONET rings in large metropolitan areas where they have a concentrated presence.

IP

The Internet Protocol (IP) is widely deployed throughout LAN and client-server networks today (as well as being the underlying protocol for the world's largest network — the Internet). While IP is not, by definition, supposed to be a multi-protocol solution, encapsulating different protocols such as IPX, AppleTalk, SNA, and others into IP for transmission over a network isn't uncommon. IP can operate at speeds ranging from dial-up to 45 Mbps and beyond.

IP is a connectionless protocol that is designed to carry an end-to-end session over a non-deterministic network. However, vendors are developing enhancements to IP that may make it more friendly to applications that require predictable levels of bandwidth and response times. IP already supports multimedia applications, including packet-based desktop conferencing and Web-based video and audio. IP is a viable alternative to ATM in some networks, especially networks that are nearly 100 percent IP in nature (not multiprotocol) and don't need the quality of service attributes offered by ATM.

Switching IP

Switching IP traffic is a concept that recently emerged to combine the hardware-switching of ATM with the intelligent routing of IP. Switching IP takes its economical hardware-switching for speed and scalability from ATM. IP offers a well-known, widely deployed protocol that already handles routing, address resolution, and all the many other requirements of a network backbone.

Two flavors of switching IP have emerged: IP switching and tap switching. Each takes advantage of the existing routing infrastructure and the connectionless nature of IP as the default state of the network. To this existing capability, switching IP adds a connection-oriented approach from ATM for any long, continuous stream of IP packets. When the transmission stream is long, layer two switching is much more efficient than the individual routing of packets at layer three. Switching IP is a technology that can route or relay IP, depending on the nature of the application being supported.

For environments that are totally or predominately IP (or where all other protocols are encapsulated into IP), switching IP can be a viable solution for economically scaling IP routing into the local or wide area network. You still need your ATM switch for the cut-through routing of the long streams, but you may be able to avoid the expensive purchase of a high-end router. As a very young technology, switching IP's capabilities will continue to aggressively expand. Chapter 23 further explores the roles of IP and ATM in networks.

Native LAN

Many users are finding that native LAN services give them the benefits of ATM without the complexities and hassles of a direct connection. Native LAN services present a traditional LAN interface (such as Ethernet, token ring, or FDDI) to the subscriber for wide area connectivity within a city or nation or even between nations. The wide area connectivity looks like just another LAN segment of the network. A hidden ATM backbone network supports the service in the carrier's infrastructure. The service provider owns and configures all necessary equipment, including the access devices and backbone ATM switches.

Native LAN services are available from a limited number of providers, primarily in the U.S. The benefit of these services is their inherent simplicity. The user receives a high bandwidth service without designing a large virtual network with multiple classes of service. If carriers made stronger commitments to these services, they might increase their popularity, especially for smaller customers. If LAN interconnect is the only application requirement, native LAN services can be very economical, compared to traditional ATM offerings, because emergent carriers such as CAPs (competitive access providers) and CLECs (competitive local exchange carriers), rather than traditional LECs and IXCs, generally offer these solutions. A sidebar in Chapter 12 "Alternatives to ATM," describes one user's experience with native LAN services.

ATM Alternatives in the LAN and Campus Backbone

For more details on the alternatives to ATM in the LAN and campus backbone and the practical trade-offs between the options, see Chapter 13.

FDDI and FDDI-II

At the time of this writing, FDDI is the most widely deployed high-speed LAN backbone technology, at least in the U.S. FDDI has been available for over seven years, uses a variable-length packet, offers a highly available and reliable solution, and includes a "fair" way to allocate and share bandwidth: a token-passing contention algorithm. The FDDI topology is typically based on two counter-rotating rings to protect against network failures and to provide a path over which to automatically reroute traffic.

FDDI is not as scalable as ATM; it is defined to operate at 100 Mbps. FDDI also doesn't offer the capability to designate different qualities of service or guarantee bandwidth to different applications. Like ATM, implementing FDDI for the first time means acquiring new protocol expertise.

FDDI-II is a standard that enhances FDDI with the option to run on fiber or twisted pair copper and supports real-time, constant bit rate bandwidth streams. FDDI II has not been widely accepted by the marketplace, and many predict a short life for it as alternatives, such as ATM, become available.

Switched Ethernet (or token ring and FDDI)

Switched Ethernet is Ethernet with 10 Mbps dedicated to each desktop. The advantages are that the shared nature of the topology is no longer a limitation, because each user gets full use of the 10 Mbps connection, and upgrading to switched Ethernet from Ethernet is very inexpensive. The Ethernet NIC at the desktop and popular star wiring is reusable. You only need to upgrade the wiring hub. Switched Ethernet is the migration solution of choice, compared to a traditional Ethernet solution, when a little more bandwidth is needed and qualities of service are not required. It is a desktop solution, not intended as a high-speed campus backbone technology.

Other switched LAN solutions are available, including switched token ring and, most recently, switched FDDI. These solutions operate similarly to switched Ethernet, dedicating an entire LAN segment to a single user.

Fast Ethernet

Fast Ethernet is an Ethernet standard defined for 100 Mbps and is part of the IEEE 802.3 standard, which means that fast Ethernet can use existing 10BaseT copper wiring and easily interoperate with traditional Ethernet desktops. Like Ethernet, fast Ethernet uses a shared bus architecture and doesn't dedicate bandwidth to individual workstations, as ATM does. However, fast Ethernet can be deployed so that only a single or a few workstations share the LAN, and switched fast Ethernet is becoming available from vendors.

The advantage of fast Ethernet is that it is Ethernet, only faster. Existing Ethernet users don't have an exorbitant learning curve to ascend, so fast Ethernet enjoys tremendous industry support and is currently the high-speed solution of choice for desktop connections upgrading from 10 Mbps Ethernet solutions. While it isn't an ideal campus backbone technology for companies needing scalability above 100 Mbps, fast Ethernet is often more practical than ATM in the LAN.

Although not widely available, gigabit Ethernet is another solution visible on the horizon. Gigabit Ethernet increases Ethernet's speed 100 times to 1,000 Mbps. Successful implementation of this emerging technology will provide network managers with yet another alternative for supporting their local area network connections.

100VG-AnyLAN

Hewlett-Packard developed a new MAC-level, high-speed LAN protocol (called Demand Priority Access Method, or DPAM) to support delay-sensitive applications such as multimedia and environments such as server farms. The new protocol is called 100VG-AnyLAN, where the *VG* stands for *voice grade,* and indicates that the protocol is compatible with four pair of Category 3 wiring. 100VG-AnyLAN falls under the 802.12 committee and operates at speeds of 100 Mbps, as the name suggests, but it has support from only a handful of vendors.

Chapter 23

Ten Drivers, Influencers, and Supporters of ATM

---

*A*TM is really just a small piece of everything that makes up a network. The success of ATM in the marketplace very much depends on the fate of other existing and emerging technologies. These technologies push the bandwidth accelerator and drive QoS requirements — ATM's strengths in the networking playing field. The market arrival and success of other technologies significantly impact the need for ATM.

If you want to forecast how ATM will fare in the marketplace or how soon you might need it somewhere in your own network, you need to consider these critical drivers, influencers, and supporters of ATM.

Driving Miss ATM

The following technologies may have a positive impact on the deployment of ATM infrastructures because they drive and support new high-speed services and applications to families, home office users, and businesses. Many users also need their networks to support new real-time video applications, further stressing the traditional data network to support different types of traffic. The faster these technologies are deployed and adopted, the sooner networks may require the high bandwidths and quality of service of ATM.

Desktop conferencing

The industry has been projecting since the early 1990s that desktop data and video conferencing will become a major market trend, but these technologies haven't yet caused the expected paradigm shift in the way people conduct business. We can come up with several reasons why widespread desktop conferencing hasn't yet emerged.

Video quality, even in a LAN-friendly, packetized format, can be poor over a wide area network that throttles down the connection. The interactive document editing and whiteboard functions that typically accompany desktop conferencing software have the same problems. In addition, early desktop conferencing solutions depended upon proprietary schemes, so users had to use similar equipment.

Recent developments may give video conferencing and desktop data a push. The recently approved standards by ITU (H.261/H.263, H.323/H.324, and T.120) enable improved interoperability between different desktop conferencing systems. Planned developments by microprocessor giant Intel may eliminate a third issue — cost. Intel's MMX puts video digital signal processing and other advanced multimedia processing capabilities into your PC.

Desktop conferencing may be a driver for ATM, or it may not. If each desktop is equipped with videoconferencing and people actually use it, the need for more bandwidth in the network and for better qualities of service for the real-time components of the application grows quickly. This growth, in turn, drives up the sales of high-speed ATM and ATM-based services.

On the other hand, ATM equipment and services or other high-speed solutions may have to be deployed *before* people start taking advantage of desktop conferencing tools on a regular basis. In this future scenario, ATM enables the adoption of desktop conferencing as opposed to desktop conferencing being a driver of ATM.

The Internet, intranets, and the Web

The Internet and its close siblings, business intranets, are key applications for ATM because they drive bandwidth increases — especially since the World Wide Web exploded onto the Internet scene and changed, practically overnight, the way businesses view the Internet. The Web transformed the Internet from a place where information and e-mail messages are exchanged by advanced computer users to a place of advertising and commerce for the ordinary PC owner. Companies are finding more and more ways to use the Web to educate consumers, display products and ideas, sell goods and services, and attract resources. They are also rapidly adopting the technologies in-house to better facilitate communication within the business.

Both an increasing number of users and emerging capabilities to better support image and graphics further feed users' appetites for more bandwidth. The capabilities of Intel's MMX technology increase the use of image and video not only in PC software applications but also on the Internet. Users downloading an Adobe-based presentation or a QuickTime movie chew up the available bandwidth transferring the multimegabit files. The latest rave of the Internet, Java and its applets, are not expected to be bandwidth hogs, but each new application adds to the aggregate load. The high speeds offered by ATM are especially important in supporting the Web servers and server farms that host individual companies and groups of companies on the Web. You can find out more about the growing popularity of the Internet and intranets in Chapter 6.

An industrial-strength Internet becomes mandatory as businesses rely ever more heavily on the Internet and the Web. The industrial-strength Internet provides a higher-performing, more reliable network than do today's less mature solutions. ATM is a logical underlying platform for this next generation Internet, enabling the Internet to support multiple qualities of service and the total level of aggregate bandwidth that is demanded.

ADSL

Asymmetrical Digital Subscriber Line (ADSL) is a new access protocol that delivers high-speed communications over a standard two-wire copper local loop, like the one the phone company uses to deliver dial tone to your home phone.

ADSL squeezes 1.5 to 6 Mbps of bandwidth from a simple phone line, the same one that your current modem uses to deliver your 14.4 or 28.8 Kbps Internet access connection. (If you thought your 28.8 Kbps modem gave you screaming Internet access, you'll be blown away with ADSL connections that provide over 100 times the bandwidth!) The transmission speed is asymmetrical, as the name says, and only delivers a fraction of this speed (up to 1 Mbps) in the return direction. However, this variance isn't a problem for supporting asymmetrical applications such as Internet access or remote LAN/server access.

Many local service providers have a staggeringly large installed base of copper wire to residential districts (such as your house and just about everybody else's, unless you have a very new house in an area that is undergoing a high-speed services trial). These providers are looking at ADSL as a means to cost-effectively deliver high-speed data, video, and interactive services to homes. Cable companies that are threatening to get into the telephone and data services business are further spurring the incumbent telco providers to ADSL action. Large deployments of ADSL may begin in 1998.

So where does ATM fit in? As a backbone infrastructure, of course. ATM is one of the options for aggregating all the high-speed ADSL traffic onto a backbone network in a cost-effective manner. Its scalability and statistical multiplexing are critical when you start looking at supporting millions of users who want service for $50 a month or less.

The question of where cellification takes place is still being debated. Some implementation plans call for cellification to occur at the customer's premises, which is the home or small business in most cases. The only problem is that a low-cost, easily configured, remotely manageable ATM device hasn't been developed for this market yet. Others plan to use ATM in the first serving wire center; still others think that frame relay may be more economical in the first serving wire center, with ATM providing high-speed switching deeper in the backbone and supporting the applications servers. The jury won't be in for some time and probably won't be unanimous when it does come in. Implementations will vary, depending on the unique needs of the service provider and the area (and who is playing golf with whom).

If you want to find out more about ADSL, turn to Kieran Taylor's "Inside ATM" feature at the end of Chapter 5.

Cable modems

Like the local phone company, the local cable TV provider wants to sell you a whole suite of new services, including Internet access, interactive TV, video telephony, and more. Cable modem technology was developed to enable cable TV providers, and other service providers using coaxial cable to the home or business, to support two-way, high-speed, interactive data over coax cables.

If you want even faster speeds than what are possible with ADSL, cable modems can provide 2 Mbps upstream and 10 Mbps downstream. Faster modems of 30 Mbps downstream and higher are on the drawing boards. Manufacturers are still testing designs and modulation schemes. Additionally, developers are considering including advanced networking capabilities such as tuners, bridging, routing, SNMP agents, and encryption/decryption.

The result may be a wide variety of modems that cannot interoperate. However, most cable companies intend to include the modems and their installations as part of their high-speed offerings (much like a converter box is part of your cable service), so this interoperability won't necessarily be an issue. The modem will probably connect to your PC via an Ethernet 10BaseT port and to your cable outlet in the wall.

Like ADSL, large deployments of cable modems may begin in 1998. The cable modem networks may include high-speed applications servers that support interactive programming interfaces for users. Many people again envision ATM as the underlying backbone network infrastructure, and the debate continues about where cellifications occur in the network.

Frame relay

Frame relay and ATM are highly complementary. Frame relay traffic can actually ride over an ATM network backbone by using network interworking. This traffic transfer is becoming very common in large frame relay networks, especially large public frame relay service networks. The underlying use of ATM can provide more scalability, faster switching, greater transmission speeds, and more efficient class of service support than is possible with end-to-end frame switching.

Networks using both frame relay and ATM to connect locations are also becoming quite common. Frame relay is ideal for connectivity to remote locations, while ATM fits at locations that require very high speeds and/or the quality of service attributes of ATM. The ATM switch, frame relay switch, or router provides the transparent protocol conversion between the two technologies, as specified in the implementors' agreement for frame relay to ATM service interworking. So the continuing surge in frame relay sales may lead to greater ATM service demand.

Network managers may also use a frame relay network with interworking when they need ATM in the local or campus network but cannot justify it in the wide area network. In this case, a frame relay service provides the wide area networking of the ATM network.

TCP/IP

Although a few IP zealots prophesy that ATM is rapidly headed to a dead-end future, most people in the industry view IP and ATM as complementary. The raging debate is about how the two best fit together. Arguments range between the following two viewpoints:

- ✔ IP is good for organizing and addressing a network and to signal required QoS of applications; however, its packet-transfer mechanism is too slow, expensive, congestion-prone, and unreliable. Lower-cost ATM is the right technology to replace the IP packet-transfer mechanism in the network backbone.

- ✔ ATM delivers good, low-cost high-speed switching hardware, but the implementations of the future continue to rely on the advanced, proven routing software of IP through technologies such as IP and tag switching. These technologies use well-established routing protocols throughout the network on fast, efficient ATM hardware.

In the first viewpoint, IP routing is important at the edge of the network, but ATM switching and signaling protocols provide the best way to move traffic across the network backbone. In the network core, ATM offers efficient, cost-effective express lanes to move traffic between the edge routers without all the packet handling complexities of IP. At the network edge, IP is still necessary to provide individual end station (and application) addressing, organization of the network units, manageable and secure subnets, and application-based signalling of QoS through emerging programming interfaces such as Winsock.

In the second viewpoint, only ATM's fast, cost-effective hardware has value — IP's routing is still the right technology for moving traffic across the backbone. The value of ATM's switching hardware comes from its low-cost implementation in silicon. Mass production of ATM switching matrices that quickly move traffic in hardware between switching ports have met their objective of being very cost-effective. Meanwhile, ATM software still requires significant investment to incorporate the new traffic management and signaling capabilities of the ATM

Forum's version 4.0 documents. Those who advocate various forms of switching in IP (such as IP switching and tag switching) insist that these ATM software developments aren't even necessary.

Whichever viewpoint emerges as the more accurate, ATM will play a critical role in the large IP networks of the future, such as the Internet and corporate intranets. The dogfight is over the distribution of the connection management intelligence between IP and ATM on the network backbone.

Regardless of the outcome between ATM and IP connection management, ATM's success is dependent on the continuing success of IP protocols and applications. The most diehard ATM evangelists look forward to new enhancements for IP which enable IP applications to support real-time applications and multiple service classes. These include RSVP (resource reservation protocol), which is a draft-IP standard giving an application the ability to request reserved bandwidth and prioritization in the network. Another important enhancement is RTP (real-time transport protocol), a transport protocol for real-time traffic. These enhancements deliver traffic that can take advantage of an ATM network's QoS capabilities and could serve as an important driver of ATM networks.

Driving under the influence

In Chapter 22, we discuss alternatives to ATM. Each new alternative takes another bite out of ATM's potential market share, and some bites hurt more than others. Each alternative has a strong influence on ATM's future success, and two other major factors may also negatively impact the deployment of ATM technology and services.

Photonic switching

Photonic switching is considered by some to be the next great networking technology on the far horizon. A major leap forward in photonic switching would have a negative impact on ATM. Photonic switching is much too complicated to describe in a few short sentences or paragraphs, but here's our best shot.

With photonic switching, each connection through a network is achieved by switching flashes of light. The photonic switch distinguishes the flashes of light representing the connections by using both the light wavelength and encoding scheme. These connections may be in a single machine, across a LAN or campus backbone, or over a wide area network. Photonic switching delivers a semi-dedicated optical connection to each application being transmitted over the network.

This technology is still in university laboratories and is the stuff of scientists' dreams. However, advances in this technology in the near future may make ATM far less important (in much the same way that ATM may make TDM switching technology far less important for enterprise networking).

The last miles

The cost and availability of high-speed local and access connection alternatives continues to have a big impact on the success of ATM in metropolitan and wide area networks. If the cost of high-speed access remains high and the availability remains low, user adoption of ATM may go slowly.

Conversely, because the cost of access has been a major hurdle in the deployment of ATM to date, high-speed access services that substantially drop in price can really help to spur the market for public ATM services. Given the new regulatory rules for local providers, competition in the loop may force prices down and increase the number of fractional speed alternatives available between 1.5 and 45 Mbps. Many new high-speed networks are being locally deployed by traditional RBOCs and LECs and by newer competitive access providers (CAPs) and competitive local exchange carriers (CLECs), so this scenario is not a far-fetched proposition — at least in the large metro areas. Cable companies are also getting into the act, becoming a popular source of dark fiber, especially in the suburbs, which have limited fiber deployed by the local telcos. The cost of access may also be influenced by how successfully and aggressively various providers deploy ADSL and cable modem technologies in the business loop.

Supporting technologies

In this section we discuss a service and technology that complement ATM and support its deployment as a backbone infrastructure in both corporate and carrier networks.

Private lines

Private leased lines often provide the underlying physical TDM infrastructure for ATM networks. The ATM protocol runs over the private line so that, within the private line, the statistical cell multiplexing of ATM enables the bandwidth to be dynamically allocated and shared among active applications.

Whether you're building a private ATM wide area network or connecting to a public service, TDM physical lines are an essential element. You probably use private lines to connect your private ATM switches together or to connect your premises equipment into a public ATM service. You can use SONET connections instead of traditional private lines, but few, if any, networks are constructed using only SONET.

In addition to providing the underlying physical infrastructure, private line networks can coexist with ATM networks. This coexistence is typically referred to as a *hybrid configuration*. Hybrid networks are like having your cake and eating it, too. If you need the benefits of ATM between some locations, then you can use a private and/or public ATM solution between these sites while you continue to rely on the existing private lines between other locations. This type of hybrid may also be found when ATM is needed in the LAN or campus network but not needed in the wide area network.

SONET

Synchronous Optical Network (SONET) provides an underlying physical infrastructure for many ATM networks. SONET connections are defined at very high speeds, typically starting at 155 Mbps. Today, some ATM public and private networks are built using traditional DS-3 (or E3) private lines. The problem with this method is that the DS-3/E3 backbone infrastructure is too low-speed (45/34 Mbps respectively) and quickly becomes congested when the network must support same-speed DS-3/E3 connections to the users. The only way to support a large number of DS-3 (or E3) network interfaces is to use the higher-speed backbone infrastructure of SONET.

SONET is also critical when carriers depend upon ATM as their underlying infrastructure for many different services on an integrated ATM network. ATM needs both the high speeds provided by SONET and the added level of physical network protection. SONET networks based on ringed topologies can self-restore in a few milliseconds in the event of a network failure. This recovery time is faster than that which can be supported by a self-healing ATM network because the SONET network typically reroutes at the physical level, not on individual logical paths and channels. Carriers must successfully outlaw backhoes (and we have many ops friends who support this campaign) or backbone fade will continue to be a common source of network trouble. (We have one friend who believes that a backhoe driver can find a 3-foot strand of buried fiber in a one-acre plot, blindfolded). SONET rings provide a stable physical infrastructure, despite the backhoe hits.

SONET can also provide very high-speed access connections into an ATM network. In this case, SONET backbone circuits are needed as well — although an OC-3s (155 Mbps if you forgot your conversion table) worth of bandwidth is still pretty difficult to fill up in one giant network surge. By the way, we provide more information on SONET in Chapter 8.

Chapter 24

Ten Tips from the Pros: Advice from Those Using the Technology

In This Chapter

▶ Finding out what to do with ATM

▶ Seeing what NOT to do with ATM

▶ Figuring out why to do it (or not to do it) with ATM

*I*f you've read other chapters, you may have noticed that we took a slightly different approach to writing this book. Instead of just loading you up with bunches of facts, figures, and definitions (though we did our share of that), we also tried to anchor the information with real life experiences and opinions of others in the industry.

So to continue the tradition, we want to offer you some words of wisdom from professionals who are already using ATM successfully. These aren't necessarily technical tips — you won't see anything along the lines of "make sure you flip the ON-OFF switch to the ON position" — but instead, you see the big-screen views that you need before you plunge into ATM. In fact, these tips are useful across the entire realm of networking, so they'll be helpful for whatever networking technology you decide to use!

Three Tips from the North

Alex Tashayod, Senior Communications Analyst for Royal Bank of Canada, has three recommendations for anyone planning on implementing an ATM network.

> "1) ATM is not a panacea in networking.
> 2) Don't try to fit ATM in every part of the network.
> 3) Test, test, test."

You can find out more about Royal Bank's implementation of ATM in Chapter 16.

Tales from the FOREfront

Joe Skorupa, Vice President of Marketing at FORE Systems always tells his customers the following:

> "There are only three criteria for choosing a networking technology
>
> 1) the requirements of the applications,
> 2) the requirements of the applications, and
> 3) the requirements of the applications,
>
> with one other consideration and that is to cover your planning horizon."

Learning from the Educators

> "Work with a vendor who knows what they are doing and can keep you out of trouble,"

is the sage advice from Steve Glick, Manager of Networking and Distributed Communications at Dallas Community College. Find out more about Dallas Community College's implementation of ATM in our case study chapter (Chapter 16).

Keep Your Focus

Daniel Gasparro, Chief Technologist for Booze, Allen, Hamilton wants his staff to,

> "Spend time focusing on applications and how they are going to support the business."

He wants to leave the networking expertise to reliable suppliers who support many different networks and customers. To check out additional information about the Booze, Allen, Hamilton network implementation, turn to the "Native LAN" sidebar in Chapter 12.

Trial of the Century

Bill Brasuell, Network Technologist at Tandem gave us the following perspective on trying out ATM.

> "Trials are a very good way to show management what the business improvement is, and trials get the end users to state the benefits. It's a hard sell when it's all theory."

You can read more about his ATM experiences in the *Inside ATM* feature at the end of Chapter 14.

From the Indiana Retreat

Indiana University's (IU) own Allen Robel, senior network analyst has implemented three ATM projects. He also maintains the popular cell relay site for ATM at

```
http://cell-relay.indiana.edu
```

He offers the following points of wisdom.

> "Make sure you are in tune with end-user needs. Until you have a good understanding of their requirements, don't make a decision. Determine what you are trying to solve and then apply the right technology; which may or may not be ATM."

Allen has found ATM to be a good fit for the following projects:

- **A WAN backbone** that supports room-based H.320 videoconferencing and high-speed data between two IU campuses.

- **High-quality desktop videoconferencing** between selected desktops and H.320 room-based systems over the campus area network and over the WAN. This application uses LAN Emulation (LANE) for address resolution but diverges from LANE by setting up VBR-RT connections for video and CBR connections for voice.

- **Delivery of CD-quality digital audio** to 40 client PCs at the IU Music Library, the largest in the country.

- **Centralization of campus server resources.** This ATM application uses LANE to connect central servers with client subnets (VLANS), saving router hops and improving performance while allowing consolidation of server hardware, environmental infrastructure, and human resources.

Seising the Earth

Amoco Corporation initiated the ARIES (ATM Research & Industrial Enterprise Study) project in 1993, under its very knowledgeable project manager David Beering. ARIES explores the usefulness of ATM in improving the accuracy and speed of seismic reading analyses that evaluate the potential of oil field locations. The project has now expanded to include all the members of the American Petroleum Institute. David offered his tip based on his years of experience in demonstrating ATM technology to both fans and skeptics.

"A persistent presence of ATM is necessary to convince everyone of ATM's benefits. The capabilities need to be available anytime users want them to demonstrate ATM's real value in assisting with their work."

You can read other thoughts from David in his feature that closes Chapter 16.

Netting It All Out

When we talked to Phil Lawlor, President and CEO of AGIS, he had the following two tips to offer to other Internet providers and any large IP network operator considering ATM.

"It's wise to overprovision the bandwidth of your virtual circuits to start. The route you believe is using 5 megabits/second may actually be using 10 megabits/second. Determining true IP usage can be very difficult. You won't want a bandwidth bottleneck confusing your life as you're ascending the ATM learning curve."

"Follow the Forum, and buy mature equipment. You'll want to select a vendor whose implementation closely follows the standards work of the ATM Forum. Be sure to choose a UNI version with which you can live. Also, look for equipment that is mature. Although difficulties are becoming fewer, early versions of hardware and software were susceptible to unexpected deficiencies, bugs, and frequent upgrades."

You can find out what else we learned in our interview with Phil in Chapter 6.

Testing ATM's MAGIC

Victor Frost, who is a professor of Electrical Engineering and Computer Science at the University of Kansas and who also helped us out by serving as technical editor for this book, has been exploring ATM technology for over seven years. His many ATM projects include work on the MAGIC testbed that runs all the way from Minneapolis, MN, past several other midwestern sites to his lab in Lawrence, KS. He offers this tip to fellow ATM users.

"After several years of testing and performance evaluation of national scale ATM WANs we have learned that the parameters of all elements of the network, including the host operating system, must be appropriately set in order to realize the full potential for high-speed long distance ATM communications."

Part V
Appendixes

The 5th Wave — By Rich Tennant

"NOW JUST WHEN THE HECK DID I INTEGRATE *THAT* INTO THE SYSTEM?"

In this part . . .

Check out Part V for information on the ATM Forum (that all-important, pro-ATM organization) in Appendix A and a glossary of terms related to ATM (and to networking in general) in Appendix B. You may find the glossary particularly helpful — that is, unless you're planning to spend the next six years memorizing all those acronyms.

Appendix A

All About the ATM Forum

• •

*A*s we mention throughout this book, the ATM Forum is one of the best and most important sources for information about ATM that you can find anywhere (besides this book, of course). The Forum is made up of just about all the makers of ATM hardware (networking equipment like switches), software (a far-ranging group, including network management software), and service providers (all those MAN, WAN, and public network providers), as well as government agencies, research institutes, and even end users.

What Does The ATM Forum Do?

The easiest way to start explaining what the ATM Forum does is to give you the group's own words:

> The ATM Forum is an international non-profit organization formed with the objective of accelerating the use of ATM (Asynchronous Transfer Mode) products and services through a rapid convergence of interoperability specifications. In addition, the Forum promotes industry cooperation and awareness.

This description is pretty complete, as far as we're concerned. Like proponents of other emerging technologies, the proponents of ATM realized early on that they'd never get anywhere without a body in place to ensure standard ATM offerings. That is, early ATM enthusiasts wanted to prevent a thousand different companies from offering a thousand different flavors of ATM. Of course, everybody with a financial stake in a new technology (like ATM) would like their particular vision of it to become THE standard. Who doesn't want to become the Bill Gates of their own little (or huge) technological land? But the ATM advocates also realize that plenty of other competing technologies can get a leg up on ATM *if users can't count on the version of ATM that they buy working with someone else's version.* Interoperability, then, is really where it's at!

So the ATM Forum promotes interoperability, and ATM technology in general, to a wider audience. Who's that audience? Probably you are, if you're reading this book. So take advantage of the Forum and its resources when you're looking at ATM as a solution to your particular networking needs.

The Forum consists of several groups and committees, all working toward the mission statement that we quoted near the beginning of this section. The Forum includes these groups:

- **A Technical Committee:** This committee is designed to provide a single, worldwide body that can work with ATM vendors and with standards bodies like ANSI and ITU to help establish and propagate appropriate ATM standards.

- **Three Marketing Committees:** These committees, which cover specific geographic regions (North America, Europe, and Asia/Pacific), are the other side of the ATM Forum coin — it takes more than just technical superiority to sell a technology. The Marketing Committees provide educational materials, publish an ATM newsletter (called *53 Bytes*, appropriately enough), coordinate demonstrations of ATM technology, and provide an interface between the Technical Committee and the third arm of the Forum, the Enterprise Network Roundtable Committee.

- **ATM Ambassadors:** The ambassadors are the folks who go out and testify at trade shows, conferences and the like — spreading the good news about ATM to any and all. We're using that old-time revival language in describing the ambassadors because they're sort of like the evangelists that Apple Computer used so effectively in their heyday (and are using once again to try and regain their position in the computer marketplace).

- **The Enterprise Network Roundtable Committee:** This group provides a place for end users of ATM technology (perhaps you, some day soon) to discuss their real-world experiences with ATM, like some of the experiences we talk about in this book. (See Chapter 16 for real-world ATM stories.) And through this group, end users can provide feedback to the Marketing Committees and, indirectly, to the Technical Committee.

Who's In The Forum?

Who's in the ATM Forum? Just about everybody, actually. The Forum started with just four member companies in 1991, the year it was founded, and has rapidly grown to include over 700 members. We could fill up a whole bunch of pages here by listing all those members, but instead we just give you a quick synopsis:

- **Equipment Providers:** A long list of *who's who in networking*, including 3Com, Alcatel, Bay Networks, Cabletron Systems, Cascade Communications, Cisco Systems, Lucent Technologies, Motorola, Newbridge Networks, Northern Telecom, Nortel, and many more.

- **Carriers:** Just about every major public local, long distance, and global network provider is a member of the Forum, including AT&T, CompuServe, MCI Communications, MFS Communications, NTT, and Sprint.

✔ **Networking hardware and software providers:** Many major players in the computer networking world are members, including Apple Computer, IBM, and Microsoft Corporation.

The preceding is really just a partial listing — if you take the time to peruse through the complete list of members, you find government agencies, research facilities, dozens of universities . . . the list goes on and on.

Should My Company Join the Forum?

Because ATM Forum membership costs a minimum of $1500 per year, we'll make the assumption that you are considering a membership to the Forum for your company. (You'd have to be a pretty hard-core ATM nut to join as an individual.) Before you decide whether you want to join, take a look at Table A-1, which lists the different membership levels.

Table A-1	ATM Forum Memberships	
Membership Level	**What It Costs**	**What It Gets You**
Principal Member	$10,000 per year	Decision-making involvement in the nuts and bolts of the Forum, including voting in General Forum meetings, and participation in the technical and marketing commitees. (Principal members are usually organizations with a BIG interest in ATM.)
Auditing Member	$1,500 per year	Convenient access to information on the latest in ATM standards and development, without being involved in committees or voting on general Forum issues. (Like auditing members of a college class, auditing members of the ATM Forum go to class and read the textbook, but they don't get a grade or credit for the course.)
User Member	$1,500 per year	Access to the Enterprise Network Roundtable Committee for expressing wants, needs, thoughts and experiences with ATM. User members provide feedback through the Marketing Committee. (User memberships are generally for end users of ATM technology.)

So should you become a member company? Well that all depends upon the specifics of your situation, but we offer this general advice: If your company needs to be a principal or auditing member, you probably already know it (because you're probably already involved in developing or providing ATM products and services).

Should your company join the Forum as user members? If you're serious about adopting ATM and want a voice in the standards process, by all means, *yes*. If you're with a smaller company, or not really sure of your company's strategic direction regarding ATM, we recommend that you at least investigate some of the free resources that the Forum offers (like the newsletter, *53 Bytes*), and then decide (or let the accounting department decide).

Where to Go to Find Out More

The first place to go is to the ATM Forum Web site, at www.atmforum.com At this Web site, you find lots of information and goodies, including mission statements, memberships listings and applications, ATM educational materials and white papers, and even an online version of the Forum newsletter, *53 Bytes*.

If you have e-mail, but not Web access — must be a tight fisted MIS department in your office — then send e-mail containing your name, company, street address, and phone number to info@atmforum.com and you can get a free subscription to the newsletter.

You can also receive information about the Forum by dialing their Fax-On-Demand service at +1.415.688.4318. A full listing of the information available can be found on the Web page.

Finally, if you prefer snail mail or the telephone, the Forum's addresses and telephone numbers are

World Headquarters
2570 West El Camino Real, Suite 304
Mountain View, CA 94040-1313
Phone: +1.415.949.6700
Fax: +1.415.949.6705

Europe Office
Boulevard Saint-Michel 78
1040 Brussels, BELGIUM
Phone: +32.2.732.8505
Fax: +32.2.732.8485

Asia-Pacific Office
Hamamatsucho Suzuki Bldg 3F
1-2-11 Hamamatsucho, Minato-ku
Tokyo 105, JAPAN
Phone: +81.3.3438.3694
Fax: +81.3.3438.3698

Appendix B

Glossary

● ●

AAL (ATM Adaptation Layer) The top layer of ATM functionality in the ATM protocol stack. The ATM adaptation layer packages higher layer information such as voice, data, and video into the payload of the 53-byte ATM cell.

ABR (Available Bit Rate) Supports bursty applications such as LAN interconnect and Internet access. ABR uses internal and external network feedback mechanisms to manage traffic. *See also* service category.

adaptation Defined methods for packaging user information into ATM cells. The most common adaptation scheme is AAL5.

ADPCM (Adaptive Differential Pulse Code Modulation) A more efficient variant of PCM audio encoding. *See also* PCM.

ADSL (Asymmetrical Digital Subscriber Line) A new access technology that delivers high speed communications (1.5 – 6 Mbps) over a standard two wire copper local loop.

alternate routing The capability of a connection-oriented system to automatically set up alternate connections if the original circuit fails.

ANSI (American National Standards Institute) A U.S. standards body.

API (Application Programming Interface) Provides a way for an application to request and use the resources of a network.

ATM (Asynchronous Transfer Mode) A high-speed networking technology that utilizes packets of a fixed-length (cells). ATM uses logical connections to provide quality of service guarantees which enable disparate traffic such as data, voice, and video to be carried over the same local or wide area network.

ATM access switches, concentrators, and muxes ATM devices for integrating multiple incoming data, voice, and video lines into a single ATM connection.

ATM backbone switches ATM switches for building corporate LAN backbones on a campus.

ATM DSU (Data Service Unit) ATM equipment for connecting one-two data lines into an ATM network.

ATM Forum The most important standards organization for ATM, with over 700 members. Fourteen technical working groups generate a variety of key specifications for building and enhancing ATM networks and services.

ATM layer Middle layer in the ATM protocol stack. The ATM layer creates the ATM cells and is responsible for their transport across the network.

ATM workgroup switches ATM LAN switches for small workgroups of generally less than 24 users who require high networking performance.

B-ICI (Broadband ISDN Inter-Carrier Interface) Defined interface for connecting two ATM networks (such as when one ATM service provider connects to another).

B-ISDN (Broadband ISDN) A high-speed (above 1.544 Mbps) network standard that grew from traditional Narrowband ISDN. The ITU standards for ATM services are its B-ISDN recommendations.

burst tolerance Maximum length of time that a connection can send at the peak cell rate. The parameter measures how long a connection may exceed the SCR.

bursty Traffic that arrives in intermittent, unpredictable bursts. This term typically refers to LAN traffic, which can vary widely depending on how often users press the Enter key and how much traffic this single action generates.

BUS (Broadcast and Unknown Server) Server within an ATM emulated LAN which handles all broadcast traffic as well as unicast packets sent by a LEC before connection to the destination ATM address is established.

CAC (Connection Admission Control) A system which determines, during the call setup procedure, whether the network has the resources to accept the connection.

campus network A high-speed network connecting multiple LANs within a building or close cluster of buildings.

CBR (Constant Bit Rate) Supports a constant or guaranteed rate to transport information. Used for services such as traditional video or voice which require rigid bandwidth and low latency.

CDV (Cell Delay Variation) The change in the interarrival times between cells at the peak cell rate. *See also* QoS.

cell The fixed-length packet used to carry data across an ATM network, a cell consists of 53 bytes, 5 of which carry header information.

cell relay A communications protocol using small, fixed-length packets, or cells. ATM is the most well-known cell relay protocol, and the two terms are often used interchangeably.

CIF (Cells In Frame) Specification for carrying ATM cells over an Ethernet interface.

CIR (Committed Information Rate) Frame relay term also used to refer to the SCR measured in Mbps in ATM.

circuit emulation Method to carry TDM circuits in an ATM network. Circuit emulation requires reservation across the network of the full bandwidth of the connection.

classes of service An older term for service categories. New terminology of Traffic Management 4.0 prefers the newer term *service categories.*

Classical IP Reference to traditional IP protocol definitions, which require all traffic crossing between subnets to pass through a router.

CLP bit (Cell Loss Priority bit) Cell header field identifying cells with a lower priority. The network drops marked CLP bit cells before unmarked cells during network congestion.

CLR (Cell Loss Ratio) The percentage of cells lost during a transmission. *See also* QoS.

compression Reformats information so that a fewer number of bits are necessary to represent it.

connection oriented A network that establishes, either permanently or on a call-by-call basis, a specific circuit path for transmission. Connection-based networks use switches. Examples of connection-oriented networks include ATM, frame relay, and the Public Switched Telephone Network (PSTN).

connectionless A network that sends individual packets from one location to another on the best path as determined by the devices along the way. Unlike connection-based networks, the network never reserves an end-to-end path. In a connectionless network, like the Internet, two packets in the same transmission may take completely different routes to the same location.

CPE (Customer Premises Equipment) End user equipment within the customer's building. CPE is usually owned by the customer and not the carrier.

CTD (Cell Transfer Delay) The end-to-end delay introduced by transmission across the network. *See also* QoS.

cut-through routing Allows end devices attached to an ATM network to communicate directly with each other, even when the devices are on two different subnets. This compares to routing in Classical IP, which always requires traffic moving between subnets to pass through a router.

DS0 (Digital Signal, Level 0) The smallest unit in digital transmission systems. A DS0 provides 64 Kbps of bandwidth.

DXI (Data Exchange Interface) Specification to split the functions of the adaptation layer between an existing router and an external device commonly referred to as an ATM DSU (Data Service Unit).

E1 The standard European carrier for transmission at 2.048 Mbps. An E1 consists of 32 DS-0 channels. Compares to a T1.

E3 The standard European carrier for transmission at 34.368 Mbps. The E3 connection can carry 16 E1s.

echo cancellers Equipment that removes the echo introduced into a voice call by telephone handsets and exaggerated by network delay.

encapsulation Wrapping information into another protocol for transport across a network.

Ethernet LAN protocol to connect desktop computers and other computing equipment over shared wiring providing a total speed of 10 Mbps. Ethernet is the most popular LAN protocol today.

fast Ethernet Ethernet standard for bumping up the speed of the shared LAN wiring from 10 Mbps to 100 Mbps.

FDDI (Fiber Distributed Data Interface) A 100 Mbps local area network standard which carries its signal over fiber optic cable.

frame relay Wide area networking interface protocol that statistically shares bandwidth by transporting variable-length packets over virtual connections. Frame relay speeds span dial-up to 45 Mbps in 1996 implementations.

FUNI (Frame User Network Interface) This interface specification was developed after the ATM UNI to accommodate low-speed connections (such as T1/E1 and below) into an ATM network. The FUNI uses variable-length packets (frames) instead of cells to avoid the *cell tax* of ATM on the access portion of the connection.

GCRA (Generic Cell Rate Algorithm) Defines the relationships between the different bandwidth rates (PCR and SCR) and variances (cell delay variation and burst tolerance) of ATM.

gigabit Ethernet Ethernet standard for bumping up the speed of the shared LAN wiring from 10 Mbps to 1 Gbps.

HAN (Home Area Network) A high-speed network connecting personal computing equipment and possibly other networked-devices (such as the TV of the future) within the home.

header The first 5 bytes of ATM cells, which contain primarily addressing information.

HSSI (High Speed Serial Interface) Physical interface primarily used on routers and supporting transmission up to 52 Mbps.

IAM (Inverse ATM Mux) A defined standard for transporting an ATM cell stream over several T1 or E1 lines.

IEEE (Institute of Electrical and Electronics Engineers) A worldwide electronics industry publishing and standards-making body.

IETF (Internet Engineering Task Force) An organization that develops and approves standards for the Internet and TCP/IP networking.

ILMI (Integrated Layer Management Interface) Allows ATM devices to exchange fault and performance management information over a UNI interface.

IMUX (Inverse Multiplexing) Used to provide service bandwidths that lie between traditional offerings (like DS0, T1, or T3). IMUX combines several smaller bandwidth transmission facilities that behave as a single, unified facility of the desired size.

Internet A worldwide network of networks using the IP family of standards to enable communications among users. Users access the network through Internet Service Providers (ISPs).

intranet Corporate network using the technologies of the Internet in private implementations. Commonly adopted technologies include browsers, web pages, and e-mail on a secure IP network.

IP (Internet Protocol) A connectionless networking protocol. IP is the protocol of the Internet and other connectionless networks, including many corporate LANs and wide area data networks.

IPv6 The replacement for the current version of IP (which is also known as IPv4).

ISP (Internet Service Provider) Provides subscribers connectivity to the Internet.

ITU (International Telecommunication Union) A U.N.-sanctioned international organization of member states that creates standards for international telecommunications systems.

IXC (Inter-exchange Carrier) A long distance telephone company.

LAN (Local Area Network) High-speed network connecting personal computers, printers, and other data equipment within an office or campus.

LANE (LAN Emulation) Specification allowing devices attached to traditional LANs (that is, Ethernet and token ring) to communicate with devices connected to ATM networks, and the connectivity of traditional LANs over an ATM backbone.

LEC (Local Exchange Carrier) A local telephone company. In the U.S., LECs include the seven Regional Bell Operating Companies (RBOCs) and various other independent providers.

LEC (LAN Emulation Client) End station belonging to an emulated LAN. The LEC may be an ATM end station or a proxy representing devices on a traditional LAN. This version of the LEC acronym is used only in very specific technical discussions of ATM LAN emulation.

LECS (LAN Emulation Configuration Server) Dynamically assigns different LECs to different emulated LANs as they join the network.

LES (LAN Emulation Server) Primarily responsible for registering and resolving MAC addresses to ATM addresses in LANE.

LNNI (LAN Emulation Network-to-Network Interface) A standard to define communications between the different servers in a LAN emulation network.

LUNI (LAN User-to-Network Interface) The interface between a user and the services of an emulated LAN network.

MAC (Media Access Control) Determines which end station can transmit over the shared transmission medium of a LAN at any time. Different types of LANs (such as Ethernet, token ring, and FDDI) have different MAC mechanisms.

MAN (Metropolitan Area Network) High speed network connecting data equipment within a local region that does not extend over 50 kilometers.

MBS (Maximum Burst Size) The maximum number of cells that a connection can send at the peak cell rate. The parameter measures how long a connection may exceed the SCR.

MCR (Minimum Cell Rate) The minimum rate of transmission on an ABR connection. The ABR connection can burst above the MCR up to the PCR.

MPEG (Motion Pictures Expert Group) A standard for compressing and digitizing audio and video streams.

MPOA (Multiprotocol over ATM) Specification connecting virtual ATM LANs together using cut-through routing.

multimedia A communications exchange requiring the transport of various media such as voice, text, image, and video.

multiplexing A process which combines multiple network sources onto a single stream of information for transport over a transmission facility. Multiplexing devices are often referred to as *muxes*.

multipoint connection Connection linking a single source to many different destinations. Traffic may flow only from the source to the destination. Also known as a point-to-multipoint connection.

native LAN Carrier service providing a traditional LAN interface (such as Ethernet, token ring, or FDDI) to the subscriber for wide area connectivity within a city or nation, or even between nations

network management The capability to monitor and control a network. Network management functions provide alarm, performance, configuration, accounting, and security information.

NHRP (Next Hop Resolution Protocol) Provides methods for routers to communicate among each other to determine unknown IP-to-ATM address mappings regardless of the IP subnet of the end devices. NHRP was defined specifically for non-broadcast networks which allow many users to directly attach to the network (such as ATM, frame relay, and X.25).

NICs (Network Interface Cards) Adapters used to interface desktop devices (such as personal computers, workstations, and printers) to a LAN.

NNI (Network-to-Network Interface) A general term referring to a connection between two switches or two networks. NNI is not a specifically defined ATM standard, but is still used because it is a part of the frame relay standards and jargon. NNI is also sometimes called Network Node Interface.

non-real time A communications exchange without any delay requirements. Non-real time applications easily tolerate significant network delay. Examples include e-mail and batch file transfers.

OAM (Operations Administration and Maintenance) A system of network management functions that allow network administrators to troubleshoot and monitor network performance.

one-armed router A router attached to an ATM switch through a single ATM connection to provide routing between the different subnets connected to the switch. Traffic moving across subnets must pass in and then back out of this router before proceeding to its destination.

overhead Any extra bits added to the actual user data for transport across the network. Each networking layer typically adds its own overhead. The ATM layer adds a considerable 10 percent overhead sometimes called the *cell tax*.

PBX (Private Branch Exchange) The switching equipment which provides a company with internal voice call routing and other voice related services.

PCM (Pulse Code Modulation) An audio encoding algorithm to digitize voice or other audio by sampling the analog signal.

PCR (Peak Cell Rate) The maximum transmission speed of a virtual connection as measured in cells. Certain service categories make use of idle network resources by bursting above their normal connection rate up to the PCR.

physical layer The lowest layer in the ATM protocol stack. The physical layer primarily identifies the transmission protocol in any network.

PNNI (Private Network-to-Network Interface) ATM network routing and signaling protocols that allow interconnection of ATM switches from different vendors.

policing Method for determining the conformance of ATM cells entering a network. Cells are said to conform if their cell rates and variances are equal to or less than values previously agreed-to by the user and service provider.

private line A carrier service providing a point-to-point TDM connection (exception is multipoint/multidrop for DS0 and lower speeds). Private line speeds span 2.4 Kbps to 155 Mbps.

PVC (Permanent Virtual Circuit) A logical connection manually defined by network administrators. The ATM network maintains the connection at all times, regardless of actual traffic flows. *See also* SVC.

QoS (Quality of Service) A unique feature of ATM compared to most other networking technologies, QoS parameters ensure minimum levels of network performance for carried traffic. QoS parameters include CDV, CLR, and CTD.

real-time A communication exchange without any noticeable delays induced by the network. Examples include phone calls, videoconferences, and ideally, Web browsing.

RM cells (Resource Management cells) Management cells used to share congestion and flow control information in the ABR service category.

router A computer that forwards packets through a network using information contained in the packet headers. A router typically maintains *routing tables* which enable it to select the best outgoing link for forwarding the packet to the next router.

RSVP (Resource Reservation Protocol) A draft IP standard that allows an application to request bandwidth and prioritization for real-time information flows.

RTP (Real-time Transfer Protocol) Provides end-to-end transport of real-time traffic on an IP network by including in the message timing information necessary for reconstruction at the far end.

SAR (Segmentation and Reassembly) Method of breaking up and then rebuilding high-layer information into fixed-length units for transport across an ATM network. SAR is a function of the adaptation layer.

SCR (Sustained Cell Rate) The expected rate of cell transmission on a VBR connection.

Service Category A known grouping of generally defined network performance attributes (that is, QoS parameters). The defined ATM service categories are CBR, VBR-RT, VBR-NRT, UBR, and ABR.

shaping Modifying the cell rates and variances of the traffic stream sent over an ATM logical connection to meet previously agreed to conformance values.

silence suppression Removes the pauses in speech before transporting voice traffic over a network.

SMDS (Switched Multi-Megabit Data Services) Connectionless public network offering that operates similarly to a LAN. SMDS speeds span 56 Kbps to 45 Mbps in 1996 implementations.

SNA (Systems Network Architecture) Networking protocols and techniques defined for connecting IBM equipment including mainframes and terminals.

SNMP (Simple Network Management Protocol) A network management protocol originally designed for TCP/IP networks which is now used in a wide variety of networking environments.

SONET (Synchronous Optical Network) An ANSI standard for transmitting bits over fiber optic cable.

SVC (Switched Virtual Circuit) A logical connection established via signaling. Users request SVCs through messages sent to the network, identifying the destination address and desired performance attributes (similar to dialing a phone number). The network tears down SVCs after the users complete their call. *See also* PVC.

switch A computer that maintains circuits by matching an input port to an output port for each connection. The switch contains *switching tables* to track this information.

switched Ethernet LAN protocol that provides a 10-Mbps dedicated Ethernet connection to each desktop, providing non-contested bandwidth to each user.

T1 The standard North American carrier for transmission at 1.544 Mbps. A T1 consists of 24 DS0 channels. *See also* E1.

T3 The standard North American carrier for transmission at 44.736 Mbps. The T3 connection can carry 28 T1s. *See also* E3.

tagging The process of marking the CLP bit of cells entering an ATM network because they do not conform to the subscribed traffic contract.

TCP (Transmission Control Protocol) Networking protocol providing end-to-end transport through a connectionless IP network. TCP includes controls for security, reliability, and performance.

TDM (Time Division Multiplexing) A network transmission method assigning transmission facility bandwidth among users through time slots. TDM is the traditional method of sharing physical bandwidth resources.

token ring LAN protocol to connect desktop computers and other computing equipment over a shared ring that provides a total of 4 or 16 Mbps of bandwidth.

Traffic Management Disciplines and methodologies for controlling traffic load and balance across the network.

UBR (Unspecified Bit Rate) Offers no traffic related service guarantees.

UNI (User-to-Network Interface) A protocol which defines how ATM end users connect to private and public ATM networks. The UNI defines the available capabilities for ATM transport.

UPC (Usage Parameter Control) A set of functions to monitor cells entering a network. Cells are said to conform if their cell rates and variances are equal to or less than values previously agreed to by the user and service provider.

VBR (Variable Bit Rate) Supports predictable data streams within bounds of average and peak traffic constraints. Used for delay- and loss-sensitive data transmissions (like SNA) and packetized voice/video. This category may be broken into two: VBR Real-Time and VBR Non-Real-Time.

VC (Virtual Channel) The lowest-order logical address in ATM. It refers to a given circuit on a link.

VCC (Virtual Channel Connection) A series of virtual channels connecting two users on the network.

VCI (Virtual Channel Identifier) The field of the cell header storing the VC address.

VLAN (Virtual LAN) Provides LAN communications between end users that are logically grouped because of shared interests instead of defining LANs based on physical location.

VP (Virtual Path) The highest-order logical address in ATM. It refers to a given group of circuits on a link.

VPC (Virtual Path Connection) A series of virtual paths connecting two users on the network.

VPI (Virtual Path Identifier) The field of the cell header storing the VP address.

VTOA (Voice and Telephony over ATM) Specification defining a standard method for carrying traditional voice circuits over an ATM network.

WAN (Wide Area Network) High-speed network connecting communications equipment nationally and internationally. The biggest difference between a MAN and a WAN is the physical distance of the region covered.

Winsock 2 An API (Application Programming Interface) allowing software applications to request the quality of service and bandwidth of their networking connection.

X.25 Wide area networking interface protocol that statistically shares bandwidth by transporting variable-length packets over virtual connections. X.25 provides error recovery and other advanced features to safely transport traffic over unreliable physical links. X.25 speeds span analog dial-up to 2 Mbps.

Index

IDG BOOKS WORLDWIDE REGISTRATION CARD

Visit our
Web site at
http://www.idgbooks.com

Title of this book: **ATM For Dummies®**

My overall rating of this book: ❑ Very good [1] ❑ Good [2] ❑ Satisfactory [3] ❑ Fair [4] ❑ Poor [5]

How I first heard about this book:

❑ Found in bookstore; name: [6] _____ ❑ Book review: [7] _____

❑ Advertisement: [8] _____ ❑ Catalog: [9] _____

❑ Word of mouth; heard about book from friend, co-worker, etc.: [10] _____ ❑ Other: [11] _____

What I liked most about this book:

_____

_____

What I would change, add, delete, etc., in future editions of this book:

_____

_____

Other comments:

_____

Number of computer books I purchase in a year: ❑ 1 [12] ❑ 2-5 [13] ❑ 6-10 [14] ❑ More than 10 [15]

I would characterize my computer skills as: ❑ Beginner [16] ❑ Intermediate [17] ❑ Advanced [18] ❑ Professional [19]

I use ❑ DOS [20] ❑ Windows [21] ❑ OS/2 [22] ❑ Unix [23] ❑ Macintosh [24] ❑ Other: [25]_____

(please specify)

I would be interested in new books on the following subjects:

(please check all that apply, and use the spaces provided to identify specific software)

❑ Word processing: [26] _____ ❑ Spreadsheets: [27] _____

❑ Data bases: [28] _____ ❑ Desktop publishing: [29] _____

❑ File Utilities: [30] _____ ❑ Money management: [31] _____

❑ Networking: [32] _____ ❑ Programming languages: [33] _____

❑ Other: [34] _____

I use a PC at (please check all that apply): ❑ home [35] ❑ work [36] ❑ school [37] ❑ other: [38] _____

The disks I prefer to use are ❑ 5.25 [39] ❑ 3.5 [40] ❑ other: [41]_____

I have a CD ROM: ❑ yes [42] ❑ no [43]

I plan to buy or upgrade computer hardware this year: ❑ yes [44] ❑ no [45]

I plan to buy or upgrade computer software this year: ❑ yes [46] ❑ no [47]

Name: _____ Business title: [48] _____ Type of Business: [49] _____

Address (❑ home [50] ❑ work [51] /Company name: _____)

Street/Suite# _____

City [52]/State [53]/Zipcode [54]: _____ Country [55] _____

❑ **I liked this book!** You may quote me by name in future
IDG Books Worldwide promotional materials.

My daytime phone number is _____

IDG
BOOKS
WORLDWIDE

THE WORLD OF
COMPUTER
KNOWLEDGE®

 # YES!

Please keep me informed about IDG Books Worldwide's
World of Computer Knowledge. Send me your latest catalog.